JAZZ on **CD**

THE ESSENTIAL GUIDE

John Fordham is a jazz critic, writer and broadcaster, who has been writing about jazz for nearly 20 years, initially for the London listings magazine, *Time Out*, and then for a variety of papers including *Melody Maker*, *Sounds*, *Zig-Zag*, *Wire* and *Q*. Since 1978 he has been a regular jazz correspondent for *The Guardian*, and more recently, for *The Listener*. His biography of Ronnie Scott, *Let's Join Hands and Contact the Living*, was published by Hamish Hamilton in 1986 to enthusiastic reviews, and an illustrated jazz history, *The Sound of Jazz*, was published by Hamlyn/Octopus in 1989. He has acted as a jazz adviser for the Arts Council of Great Britain, and the Greater London Arts, and was also editor of *Time Out* from 1978 to 1981, and co-editor of *City Limits* from 1981 to 1986. He scripted and presented a documentary to celebrate the 30th anniversary of Ronnie Scott's Club for BBC's Omnibus series in 1989, regularly presents jazz items on Radio 4's Kaleidoscope, and is currently working on a six-part BBC TV series on new British and American jazz players, to be broadcast in 1991.

ƒAZZ on **CD**

THE ESSENTIAL GUIDE

JOHN FORDHAM

First published in Great Britain by
Kyle Cathie Limited
3 Vincent Square, London SW1P 2LX

Copyright © 1991 by John Fordham

ISBN 1 85626 014 3

A CIP catalogue record for this book is available from
the British Library

Designed by Lorraine Abraham
Typeset by DP Photosetting
Printed by Cox & Wyman Ltd.

CONTENTS

PREFACE

IN AUTUMN 1987, I wrote a guide to jazz on CD for *Q* magazine, listing my idea of the most representative fifty discs to form the nucleus of a jazz collection in the new format. It wasn't the hardest job I've ever done. Among others, the London jazz record specialists, Honest Jon's, had the whole lot down on a pocket-sized list. You couldn't have got it on to the back of an envelope, but just the same it didn't run, as I recall, to much more than six hundred discs.

By 1990 the numbers ran into thousands. As jazz returned to something like the popularity it had enjoyed in the 1950s, record companies with large back catalogues began furiously reissuing material on CD, and many new independent labels emerged that embraced CD as an ideal combination of reliable sound quality, and ease of storage and transportation. The result has been that it hasn't been possible to come close to a fully comprehensive contemporary guide to jazz on compact disc in a book such as this. This has therefore been my personal selection, from what was available at the time of writing – and, of course, new material is emerging and earlier material being deleted every month to complicate things further.

But this is not such bad news as all that. In the rush to capitalise on the 'jazz boom', some record companies have reissued old material fairly indiscriminately, and I have tried to channel this torrent into what seemed to me the most entertaining, useful, and illuminating selections. And you can get hot-off-the-presses updates on the most recent issues in the review pages of such useful publications as *Wire* magazine, *Jazz Journal*, and *Jazz FM* magazine, which also run advertising that will help you locate the specialist dealers.

Organising material in a book like this one is always a journey into a minefield. In a period in which sectarianism between fans of this music or that appears to be lessening, it might have seemed appropriate to forget all considerations of genre or generation, and run all these selections as an alphabetical directory. After much consideration, however, I wound up concluding that a basic breakdown according to a rough chronology of jazz history might help this wonderful music's many new fans to find their way around. *Jazz on CD* also includes introductory essays to each area of the music, and brief biographies of the musicians to the same end.

I have thus divided the book into sections dealing with the earliest recorded jazz; the development of Swing music and its recordings both by pioneers of the idiom and younger revivalists; the Forties modernist shockwave of Bebop, and its many variations; the 1960s Avant-Garde, a tumultuous expressionist development now largely subsumed into current jazz styles; and the wide world of Contemporary jazz, from those variations close to disco music, to the jazz played by Bulgarian wedding bands, free-improvising players, off-duty Russian classical musicians and many others. Entries are alphabetical within each section, and names in capital letters denote a cross-reference elsewhere in the section, though not throughout the book. The index will guide you to making connections throughout *Jazz On CD*. I have, regretfully, not included blues musicians, subjects for a CD book of their own.

As for gratitude to those individuals and organisations that made this marathon possible, this is the most necessarily cursory of lists and I would like to thank everyone with whom I've shared the mercurial fascination of jazz over the years. But special mentions should go to: Val and Jane at BMG Records; Jo at EMI; Ron at Harmonia Mundi distributors, and all at New Note; Ron Atkins and John Jack; *Q* magazine, *The Guardian*, *New Statesman* and *Wire*, in which, in other forms, some of these reviews were previously published; my angelically patient publisher Kyle Cathie and copy editor Marcus Bell; and Ros, Fred and Leo, who had to live with the mess, bad temper, and fitful baffling cries of 'yeaahhh!!'

John Fordham
London 1991

INTRODUCTION

FAREWELL TO THE BLACK PLATTER?

I n his book, *The Recording Angel*, the New York writer, Evan Eisenberg, describes a man on the wilder shores of fetishism. Clarence Browne is the impoverished son of a big-time Cadillac salesman, a hibernating obsessive, who has spent a considerable inheritance in accumulating three quarters of a million records, within the crumbling walls of the family home. The Long Island building, now mostly hocked to a landlord, has blocked drains and no heating. But Clarence's collection of vinyl, shellac and Edison cylinders, still warms his heart amid the chaos.

Not every record collector lets the preoccupation take over as much as Clarence. But to judge by the correspondence columns of *The Gramophone*, during 1989, plenty of admirers of the old-fashioned black vinyl disc fervently reject the suggestion that their pastime has become an anachronism. The correspondence was triggered by Deutsche Gramophon's decision to switch its operation away from vinyl and into compact discs, an increasingly popular move with companies widely involved in the reissues market. The move initiated a flurry of press reports, which, perhaps over-hastily, intoned the last rites over the black platter.

All these changes have happened within ten years. When the compact tape cassette was first introduced it was thought unreliable, prone to jamming and tape hiss, and devoid of any of the fetishistic pleasures of the album sleeve, with its panoramic photography and more or less helpful information. Then came state-of-the-art tape technology, falling cassette player prices, high quality pre-recording of tape, 'in-car entertainment' and, most significant of all, the Walkman. In 1983, sales of pre-recorded tapes stood at 35.8 million a year. In 1988, the figure was 91 million. For compact discs the development has been slower, because both the hardware and the software were expensive, when the idea was launched in 1982 (this wasn't just a question of passing on high development costs, the record companies liked the profit margins of sustaining a prestigious ABCI clientele even after the unit costs started to drop), but CD sales now are certainly demonstrating the kind of rise to justify the London *Evening Standard* headline 'Vinyl's Final Spin'. Every year, vinyl sales continue to drop, and CD sales now outstrip both vinyl and cassette tape.

Concurrently with the CD boom, has been the jazz boom. A form of music that was of little interest to the major record companies during the 1970s (except in its pop and fusion guises) it now has a high profile in the record industry – predominantly as a source of reissues, but, to an increasing extent, of new artists as well. Jazz and CDs have now resoundingly found each other. Unlike pop, the extended forms the music frequently takes has ideally suited the 60-minute playing time of CDs. On a live recording, the high level of ambient 'presence' on a CD, and the precision of detail (unmusical and fussy to some) can heighten the illusion of being in the front seat in a club.

Every month now, a swelling flood of new, and reissued, jazz discs from the big companies (EMI, RCA, CBS, Warners) hit the racks, as well as frequently more adventurous and contemporary material from middle-sized enterprises (Island/Antilles, Virgin/ Rough Trade) and the output of the small independents (Incus, Spotlite, Steam, Miles etc etc) dealing with everything from little-known conventional players, to the wildest shores of the avant-garde. Almost all this material is available on CD. For all its yuppified image, the CD has proved as invaluable to the cottage-industry labels for its ease of storage and handling, as it has to the majors.

Some record company insiders still believe that vinyl will be around in ten years time – almost certainly more expensive than CDs, by then, because production facilities will be fewer and costlier, but still representing a service to those who have invested in expensive record-playing equipment and have extensive and possibly rare collections. And some listeners simply don't like the CD sound. Compact discs are currently produced by recording a sound-wave form, as numbers. The present process involves losing the upper frequencies, above 20 kilohertz – not on the face of it a serious problem, because most people over thirty probably can't hear that high anyway. Critics of the process, however, take the view that such an operation disrupts the harmonics in such a way, as to cause a disagreeable steeliness at higher frequencies.

But in the end it won't be sentiment that keeps the record companies operating their vinyl pressing plants, but economics. As more and more CD purchasers come into the market place every day, because they've bought a space-saving new stacking hi-fi system to fit in that awkward corner and found that a CD player comes as part of the deal, the demand for vinyl will inevitably dwindle. And the transformation doesn't just have mass-market implications. As it becomes cheaper to press CDs, more independent, small scale, record producers will turn to it for their modest production runs of new, uncelebrated or avant-garde music. The improvising guitarist Derek Bailey administrates Incus Records, a label that has been documenting the work of many of the world's free-improvising musicians for twenty years. From Bailey's point of view, as he runs a largely mail-order based operation single-handed, CDs couldn't have arrived too soon. 'Like desktop publishing', Bailey says, 'CDs are perfect for a cottage industry like this. Small recording and distributing operations all over the world are turning to them because they're easy to package and transport. And the practical implication of CD, other than from the handling point of view, is that you know if you've got a good master you'll almost certainly find that a CD does justice to it, which isn't always the case with an LP by any means.'

The little silver disc is an emblem of the recording future. Even the scare over the durability of CDs recently died down, when the actual incidence of dud records, over the seven years or so of production, turned out to be miniscule. And the implications for jazz collectors are immense. Some inside the record industry have opined that virtually every jazz record, of any quality, will be reissued on CD, by the mid Nineties – and even though a long argument could be embarked on as to what counts as 'jazz' and what counts as 'quality', that's going to amount to a very large slice of the important jazz sessions of the past seventy years.

1

NEW ORLEANS TO CHICAGO

NEW ORLEANS is usually taken to be the exclusive birthplace of jazz, which is something of an overstatement that avoids the complicated history of the people of the southern United States in the 19th century and their music. What's more, jazz music has such a mixed parentage and its history, in the era before sound recording, is so erratically documented, that debates about its family tree have become a controversial business.

However the importance of New Orleans, and its surrounding state Louisiana, to the development of assorted strands of ethnic music into an international musical language, is undisputed. Louisiana's geographical location both made it a political bargaining chip for the French and Spanish (sometime landlords of the place) and the emerging United States, and gave it a multinational community of immigrants and itinerants embracing many cultures. It had two principal black populations – freed French-speaking slaves or Creoles, and American negroes only liberated after the Civil War. The French strand had inherited traditions of European classical music, popular songs, opera (New Orleans was an opera city earlier than anywhere else in the States, with blacks and whites attending the opera house) and dance.

From the American slaves came another musical line – the music of Africa, adapted by contact with church music in the States and by the working conditions suffered under slavery. African music reversed the European supremacy of melody and harmony over rhythm, featured an elided, bent-note intonation (often attributed to a culture in which spoken language is dependent on pitch as well as vocabulary for meaning), and had a tradition of songs accompanying everyday labours. It also had a preference for grouping notes in threes over a single beat (triple

4

time) rather than the European two-to-a-beat (duple) rhythms. Later graftings on to this tradition were two new scales, somewhere between the five-note scales of African music and the seven-note European one, with some notes of indeterminate pitch. These became the 'spiritual' and 'blue note' scales.

These strands in the emerging music of America produced 'ragtime' – primarily a descendant of Creole culture – and the blues.

Ragtime became an obsession in the States in the late 19th century. The word meant what it said – ragged time. An even-tempo, European-derived pulse would be played in a pianist's left hand, while the right played the normally soft beats hard and softened the ones usually emphasised, in a 'syncopation' of the beat. The melodies were mutations of the piano music of Chopin and Liszt among others, and they became known across America before the century was out, played by saloon-bar pianists and on the 'piano-rolls' that activated automatic player-pianos. The most famous ragtime composer, Scott Joplin, wrote over six hundred rags and two operas, including widely-loved themes such as 'The Entertainer', 'Solace' and 'Maple Leaf Rag'. But ragtime – a wholly composed music – wasn't jazz, although the terms are treated as interchangeable in some histories of early jazz. Neither was the blues, though it too was a crucial part of the chemistry from which jazz erupted.

In the southlands of America these musics lived side by side, along with the work songs and spirituals of the plantations, the folk-blues of the travelling banjo players, the boogie woogie style of saloon-bar pianists – and, in New Orleans, the traditional songs of the French, the Spaniards, Africans, English, Italians and, later, Germans and Slavs. The southern European custom of playing respectful slow marches on the outward journey to a cemetery and a celebratory romp on the way back, also survived into New Orleans life and provided an opportunity for collective and professional music making in the locality. The other big employer of musicians was the red-light district; given a municipal go-ahead by Alderman Sidney Story in 1898, and thereafter immortalised as 'Storyville'.

The makeup of the proto-jazz band was a mixture of high-culture Creole influences (audible in the prominence of the clarinet) and military-band instrumentation – the latter having received a boost from the sales of cheap secondhand brassware following the demobilisation of American forces after the Spanish–American war in 1898. The ensemble playing suggested a louche mutation of European polyphony – there would normally be three melody lines combined, from the cornet, trombone and clarinet, though the intonation would be quite unlike the 'pure' pitching of conservatoire music. Rhythmically it was still primitive, resembling parade and circus music. And the New Orleans pioneers of the movement around the turn of the century were mostly black – men like bandleaders Charles 'Buddy' Bolden, Bunk Johnson and Freddie Keppard, all playing a distinctively phrased music of unusual tonality but pedestrian in rhythm. The style became popular musical currency around Louisiana in the early years of the 20th century. By 1913, the word 'jass' – usually taken to have had a sexual meaning originally – was beginning to be associated with it. It was, however, a prominent white New Orleans bandleader, Papa Jack Laine, who launched the career of a man who in turn put jazz on the world map. Laine's band featured a powerful, but limited, self-taught trumpeter called Nick LaRocca. LaRocca eventually found himself in another band which was spotted by a Chicago impresario, and a modified version of it was duly hired for New York's Reisenweber's Restaurant in 1917. The group instantly became a runaway hit, was renamed the 'Original Dixieland Jass Band', and became the first jazz group to exploit the newly-invented record-producing technology with 'Livery Stable Blues' and 'Dixieland Jass Band One-Step'.

That a white, Chicago based, jazz group should have made a world-wide craze out of the new ideas of only a few hundred southern States musicians, far more of them black than white, was a travesty that nevertheless accurately reflected the race relations of the day. The ODJB, though it displayed a kind of frantic heat, was the vehicle for a palatable kind of jazz with little of the characteristic abrasiveness of the black bands. The group that truly synthesised the volatile musical energies of the south into a thrilling new concept quite different from the sum of its parts was just around the corner.

King Oliver's Creole Jazz Band

Joe 'King' Oliver was a cornettist who, by 1910, had proved himself adaptable enough to work in the best of the New Orleans brass bands and dance outfits. In the wake of the ODJB's successes in Chicago and New York, Oliver was brought to Chicago, became a familiar feature of the city's nightlife and in 1922 got the chance to lead a band of his own. King Oliver's first Creole Jazz Band (with Johnny Dodds, on clarinet, Baby Dodds, on drums, Honore Dutrey, on trombone, Lil Hardin, on piano, and Bill Johnson, on bass) was a revelation for the emerging jazz audiences. It was raucous, exultant, witty and swinging, its polyphonic ensemble sound of multiple melody lines rolling and diving over a beat that was beginning to disengage itself from the regularities of street-music. To add further variety, Oliver brought in a young discovery from New Orleans to create a two-cornet front line. The young man was Louis Armstrong, grand-child of slaves, raised by an aunt in the New Orleans ghetto, and later recipient of a rudimentary musical training at the Colored Waifs' Home. Armstrong had learned about four-part harmony from singing in a vocal group on the streets, his harmonic sense was such that he could improvise a counterpoint to melodies he was hearing for the first time, and he used this skill to devastating effect in improvising against Oliver's theme statements. Armstrong, Oliver and the Creole Jazz Band recorded for the first time in 1923, producing the first classics of jazz.

The Jazz Age began. Armstrong's genius soon led him to pursue a career of his own, and recordings of his Hot Five and Hot Seven bands rank among the most astonishing displays of spontaneous composition in jazz history. Under pressure from Armstrong's blazing virtuosity, the New Orleans contrapuntal ensemble style began to give way to jazz forms designed to high-light the soloist. But at the same time, more complex ensemble writing for improvisors to expand on was beginning to be developed by pianist Jelly Roll Morton with his Red Hot Peppers, and a larger ensemble was on the verge of being glimpsed by bandleaders such as Fletcher Henderson and Duke Ellington.

The earliest period of jazz is documented on CD – up to a point. Australian sound engineer Robert Parker's use of a Sony Digital Reprocessor to rescue crackly old masters (notably for the BBC's

7

'Jazz Classics in Digital Stereo' series) has made remarkable improvements to the quality of material that usually sounds as if it's coming from the house next door in a hurricane. But some enthusiasts dislike the imposition of stereo effects on mono originals, and the representation of early jazz for the specialist and collector is still overwhelmingly superior on vinyl.

Ammons, Albert C

(Born Chicago, September 23, 1907; died December 2, 1949)
Boogie-woogie piano developed in the southlands. It was originally a highly rhythmic and rough-and-ready blues style based on a repeated ostinato eight-beat figure in the left hand, decorated by improvised blues melody in the right, and it existed in some primitive form in the railhead bars long before jazz as a recognisable idiom was born. Boogie was big in the 1920s, dipped in the Thirties and came back with the jazz revivalist movement in the 1940s.

One of boogie's most imposing later practitioners was Albert Ammons, the rock-steadiness and booming vigour of whose left-hand figures (lessons learned from an earlier boogie star, Jimmy Yancey) made him one of the most consistently exciting exponents of the style. Ammons was internationally known by the end of his life, having come to the fore in the Twenties, with Francois Moseley's Louisiana Stompers. He ran bands of his own between 1934 and 1938 in Chicago, and was taken up by the impresario and talent-scout John Hammond, who persuaded him to move to New York and work in partnership with two other blues pianists, Meade Lux Lewis and Pete Johnson. These musicians performing in duos and trios were a considerable hit with audiences, and the boogie idiom became something of a craze, figuring in the repertoires of several of the Forties big bands. Ammons recorded with Lewis and Johnson for Hammond's *Spirituals to Swing* series, for the Library of Congress in 1938, and for the beginnings of the Blue Note label a year later. Between 1941 and 1944 Ammons' recording career was hampered by the Musicians' Union recording ban, but he returned to the studios frequently between 1944 and the end of his life, touring with the Lionel Hampton band in his final year, 1949.

★*Boogie Woogie and the Blues* (Commodore Class 824 297)

Ammons' return to recording after the Musicians' Union ban. This set features a mixture of strong solo performances and exchanges with a group of powerful partners, including Don Byas, on tenor, Hot Lips Page, on trumpet, and Sid Catlett, on drums. Tracks like 'Boogie Rocks' and 'Albert's Special Boogie', though not in the same league as earlier triumphs like 'Boogie Woogie Stomp' and 'Suitcase Blues', confirm Ammons' steely touch and unflagging beat; and Catlett's propulsive drumming mirrors the pianist's careering vigour on 'Bottom Blues'.

Armstrong, Louis Daniel

(Born New Orleans, July 4, 1900; died July 6, 1971)
Louis Armstrong revolutionised the sound of jazz. His boldness, melodic audacity, technical range and spontaneous sense of structure was in a different league even to the work of a vigorous, but more static, performer, his boss King Oliver. Armstrong's solos developed like well-told stories, full of sub-plots, diversions and grand finales, often with an integrating motif, characteristic to the tune, recurring, with minor variations, in chorus after chorus. He also played with equal fierceness in all registers and with astonishing volume – testified to by the now famous account of the Oliver band's early recording session in which Armstrong was placed fully twenty yards behind the others to avoid upsetting the sound balance. Such a virtuoso found it hard to inhabit the predominantly collective world of New Orleans jazz. Armstrong's arrival had a lot to do with the transformation of jazz, in the later Twenties, into a music of soloists and accompanists.

Since his mother's paid employment, in the New Orleans ghetto, included domestic service and prostitution, the young Armstrong was raised by an aunt, in low-life surroundings that appeared to dampen his characteristic amiability and optimism hardly at all. As a boy he raised money by singing in a harmony group on the streets, and when he fired a revolver into the air to help celebrate New Year's Day, 1913, and was committed to the Colored Waifs' Home, his musical progress soon proved highly unusual. From rapid promotion to the role of Waifs' Home bugler, Armstrong moved to being leader of its band, by now on cornet.

This kind of progress made a mark even in a seething musical environment like New Orleans. The teenage Armstrong began to find work as a musician in Storyville, and, at eighteen, joined the band led by local trombonist KID ORY. Through Ory he met King Oliver, who helped him further his education in the rudiments of jazz ensemble technique and the essentials of the repertoire.

Armstrong stayed in New Orleans – gaining experience by working on the riverboats with Fate Marable – when the first migration of black musicians started northwards. But when he got the call from Chicago to join King Oliver there, one of the most influential careers in jazz truly began. In 1923, when Armstrong was only twenty-two, the Oliver band made its first, historic, recordings for the Gennett Company of Richmond, Indiana, and the young Armstrong quickly demonstrated his incisive musical logic and often blistering sound despite the collective structure. After two years as 'second cornettist' to Oliver, Armstrong left to join the increasingly popular Fletcher Henderson dance band, and helped transform that organisation into a 'hot jazz' outfit, alongside other fast-rising stars like, saxophonist, Coleman Hawkins. With Henderson, Armstrong began to record hair-raising solos that frequently carried the band more than did its rhythm section, and his empathy and ability to listen creatively to another artist was also demonstrated in accompanying work with singers, most notably Bessie Smith.

The trumpeter's developing independence led him next to the formation of his Hot Fives, and then Hot Sevens, the bands that in the course of three years cut the most memorable music of the first phase of jazz. Recordings made in 1928 with Armstrong's Savoy Ballroom Five, and in 1929 with the CLARENCE WILLIAMS Blue Five, that included SIDNEY BECHET, also produced startling work. From the Thirties onward, the Louis Armstrong story was largely a catalogue of consistently remarkable solo performances against a variety of backdrops, many of them otherwise ordinary. Armstrong also became celebrated as a singer, credited with inventing the wordless 'scat' style, when he dropped his lyric sheet on the floor during a recording session.

Armstrong toured extensively during the 1930s, captivating European as well as American audiences. But he began to suffer with lip problems that hampered his old blazing virtuosity, and his solos became more epigrammatic, though still demonstrating that characteristic shapeliness. These instrumental restrictions led Armstrong to sing more, but he was such an inimitable improvisor in that role that it rarely seemed like second best. The collapse of the big band era, in the Forties, led Armstrong to continue his touring life with various lively small bands, dubbed the All-Stars, the first version memorably including cornettist, Bobby Hackett, trombonist, Jack Teagarden, and drummer, Sid Catlett. All-Stars tours could be routine affairs (driving away Earl Hines in 1951) but Armstrong proved he could still rise spectacularly to unique occasions, such as tributes to WC Handy (1953) and Fats Waller (1955). In the Fifties and Sixties Armstrong, as one of American music's best-loved ambassadors, toured the world, appeared in over thirty movies, received awards and citations everywhere, and was the subject of many documentaries and books. In his later years ill-health forced him to replace much more of his trumpet playing with vocals, but the two major hits he had with these ('Hello Dolly' and 'What A Wonderful World') endeared him to a far bigger public than he could ever have reached with jazz alone. He died peacefully in 1971.

Louis Armstrong – Great Original Performances 1923–1931 (BBC CD 597)

Tracks here include 'St Louis Blues', 'Muggles' and 'West End Blues' (with the most celebrated cadenza in jazz history in its opening bars), and the disc features all of Armstrong's timeless virtues crisply reproduced – urgent, declamatory tone, passionate blues feeling, immense audacity of phrasing. The compilation includes King Oliver's band ('Snake Rag'), eight tracks from the Hot Fives and Sevens (including the majestic but flawed 'Wild Man Blues', the flamboyant 'Muskrat Ramble', the perfectly poised 'Willie the Weeper' and 'Struttin' with Some Barbecue') and two by the Savoy Ballroom Five ('Save It Pretty Mama' and 'St James' Infirmary').

Louis Armstrong Hot Five and Hot Seven 1925–28 (Giants of Jazz/ Hasmick GOJCD 0242)

'Wild Man Blues', 'Willie the Weeper' and 'West End Blues' are also included in this selection, taken solely from Hot Five and Hot

Seven sessions, but so are 'Melancholy Blues', 'Cornet Chop Suey', 'Skid dat de dat' and 'I'm in the Barrel'. 'Cornet Chop Suey' is one of Armstrong's most sensational displays of virtuosity and became a model for aspiring trumpeters to copy. 'Skid dat de dat' is a novelty song featuring the leader's scat singing as an effortlessly blended instrumental voice, and 'I'm in the Barrel' was one of the opening cuts of that historic first Hot Five session, on November 12, 1925 – a blend, on Armstrong's part, of an initial minor mood transformed into a raucous blues, followed by poignant Johnny Dodds choruses on clarinet and resolved devastatingly by the trumpeter's final breaks. 'Potato Head Blues', with its roller-coaster of tension and resolution in Armstrong's solo, and his daring placing of accents on weak beats, is a display of genius at work.

★*Laughin' Louis* (Bluebird/BMG ND 90404)

Orchestra recordings between 1932–33, representing the final episode of Louis Armstrong's volcanic first creative period. Though the accompaniment is now more orderly and not prone to the occasional fluff, the sense of group endeavour is mostly gone and the pieces are showcases for the leader's by now utterly assured improvisation with trumpet or vocals. But Armstrong's solos are often breathtaking in their clarity of thought and panache, frequently on songs that have become mainstays of the standard repertoire – like 'I Got the World on a String' and 'I Gotta Right to Sing the Blues'.

★*Pops: The 1940s Small Band Sides* (Bluebird/BMG ND 86378)

The period during which Armstrong, like many other artists, found big band company too expensive and opted for a streamlined ensemble. Included is the music he recorded for the 1947 Arthur Lubin musical, *New Orleans*, including the tune Billie Holiday made her only feature film role, 'Do You Know What It Means To Miss New Orleans'. Armstrong's delightful reunions with trombonist Jack Teagarden (from the first All-Stars line-up) are the primary feature of the 1947 tracks, including exchanges with Teagarden, of an intensity worthy of the trumpeter's earliest days, on the justly celebrated Town Hall Concert material from May of that year.

★*Complete Louis Armstrong/Duke Ellington* (Roulette/EMI CDP 793 844-2)

A producer's idea of a good time rather than an artist's perhaps – this was Bob Thiele's attempt to find common ground between Armstrong and Ellington in 1961, and generally it can't be said to have been an unqualified success. But since Armstrong's reputation was mostly associated with pop hits after this, it's notable as one of his last unreservedly jazzy achievements, and for his scat vocal on 'Cotton Tail', embellishment of 'Mood Indigo' and nostalgically punchy treatment of 'Black and Tan Fantasy'.

★*Satch Plays Fats* (CBS 450 980-2)

Armstrong and the All-Stars, in 1955, with Trummy Young having replaced Jack Teagarden and with Billy Kyle on piano following Earl Hines' departure. In a period in which touring pressure was leading Armstrong bands to sound a shade tired, a special stimulus was necessary to get a little extra – and this happened on the Fats Waller tribute, with the musicians appropriately reflecting Waller's bounce and the leader inspired in his performance of 'Blue Turning Grey over You'.

★*What a Wonderful World* (Bluebird/BMG ND 88310)

By 1970 Louis Armstrong had stopped playing the trumpet, but his vocal style still transformed classic songs. He was by this point a much-loved institution, virtually beyond criticism, having influenced the course of 20th century music more substantially, in his most active years, than anyone had a right to expect. These tracks were recorded for Armstrong's newer audience, some of whom may never have known that he even played the trumpet. The title song was a hit for Armstrong twice, once in 1961, and then again twenty years later with the success of the movie *Good Morning Vietnam*, in which it was featured. Oliver Nelson conducts a supporting orchestra, and the choir accompanying 'We Shall Overcome' even includes such illustrious guests as Miles Davis and Tony Bennett.

Bechet, Sidney

(Born New Orleans, May 14, 1897; died May 14, 1959)
John Coltrane, listening to a soprano saxophone recording of Sidney Bechet's, is reputed to have said in wonderment 'did all those old guys swing like that?'. Bechet was, quite simply, *the* horn virtuoso of the early jazz, with an ability to disrupt the rigid accents that New Orleans had inherited from ragtime and to deliver his rhythmically audacious solos with a blazing tone and emotive vibrato equalled only by LOUIS ARMSTRONG. Bechet was the only serious competitor to Armstrong for the title of supreme architect of the early jazz. He established a substantial soloists' role for the saxophone (shifting from the popular clarinet to the rarely-played soprano saxophone in 1919), his compositions were probably better than Armstrong's, and he built an improvisors' language for his chosen instrument virtually singlehanded. But unlike Armstrong, he was temperamentally fragile, lacked the trumpeter's popular appeal, and spent the postwar years out of America. In his adopted France, in the Fifties, he was treated with much the same respect accorded to Maurice Chevalier.

Bechet grew up in the pre-jazz years in New Orleans, hearing the powerful, assertive street-band trumpeters as well as the reed players, and the experience may have helped him to cultivate his fierce, incandescent sound. Bechet learned clarinet with a famous local teacher, Lorenzo Tio, by twelve or thirteen he was able to take on virtually any kind of New Orleans band work and not long afterwards was teaching the instrument himself. Bechet moved to Chicago (in 1917), where he joined the orchestra of Will Marion Cook, and went with Cook to Europe with the Southern Syncopated Orchestra. Ernest Ansermet, the Swiss conductor, heard Bechet and instantly dubbed him a genius.

In JF Lafleur's Wardour Street music shop in London, Bechet found his first soprano saxophone, had a double-octave key added to it, and thereafter largely replaced the clarinet with it. He played to royalty in London, but ended up being deported from Britain after a fracas. Work with Duke Ellington and James P Johnson in New York followed, and with the CLARENCE WILLIAMS Blue Five, from 1923 onwards, Bechet (sometimes in partnership with Armstrong and various singers) gave early warning of his violently ecstatic manner of playing. At the end of the Twenties he travelled extensively in Europe, again as a sideman, with the Revue Nègre. By this point his improvising style was fully formed. He had subverted the rhythmic regularity of ragtime and was accenting notes in a wilful, but utterly deliberate manner; ideas seemed to be tumbling over each other in the effort to escape from the horn, and his tone was a colourful mixture of distortions, exultant and admonishing sounds, and massive, suspenseful vibrato. The New Orleans Feetwarmers, the band he formed in 1932 with trumpeter Tommy Ladnier, displayed Bechet in the full flood of this mature style.

Through the Thirties Bechet's fortunes were mixed (at one point he gave up and opened a New York tailor's shop with Ladnier) but he recorded some historic tracks in a competitive meeting with Armstrong in 1940. Club work followed in the postwar years, but not enough of it to prevent him from having to teach for a living as well. Bechet did however record for the then new label Blue Note (available as *From Boogie to Bop*, Blue Note CDP 792 465-2); his version of 'Summertime' being a hit for the company. But when Bechet visited the Paris Jazz Festival in 1949 (on that occasion even performing with Charlie Parker) and was greeted rapturously, he decided to emigrate to a place that appreciated him. He remained in France until his death, a celebrated entertainer through hit records like 'Les Oignons' and 'Petite Fleur' (allegedly composed while Bechet was seated on the lavatory) and toward the end of his life even a composer for a ballet, *La Nuit Est une Sorcière*. In Antibes, a town square was named after him.

Unlike Louis Armstrong, Bechet is so far poorly represented on CD, though the RCA/Bluebird recordings cover a spectacular eleven-year display of much of his best work, and there are some interesting, but more erratic, sessions on the Vogue label from the period in France.

★*The Bluebird Sessions 1932–1943* (BMG/Bluebird ND 90317)

This collection, excluding as it does Bechet's earlier and later periods, thoroughly documents the developments of his mid-career, from prolific recording opportunities in the early Thirties, through semi-retirement by the end of the decade, and then resurgence with the New Orleans revival that partly occurred as a backlash to bop. It features nineteen bands on eighty-four tracks, some of them represented in several takes, and it vibrates with Bechet's impassioned, impulsive and inimitable sound; from the sultry, liquid clarinet on 'Blues In the Air', through the soaring, violin-like soprano sax high register, with his 1941 New York trio, on 'Strange Fruit'. On 'I Found a New Baby', Bechet's spinechilling vibrato and sheer penetration provoke trumpeter Tommy Ladnier into almost desperate wailing, and 'Maple Leaf Rag' and 'Shag' are streams of lyrical consciousness, with the latter (based on the famous 'I Got Rhythm' sequence used by the beboppers) representing one of the first themeless jazz recordings. JELLY ROLL MORTON's 1939 band is featured too.

★*Platinum For Sidney Bechet* (Vogue VG 600 026)

One of the saxophonist's better French sessions (his tendency to play rather melodramatic rehearsed solos in later years was often attributed to the effort needed to stimulate lagging rhythm sections) dating from Bechet's arrival in France in 1949. This includes the first of the American's many recordings with French bandleader, Claude Luter, and finds Bechet in robust form on the 'Summertime'-like, 'Bechet's Creole Blues', and an amiable rendition of the attractive theme, 'Les Oignons', which was to become such a success in France. The saxophonist's other popular recording, 'Petite Fleur', is also included.

Morton, Ferdinand Le Menthe (or Lemott) 'Jelly Roll'

(Born New Orleans, October 20, 1890; died July 10, 1941)
The great ragtime players – of whom the most fertile and creative was Scott Joplin – didn't really fall into even the widest definitions of jazz because their music was primarily composed. Pianist Jelly Roll Morton was one of the most significant artists to have accelerated the evolution of ragtime into jazz, and it helped that his primary influences were both ragtime and the blues. A pimp, a vaudeville artist, a music publisher, boxing promoter and gambling-house manager, Morton nonetheless achieved more in his musical career (unappreciated though it was by the end of his life) than many early jazz figures who had pursued their craft

with fewer diversions. The ragtime antecedents are clear in Morton's work, but he disrupts its even pulse and he improvises. And as a writer and arranger, he developed the resources of the standard New Orleans instrumentation, augmenting the lineup at times, creating a clarinet 'section', blending improvisation and composition and anticipating the future by the use of the repeated ensemble motif (the 'riff') behind soloists and the brief unaccompanied improvisation (the 'break') between abruptly stopped and started ensemble sections, both of which featured strongly in the big-band 'swing' era.

Morton learned the piano as a child, being from a middle class Creole background, his parents patrons of the opera. But this wasn't the kind of New Orleans life the young Morton cared to be part of. By his teens he was playing the piano in the 'sporting-houses' of Storyville and in 1923 he joined the exodus to Chicago. He began recording some sensational piano solos for the Gennett Company (including classics like 'King Porter Stomp', 'Kansas City Stomp' and 'The Pearls') followed up three years later by the first Red Hot Peppers sessions. The pieces are remarkable for their variation of pace and texture, for their interwoven and contrasting themes and for the blend of solo and ensemble energy – Morton being considerably assisted by the presence of excellent and understanding sidemen like trumpeter, George Mitchell, and clarinettist, Omer Simeon.

But by the beginning of 1930, with the move toward more soloistic music and demand for more elaborate jazz using bigger bands, Morton's fondness for elaborations on the old New Orleans style was going out of fashion. He attempted unsuccessfully to run a big band as the Depression hit, his record contract expired and he was soon scuffling for orchestra-pit work. Morton was eventually tracked down in Washington by the archivist Alan Lomax and committed his thoughts and music to record for the Library of Congress in 1938. Though he recorded again (notably with SIDNEY BECHET, see page 16) Morton was a disillusioned man. He drove west in 1940, already suffering from asthma and a heart condition, hoping that warmer climes would put him right. He died the next year in Los Angeles. His grave was not marked until ten years after his death, at the instigation of the Jelly Roll Morton Society.

★*The Pearls* (Bluebird/BMG ND 86588)

Brilliant Morton tracks from the Red Hot Pepper sessions – including the classics, 'Black Bottom Stomp', 'The Chant', 'Grandpa's Spells' and 'Doctor Jazz'. These sessions were high points of the most sophisticated early New Orleans music, and their blends of composition and improvisation, deft rhythmic shifts and subtle interweaving of the trumpet/clarinet/trombone front line, give the music a constant vividness and vivacity. Morton skilfully avoids repeating devices within the same piece and engineers numerous shifts of tone colour to effect a previously unheard-of variety within the span of a three-minute recording. Trombonist KID ORY and clarinettist Omer Simeon are regular Peppers members, and on 'Steamboat Stomp' and 'Sidewalk Blues' two extra clarinettists are added (Darnell Howard and Barney Bigard) to produce Morton's revolutionary pre-big band reed 'section', albeit only briefly. The set also includes two tracks featuring Morton in collaboration with Sidney Bechet, in 1939.

★*New Orleans Memories* (Commodore AG6 24062)

Morton on piano in 1939, in a session that displays both the artist's compositional genius on magnificent blues like 'Mamie's Blues' and 'Winin' Boy Blues' and examples of the music that he so resoundingly helped to transform – early ragtime. Morton's modifications of the inexorable beat of ragtime confirms (if not the musician's own contention that he created jazz out of ragtime singlehandedly) the audacity of his rhythmic development of those materials, the left hand urgently pressing the beat, the right unfolding graceful, intricate runs of far greater complexity than the steady clang of the originals.

Original Dixieland Jazz Band

Justly, or unjustly, the ODJB was where the Jazz Age began. Though musically the band was nowhere near the jazz equal of many of the black groups of the day (or some of the white ones) the mixture of fortuitousness and bravura that took it into Resenweiber's restaurant in New York in 1917, set the jazz message reverberating around the world.

The five founding members of the band were Nick LaRocca (cornet), Larry Shields (clarinet), Eddie Edwards (trombone), Henry Ragas (piano) and Tony Spargo (drums). All of them were white, and had served a loose apprenticeship in the bands of local bandleader Papa Jack Laine, as well as closely attending to the work of King Oliver. LaRocca in particular, as well as being a trumpeter of determination, was also a ferociously energetic and ambitious man, and his application galvanised the ODJB's career. In 1916 LaRocca, Ragas and Edwards, plus drummer Johnny Stein and clarinettist Alcide Nunez, went to Chicago for a nightclub season, then moved to New York to Resenweiber's, helped by the encouragement of Al Jolson. With a mixture of virtuosic musicianship (Larry Shields, who replaced Nunez, was the most reliable exponent of it) and vaudevillian horseplay, the band provided diverting, and engagingly anarchic, entertainment and was soon a big commercial success. The enthusiasm it engendered resulted in the band entering the Victor studios, in New York, on February 26, 1917, to cut the first ever jazz record. It sold over a million copies and jazz became a national, then international, craze.

The ODJB's overnight success led to a trip to Britain (it performed privately for members of the Royal Family) touring vaudeville theatres and holding down a nine-month residency at the Hammersmith Palais. Returning to the States in 1920, the ODJB continue to record and tour, but in 1921 Shields dropped out, followed in 1925 by LaRocca, at which point the group disbanded. It had sparked an enthusiasm for jazz in innumerable musicians (notably cornettists Red Nichols and Bix Beiderbecke) but was being overhauled not long after its arrival by the more spontaneous and vital playing of the black bands, and the more sophisticated ensemble sound of white groups like Paul Whiteman's. Various members of the ODJB participated in occasional revivals in the 1930s and 1940s, but the early sparkle was never recaptured.

*Sensation (Living Era/Academy Sound and Vision CD AJA 5023)

Most of the ODJB's successful early pieces are included on this set, and though much of it sounds archaic and clumsy today ('Livery

Stable Blues' and 'At the Jazz Band Ball' are particularly quaint combinations of crass instrumental effects and studied informality) there are moments of genuinely musical uplift on later tracks, such as 'I've Lost My Heart in Dixieland'. In general a disc of more historical than musical value, but as the starting point of recorded jazz, the historical value amounts to quite a lot.

Ory, Edward 'Kid'

(Born La Place, Louisiana, December 25, 1886; died January 23, 1973)

One of the most astute and successful of early New Orleans musicians, Kid Ory was also a basic but immensely powerful and effective trombonist in the gruff, relaxed manner required of the instrument in its collective-ensemble guise. He played with the very best of the first wave of musicians, including ARMSTRONG, JELLY ROLL MORTON and blues singer Ma Rainey, then dropped out of the business during the swing band era of the Thirties, but returned to become one of the most acclaimed defenders of New Orleans music in the revival that began in the 1940s.

Ory was a banjo player originally, and always believed that if there was a market for the increasingly popular idiom of jazz, it should be properly handled – that meant good presentation, and it also meant suitably profiting from the music's desirability. He had a talent for self-promotion, and was impatient with unsuitable musicians – but with those who did suit him (notably King Oliver and Louis Armstrong) he was a robust and sometimes enthralling performer. In California, in 1922, Ory's band was the first black New Orleans-style outfit to make a jazz record, and later in the Twenties the trombonist appeared on Armstrong's Hot Fives and Sevens, as well as collaborating successfully with clarinettist Johnny Dodds and with Jelly Roll Morton's Red Hot Peppers. Though he retired to run a chicken farm in the Thirties, he was back with a fine band of his own in the mid Forties, appearing to great acclaim on the Orson Welles radio show. Ory toured Europe several times, his most famous composition 'Muskrat Ramble' was a revivalist hit in the Fifties.

★*Echoes from New Orleans* (Giants of Jazz CD 53037)

Vigorous work by Ory's Creole Jazz Band, the outfit he led from the late Forties until he quit in 1961. Though ensemble democracy is the priority, Ory's firmness, booming tone and unfailing comprehension of when to apply the pressure as a group player, give the entire session much of its verve. Excellent, infectious pieces include 'Oh Didn't He Ramble', 'High Society', 'Maryland My Maryland' and 'Bugle Call Rag'.

Williams, Clarence

(Born Plaquemine, Louisiana, October 8, 1893; died November 6, 1964)
Williams was a New Orleans pianist and composer who probably didn't receive his due recognition because the illustrious artists he performed with eclipsed him – particularly LOUIS ARMSTRONG and SIDNEY BECHET. But he wrote many of the most famous tunes of New Orleans music (including 'Baby Won't You Please Come Home', 'Everybody Loves My Baby' and 'Royal Garden Blues'), accompanied Bessie Smith on her recording debut, and was highly influential behind the scenes, as well as on the bandstand, in the difficult early days of recording black American music.

Williams was a shrewd operator as well as a good musician (his family were hotel-owners, and Williams often ran sideline operations such as cleaning businesses alongside his musical career) and when he made $1600 in 1916, as a royalty payment from a successful New York band for one of his compositions, he used the money to found a music publishing company in Chicago. From 1923, Williams was handling new signings to the so-called 'race' division of Okeh Records as well as running his own bands, and though his fortunes declined with the movement away from New Orleans styles in the Thirties, Williams profitably sold his catalogue to Decca Records and opened a record shop in Harlem.

★*Jazz Classics in Digital Stereo* (BBC CD 721)

Wide selection of Williams' music with his celebrated Washboard Band, including such tunes as 'Organ Grinder Blues', 'Trouble' and 'I Can't Beat You Doin' What You're Doin' To Me'.

2

THAT WAS THEN AND THIS IS NOW: OLD AND NEW MEANINGS OF SWING

LOUIS ARMSTRONG towered over jazz in the early Twenties, and his virtuosity and insight were the principal catalysts shifting the traditional New Orleans contrapuntal ensemble style toward jazz forms showcasing soloists. The result was that, at the end of the 1920s, jazz stood poised to develop on several tumultuous fronts at once. Following Armstrong's lead, some of the most diligent white musicians (most notably cornettist, Bix Beiderbecke) were developing a more soloistic, small-band music in New York. A pianistic genius, Art Tatum, was indicating new and richer resources for improvisation, using the underlying harmonic structures of songs rather than the melody lines themselves. Sidney Bechet's example on the saxophone, a hitherto little used instrument, was beginning to be paralleled by reed virtuosi, such as Johnny Hodges and Coleman Hawkins. Pianist/arrangers Fletcher Henderson, Duke Ellington and Luis Russell, started expanding the jazz ensemble, dividing the band into meshing blocks or 'sections'.

And it was this development that overwhelmed the jazz scene for most of the 1930s. Bandleaders like Benny Goodman, the Dorsey Brothers, Count Basie and Duke Ellington, were frontrunners in a big-band boom that, at its height, saw dozens of sizeable orchestras working flat out in every corner of the United States. From these bands emerged great instrumental soloists (saxophonists Coleman Hawkins and Lester Young, trumpeter Roy Eldridge) and powerful improvising singers too (Billie Holiday, Ella Fitzgerald).

Duke Ellington, though he wasn't the most commercially popular of the orchestra leaders during the boom, was ultimately the artist who rewrote the book of what was possible for a large orchestra of jazz instrumentalists. Ellington's method of composi-

22

tion owed little or nothing to orthodox classical music or conservatoire methods, but drew its energies from the core of jazz, since his development of fragments of themes into rich tapestries of orchestral sound was often based on a trial-and-error exploration of harmonic options, in rehearsal with his musicians. Sidemen of the creative quality of Johnny Hodges, Tricky Sam Nanton and Bubber Miley, were therefore crucial to Ellington's conception, and timeless classics like, 'Creole Love Call', 'Mood Indigo', and, 'Sophisticated Lady', came from such collaboration.

But Ellington's wasn't the only kind of big-band jazz, and less impressionistic versions of it than his tended to do better at the box office. Bands like Bennie Moten's and Count Basie's, used the repeated, rhythmically insistent chordal figure behind soloists, a device that came to be known as the 'riff'. Clarinettist Benny Goodman's band drew on New Orleans music and the riff-dominated style associated with Kansas City musicians. Much of the appeal of the big-bands depended on the quality of their soloists, and competition to be a bigger drawing card was intense.

The bottom fell out of the big-band business, in the tough, postwar economic climate. Leaner times required slimmed-down music production, which is one good material reason for the development of a predominantly, small-band music – bebop – from the 1940s onward. By the mid-1950s, several strains of jazz were coexisting, not always amicably. Some big-bands struggled to continue, if necessary in pared-down form, as Count Basie's was forced to do for a time. Some of the surviving musicians, of the early New Orleans era, enjoyed a comeback as those jazz fans who disliked the complexities of modernism embraced them again in a revivalism that was to result in a good deal of controversy between 'modern' and 'trad' fans. As younger musicians developed, they faced the choice of whether to burnish and develop the older styles or throw in their lot with bop. The result was a current of jazz that came to be known as the 'mainstream', involving both the original practitioners of earlier styles and later generations of musicians who sought to protect them.

Allison, Mose John

(Born Tippo, Mississippi, November 11, 1927)
Mose Allison's singing, an influential triumph of artlessness

23

(Georgie Fame has been his most respectful interpreter in this country) is rarely far from the blues. He was once a bebop pianist, accompanying Stan Getz and Gerry Mulligan in the Fifties, but his allegiances are with simpler and earthier forms. Allison's piano playing, a mixture of hopping, emphatic on-the-beat accents, rattling triplet runs like coaches travelling fast over points, and baleful bluesy trills, suggests a confection of saloon-bar blues pianists and the work of ELLINGTON and Thelonious Monk. His singing is influenced by Sonny Boy Williamson and Tampa Red. but with a diffident, though always swinging, delivery that implies private musings rather than performance, if of an acerbic, ironic and penetrating kind.

Allison played piano as a child, and was a Dixieland trumpeter at school, but blues was an inevitable accompaniment to life in the Mississippi Delta. He played throughout the region until 1956, when he moved to New York to work with Getz, Mulligan and others, but performed with his own trios from the Sixties onward, honing his unique style and expanding on a collection of brilliant original compositions including 'Parchman Farm', 'Look What You Made Me Do' and 'Everybody Cryin' Mercy'. His classic 1957 Prestige album *Black Country Suite* isn't available on CD.

★*Ever Since the World Ended* (Blue Note CDP 748 015-2)

Mose Allison had a lean time in the 1970s, and his signing to Blue Note for a debut album, in 1987, was a long-overdue recognition of his talents. Not only did this disc feature Allison's uniquely gentle perversity and ironic vision in full spate, but it included some new compositions and assistance from altoist Arthur Blythe, saxophonist Bennie Wallace and guitarist Kenny Burrell. Burrell excepted, this amplification wasn't really necessary and only suggested that the label didn't have confidence in Allison selling on his own – but the session worked well enough, and showed the leader's independent spirit to be still firmly in charge.

Barber, Ball and Bilk

Chris Barber (born Hertfordshire, April 17, 1930)
Kenneth 'Kenny' Ball (born Essex, May 22, 1930)

Bernard Stanley 'Acker' Bilk (born Somerset, January 28, 1929)
These three musicians developed their careers quite separately, as
distinctive exponents of the British revivalist music of the 1950s
and 1960s, yet they are united by age, by aptitude for adapting
their enthusiasms in early jazz to a commercial market in a rock
dominated period, and by the possession of far more sophisticated
instrumental skills than they're often given credit for.
Trombonist Chris Barber was one of the most influential figures
in the British 'trad boom' of the Fifties, originally a defendant of
unadulterated New Orleans playing, but later the leader of a
vigorous and entertaining band that intermingled rhythm 'n'
blues, Ellingtonish ensemble ideas and programmatic accounts of
the early development of jazz. Trumpeter Kenny Ball, began
leading his own groups in 1958, and ten years later was virtually
a household name with a string of pop hits, from catchy tunes
given a streamlined trad treatment, and regular appearance on
TV. Clarinettist Acker Bilk, has similarly enjoyed a career as a
serious and knowledgeable exponent of early jazz instrumental
skills, fitfully interrupted by pop success – his biggest hit being a
lilting, vibrato-packed ballad called 'Stranger on the Shore', which
made Bilk the top-selling artist of the trad boom.

The emergence of the Beatles in England, and all the rhythm 'n'
blues groups that came in their wake, swept revivalist jazz aside,
and these musicians and others retired to clubs and to audiences
of loyal fans. They have all continued to produce good music
however, often in collaboration with visiting Americans of the
same inclinations.

★*The Ultimate* (Kaz Records KAZ CD4)

Barber, Ball and Bilk in a collection that includes: Ball's lively, early
Sixties dancefloor hit, 'Midnight in Moscow'; Bilk's rhapsodic
'Stranger on the Shore'; and a selection of standard revivalist fare
including 'When The Saints Go Marching In', 'Muskrat Ramble'
and 'St Louis Blues'.

★*Chris Barber – Mardi Gras at the Marquee*
(Timeless CDTTD 5546)

An Eighties project of the energetic Barber's, whose performances were frequently historical tours around New Orleans music. But Barber has rarely been content simply to replicate early material, and in this session from the London Marquee Club, his band vivaciously rolls through a repertoire of originals by the blues singer and pianist Dr John, also present on the date.

Basie, William 'Count'

(Born Red Bank, New Jersey, August 21, 1904; died April 26, 1984) If the sound of any outfit came to define big band jazz, it was the orchestra of William 'Count' Basie. Universally loved, it turned on succeeding generations to a way of making music that was quintessentially American. Six years after Basie's death, and now led by saxophonist Frank Foster, it still bristles with those classic Basie virtues of the blues, uninhibited soloing, simplicity, spontaneity, laid-back expertise and wit, and tireless capacity to swing.

William Basie, a one-time vaudeville pianist, got his jazz break with the successful Benny Moten band, one of the exciting Kansas City ensembles of the 1920s that showed New Orleans wasn't the only home of jazz. Basie displayed the 'stride' style of FATS WALLER, but unlike most young pianists preferred selectiveness, surprise and humour to technical fireworks. When Moten died unexpectedly during a tonsillectomy in 1935, Basie formed a new band out of the old one. Encouraged by the critic John Hammond to tighten up a rather haphazard collection of arrangements, the Basie band became by 1937 a brisk, disciplined and furiously rhythmic outfit, with players of the calibre of LESTER YOUNG and Herschel Evans on saxophones, Buck Clayton on trumpet and a dazzling rhythm section (always the heart of a Basie band) with the leader on piano, Freddie Green on guitar, Walter Page on bass and Jo Jones on drums. Driving and purposeful but light as a feather, those musicians came to define the swing beat, and Basie's doodling fill-ins and sidelong introductions became an indelible trademark.

In the hard postwar years, Count Basie rebuilt his orchestra with more complex arrangements (featuring, among others, those of Neal Hefti and Johnny Mandel) but without sacrificing its characteristic punch. The revitalised Basie band also introduced a new tenor player in 1953, the Cincinnati-born Frank Foster.

Foster stayed with Basie until 1964, and rejoined as keeper of the flame after the first inheritor of the Basie mantle, trumpeter Thad Jones, died a year into the job. A gifted arranger as well as a good soloist, Foster has written around 125 of the charts over the years, scored a Basie album all to himself with _Easin' It_ in 1960, and wrote some of the ensemble's showpieces including 'Shiny Stockings' and 'Allright OK You Win' for the band's majestic blues singer of the day, Joe Williams. Foster has also written a glowing but entirely appropriate tribute to the maestro, the 'Count Basie Remembrance Suite', a celebration of the high periods of the orchestra.

★_The Atomic Mr Basie_ (Roulette/EMI CDP 793 273-2)

One of the later Basie band's greatest recordings, a session from 1959 that featured some of the best of the outfit's soloists on some of the most fitting material, its insistent rhythmic grace in full flow, its dynamic leaps constantly exhilarating. Eddie 'Lockjaw' Davis is grittily garrulous on 'Whirly Bird', Frank Wess on 'Splanky', and trumpeter Thad Jones and Basie himself make a delectable job of variations on 'The Kid From Red Bank'. State-of-the-art big band music, though the nuclear explosion on the sleeve hasn't worn well as a piece of upbeat artwork.

★_For the First Time_ (Pablo J33J 20051)

Basie was a much better pianist than many of his listeners took him for, with a Waller-derived stride style that used space and prolonged silences with an audacity that made the pianist's eventual statements seem positively loquacious. Jazz impresario Norman Granz appreciated Basie's keyboard work, and set him with a vigorous trio (bassist Ray Brown and drummer Louis Bellson) for this attractive session, including 'Lady Be Good' and 'Royal Garden Blues'.

★_Count Basie – Compact Jazz_ (Verve 831 364-2)

More of _The Atomic Mr Basie_, but generally a good-value 55 minutes or so of cuts from 1956 to '64 with Thad Jones, Frank Wess and Frank Foster among the soloists and the band demonstrating much of its relaxed and effortless swing. No Joe Williams however, the blues singer who did much to restore the post-war fortunes of the Basie outfit.

Beiderbecke, Leon Bix

(Born Davenport, Iowa, March 10, 1903; died August 7, 1931) The legend of trumpeter Bix Beiderbecke is now hard to disentangle from Hollywood cliche. As the first white soloist to make a dent in the world of jazz, he set the legend in motion by dying young. Before that, his clean, precise and glistening sound on cornet had transfixed itself in the minds of all who heard it, while his even-paced, almost matter-of-fact phrasing held implications for the future that took decades to work through.

Beiderbecke's mother was a pianist, though the boy was a self-taught musician, originally inspired by the recordings of the Original Dixieland Jazz band and its trumpeter Nick LaRocca, and also hearing Louis Armstrong during his riverboat-playing period before his move to Chicago. Beiderbecke's career on record began in 1923 with the Wolverines, a somewhat stodgy outfit that he pulled imperiously into shape during the ensembles. Comparing the band's version of 'Jazz Me Blues' and Beiderbecke's own 1927 recording, reveals the extent to which he was developing a solo style more independent of the lead-cornettist's role, and with more of an Armstrong influence in the dynamics. From the same year came the classic ballad 'Singin' The Blues', that places his tone in its most perfect setting. A few more sides from that year, including 'I'm Coming Virginia' and 'At the Jazz Band Ball' constitute the best of the Beiderbecke legend, not forgetting poignantly impressionistic piano solos like 'In A Mist', then derided as not jazzy enough. Beiderbecke joined the symphonic-jazz orchestra of bandleader Paul Whiteman, in the later stages of his brief career, but alcoholism affected his consistency with the band. A sort of memorial to Beiderbecke exists in the form of one of the most popular of popular songs, 'Stardust' by his friend Hoagy Carmichael. The entire song, especially the verse, sounds like one gloriously extended melodic statement by Bix at his best.

★*Bix Beiderbecke – Jazz Classics in Digital Stereo* (BBC CD 601)

Beiderbecke recordings from 1924 to 1930. Where Armstrong

approaches his solos like a man charging through a swing-door, a dreamer but with a pragmatic zest for life; Beiderbecke at his peak was like an illustrator able to draw a free-hand circle – his solos were as finely balanced as compositions, his tone like a chime, and his mood reflective, but reflective on an unattainable grace. Beiderbecke is sometimes found here in one of his most fruitful partnerships – with the equally wistful saxophone Frank Trumbauer, an influence on LESTER YOUNG. The disc features 'Jazz Me Blues' and 'At the Jazz Band Ball', but not 'I'm Coming Virginia'.

★*Bixology* (Giants of Jazz GO JCD 53017)

'Tiger Rag', the piano classic 'In A Mist' and 'I'm Coming Virginia' are included on this selection of vintage Beiderbecke.

Berigan, Rowland Bernart 'Bunny'

(Born Wisconsin, November 2, 1908; died June 2, 1942)
Like BIX BEIDERBECKE, Bunny Berigan was a white trumpeter of prodigious talent who only partially developed as a jazz artist before drink and a diffidence about applying himself to details wrecked his career. Berigan lived longer than Beiderbecke, but not by much.

Berigan's sound at its best was both majestic and emotional, his dynamic range immense (he was one of the loudest players in the business, as well as one of the most melodically subtle) and his speed of thought such that much of his work seemed to consist of throwaway phrases that could have formed the start of innumerable trumpet solos on their own. His career began at the end of the Twenties when he joined Hal Kemp's dance-band for a European tour and, in 1931, he joined the prestigious Paul Whiteman outfit as a replacement for Beiderbecke, then the fast-rising BENNY GOODMAN four years later. Berigan was restless in other people's groups and formed his own big band, with mixed results, in 1937. That year he also made a second recording of a classic song, perenially associated with him – 'I Can't Get Started'. Berigan's career went on the slide during the war years. TOMMY DORSEY paid for the trumpeter's funeral. Very little Berigan is available on CD.

★*Portrait of Bunny Berigan* (Academy Sound & Vision AJA 5060)

Recordings by Berigan in a variety of contexts between 1932 and 1936, on tunes such as 'King Porter Stomp' and 'Prisoner's Song', plus the first (and less convincing) version of 'I Can't Get Started'.

Berry, Leon 'Chu'

(Born Wheeling, West Virginia, September 13, 1910; died October 30, 1941)

If Chu Berry had not died in a road smash, he would almost certainly have gone down in the jazz histories as on close to equal footing with tenor saxophone giants such as COLEMAN HAWKINS, BEN WEBSTER and LESTER YOUNG. He had an opulent tone, mingled with a fragile high-register delicacy, he was fast, and – like Hawkins – it's likely that his technique and inclinations would have led him to embrace the development of bebop. Berry came to New York in 1930, joined BENNY CARTER's band and then rejected an offer from DUKE ELLINGTON in favour of FLETCHER HENDERSON, following that stretch with the period in CAB CALLOWAY's band that lasted until his death. It was with Calloway that Berry made some of his finest recordings, developing a productive relationship with the trumpeter ROY ELDRIDGE, and with pianist Teddy Wilson. Berry's work on disc reveals him to be, if not independent of the inexorable Hawkins momentum, a gentler exponent of it.

★*Giant of the Tenor Sax* (Commodore 824 291)
Chu Berry with the Little Jazz Ensemble from 1939 to 1941. The disc features a good deal of previously unissued material, as well as one of his finest and most feverishly intense solos on '46 West 52nd Street', which is represented by two takes. Berry's account of 'Body and Soul' is also here, though he's too lush and sentimental as a ballad player.

Braff, Reuben 'Ruby'

(Born Boston, March 16, 1927)
Cornettist Ruby Braff is the kind of jazz musician commonly

overlooked because he didn't do what the rest of his generation did and thus appears to be a confused revivalist. Braff is a year younger than Miles Davis, but he plays swing. The Boston musician can play ballads with a subtlety all but lost in the post-bop compulsion to perform everything in double-time, and his tone blends the vigour of Armstrong, with the bell-like sound of BEIDERBECKE. In his chosen field, he is one of the most evocative, hypnotic brass-playing storytellers in jazz.

Because of his avoidance of bop, Braff didn't appear in concert very much in the Fifties, but he recorded some excellent music, sometimes partnering illustrious elders – like fellow trumpeter ROY ELDRIDGE. Braff's warm sound and gently-paced elegance makes him gleam almost regardless of the playing circumstances, and the public seemed to acknowledge this from the Sixties onward, when he became a regular member of George Wein's Newport package, and then a softly emotional partner of guitarist George Barnes in the Braff-Barnes quartet. *Two By Two*, Braff's duet with pianist Ellis Larkins, deserves CD release.

A Sailboat In The Moonlight (Concord CCD 4296)
A 1986 meeting between Ruby Braff's graceful trumpet and the equally poised mainstream tenor of SCOTT HAMILTON. Braff is inventive and original throughout, and Hamilton both shadows him and burnishes his work. For all their devotion to the past, neither man has time for cliches and, as a celebration of old-style lyricism, this collaboration is a delight.

Byas, Carlos Wesley 'Don'

(Born Oklahoma, October 21, 1912; died August 24, 1972)
Like CHU BERRY, Don Byas was a supreme technician with a considerable debt to COLEMAN HAWKINS, but he was more a modernist in conception than Berry, and his harmonic ear was very sophisticated – partly a result of absorption in the work of pianist ART TATUM. Byas took on the implications of bebop, though – like Hawkins – his Thirties notion of the even placement of accents didn't permit him to take the liberties the bebopper did. But Byas' big tone and fast construction made him an influence on

both John Coltrane and Sonny Rollins, and his music almost always gave off energy and conviction. He was a violinist originally, but took up saxophone as a teenager and was appearing with mid-West big bands before he was twenty. Moving to California, Byas worked with LIONEL HAMPTON, Ethel Waters, Don Redman and others before joining first Andy Kirk's band, then COUNT BASIE's. Byas played the 52nd Street bebop clubs in the Forties, appearing on early bop record dates, then toured Europe with the Don Redman band in 1946, which led him to settle in France, and then in Holland. Byas was busy into the Seventies, working briefly with Art Blakey's Messengers on a 1971 Japanese tour.

★*Tenderly* (Vogue VG 600 088)

Trio and quartet recordings by Don Byas, dating from his arrival in Paris in the late Forties. Byas' Paris recordings often set him with strings, and presented him largely as a ballad player. These excellent sessions show that, when he was supported only by a rhythm section, he retained all the fullness of tone and harmonic ingenuity that had built his reputation.

Calloway, Cabell 'Cab'

(Born Rochester, New York, December 25, 1907)
Bandleader Cab Calloway has had a remarkably sustained career in the jazz world, and on the fringes of it. His work has had as much in common with vaudeville as jazz, and he is best known to the public for a variety of novelty-vocals that have become entertainment-business landmarks, most notably, 'The Hi De Ho Man', which became a catch-phrase that swept America. But, like many showmen with an interest in jazz, Calloway frequently hired excellent partners, his most illustrious soloist being saxophonist, CHU BERRY.

He began in vaudeville with his sister Blanche, and also worked as a sometime drummer and MC in clubs, but it was as a bandleader-singer that he made his mark. 'Minnie the Moocher – the King of Hi De Ho' is the recording that has been more indelibly imprinted on the CV of Cab Calloway than any other. Calloway worked successfully at the Cotton Club during the early

Thirties, and he sustained a big band (at times including Chu Berry) until 1948, after which he took to touring the world, with a small group, playing a London Palladium season in 1948. He was in the original cast of the musical *Porgy and Bess*, played opposite Pearl Bailey, in *Hello Dolly*, and, in more recent times, featured in John Belushi and Dan Ackroyd's film *Blues Brothers*, as well as making regular appearances on 'Sesame Street' and 'The Muppet Show'.

★*The Cab Calloway Story* (Deja Vu DVRECD 22)

More Calloway's rather gimmicky and dated-sounding singing, than a real representation of the powers of his bands in the Thirties, but it nevertheless contains the famous, 'Hi De Ho', as well as 'Minnie the Moocher', 'Stormy Weather', and, 'Birth of the Blues'. Calloway's jazzier recordings are not well represented on CD.

Carter, Benny

(Born New York, August 8, 1907)
Benny Carter has always been hugely admired for all-round musical ability by his peers, many of whom happily endorse his sobriquet of 'King Carter'. He is nearly as proficient on trumpet as on alto-saxophone, and led a successful swing band for which he arranged most of the material as well. Reissues of his early music seem still today, remarkable displays of the bandleader's overall command of resources, and strong themes put together with an innate sense of form. Carter's 'Symphony In Riffs', for instance, merges two contrasting melodies plus solos, with superb aplomb, all within the three minutes available on a 78 rpm disc.

Benny Carter was brought up in New York City, and began as a trumpeter through his friendship with DUKE ELLIINGTON's Bubber Miley. He formed his first band in 1928, and also worked and recorded with Charlie Johnson, McKinney's Cotton Pickers, the Chocolate Dandies, and others, before travelling to Europe, as COLEMAN HAWKINS did, spending the late Thirties there. This period included a spell in London as arranger to the BBC Dance Orchestra. On a recording from this period, Elizabeth Welch sings the original version of Carter's best-known song 'When Lights

Are Low'. And in Holland, Carter put together the first jazz orchestra that was both international and multi-racial, with the young Scots musician George Chisholm taking the trombone solos.

Carter returned to America and to bandleading, featuring emerging talents like Max Roach, JJ Johnson and Miles Davis, alongside those from the swing era. Settling in Los Angeles, he became the first black musician to break into the lucrative field of film and television scores, and movie appearances include a shot of Carter serenading Gregory Peck in *Snows Of Kilimanjaro*. Carter still plays superbly, being much in demand for festivals and jazz cruises and generally getting the recognition he deserves. Critics and their followers who took extreme positions tended to undervalue his solos, spun out with a logic concealed behind his effortless technique and affable tone that seemed too much at ease with the world. In today's climate of attention to the jazz past, opinion has swung back in his favour.

★*Central City Sketches* (Music Masters CIJD 60126 X)

A 1987 concert dedicated to the achievements of Benny Carter, which ironically had to wait until his eightieth year. Performed by Carter in collaboration with the American Jazz Orchestra, it was an opportunity for the veteran musician to direct an extended programme of his own music, including the new commission of the title. Carter, still definitively on the case, grasped it whole-heartedly and his luminous writing for saxophone sections remains undimmed.

Christy, June (Shirley Luster)

(Born Springfield, Illinois, November 20, 1925)
Singer June Christy has always been associated with the ambitious and idiom-stretching orchestra of STAN KENTON, though she made some convincing recordings of her own with small groups. Influenced primarily by ANITA O'DAY as a singer, Christy developed a cooler and more refined style as she grew older, and the appeal of her easy swing and distinctive phrasing brought her a new audience among younger jazz listeners in the years before

she died. Christy worked as a teenager in bands around Chicago, and replaced Anita O'Day in the Kenton Orchestra in 1945. Through the Fifties she occasionally worked with reformed versions of the Kenton band, though more frequently with her husband, saxophonist Bob Cooper. She more or less retired at the end of the Sixties, but returned in the mid-Eighties to considerable acclaim.

★*Best of June Christy – The Capitol Years*
(Capitol/EMI CDEMS 1336)

Selections from several Capitol albums recorded with Kenton musicians, including some of the songs that made her one of the most popular of big-band singers. A Christy/Kenton classic 'Something Cool' is alongside a collection of standards, including 'Give Me The Simple Life', 'They Can't Take That Away From Me' and 'Do Nothing Till You Hear From Me'.

Cole, Nat 'King' (Nathaniel Adams)

(Born Montgomery, Alabama, March 17, 1917; died February 15, 1965)

Through enduring interpretations of standard songs as a vocalist, and through a tradition that continues through the work of soul and funk vocalists like George Benson, Nat 'King' Cole is largely remembered as an elegant romantic singer. But – just like Benson as a guitarist – Cole was a gifted improvising pianist before his pop successes, and it is this side of him that influenced subsequent pianists from OSCAR PETERSON to Bill Evans. Cole's style was derived from EARL HINES – using the right hand to approximate the melody lines of the increasingly virtuosic horn players of the Thirties, but in Cole's hands the process was smoother and less rhythmically surprising. He recorded extensively with trios in the late Forties, worked with LESTER YOUNG, and on Normal Granz' early Jazz At The Philharmonic tour packages. But from the 1950s onward King was a pop star, and rarely worked in jazz contexts again. He was, however, the first black singer to dominate the pop market so successfully.

★*After Midnight* (Capitol/EMI CDP 748 328-2)
Digitally remastered Cole piano performances, from 1956, with
his trio and guests including trumpeter Harry Edison.

Colyer, Kenneth 'Ken'

(Born Norfolk, England, April 18, 1928; died March 10, 1988)
Ken Colyer, the most unwavering and dedicated of British jazz
traditionalists, seemed to occupy a place on the jazz circuit
unshiftable by fashions, economics or mortality. A resolute
musical fundamentalist, Colyer's preoccupation was the sound of
Bunk Johnson, a trumpeter from the pre-recording period of jazz
whose music enjoyed a resurgence in the 1940s as part of the
backlash against bebop. Devoted to the New Orleans music that
preceded Louis Armstrong, Colyer admired a collectively improvised contrapuntal music in which no-one stood in the spotlight.
It was also rhythmically far closer to the marching bands and
funeral bands of turn-of-the-century New Orleans, than it was to
the driving tempos and unpredictable placing of accents that
coined the term 'swing'.
   Colyer formed the Crane River Jazz Band, in the early Fifties
(which he named after a stream running near his home in
Hounslow), was nicknamed 'The Guvnor' by all the serious
adherents of the idiom, and rejoined his old service, the Merchant
Navy, in order to wangle a trip to New Orleans. He deserted once
he got there, played with many of the surviving veterans of the
music, was jailed and deported back to England – to a hero's
welcome from the cognoscenti. He rejected the 'skiffle' craze that
made money for many traditional jazz musicians in the Fifties, and
though his mind was clearly closed to much of what was going on
in jazz, his devotion to purely musical values and his indifference
to compromise were an example even to players light years away
from his style.

★*The Guvnor* (Polydor 830 782-2)
Late Fifties and early Sixties recordings by the Colyer band, in full
inexorably collective flow. Despite the rigour of the Colyer
method however, the results are highly musical, early gems of
jazz lovingly polished to a gleam.

Connor, Chris

(Born Kansas City, November 8, 1927)
Like JUNE CHRISTY, Chris Connor built her reputation on a period as a popular vocalist with the STAN KENTON band, following Christy into the orchestra in the 1950s. She had begun with arranger CLAUDE THORNHILL's vocal band The Snowflakes, and her singing developed under the influence of the emotionally restrained, melodically subtle methods of Fifties cool jazz. Like Christy, Connor found that there wasn't room for her delicate artistry in the music business in the Seventies, but she reappeared on disc in the next decade and turned in some excellent performances on the Contemporary label.

★*Cool Chris* (Charly CDCHARLY 115)

Connor's quality is to get inside the meanings of songs rather than simply use the themes as vehicles for improvisation. She demonstrates that skill here in a fine collection of standards, including 'Lullaby of Birdland', 'Lush Life' and 'Stella By Starlight'.

Crosby, George Robert 'Bob'

(Born Washington, August 25, 1913)
Bob Crosby was barely a musician – he had qualified as a lawyer and became a passable singer (though not in the same league as his brother Bing) but his bandleading career was launched when he took over a group of dissaffected musicians from the Ben Pollack orchestra. Whatever his lack of technical skills, Crosby had an ear for a popular mix, and the band developed a repertoire of tight, breezy New Orleans music in the soloistic Dixieland style. Within the orchestra, Crosby also developed a sub-group, the Bobcats, which played the most spontaneous and flexible jazz material, and the music that has lasted best. Crosby's enterprise fell apart in the big-band slump of the Forties, and he became a TV and radio personality, and eventually left the music business altogether – though he has occasionally fronted Crosby revivals.

★*Bob Crosby – Jazz Classics in Digital Stereo* (BBC CD 688)

A mixture of novelty music and gimmicks and some driving

Dixieland with fine soloists, this selection includes 'Fidgety Feet' and 'Honky Tonk Train Blues' among many others, and the classic vaudeville-jazz hit 'Big Noise From Winnetka', with drummer Ray Bauduc playing with sticks on the strings of Bob Haggart's bass.

Davison, William Edward 'Wild Bill'

(Born Defiance, Ohio, January 5, 1906; died November 14, 1989)
Cornettist Wild Bill Davison, who on occasion played mellophone, banjo, guitar and mandolin as well as cornet, was one of the foremost white musicians of the 'Chicago school' of the 1920s, and continued to promote and by all appearances revel in that crisp and well-turned brand of jazz until into his eighties. He proved it in 1986 on the New York Jazz Festival, which had run a tribute concert in his honour.

Davison began picking up regular commercial work in Chicago around 1927. He was inspired by BIX BEIDERBECKE rather than Armstrong, though his clipped, corner-of-the-mouth phraseology, full of spurting phrases and long pauses, owed a lot to a more primitive trumpet pioneer, Freddy Keppard. Davison's skills and forceful personality quickly made him a crucial part of the white Dixieland scene of the 1930s. But it was in New York, in the Forties, that his reputation grew, partly through association with the influential white bandleader Eddie Condon. Working with pianist Art Hodes and supporting the sublime saxophone voice of Sidney Bechet in 1945, Davison committed some of his most convincing performances to disc. Between this point and 1951, Davison also recorded other memorable performances at Eddie Condon's own club, including a reverberating version of the classic Beiderbecke vehicle, 'I'm Coming Virginia'. From 1960 onward, feeling dislocated from the action by his move to California, Davison took to touring the globe, appearing with over a hundred different bands between 1965 and 1975, always willing to discuss the traditions and development of jazz with his audiences as well as play. European defenders of the Chicago idiom, like Freddy Randall and Alex Welsh, owed him a lot.

★*Together Again* (CMJ CMJCD 003)

Brisk session featuring the engagingly abrasive Davison touch, in collaboration with an excellent pianist of the Harlem stride style, Ralph Sutton. The two make crisp and exuberant work of 'Three Little Words', 'I've Got the World On A String' and 'Rockin' Chair' among other pieces.

Dirty Dozen Brass Band

For years visitors to New Orleans were able to witness the town's veteran musicians playing the way they had in their youth, and sustaining the energies of Southlands street music as both a musical tribute and a tourist attraction. But as time took toll of them, younger players who also loved the tradition but believed it could be combined with more recent music began to emerge. Though purists would continue to reject such hybrids, they were immensely attractive to younger audiences and many of them were at least as musically resourceful as their forbears and in several cases more so.

One of the best examples of 'contemporary revivalism' is the Dirty Dozen Brass Band, which was formed in New Orleans in the early 1970s by a group of young players involved in cajun music, street music, funk, bebop, and the kind of John Zorn-like mischief-making that led to the inclusion of the 'Flintstones' theme in their repertoire. A delightful band in live performance, describing its curious chemistry as 'jazz gumbo', the Dirty Dozen has made friends wherever it has travelled, ensuring that jazz history doesn't remain simply a collection of dusted-off museum pieces.

Mardi Gras in Montreux (Rounder CD 2052)
The Dirty Dozen as it should be heard, in live performance at the Montreux Festival in 1985, roaring through an unbroken stream of music from its members' tireless ransacking of many traditions. It's regarded by some as one of the most vivid and exciting concert recordings of the past decade.

Dorsey, Thomas 'Tommy'

(Born Pennsylvania, November 19, 1905; died November 26, 1956)
A brilliant trombonist with an ethereal delicacy at the top end of

the range, Tommy Dorsey was also one of the most successful of the swing-era bandleaders. Both he and his brother Jimmy led swing bands (originally they co-led one, but violent disagreements between them broke it up) and it was Tommy Dorsey's that retained the greater jazz content. Some of the finest jazz musicians spawned by that period came through Dorsey's group, including trumpeters Charlie Shavers and BUNNY BERIGAN, drummers BUDDY RICH, Gene Krupa and Louis Bellson, and singers Frank Sinatra and Jo Stafford. Dorsey's band was tight and orderly, his business and promotional sense was acute, and a string of hits including 'I'm Getting Sentimental Over You' and 'Sunny Side of the Street' followed his reunification with Jimmy in 1937.

★*Greatest Hits* (BMG ND 90310)

It doesn't include the biggest hits of all, like those mentioned above or 'Song of India', but this RCA collection of Dorsey music is an otherwise good example of his sharp, well-drilled orchestral style, and it features a young Frank Sinatra.

Eldridge, David 'Roy'

(Born Pittsburgh, January 30, 1911; died February 26, 1989)
It's doubtful if anyone called Roy Eldridge a missing link to his face, but some commentators imply his importance lay in being a kind of bridge between Louis Armstrong and Dizzy Gillespie. At least such neat categorization does suggest he must have unearthed something new. He was, in fact, a soloist of tremendous character as well as originality, the most admired trumpet player of the later 1930s and one who could still turn it on almost up to his death.

Eldridge developed a style more mobile than his predecessors. He played high and with a hot, sometimes gritty sound into which he packed a barrelful of emotion – though the extremes of his playing were sometimes dismissed as poor tone and lack of taste. Much of Eldridge's inspiration came from saxophonists COLEMAN HAWKINS and BENNY CARTER, who were setting new levels of harmonic improvisation that Eldridge translated to the trumpet.

He worked and recorded with FLETCHER HENDERSON and Teddy Hill, formed a band of his own from which came classics like 'Heckler's Hop' and the feverish 'After You've Gone', and became one of the first black musicians to be featured with a white orchestra when he joined Gene Krupa. He later toured with Jazz At The Philharmonic, often forming an ebullient partnership with Coleman Hawkins, and spent the last of his playing years holding the fort at Jimmy Ryan's club in New York.

★*The Nifty Cat* (New World NWCD 349)

Eldridge got the opportunity to record under his own name far less often than he should have. This was a 1970 session (including Budd Johnson on tenor and Benny Morton on trombone) that proved how negligent the record business had been, with 'Little Jazz' hustling his way through six mainstream features with so little blunting of his old panache that the passage of the years was rendered as meaningless as it was with Benny Carter or Gil Evans.

Ellington, Edward Kennedy 'Duke'

(Born Washington DC, April 29, 1899; died May 24, 1974)
No orchestra leader in the history of jazz more imaginatively explored texture, idiomatic variety, the idiosyncrasies of soloists or the possibilities of art and pop as comprehensively as Duke Ellington. His compositions run to thousands – but unlike most composers he made his writing options harder by running a band on the road at the same time. Ellington (dubbed 'Duke' for his snappy dress sense) was taught piano as a child, and though he had wanted to be a painter, by his late teens he was a musician specialising in rags and dance music. By the mid 1920s he had moved to New York, and was running a band for which he had acquired the, King Oliver-influenced, growl-trumpet specialist James 'Bubber' Miley and saxophonist Sidney Bechet, two players who revealed much of the essence of jazz to Ellington, as did hearing the King Oliver band live in Chicago on the famous 1922 engagement.

Ellington's most important early gig was a five year apprentice-ship at Harlem's Cotton Club, mostly providing the backdrop for 'jungle' dance-routines popular with white audiences. Helped by bandleader Will Vodery and composer Will Marion Cook (the latter the boss of the Southern Syncopated Orchestra which featured Sidney Bechet as a soloist) Ellington, the man with the painter's perception of jazz, soon developed into a master of tone colour. His combinations of instrumental textures were quickly recognised as richer and more subtle than anything previously attempted in jazz. His melodic sense was strong, he would vary his key centres and rhythmic patterns more than was common in the music, to a degree that stretched the risk-taking of dance-music to the limit. During the Cotton Club years, Ellington recorded some of his best early pieces, including 'The Mooch', 'Rockin' in Rhythm', and 'Mood Indigo'. As the swing era developed, Ellington's was not as commercial an orchestra as BENNY GOODMAN's or the DORSEYS', but the romantic, balladeering side of pop was strengthened in his band by the arrival of such sumptuously-toned saxophonists as altoist Johnny Hodges (one of the most moving instrumentalists in jazz) and baritonist Harry Carney, and one of his finest songs, 'In A Sentimental Mood', was written during this period.

The Forties represented Ellington's Golden Age. At precisely the point when the big band movement was being undermined by wartime economics and the arrival of bebop, Ellington's rhythm section was transformed by the addition of a double-bass genius in Jimmy Blanton (the pioneer of counter-melodic virtuoso bass playing) and 'Concerto for Cootie', 'Harlem Air Shaft' 'Take the A Train' and 'Warm Valley' materialised during this period of intense, concise, structurally elegant and moving work. Hodges left the band in 1951 and its progress stumbled from then until his return in 1955, when the reintroduction of his sensuous sound – and tenorist Paul Gonsalves' famous 27 blues choruses on 'Diminuendo and Crescendo in Blue' at the 1956 Newport Jazz Festival – put the band back on the map and on the cover of *Time* magazine.

Ellington began to compose again, prolifically. He wrote 'Such Sweet Thunder' as a dedication to Shakespeare, toyed with rearrangements of Tchaikovsky and Grieg, introduced non Afro-American elements after extensive global touring in his 'Far East Suite' in 1956, and composed a good deal of religious music in his later years.

★*Jazz Classics in Digital Stereo* (BBC CD 686)

Though the period around 1940 is often regarded as a high point for Ellington, the more formative years are a better insight into the mountain he actually moved to achieve what he did, and the music – a mixture of the cultivated 'primitiveness' of the pre-swing era and the cooler and more fluid sounds that followed – is often dazzling. 'The Mooch', a swirling, wraith-like ensemble sound that breaks into a cruising mid-tempo dance and glows with the solo voices of Johnny Hodges and Barney Bigard, is a virtual definition of the Cotton Club sound of the late Twenties. By 1934 the choppy rhythms of swing and the clout of the bigger orchestra point to the future.

★*The Blanton-Webster Band* (Bluebird/BMG PD 85659)

A three-disc boxed set covering the most exciting period in the life of the Duke Ellington Orchestra. There are 66 tracks on it, featuring the remarkable chemistry of BEN WEBSTER on tenor, Jimmy Blanton on bass, trumpeter Rex Stewart and the compositional talents of Billy Strayhorn. If there's an essential Ellington collection, this is it. Tracks include 'Ko-Ko', 'Cotton Tail' and 'Take The A Train'.

★*Solos Duets and Trios* (Bluebird/BMG ND 82178)

Ellington's impact on orchestral jazz was so substantial that his piano playing is sometimes sidelined by it. But though he was a peerless ensemble player, he was also a fine and often inspired stride-derived swing pianist. On this set, covering more than thirty years of his piano playing, he is heard in partnership with Jimmy Blanton on all their most memorable collaborations, with EARL HINES, and unaccompanied.

★*New Orleans Suite* (Atlantic/WEA 781376-2)

Fine late-Sixties suite in which Ellington paid tribute to the music that had put him on the road. Not only does the orchestra catch the ensemble bounce and sparkle of the early New Orleans bands, but Paul Gonsalves successfully recalls the mercurial Sidney Bechet, and Cootie Williams the mixture of fire and poise that characterised Louis Armstrong.

★*Far East Suite* (Bluebird/BMG ND 87640)

Ellington's 1966 collection following an extensive period of world touring. Unlike many jazz journeys into unjazzlike territory, the 'Far East Suite' isn't precious, sycophantic or condescending, and Harry Carney's saxophone is a mixture of majestic and tremulous on 'Agra', while the great Johnny Hodges is at his rhapsodic best on 'Isfahan'.

Fitzgerald, Ella

(Born Virginia, April 25, 1918)
Ella Fitzgerald's popularity burst the definitions of 'jazz' a long time ago. She includes Bing Crosby, Frank Sinatra and Elton John among her fans, and she has set standards for the performance of popular song that expanded the meanings of good songs and camouflaged the weaknesses of bad ones. All this has been possible largely because of her remarkable range, and pitching of a certainty and accuracy rare among jazz singers attempting to emulate the flexibility and speed of instruments. She also understands harmony well enough to improvise freely on it, and has always swung furiously. But for all this expertise, she has nevertheless managed to retain an artless, relaxed innocence, an informality that instantly establishes a rapport with listeners.

Ella Fitzgerald was spotted as a sixteen year old singing in the amateur hour at the Apollo Theatre in Harlem, and shortly afterwards she began working for the drummer Chick Webb, a leading figure in the big-band business. Fitzgerald and the Webb band became nationally famous through their shows at the Savoy Ballroom, late night radio broadcasts and then recordings. Collaborating with arranger Van Alexander, Fitzgerald turned a children's song into a huge hit with 'A-Tisket, A-Tasket'. Chick Webb died young, and Fitzgerald fronted the band for three years until the big-band boom ended and the singer became a solo artist.

In 1946 Fitzgerald began working for impresario Norman Granz' early 'Jazz At The Philharmonic' packages, as well as working in less populist circumstances with small groups, notably featuring the pianist Hank Jones. Her recordings on Granz' Verve label of the 'Song Books' series remains her greatest achievement. They were celebrations of the best of American pop – the works of Jerome Kern, Cole Porter, Rodgers and Hart, Irving Berlin, DUKE ELLINGTON, Johnny Mercer, Harold Arlen and Frank Loesser, and there were five volumes devoted to the Gershwins. In recent times Ella Fitzgerald has continued to perform and record, broadcasting on occasion with Frank Sinatra and Duke Ellington, performing with ensembles as different as symphony orchestras and COUNT BASIE's band. She has also worked in small scale but delicately detailed ensembles, with pianist Tommy Flanagan, usually performing standards.

★*Ella With . . .* (Living Era/Academy Sound & Vision CD AJD 055)

Early Ella with a variety of bands, including her Savoy Eight, Chick Webb and BENNY GOODMAN. It doesn't include 'A-Tisket, A-Tasket', but has most of the other recordings she made with Webb in 1936.

★*The Songbooks* (Verve 823 445-2)

Compilation from some of the Verve songbooks material, which in its original form is currently mostly deleted on CD. Fitzgerald's relaxation with the work of virtually any songwriter of the swing era is apparent from these breezy renditions of 'Lady Be Good', 'Fascinating Rhythm', 'The Lady Is A Tramp' and many other classics.

Francis, David Albert 'Panama'

(Born Miami, December 21, 1918)

When BUDDY RICH and Jo Jones died, Panama Francis became the finest surviving swing-band drummer – but the band with which he is associated, the Savoy Sultans, had been described in reverential tones by jazz musicians since 1937. Reputed to be the first to use the term 'jump music' to describe that riff-packed, highly rhythmic idiom that was the precursor of rock 'n' roll, the Sultans were a peerless dance band, but they also featured soloists who could imaginatively bridge swing and bebop.

Panama Francis was originally a church musician, then a swing player who worked with trumpeter ROY ELDRIDGE from 1939 in New York. Working with Lucky Millinder at the Savoy Ballroom in the war years, Francis heard the Sultans at close range and loved their sound to the extent of trying to form a replica in the Fifties. It didn't work, and Francis retired to the studios, eventually becoming a rhythm and blues drummer and working with Ray Charles. But in 1974, anxious that his jazz past shouldn't be forgotten, Francis re-formed a version of the Savoy Sultans to play at a concert by the New York Jazz Repertory Company in 1974, and the aftermath was dynamic, particularly with the European festival audiences. Francis' version preserved the intense ensemble interplay and empathetic soloing, and he featured George Kelly, a powerful COLEMAN HAWKINS-like saxophonist who had played in the original Sultans in the Forties.

★*Get Up and Dance* (Stash STCD 5)

Good Sultans set from the mid-Eighties, featuring not just old Sultans hits but material from other artists of the swing era. The band's emphasis has always been on the beat and on spirited delivery, and there's plenty of both on this set.

Garner, Errol Louis

(Born Pittsburgh, June 15, 1923; died January 2, 1977)

Errol Garner combined the rich orchestral self-sufficiency of the swing pianists with a broadmindedness about material and a rhythmically infectious percussive technique that brought him commercial success he almost certainly never sought to engineer. The dancing rhythmic figures of his left hand and the churning melodic eloquence of his right made him one of the happiest-sounding pianists in jazz, and the impact of that vivacity on sales was inevitable.

Garner taught himself piano as a child, and appeared on a children's radio show playing piano at the age of ten. He moved to New York when he was twenty three and began to work steadily in nightclubs. This was predominantly Garner's chosen setting for the rest of his career, though he made guest appearances on the recordings of others, notably an unsuitable but intriguing one with Charlie Parker on a Dial session in 1947. On his own or with a trio, Garner's performances unfolded with gleeful drama. He would play elaborate, whirling overtures to his pieces, then explore them at relentless rhythmic pressure, hurling in pearly runs, furious trills, left-hand and right-hand figures that would seem to be galloping in resolutely opposite directions until their deft and inevitable reconciliations. 'Misty' was Garner's most famous composition, and *Concert By The Sea* his best known recording.

★*Errol Garner – Immortal Concerts* (Giants of Jazz GOJCD 53034) Good budget-priced selection of live Garner work from concerts in 1955, 1963 and 1969. Themes include 'Autumn Leaves', 'Girl From Ipanema', 'Lover Come Back To Me' and his much-loved 'Misty'.

Goodman, Benjamin David 'Benny'

(Born Chicago, May 30, 1909; died June 13, 1986)
As most of the world knows, clarinettist and bandleader Benny Goodman's name was interchangeable with the title 'King of Swing', a contentious accolade that had come about because, in the period in the 1930s when big-band jazz received public endorsement on the scale of rock 'n' roll two decades later, Goodman did the best business. But he also appealed to classical-music lovers. A clarinet virtuoso, he was as comfortable with classical pieces as jazz, and often used the former in practice sessions.

Goodman was one of twelve children, descended from Russian Jews. His family was nearly always broke, and the children were encouraged toward music in the dance-band era as a possible route out of the ghetto. Benny learned so fast that he was a full-time professional by the age of fourteen and his first big-time engagement, a year later, was with the briefly successfully Ben Pollack orchestra. But unlike many dance band musicians, Goodman was fascinated by the seductive art of improvisation, and even in his early recordings he would quickly stray away from written themes. The tension between the adventure of improvising and the security of a popular repertoire, driven by the

47

hustling, frantic quality that fuelled the swing craze, was Goodman's musical chemistry.

Goodman began leading his own big band in 1934 and by judicious purchase of swing arrangements (FLETCHER HENDERSON's, among others) his career took off to the point where huge audiences were devoted to the point of hysteria. But though his big band was his most famous achievement, some of Goodman's most enduring jazz music was recording with small groups, the clarinet winging its way over the crisp insistence of accompanists like pianist Teddy Wilson, drummer Gene Krupa, vibist LIONEL HAMPTON and guitarist Charlie Christian. Goodman became a jazz ambassador during the Fifties, touring extensively. He also maintained his relationships with classical composers – having worked with Hungarian modernist Bela Bartok, performed with the Chicago Symphony Orchestra, he eventually commissioned concertos for his clarinet from Aaron Copland and Paul Hindemith.

★*Sing Sing Sing* (Bluebird/BMG ND 85630)

Goodman's orchestra as the swing bandwagon began to roll in the mid-Thirties. BUNNY BERIGAN, Harry James (later to have a hit of his own with this title track) and Gene Krupa are in the band, and the tracks include the classic 'King Porter Stomp'.

★*Trio and Quartet Sessions* (Bluebird/BMG 85631)

Goodman's small-group recordings displayed his remarkable clarinet technique at its best, and his improvisor's imagination as well. These sessions from the mid-Thirties find Goodman in relaxed collaboration with the pearly-sounding Teddy Wilson on piano and Gene Krupa on drums, and the quartet tracks add the graceful sway of Lionel Hampton's vibes. 'China Boy' and 'Moonglow' are among the best known tracks.

Grappelli, Stephane

(Born Paris, January 26, 1908)

A walking definition of grace, swing and orthodox tunefulness, violinist Stephane Grappelli has been entertaining audiences inside and outside the jazz fraternity since the 1920s. He took up the instrument at twelve, went to the Paris Conservatoire as a teenager and soon after joined a jazz-influenced dance-band (The Gregorians) first as a pianist, then as a violinist. Grappelli met the gypsy guitarist Django Reinhardt, and began a casual improvising partnership with him that ended up as the Quintet du Hot Club de France – a band that became influential all over the world in the Thirties and Forties, though its rhythmic rigidity hasn't aged well. Grappelli stayed in London during the war years and tried with mixed success to rebuild his always unsteady relationship with Reinhardt until the guitarist's death in 1953. During the Sixties Grappelli continued to tour in Europe, but it was the reconstruction of the Hot Club format with guitarist Denny Wright that led to Grappelli's resurgence in the next decade – appearing with artists such as vibraharpist Gary Burton and classical virtuoso Yehudi Menuhin among others.

*_Hot Club De France_ (Vogue VG 651)

Early Hot Club work between Grappelli and Reinhardt – from the era that tends to display Reinhardt as consistently rising above rather mediocre surroundings, and Grappelli's more formal technique still trying to slot into them. Nevertheless, the empathy between the two is clear, and Grappelli's swooning romanticism is always undercut by his own rhythmic momentum and tight melodic intelligence.

*_Live in Copenhagen_ (Pablo J33J 20041)

Excellent concert session for Grappelli with bassist Neils Henning Oersted Pedersen and guitarist JOE PASS. Grappelli demonstrates that the passage of the years seems to improve him and the interplay with Pass and Pedersen shows how flexible and accommodating his playing has remained.

Hamilton, Scott

(Born New England, September 12, 1954)
If any jazz musician under forty personifies the mainstream that

idolised the sound of BEN WEBSTER and COLEMAN HAWKINS it's Scott Hamilton. Unlike the jazz classicists of the Marsalises generation, Hamilton has hardly sought to alter the musical legacy of his heroes at all, and has contented himself instead with perfecting a big, lazily-moving sound in which the articulation of every note is important and spaciousness is crucial to melodic development. Hamilton might have disappeared behind a smokescreen fuelled by the reputations of all his departed heroes, but he turned out to be a good enough improvisor to rescue a sound of his own from such a respectful apprenticeship. Hamilton's musical circle has always been rooted in swing, and it was the acquaintance of trumpeter ROY ELDRIDGE, guitarist Tiny Grimes and pianist John Bunch that got him started. Hamilton joined BENNY GOODMAN's band in 1977 and began recording extensively for Concord the following year, sometimes with a cornet-playing partner almost as highly thought of as a revivalist as he is – Warren Vache.

★*The Second Set* (Concord CCD 4254)

Hamilton in live performance in Japan in 1983, with his regular group featuring John Bunch on piano, Chris Flory on guitar, Phil Flanigan on bass and Chuck Riggs on drums. Crisp, organised and as smooth as a limousine, but with the leader's gracefully scattered and rather cultivated idiosyncrasies constantly edging it along.

★*Scott Hamilton Plays Ballads* (Concord CCD 4386)

Hamilton in perhaps his most flattering light. An excellent thematic improvisor, he develops solos by using his characteristic full-bodied tone and subtle placing of notes to stitch together a series of resonating motifs. As if to demonstrate his liberation from the shadow of Coleman Hawkins, Hamilton even applies those skills to 'Body and Soul', and makes a strikingly independent account of it.

Hampton, Lionel

(Born Louisville, Kentucky, April 20, 1908)
Drummer, pianist, singer, vibraharpist and all-round showman

Lionel Hampton has led the longest-running jazz orchestra in the music's history, and attained some of the most spectacular peaks of audience excitement with it. Hampton is often dismissed as showy to the point at which musicality evaporates, and his band's performances undoubtedly are celebrations of technique, volume, energy and the constant crescendo. But he has frequently turned in impressive performances of his own, and nurtured many excellent musicians, not to mention converting countless new jazz fans everywhere he has travelled over the years.

Hampton is probably unique among big-time jazz drummers for having been taught snare technique by a Dominican nun. He learned marimba later, but was a drummer when he backed Louis Armstrong in Los Angeles as a member of the Les Hite orchestra. At his wife's recommendation, Hampton also took up vibes, and interrupted his career to study music at college. In 1936, whilst performing in an LA club, Hampton found himself backing BENNY GOODMAN and shortly afterwards he was a member of the Goodman band. Hampton was quickly popular, and secured a deal to record with whoever he liked. In 1940 Hampton formed his own big band and the likes of Charles Mingus, Art Farmer, Dexter Gordon and Dinah Washington passed through it. The band has constantly played festivals all over the world, and in recent years Hampton has attempted to plough back some of his success into New York's black community through housing and educational projects.

★*Hot Mallets Vol 1* (Bluebird/BMG ND 86458)
Some of the results of Hampton's recently-discovered extraordinary record deal with RCA, that enabled him to cut a series of small-band recordings with passing celebrities that amount to some of the best swing playing of the entire period. Hampton gets an Ellingtonish ensemble sound on 'Buzzin' Around With the Bee', with ELLINGTON's trumpeter Cootie Williams and saxophonist Johnny Hodges in full flow. 'Hot Mallets' and 'One Sweet Letter From You' feature Dizzy Gillespie, BENNY CARTER, COLEMAN HAWKINS, Charlie Christian and many others. Beautiful soloing, and feline swing from Hampton himself.

★*Complete Paris Session* (Vogue VG 600 029)
A 1953 Hampton big band (the one that included Clifford Brown,

though he isn't heard here) displaying both its usual heatedness and some more fine small group work featuring the leader on 'September in the Rain' and 'I Only Have Eyes for You'.

★*Newport 78* (Timeless CDSJP 142)

More recent and typical Hampton bravura, with great emphasis on the tunes that became standbys with him – such as 'Flying Home' and 'Stompin' At the Savoy'. Noisy, blustering and uneven, but what marks it out is an excellent lineup including Doc Cheatham and Cat Anderson on trumpets, Charles MacPherson, Bob Wilber and Arnett Cobb on reeds, and PANAMA FRANCIS on drums.

Hawkins, Coleman Randolph

(Born St Joseph, Missouri, November 21, 1901; died May 19, 1969)

Though the expressiveness, tonal range and scalding intensity (in modernists' hands) of the tenor saxophone are now taken for granted, Coleman Hawkins picked up the instrument when it was used for little more than special effects, and brought it so reverberatingly to life that virtually every tenorist in the music's history either studied him directly or inherited part of his vision unawares. His sound was magisterial, deliberate, gruff and imposing, his melodic imagination more alert and fast-moving than any saxophone player in the pre-bop period.

Hawkins had a sophisticated musical education, which helped him become such an ingenious exponent of harmonic improvising. His technical skill and theoretical knowledge gave him more choices than were available to most jazz improvisors, and he avoided emotionalism or recourse to grandstanding displays. He started young (playing in public by the age of twelve), was a teenager as the migration from the South to Chicago got under way, went on the road at twenty with Mamie Smith's Jazz Hounds, and three years later was helping to build one of the most influential ensembles of the big-band era, FLETCHER HENDERSON's Orchestra. After the departure of Louis Armstrong, Hawkins was soon Henderson's brightest star, and he dominated saxophone playing in America until he left for Europe in 1934, playing in England, France and Scandinavia for the next five years. On his return to the States in 1939 Hawkins recorded one of the most famous solos in jazz, a rhapsody on 'Body and Soul' that became both a hit and a model for both arrangers and improvisors.

Hawkins didn't reject bebop – his harmonic awareness helped him grasp its logic, though its timing and accents never wholly suited him – and he performed with many of the leaders of the movement, including Thelonious Monk in 1943. He continued to tour (both as a soloist and occasionally with 'Jazz At The Philharmonic'), recorded with modernists like Max Roach and Sonny Rollins, and remained on the road until shortly before his death. Hawkins isn't so far well represented on CD.

★*Body and Soul* (BMG ND 85717)

An excellent representation of the 'Body and Soul' session itself, including all the material from the two RCA sessions that spawned it. The disc then displays Hawkins' fascinating attempts to come to grips with bebop, in appearances with Fats Navarro, JJ Johnson and Max Roach. There is also material from a more variable 1956 session in which Hawkins fronted a string section.

★*The High and Mighty Hawk* (London 820 602-2)

One of Hawkins very best sessions, set up by the critic Stanley Dance for the Felsted label in the late Fifties. Hawkins performs with a perfectly-suited small band featuring Buck Clayton on trumpet, Hank Jones on piano, Ray Brown on bass and Mickey Sheen on drums, and the saxophonist is in his indomitable prime amid the stream of arpeggios he conjures from 'Bird of Prey Blues' and a remarkable 'My One and Only Love'.

Henderson, Fletcher Hamilton

(Born Georgia, December 18, 1897; died December 28, 1952)
For a man who made an immense (if eventually underrated) contribution to jazz, bandleader Fletcher Henderson's career was more accidental and idiosyncratic than most. A scientist by

training, Henderson drifted into music, first as a record company demonstrator then as a bandleader, became a Twenties success with Louis Armstrong as his star sideman, then went broke, sold his best arrangements to BENNY GOODMAN, and watched Goodman become a wealthy celebrity.

Fletcher Henderson's mother was a music teacher, and the boy studied classical piano, but went to Atlanta University as a mathematician and chemist. Black graduates, however, found appropriate work hard to come by and Henderson wound up working for a New York music publishing company, demonstrating new songs. He later became a fixer for Black Swan Records, finding musicians for studio sessions to showcase singers such as Bessie Smith, and when these aggregations started to perform live, Henderson found himself as a bandleader. His group won an audition to Harlem's Club Alabam in 1924, though at that time still performing in the genial, stolid plod of the period's dance-music. Henderson's band for the Club Alabam included a then rather awkward-sounding COLEMAN HAWKINS, and a young clarinettist and arranger called Don Redman. When Henderson fell out with the management and moved to the nearby Roseland Ballroom, he found the establishment that was to be his home for the next decade. Henderson also had the incalculable benefit of hiring Louis Armstrong, having heard the cornettist in 1922 when the King Oliver Creole Band had performed at Chicago's Lincoln Gardens. Initially reluctant to leave Oliver, Armstrong had answered Henderson's call two years later.

Don Redman was a powerful influence on Henderson. An arranger and an expert theoretician from his teens, Redman sidestepped the regular practice of all-in melody statement followed by solos, in favour of an audacious use of 'sections' of the band to maximise contrast. Like Jelly Roll Morton, Redman ensured that even within the tight format of a three-minute piece, the contrasts and continual movements of texture and instrumentation give the music an irresistible sense of forward motion. The Henderson momentum slowed in the Thirties, many of his musicians left, and Benny Goodman re-established much of the dynamism of the old band. Henderson continued to lead bands on and off in the Forties, but his health was failing by 1950 and he never recovered his old aplomb.

*Hocus Pocus (Bluebird/BMG ND 90413)

'Sugar Foot Stomp' and 'Singing The Blues' figure among the early Henderson milestones performed here by the likes of Coleman Hawkins, trumpeters Rex Stewart and ROY ELDRIDGE, saxophonist CHU BERRY and others in the high period of the band's life from 1927 to 1936.

Herman, Woodrow Charles 'Woody'

(Born Wisconsin, May 16, 1913; died October 27, 1987)
Like BUDDY RICH, Woody Herman was an indefatiguable showbiz personality whose first appearance in the footlights had been as a child performer in vaudeville. He was billed as the 'Boy Wonder of the Clarinet' in his parents' act, and by the age of twenty three he had become the leader of his own orchestra, three years later recording *Woodchoppers' Ball*, a million-selling disc that made his reputation. After the war, Herman formed the first of his famous Herds, broadcast with it, and became a household name. The result was that Herman survived the decline of the big band era, an achievement partly due to his soloists, and partly because he was shrewd enough to perceive a potential in bebop. Herman's orchestras influenced young bop players all over the world who wanted to combine their adventurousness with dance hall acceptability. Herman was a good clarinettist and alto saxophonist himself (performing on the latter in the honeyed style of Frankie Trumbauer) and the tenor saxophone style of LESTER YOUNG underpinned his reed section, notably in the hands of Stan Getz and Zoot Sims. It was a Getz recording with Herman, a brief, fluttering, feathery solo on a ballad called 'Early Autumn' that made Getz's name and made him the most emulated of white saxophonists.

Herman's Fifties Third Herd tried to stay afloat in bad times for the big bands. But by the 1960s, helped by the muscular style of tenorist Sal Nistico, and bending toward the sound of John Coltrane, Herman's orchestra came back. It used pop music to catch a younger audience, and relished combining it with the kind of blistering ensemble playing (particularly from the brass) that a well-drilled jazz band could exhibit, but he never lost his enthusiasm for the kind of outfit that could still spring surprises.

Woody Herman did not leave jazz much changed, unlike ELLINGTON or BASIE, but he introduced it to many who would not otherwise have stumbled on it.

★*Blowin' Up A Storm* (Charly CDCHARLY 100)

A collection of Woody Herman classics from the Forties Herds, including 'Caldonia', 'Apple Honey', 'Bijou' and 'The Good Earth'. Jimmy Giuffre's serpentine saxophone display 'Four Brothers' is also here. Feathery, glancing variations on 'Early Autumn' were what launched the career of the twenty year old Stan Getz.

★*Woodchoppers' Ball* (Dance Band Days/Prism DBCD 09)

More early Herman on the Dixieland meets Swing theme, including the title – his biggest Thirties hit.

Hines, Earl Kenneth

(Born Pennsylvania, December 28, 1903; died April 22, 1983)
Though ART TATUM's was a dominant name in piano jazz by the early 1930s, Earl 'Fatha' Hines was the instrument's first great virtuoso, and he retained the loyalty and admiration of a wide public and his fellow musicians throughout six decades as an active performer. Hines developed his unique sound by listening to horn players – most notably Louis Armstrong – and evolving what became known as the 'trumpet style' on piano. Where the predominant jazz keyboard technique of the Twenties was the ragtime derivative known as 'stride', with its regular bass patterns and rocking chords, Hines loosened the left-hand to play in a more free-ranging 'orchestral' manner and his right hand runs closely emulated the wide leaps of intervals, tremelo effects and tempo-stretching ascents and descents of the New Orleans horn stars. It was a piano identity of such irrepressible, self-propelled energy that Hines, for all his collaborative exploits, became Tatum-like in a kind of glorious isolation. He sounded better on his own, and many of the recordings of the later stages of his career are preferable for just that reason.

Hines' family was musical, and he began on cornet, switching to piano and studying music formally. In the early Twenties he found work backing singers, played with Louis Armstrong's band in 1927, and then with the excellent clarinettist Jimmie Noone, producing some memorable recordings with him. But it was the collaboration with Armstrong in 1929 that produced the improvised duet 'Weatherbird' that revealed how far ahead of his contemporaries on piano Hines had come. The pianist led his own bands throughout the Thirties and into the Forties, mostly at Chicago's mob-controlled Grand Terrace Club – and when bebop arrived, he formed a band that included Dizzy Gillespie, Charlie Parker and Wardell Gray, though his bop work was hardly recorded. In the Fifties, promoters sought to rebuild the Hines-Armstrong connection, but though the pianist played with the All Stars from 1947 to 1951 it was an awkward period and Hines' natural exuberance was often stifled. The rest of the decade was a comparatively lean time for him but he resurfaced in the Sixties with some dazzling solo recordings. He worked tirelessly until the weekend of his death at the age of seventy nine.

★*Piano Man* (Bluebird/BMG ND 86750)

Earl Hines' Grand Terrace band in the period from 1939–42 (a compilation of RCA material of the period), notably featuring the hit collaboration with singer Billy Eckstine on 'Jelly Jelly' and the thunderous piano solo 'Boogie Woogie On St Louis Blues'. At times the ensemble resembles the big hands of both Jimmie Lunceford and COUNT BASIE, but any routine qualities in the overall sound are despatched by Hines' own playing, some good Armstrong-like Walter Fuller trumpet solos, and the propulsive drumming of Alvin Burroughs.

★*Live at the Village Vanguard* (CBS France 462401-2)

Hines in fine solo form in the mid-Sixties, on such pieces as 'Out of Nowhere' and 'Moten Swing' and one of the definitive explorations of 'Tea For Two'.

Holiday, Billie (Eleanora Fagan)

(Born Baltimore, April 7, 1915; died July 17, 1959)

If ELLA FITZGERALD has been jazz singing's most popular and

accessible artist, and SARAH VAUGHAN its most operatic and complete, Billie Holiday most intimately contacted the improvisational essence of jazz vocals. Her timing, her delicate twists of intonation and phrasing, her ability to maintain intensity at low volumes and with the most measured and least histrionic of methods, amounted to a style that has defied imitation. If Holiday's significance to 20th century western music is not as well understood as it should be, her vulnerability to myth-making as troubled, narcotic-dependent artist whose slow decline happened in the glare of the spotlights hasn't helped. But on musical values alone, Holiday has never been rivalled in jazz. Though an 'instrumental' singer, she inhabited the lyrics of good songs with a poignancy – and in earlier days, with an exuberance – that integrated the meanings of the words with the movements of the music.

Billie Holiday was institutionalised at ten after being raped, and drifted into prostitution as a teenager, but a move to New York, with her mother Sadie Fagan in 1929, resulted in work as a singer in the Harlem clubs. She immediately impressed listeners with a voice that was both youthful yet shaded with experience, she was bluesy without explicitly featuring blues material, she strayed provocatively behind the beat giving her work a world-weary quality, and her sound had an imposing quality out of all proportion to its small volume. BENNY GOODMAN took an interest, and played on her first recordings – but when she appeared in a film featuring the DUKE ELLINGTON Orchestra ('Symphony In Black') singing 'Big City Blues' her career took off, and a sensational appearance in April 1935 at the Apollo confirmed it. Holiday was soon finding favour with more top-flight instrumentalists than any other singer. Saxophonist LESTER YOUNG and pianist Teddy Wilson became close friends, and Holiday's recordings with Young represented one of the finest recorded partnerships in jazz.

Holiday also worked with bandleader Artie Shaw in the Forties, and made occasional appearances with Benny Goodman and Duke Ellington, but it was in small-band contexts that she was at her most incandescent. Her popularity didn't divert her from fury over racism, and with the song 'Strange Fruit' (a reference to lynched blacks) she recorded one of the most resounding of all anti-racist songs. But in the Fifties, the effects of drugs and drink were increasingly audible in the rasping awkwardness of her intonation, though if anything her communicating powers intensified as her technique broke. She died at the Metropolitan Hospital in New York, facing a narcotics possession charge on her deathbed.

★*Lady Day & Prez* (Giants of Jazz CD 0218)

A good-value package of 24 tracks from 1937 to 1941, featuring one of the most fertile partnerships in jazz – because Lester Young, a saxophonist with a musical temperament very similar to Holiday's, was not yet in the sombre phase that enveloped him after the war. Young provides such a stream of seductive intros, nudging counterpoints and complementary solos that the voices of two are inseparably entwined. The mixture of innocent expectation and weariness in her phrasing on 'The Man I Love' is pure Lady Day, and Young's solo, hovering in the low register, exactly catches her mood.

★*I'll Be Seeing You* (Commodore AG8 24291)

Three of the finest of all Holiday performances were made for the Commodore label in the 1940s and they surface here in a mixture of the spinechilling ('Strange Fruit'), the quietly distraught ('Yesterdays') and the triumphantly bluesy ('Fine and Mellow').

★*At Storyville* (Black Lion BLCD 60921)

Good compilation from Billie Holiday's season at the Boston Storyville Club in 1951, featuring a selection of standards including 'Willow Weep For Me' and 'I Loves You Porgy'. Holiday's live work by was becoming erratic by this point, but this is a better than average live representation, and features a young Stan Getz performing the Lester Young role on tenor.

Jordan, Louis

(Born Arkansas, July 9, 1908; died February 4, 1975)
Saxophonist and singer Louis Jordan is most usually remembered

now as a forerunner of rock and roll, and the 'jump music' he pioneered in the Forties has recently been revived by Eighties bands like the Deep Sea Jivers and the Chevalier Brothers in Britain. The motive-power of the music is blues, but Jordan's personality was so strong, his timing so good and his feeling for dance-music so commercial that he had a string of hit records in a rhythm and blues style throughout the Forties and into the Fifties. Originally Jordan had been a swing saxophonist, working with the drummer Chick Webb, but he founded his first jazz-based rhythm and blues group, the Tympani Five, in 1938. The band sold a million copies of 'Choo Choo Ch'Boogie'. Jordan experimented with a big gand in the Fifties but soon reverted to the Tympani Five lineup. When the rock and roll he had helped create left him behind, Jordan nevertheless continued to tour (working with the CHRIS BARBER band in Britain in the Sixties) and he enjoyed something of a comeback.

★*Golden Greats* (MCA DMCL 1734)

Jordan's biggest hits from his most successful period, including 'Caldonia' (later recorded by Woody Herman), 'Choo Choo Ch'Boogie', 'Ain't Nobody Here But Us Chickens', and 'Saturday Night Fish Fry'. Energetic, funny, spirited music.

Kenton, Stanley Newcomb 'Stan'

(Born Wichita, Kansas, February 19, 1912; died August 25, 1979)
Bandleader Stan Kenton, by deciding to avoid most of the conventional ways of organising a jazz big band, wound up with a reputation for hyperbole and pretentiousness that he didn't deserve in his most creative period but probably earned in his later years. Kenton liked massive volume, complex and highly structured works, references to contemporary classical music, and orchestras in excess of 40 players when he could afford them. But he was still a commercial bandleader, and was obliged to reconcile his ambitions and his wilfulness with the regular big-band audience. In the Forties, when he ran his first bands, the elements coexisted successfully – and by extensive radio broadcasting, Kenton became very popular, with fine sidemen like drummer

Shelly Manne and saxophonist Art Pepper compounding the impact. Toward the end of the decade the music became more impressionistic and more influenced by the classics (explicit Stravinsky and Ravel), and Kenton began declaring his intentions to be 'Progressive Jazz', moving between dissonance and conventional resolution in a manner that infuriated the critics of the period.

These ambitious flights, for all their courage and audacity (years before the flowering of 'free jazz' and in a period when only pianist Lennie Tristano showed similar inclinations) did lack integration or musical logic and Kenton went back to more jazz-inclined material in 1952 with excellent soloists like trombonist Frank Rosolino and saxophonist Lee Konitz. Despite occasional flights into Latin American music and neo-classical extravaganzas such as the Neophonic Orchestra, Kenton mostly maintained this side of his work for the rest of his life. Kenton's work is patchily available on CD, but it would be nice to hear his successfully adventurous *West Side Story* in the format.

★*New Concepts of Artistry in Rhythm* (Capitol CDP7 92865-2)

One of the best of all Kenton Bands, recorded in Chicago in 1952, and featuring Art Pepper, Maynard Ferguson, Frank Rosolino and others. Kenton had just ditched his flat-out 'progressive jazz' policy, but the 'Prologue' here finds him in typical hectoring mood, lecturing his public on his intentions and ham-fistedly emphasising them with illustrations from the players. After that things warm up, notably with excellent arrangements of 'Young Blood' and 'Swing House' by Gerry Mulligan, and a vivacious rendition of an Afro-Cuban piece 'Taboo', as a feature for Frank Rosolino and Lee Konitz.

Laine, Cleo (Clementina Dinah Campbell)

(Born Southall, England, October 27, 1927)
Cleo Laine had performed a variety of commercial music jobs by the time she auditioned for the John Dankworth Seven at the age of twenty five, at which point she was already possessed of a rich contralto, emotional warmth, wit and swing. While with the Dankworth band, one of the most commercially successful bop-

derived British groups of the Fifties, she developed her instrumental awareness and acquired a considerable feel and affection for jazz. In 1958 Laine and Dankworth married, and the singer left the band in search of an acting and solo singing career. She made a powerful acting debut in the 1958 Royal Court production of *Flesh To A Tiger*, developed as both a cabaret artist and an actress, collaborated with Dankworth (by 1965 a successful movie-score writer) on a musical setting for Shakespeare's sonnets that was an overnight success, and won a *Downbeat* magazine critics' poll. By the end of the decade Laine's repertoire embraced renditions of works by TS Eliot, Thomas Hardy and WH Auden, and she even earned William Walton's gratitude for a recording of his 'Facade', a musical setting for the poetry of Dame Edith Sitwell.

In 1972 a recording made at Carnegie Hall cemented Dankworth and Laine's reputation as international stars, though only peripherally jazz ones. Together however, Laine and Dankworth have retained an enthusiasm for communicating jazz values through performance and education, with the Wavendon All Music Plan, in Buckinghamshire, being a project devoted to breaking down the barriers between all forms of contemporary music.

★*Cleo at Carnegie* (DRG/USA CDXP 2101)

The album for which Laine won a Grammy in 1986, with more of an emphasis on standards than on the faintly precious poetry reworkings of the Seventies. The set includes an elegant Hoagy Carmichael medley, one of her most popular ballads in 'He Was Beautiful' and jazz standards such as 'Crazy Rhythm' and 'I Want to Be Happy'.

Lyttelton, Humphrey

(Born Eton, England, May 23, 1921)
The years after the Second World War were tempestuous ones in British jazz. In the pre-war years the music had been performed mainly by danceband professionals, in the busy after-hours club scene, or smuggled where possible into a commercial repertoire. It was the younger danceband players who developed the British

bebop movement, but interest in earlier jazz was principally sustained by jazz-loving amateurs, and their fans were often particular to the point of paranoia about avoiding the slightest hint of modernism. The most prominent figure on the post-war revivalist scene (though ultimately one of the least sectarian) was old Etonian ex-Guardsman Humphrey Lyttelton, who was not only a fine trumpeter in a manner initially influenced by Louis Armstrong and later by Buck Clayton, but an energetic campaigner for jazz in general.

Lyttelton joined one of the best of the revivalist bands, George Webb's Dixielanders, in the immediate postwar years, then formed a band of his own including the excellent clarinettist and cartoonist, Wally Fawkes. They specialised in remakes of New Orleans classics, but though there were bursts of individual flair, the band (like most of its relatives on the British scene) lacked the contrapuntal momentum and rhythmic elan of its American models. Lyttelton had a hit record with 'Bad Penny Blues' in 1956, but by the end of the Fifties he was parting company with the revivalist hard-liners and began to hire saxophonists – much to the chagrin of some fans, since the only reeds in a traditional New Orleans ensemble were clarinets. With excellent saxophonists such as Bruce Turner, Tony Coe, Jimmy Skidmore, Joe Temperley and Kathy Stobart, Lyttelton broadened his scope to include Ellingtonish music, and his bands from the Sixties onwards are consistently colourful and soloistically strong, though CDs have so far passed them by – and the Duke Ellington Classics band with Ray Warleigh and John Surman would be delightful to hear on the format. Lyttelton has also been prolific as a writer and broadcaster, and has done much to raise the profile of jazz music in Britain.

The Parlophone Years (Dormouse DM 21CD)

Lyttelton's early bands at work, from the days when the revivalist urge was upon them and they tended to be strong in the front line and weak in the rhythm section. For specialist interest mainly, though the set does feature the trumpeter's chart hit of 1956, 'Bad Penny Blues' and an excellent 1952 recording of 'London Blues' featuring a fine alto saxophonist, Bertie King.

McRae, Carmen

(Born New York, April 8, 1922)
Carmen McRae has displayed one of the most personal vocal styles in jazz for over forty years, a disciple of BILLIE HOLIDAY's who nevertheless retains a characteristic brusque independence that marks her out. Like Holiday, she gets inside the lyrics of songs, her stage personality has the strength of NINA SIMONE's but with an acid wit in place of the bleak defiance, and her rhythmic originality constantly changes the pace and spacing of standard songs.

Originally a pianist, she had a precocious start in the music business by writing the song 'Dream of Life' when she was sixteen, which Billie Holiday recorded. She then joined the bands of BENNY CARTER, COUNT BASIE and Mercer Ellington in rapid succession in the 1940s, briefly being married to the drummer Kenny Clarke during that period. After club jobs in the early Fifties, McRae began recording in 1953, and has worked with excellent piano trios (Ray Bryant and Duke Pearson have been among the pianists) ever since.

★*Fine and Mellow* (Concord CCD 4342)

Commercial pressures diverted Carmen McRae from the sharp end of jazz for much of her career, but in the 1980s her improvisor's quality surfaced more consistently on disc, and this live recording from California's Birdland West not only features the singer in her imposing prime on songs like 'These Foolish Things' and 'What Is This Thing Called Love' but infectious, funk-inclined accompaniment from a band led by altoist Red Holloway including Jack McDuff on organ and Phil Upchurch on guitar.

McShann, James Columbus 'Jay'

(Born Oklahoma, January 12, 1909)
McShann is principally known to younger jazz audiences as Charlie Parker's boss shortly before the saxophonist took the music world by storm. A bandleader with a strong enthusiasm for blues, McShann was both a powerful boogie-influenced pianist and a shrewd judge of his fellow musicians, and his bands were excellent examples of Kansas City danceability and directness.

McShann began touring with other leaders from the mid-Thirties but formed his own quintet (with Charlie Parker on alto) in 1937, and a bigger band in 1940. This outfit displayed a good deal of unspectacular blues singing but also the fascinating beginnings of Charlie Parker's mature style, as well as the other members of a first-class rhythm section in bassist Gene Ramey and drummer Gus Johnson. After the war, McShann ran smaller bands, still blues-oriented, with BASIE's vocalist Jimmy Witherspoon making several appearances. McShann energetically defended the memory of Kansas City jazz at festivals and concert performances worldwide, and his talents became more widely known through his performance in the excellent 1978 jazz movie *Last of the Blue Devils*.

★*Airmail Special* (Sackville/Spotlite SACKCD 3040)

Immense spirit and vigour in a McShann mix of swing classics and blues, recorded in the 1980s and also featuring the excellent bassist Neil Swainson, and drummer Terry Clarke.

Norvo, Red (Kenneth Norville)

(Born Beardstown, Illinois, March 31 1908)
For over forty years, various small-bands led by the vibraharpist Red Norvo have been performing a concentrated distillation of elegant euphoria to reverential silences from the world's jazz audiences. Norvo is a pioneer of the use of the vibraharp in jazz, and has chosen musicians over the years who have helped him sustain a music-box world of glistening harmonies, sly quotes, and gently rippling pools of sound against all the odds from an increasingly amplified popular music. Norvo, who started his career in a marimba band in the mid-Twenties, formed his first trio in 1949, assuming that even the sextet he led before was an uneconomic proposition in the music-business squeeze of the day. One of his early bassists was Charles Mingus, and that tempestuous individual still managed to fit with relative peace into Norvo's chosen formula which has always celebrated Broadway tunes, jazz classics, and technical showpieces like FATS WALLER's 'Jitterbug Waltz'.

★*Just A Mood* (Bluebird/BMG ND 86278)

Material from two key Norvo dates in 1954 and 1957 on this classic Bluebird compilation, the latter being one of the best recording sessions the vibist ever participated in. The 1957 date produced four long tracks ('The Night Is Blue', 'Easy on the Eye', 'Just A Mood', 'Sunrise Blues') in which a terrific band featuring BEN WEBSTER on tenor, Harry Edison on trumpet and the delightful Jimmy Rowles on piano, not only empathised with Norvo's notions of restrained swing and melodic delicacy but all displayed their unique virtues to the full as well.

O'Day, Anita

(Born Chicago, December 18, 1919)
Anita O'Day, whose performance (and immense feathery hat) provided some of the most enduring musical episodes and Fifties imagery of the celebrated *Jazz on a Summer's Day* Newport movie, possessed at her peak a mixture of cool vivacity, immaculate technique (the most convoluted writing couldn't throw her) and original improvisors' skills, both melodically and rhythmically. Though her influences included BILLIE HOLIDAY and ELLA FITZGERALD (and her best work is a remarkable blend of Holiday's subtlety of inflection and Fitzgerald's ebullience) she has remained a highly distinctive artist, even up to the point in recent times where her pitching has become more erratic and her stamina restricted. O'Day began in the entertainment business as a contestant in America's grisly 'dancethons' in the mid-Thirties, then took various nightclub jobs in which singing was secondary. She joined drummer Gene Krupa's band as featured vocalist in 1941, and by the mid-Forties was highly regarded as the singer with STAN KENTON's demanding orchestra. O'Day influenced several subsequent Kenton vocalists, such as JUNE CHRISTY and CHRIS CONNOR.

★*Anita Sings The Most* (Verve 829 577-2)

O'Day in 1957 with a good band including guitarist Herb Ellis and pianist OSCAR PETERSON, on a variety of standard material including 'S'Wonderful', 'They Can't Take That Away From Me' and 'Ol' Devil Moon'. A rare CD of early O'Day, with her characteristic rhythmic and tonal adventures and genuine transformation of the material, though Peterson is too busy a pianist to be an ideal partner.

Pass, Joe (Joseph Anthony Passalaqua)

(Born New Jersey, January 13, 1929)

If Joe Pass has a problem, it is that he is so comprehensively endowed with everything a bop-inclined guitarist needs to know as to have become as attractive to admirers of guitar technique as to music-lovers in general. He frequently plays unaccompanied, or in partnership with a bassist, and specialises in standards and blues, dressed in a mixture of slinky chords, walking bass lines and general embroidery. Pass was working in demanding company while still at high school and joined Charlie Barnet's swing band in 1947, but narcotics problems affected his career and he was in and out of music for much of the next two decades, though playing actively with jazz-oriented inmates in the band of the Synanon Foundation Rehabilitation Centre, in 1961.

On his release, Pass's lovely sound and full technique brought plenty of offers and some that he took up included George Shearing's, BENNY GOODMAN's and OSCAR PETERSON's. Through Peterson, Pass became closely associated with the projects of the impresario Norman Granz, and as a result he has become widely known particularly as a festival performer (sometimes with ELLA FITZGERALD). But Pass remains at his best in intimate surroundings where his delicacy and tonal subtleties are audible. He likes playing unaccompanied, and has often recorded this way, particularly covering the standards repertoire.

★*Checkmate* (Pablo CD 311-22)

A 1981 duet between Pass and the fluid, encyclopaedically knowledgeable and witty pianist Jimmy Rowles, being a valuable contrast with the interminable supplies of virtuosic work Pass has laid down over the years. The material is good ('So Rare', 'God Bless The Child') and the interplay is genuine.

Peterson, Oscar Emmanuel

(Born Montreal, August 15, 1925)
Oscar Peterson has often been criticised as a musician in thrall to
his own runaway technique, but he remains a great virtuoso of
piano jazz, and an equally effective populariser of the music
among those who might otherwise not have encountered it.
Influenced primarily by ART TATUM, Peterson's playing is similarly
a rolling torrent of arpeggios, trills, contrapuntal tug-of-war,
thundering bass figures and ignition of blazing flares of sound in
every possible chink or gap in the music. Inevitably Peterson has
become a phenomenon for this aspect of his work alone, with the
result that the most rhapsodic or contemplative of overtures will
usually turn into a roaring uptempo display before long. Yet he
has a devastating rhythmic momentum, and his harmonic ear is
highly developed. A phenomenon in his native Canada, Peterson
burst upon American audiences at Norman Granz's invitation in
1949 and – predominantly as a trio leader – he sustained this
exhausting pressure ever since. Peterson has frequently been
featured with other leading figures of jazz (Dizzy Gillespie, ROY
ELDRIDGE, COUNT BASIE and many others).

Ain't But A Few of Us Left (Pablo CD 131121-3)

A fine Peterson display in the company of a shrewd partner who
he had to take care not to swamp – vibraharpist Milt Jackson. This
collaboration from 1981 was released under Jackson's name, it
includes 'If I Should Lose You' and 'Body and Soul', and drummer
Grady Tate and bassist Ray Brown furnish inventive and eventful
support.

Digital at Montreux (Pablo CD 20014)

There are sessions in which Peterson holds his immense technique in check (usually in the company of other strong musical
personalities, like the above with Milt Jackson, or saxophonist
BENNY CARTER) but most of his innumerable albums are intended to
ensure that his virtuoso status is undimmed. This 1979 session
from the Montreux Festival is just that, and bassist Neils-

Henning Oersted Pedersen is in fleet support on 'Caravan', 'C Jam Blues', 'Satin Doll' and others.

Reinhardt, Jean Baptiste 'Django'

(Born Charleroi, Belgium, January 23, 1910; died May 16, 1953)
In a period in which European players were rarely commended by the pioneering Americans for much more than diligent plagiarism, Belgian Romany guitarist Django Reinhardt impressed the originators as the first European jazz artist of genius and his reputation has not dulled with time. Though self-taught and unable to read music, Reinhardt was the complete jazz guitarist. He executed singing fast lines with a precision that made the notes glitter, his driving chord-playing lifted his fellow musicians with its swing and bounce, his playing of trills was like a pianist's, and his melodic construction was almost infallibly graceful. The fastest tempos could not unsettle Reinhardt, and he would launch into uptempo solos with a breakneck momentum that left him no room for coasting. But his ballad playing, by total contrast, could be hypnotically poignant – rare for such a powerful technician.

Reinhardt was the son of a gypsy entertainer, and he learned both violin and guitar as a child. In one of jazz's most famous acts of fate, Reinhardt lost the use of two fingers of his left hand in a caravan fire, was forced to abandon the violin, and developed a technique for his second instrument better than that of all fully-functioning jazz guitarists of his day. He loved Louis Armstrong's, Joe Venuti's, and Duke Ellington's music from records, worked with various French semi-dance orchestras in the early Thirties, then formed his famous Quintet du Hot Club de France in 1934, with violinist STEPHANE GRAPPELLI. The QHCF recorded extensively, and Reinhardt's contribution to it was quickly recognised as ranking with the finest improvisation since the beginning of recorded jazz. The war broke the band up, and though DUKE ELLINGTON later requested his presence (Reinhardt's performances with Ellington in America weren't sensations, nor were they helped by the guitarist's notorious unreliability about turning up) his career lost its pre-war momentum. Reinhardt had partly lost interest in showbusiness, and was diverted by bebop and the electric guitar playing of Charlie Christian. He died unexpectedly in 1953.

★*Djangology* (Giants of Jazz GOJCD 53002)

Nearly seventy minutes of classic Reinhardt on this budget-priced collection, not only featuring the Hot Club band but Thirties emigre saxophone giants COLEMAN HAWKINS and BENNY CARTER as well. 'Honeysuckle Rose' and 'Crazy Rhythm' are from the Coleman Hawkins All Star band that included Carter, and some of the tracks feature trombonist Dicky Wells in what are frequently regarded as his best recorded performances.

Rich, Bernard 'Buddy'

(Born New York, June 30, 1917; died April 2, 1987)

Buddy Rich may have been one of jazz music's circus acts, but he was also one of its most compelling. People who otherwise disliked his brash, frantic big band style would watch his drumming mesmerised. His percussion introductions established a pitch of excitement that made the eventual arrival of the ensemble a climax rather than a beginning, his left-hand patterns were executed with the speed of two-hand rolls, and his solos were a blur.

Rich's reputation in his later years was established by the big-band he led from the mid-Sixties to the end of his life – an ensemble tailored to please both older swing fans and younger audiences by including both traditional material and fusion music – but he could on occasion be a fine accompanist to good soloists, a role he wasn't often invited to play. Rich's career was a hangover from the dance-hall euphoria of the swing craze, and he never lost his commitment to direct, spectacular, pyrotechnical entertainment.

Rich was a vaudeville performer more or less as soon as he was weaned, and appeared onstage with his parents as a drumming toddler, dubbed 'Baby Traps'. He was dancing and playing on Broadway when he was four and was a bandleader at eleven. Through his twenties, Rich occupied the drum chair in bands led by BUNNY BERIGAN, Harry James, ARTIE SHAW and TOMMY DORSEY, and decided to start his own big band in the Forties when everyone else was giving up. Rich's outfit didn't last either, and until the end of the Fifties he played for Norman Granz's 'Jazz At The Philharmonic' and almost became a singer. Rich's second attempt at starting a big band at an inopportune time – in the mid Sixties rock renaissance – unexpectedly took off because of a wide-ranging repertoire, and it toured to enthusiastic audiences for the rest of Rich's life.

*Time Being (Bluebird/BMG ND 86459)

Several items by a roaring Rich big band caught in motion at Ronnie Scott's Club, with both the strength of the arrangements and the leader's devastating drumming in evidence on a long workout on the title track and crisp versions of 'Straight No Chaser' and 'Dancing Men'.

Shaw, Artie (Arthur Jacob Arshawsky)

(Born New York, May 23, 1910)
Clarinettist Artie Shaw produced some of the most substantial music of the swing era, but his contemporary BENNY GOODMAN diverted most of the limelight that this complex and gifted musician might have attracted. Shaw's career was full of false starts because his commitment to the music business was ambivalent. A fine instrumentalist, with a technique rivalling Goodman's, and more originality of line at times, Shaw nevertheless constantly interrupted himself with sudden decisions to learn the guitar, write books, investigate psychoanalysis.

Shaw was a saxophonist originally, then worked in dance bands as a saxophonist and clarinettist in Cleveland, Ohio, returning to New York for recording sessions in the mid-Thirties that led to highly successful collaborations with BILLIE HOLIDAY and BUNNY BERIGAN, appearing on Berigan's celebrated first recording of 'I Can't Get Started'. In 1937 Shaw put together a big band of his own, and had such a substantial hit with a tune called 'Begin the Beguine' that he began the first of several semi-retirements, occasioned by doubts about the hype attendant on showbusiness success. In 1940 he re-formed the band, and developed a small group within it called the Gramercy Five (featuring an excellent pianist who doubled on harpsichord, Johnny Guarnieri) with which he recorded some of his most creative playing. Shaw rebuilt the group after the war, with trumpeter ROY ELDRIDGE in a prominent role, but increasingly turned to literary work from the

Fifties on. He has occasionally returned to bandleading since.

Shaw's intelligence and awareness of modernism marked him out among swing-band stars, and his courage in confronting the racial issue in the music business led to his hiring black artists (notably Billie Holiday) at a time when mixed bands were rare.

*Begin the Beguine (Bluebird/BMG ND 86274)

The title track, Shaw's biggest hit, is featured on this compilation from his RCA recordings. Quickly apparent is Shaw's disinclination to use the riff-packed crescendos and calculated hysteria common in the swing period, favouring instead more textured ensemble sounds and at times the use of strings. Trumpeter Billy Butterfield is a prominent feature of these recordings, the tunes also include 'Frenesi' (almost as big a hit as 'Begin the Beguine') and 'Stardust', and there are appearances from Billie Holiday and BUDDY RICH.

*The Complete Gramercy Sessions (Bluebird/BMG ND 87637)

The 1940 and 1945 versions of Shaw's Gramercy Five, confirming the general impression of Shaw that both his own playing and the jazz content of his music were at their most extended in these small groups. The compilation includes 'Summit Ridge Drive', which was a hit for Shaw and displays considerable imagination in the clarinet soloing, as well as the more modern-sounding 'Gentle Grifter' and 'Sad Sack' from a later session, featuring trumpeter Roy Eldridge, pianist Dodo Marmarosa (better known as a bop-oriented Parker disciple) and guitarist Barney Kessel.

Tatum, Arthur 'Art'

(Born Toledo, Ohio, October 13, 1909; died November 5, 1956) Very few jazz musicians have caused classical virtuosi to visit nightclubs and watch them in astonishment (it's a dubious accolade in any case) but if nothing else, it was certainly a testament to pianist Art Tatum's extraordinary technical command that concert artists such as Gieseking and Horowitz did exactly that. Tatum was the fastest and most elaborate jazz pianist there has ever been, with a style originally derived from stride musician FATS WALLER but which soon evolved into a shower of sound in which the harmonic basis of the song was spontaneously altered. There were constantly surprising key changes and eventual resolutions by the most circuitous of routes, and the perpetual contrasts between left and right hand conveyed the impression of more than one improvisor at work. Tatum was later criticised for sacrificing all material, good or bad, to the meat-mincer of his technique, but he remained within the spirit of the songs more often than he is given credit for.

Tatum was blind in one eye and his sight was deteriorating in the other, and he first learned music at a school for the blind before eventually studying formally in Toledo. He had his own local radio show at seventeen, began working for singer Adelaide Hall in the early Thirties, then worked clubs all over America as a soloist and with his own trio. Throughout the Thirties, Tatum cut a stream of excellent recordings, and began sessions for Norman Granz in 1953 which were largely unaccompanied and among his most remarkable work. He also recorded with excellent sidemen in the mid-Fifties and appeared to be performing at the peak of his own exacting standards right up to his death.

★*Complete Capitol Recordings Vol 2* (Capitol/EMI CDP 792 867-2)

Tatum recorded some solo work for Capitol in 1949, providing some good examples of his ability to break down the significant elements of a tune, rework them separately, build counter-melodies against them, alter the texture and then reassemble the whole lot in tumultuous resolutions. The pianist does exactly this in a version of 'Blue Skies' that nevertheless always retains the tune's identity and shape, and the ordinariness of 'Dancing In The Dark' is transformed by Tatum's treatment of it.

★*The Tatum Group Masterpieces* (Pablo CD 20034)

Tatum wasn't the perfect pianist to collaborate with others, but some of the situations that Norman Granz put him into in the Fifties were surprisingly fruitful – and this recording with BEN WEBSTER from shortly before the pianist's death was one of the best. The contrast between Webster's lazy lyricism and Tatum's energy worked perfectly, and on 'My Ideal' and 'Night and Day' they play well enough to make it a shame these two musicians from different ends of the jazz universe couldn't work together again.

Thornhill, Claude

(Born Indiana, August 10, 1909; died July 1, 1965)

Claude Thornhill was more of a dance-band arranger than a fully fledged jazz artist, yet his work was continually inflected with jazz and – as an inspiration to a truly great composer and arranger in Gil Evans – his influence filtered unmistakeably into the mainstream of the music. Thornhill was a remarkable textural artist, whose avoidance of the percussive riffing technique of big jazz bands in favour of subtly coloured orchestral effects made tone-poems of the most mundane material. He constantly perceived new ways of organising regular jazz lineups (on one occasion turning his entire reed section into clarinettists) and he introduced the French horn into arrangement, a device unforgettably developed by Gil Evans later on. Thornhill's graceful methodology stood in the shadows of the Miles Davis/Gil Evans 'Birth of the Cool' recordings of 1949. Thornhill was a trained musician who had worked for Paul Whiteman, BENNY GOODMAN and then as a session arranger, before forming his own band in 1940, Gil Evans joining him a year later. His postwar band included altoist Lee Konitz. Thornhill's later career was hampered by personal difficulties, but his earlier music is excellent and his influence on jazz immense.

Tapestries (Charly CDCHARLY 82)

Excellent Thornhill compilation with most of his best work, including a good deal of material arranged by Gil Evans. Thornhill's manipulation of the danceband repertoire is nowhere better represented than on 'Snowfall', the tune that became his theme-song – a foxtrot turned into a piece of drifting impressionism. Reflecting the changes in the Forties, 'Thrivin' On A Riff' and 'Yardbird Suite' also make fascinating appearances.

Vaughan, Sarah Lois

(Born New Jersey, March 27, 1924; died April 3, 1990)
Some artists transcend the technical demands of their craft. Sarah Vaughan was the jazz singer who made it sound easiest. Possessed of a four-octave voice, she could sound as fragile and wistful as a flute, or as luxurious and resonant as the low notes of a tenor saxophone. Her control of timbre, pitch, phrasing, dynamics and improvisation were extraordinary throughout her career. She was the operatic diva of jazz.

Sarah Vaughan began as a church singer at seven, and had piano and organ lessons at the same time. She won an amateur talent contest at the Apollo Theatre in Harlem when she was sixteen (the song was 'Body and Soul') and joined EARL HINES' band shortly afterwards, following that up with fellow-singer Billy Eckstine's bop-influenced orchestra. Vaughan understood bebop quickly, singing with Charlie Parker, Dizzy Gillespie and the 'cool school' guru Lennie Tristano, and in the Fifties with Clifford Brown and Herbie Mann. She later worked with her own small groups, but also with organisations up to the size of symphony orchestras. She was *Downbeat* magazine's Best Female Vocalist for eighteen consecutive years, and has recorded lyricists as different as Stephen Sondheim and Pope John Paul II.

★*After Hours* (Roulette CDP 7 93271-2)

Short weight for a CD, but a fine live recording by Vaughan from 1961, with Mundell Lowe on guitar and George Duvivier on bass. The spare support enhances the crystal clarity of the voice, and 'My Favourite Things' and 'In A Sentimental Mood' represents classic Vaughan.

Waller, Thomas Wright 'Fats'

(Born New York, May 21, 1904; died December 15, 1943)
As an all-round entertainer, Fats Waller is sometimes thought of as having sidelined his jazz talents, but he brought humdrum popular material to life throughout his career and it's been a particular virtue of jazz musicians to achieve such metamorphoses. He also turned the ragtime derived 'stride' piano style into

a dancing, witty and vivacious idiom that in turn influenced innumerable other pianists, as widely divergent as COUNT BASIE, ART TATUM, Thelonious Monk and Bud Powell. Waller was the son of a clergyman and learned organ first (an instrument he sometimes returned to later in his career) but he was a professional pianist by the age of fifteen, an accompanist to blues artists like Bessie Smith in the Twenties, and a successful tunesmith for musicals as well. Waller made a series of pastiche recordings of popular songs in the Thirties that brought him wider popularity, but even these exhibited his usual panache and devastating piano flights. In 'Honeysuckle Rose' and 'Ain't Misbehavin'' Waller composed two of the best-loved tunes in popular music.

★*Joint Is Jumpin'* (Bluebird/BMG ND 86288)

Waller from 1929 to 1943, with half the tracks unaccompanied piano playing. Some of his finest compositions are included, like 'Handful of Keys' and 'Ain't Misbehavin''.

★*The Last Years 1940–1943* (Bluebird/BMG ND 90411)

Extensive set representing the showbiz side of Waller that obscured the improvisor ('By the light of the Silvery Moon' 'Your Socks Don't Match') but still vivacious music.

Webster, Benjamin Francis 'Ben'

(Born Kansas City, March 27, 1909; died September 20, 1973)
One of the supreme saxophone stylists in all jazz, Ben Webster's career divides neatly into two. The first period came to a climax during his stint with DUKE ELLINGTON's orchestra, where his wide-brimmed sound transformed the reed section and where his driving solo on 'Cottontail' eventually became part of the arrangement. Webster has subsequently been thought of primarily as a ballad specialist, in which the songs are remoulded, lightly bludgeoned but ultimately caressed by one of the most lustrous sounds ever to emerge from a tenor saxophone.

In the 1930s, Webster worked and recorded with most of the major swing bandleaders, including FLETCHER HENDERSON, Bennie

Moten, Andy Kirk and BENNY CARTER. When smaller groups became the fashion, he became one of the staples around 52nd Street, both as a leader and sideman. He later toured with 'Jazz At The Philharmonic', settled in Los Angeles and worked in the West Coast studios and clubs. Webster spent his last decade or so in Europe, usually based in Copenhagen, from where he would periodically tour the continent. Never at his best at fast tempos, Webster in later years turned everything over medium pace, into a glorified rasp. Putting over a romantic ballad, he combined a robustly opulent sound, controlled down to the last scoop and slur, with a deeply-felt, deceptively casual sense of rhythm. He also had, like Armstrong, the knack of picking the choicest notes from the melody as written.

★Live In Paris 1972 (Esoldun FCD 131)

Webster with French musicians, in a selection of fine performances that enhance all the saxophonist's virtues of rich, colourful tenor playing combined with a remarkable lightness and ambiguity. The recording is good, the range of material is excellent, and George Arvanitas at the piano – one of the finest European bebop players – is almost Webster's equal.

★For the Guvnor (Charly CDCHARLY 15)

Ben Webster steadily improved with the passage of the years. Never an impulsive player, he grew into his reflectiveness and his refinement of a handful of devices as recognisable as a signature. Here he performs with characteristic subtle resonance on an excellent selection including 'I Got It Bad And That Ain't Good', 'In A Sentimental Mood' and 'Rockin' In Rhythm' (recalling his Ellington associations) as well as Thelonious Monk's 'Straight No Chaser'.

Young, Lester Willis 'Prez'

(Born Mississippi, August 27, 1909; died March 15, 1959)
If any musician was the first model for the restrained 'cool school' of improvisation that became fashionable in the 1950s it was

tenor saxophonist Lester Young. Yet Young's style, though delicate, displayed none of the chilly remoteness that some exponents of the Fifties method adopted. The diametric opposite of COLEMAN HAWKINS, his chief rival for pre-eminence in the saxophone world in the Thirties, Young not only became a primary influence on the developing Charlie Parker but later on Sonny Rollins and John Coltrane as well – all players whose styles were worlds away from 'cool' music. Young's sound on the saxophone was once memorably described as 'soundless laughter' and he brought to the tenor some of the gentler effervescence of the clarinet, which he also played. Unlike Hawkins, he was not a harmonic improvisor (working off the related scales to chords) but a player who constantly remoulded the original theme, extracting motifs from it, manipulating them, relating them to the overall picture and, in his words, 'telling a story'. Young therefore placed much of his emphasis on tone, and his vocabulary of timbre was immense, from vibrant, singing sounds to wistful, disconsolate sighs.

Young was the son of a vaudeville entertainer, and he was strongly influenced by BIX BEIDERBECKE's saxophone partner Frankie Trumbauer in his early development. He replaced Coleman Hawkins in the FLETCHER HENDERSON band in 1934 but was an insufficiently aggressive performer for Henderson, and left. Young's tenure with the COUNT BASIE made his reputation – it ended all attempts by potential employers to harden his style – and in the late Thirties he also recorded some of the most memorable duo improvisations in jazz with BILLIE HOLIDAY. Young left Basie to lead his own band in 1940, but was conscripted into the army, an experience that broke his mental health. Though he worked a good deal with 'Jazz At The Philharmonic' in the Fifties, his increasingly oblique style was underestimated in that hothouse of technical playing and he became increasingly depressed. When he died in New York in 1959 (Billie Holiday soon followed) an album with Gil Evans was planned, one of jazz's most poignant missed chances.

★*Savoy Recordings Vol 1* (Vogue 550104)

Two sessions from 1944 featuring Lester Young, one with Earle Warren's Orchestra, the other with pianist Johnny Guarnieri's.

Young's vibrant youth is past by now, but much of the music remains vigorous and inventive, and his tone is richer and wider than formerly. Trombonist Dicky Wells also puts in some substantial contributions.

★*Amadeus* (Nostalgia/Mainline CDNOST 7639)

An erratic air-shot from the late Thirties, when the Basie Orchestra was playing the Savoy Ballroom. Not perfect, it nevertheless captures the atmosphere of the Basie band in action in its heyday, and Young's dynamic part in it. The band's theme song 'Moten Swing' kicks it off, and other features include 'Swing Brother Swing', 'They Can't Take That Away From Me' and 'Bugle Blues'.

3

BEBOP

SHORTLY before the Second World War, a young New York swing drummer called Kenny Clarke* found himself looking for a job. His offence, in the drum chair of the popular Teddy Hill band, had been to change the playing of the pulse – such that, to the ears of his employer, the dancers wouldn't know where to put their feet. The established rhythm of swing tended to be four beats to the bar, with the emphasis on the first and third, and the signpost of the beat was usually the bass drum so that nobody could possibly miss it. Clarke switched the marking of the beat to his cymbals and began using the bass drum for scattered accents. It wasn't the best way to keep a swing band employer coming up with the wages.

Nevertheless, in 1940 Clarke was asked by Teddy Hill to find some young and inexpensive players to provide music at a 108th Street club, Minton's Playhouse. Clarke came up with a band that included an eccentric young stride pianist called Thelonious Monk. John Birks 'Dizzy' Gillespie, a boisterous, technically adroit swing-band trumpeter, came to the sessions after hours, as did, Benny Goodman's star guitarist, Charlie Christian. Down the road, at Monroe's Uptown House, Jay McShann's young altoist, Charlie Parker, seemed to be exploring variations on the orthodox harmonies of swing similar to the Minton's players.

Charlie Parker had worshipped the work of Count Basie's saxophonist Lester Young in Kansas City, and had learned a good many of Young's light and lyrical methods. As the 1940s

* Kenny Clarke, though one of the originators of bebop, is not currently represented on CD as a leader; therefore he has no biographical section in this book, though he is mentioned incidentally in the biographies of other players.

progressed, Parker increasingly made clear to his habitual listeners that he was likely to have the same impact on the jazz of his
time as, twenty years earlier, Louis Armstrong had had on his. He
could play in all keys (he had never been taught that it wasn't
necessary to), he was a brilliant blues player, and he transformed
the received materials of jazz so comprehensively in melody,
harmony and rhythm that no young player, even a revivalist,
could fail to respond to the difference.

Parker, Gillespie, Monk, Clarke and others began increasingly
to play together, to share ideas and deconstruct swing. The new
idiom was first called (after its symptomatic accents and jumpy
melodies) 'rebop' and then 'bebop'. Its characteristics were fast
tempos, harmonic progressions augmented by added notes on the
chords, and a shift in phrasing and accents that made it seem at
first to the unwary as if it began and ended in the wrong places.
Chord changes usually began on strong beats in swing, resolutions ended on them. Charlie Christian, Gillespie and Parker used
offbeats more and more. Eventually Parker's adventures with
accents became so ambitious that he would appear to be in
another world to his accompanists, if not for the fact that he
virtually always ended up where he meant to. Miles Davis recalls
shouting at the pianist Duke Jordan not to follow Parker's line
during a recording session but concentrate on staying in step with
drummer Max Roach, trusting that Parker would find his way
back. Often to the astonishment of his musicians, he did.

Bebop provoked sharp reactions. Many older musicians disliked
it and felt that it neither swung, nor told a story. Even some of its
practitioners found it too frenetic, notably Miles Davis, who
quickly adapted its phrasing and intonation to a much more
muted style. Davis brought an orchestra of his own to New York's
Royal Roost in 1948, performing an unexpectedly soft and velvety
arranged music, which was nevertheless embroidered on by a
diffident form of bop soloing from the leader, and from prominent
white musicians, such as Lee Konitz and Gerry Mulligan. A
Canadian arranger called Gil Evans, an Ellington fan who
vigorously educated himself in classical music and classic jazz, was
instrumental in bringing about this change, but it wasn't the only
form that this new 'cool' music took. A scholarly, single-minded
Chicago pianist, Lennie Tristano, developed a more ascetic
version (saxophonists Konitz, Warne Marsh and others studied

with him), which pursued the goal of melodic variation above all else. Tristano rhythm sections were timekeepers, not active participants, and pyrotechnics or flagwaving climaxes were considered cheap thrills and to be avoided. Another kind of 'cool' style was explored by bored Hollywood studio players on the West Coast – but though the emotional temperature of some of the music produced by players like trumpeter Shorty Rogers and drummer Shelly Manne was a few degrees down on New York bop, it was nothing like as restrained as the Tristano school and is often unfairly saddled with the 'cool' tag.

.Through the Fifties, some versions of bop moved closer to public acceptability by emphasising the blues and gospel qualities of jazz. Groups led by drummers Max Roach and Art Blakey, by pianist Horace Silver (featuring powerful soloists like virtuoso trumpeters Lee Morgan and Clifford Brown, the idiosyncratic saxophonist Sonny Rollins and the brilliant, obsessive saxophone mystic John Coltrane) performed a mutation usually called 'hard bop'. This was a version of bebop that had emerged as an antidote to 'cool' music, restoring the earlier explicit emotionalism of jazz, a wider dynamic range and a powerful independent role for the rhythm sections. Though it wasn't coherent enough in its early stages to be categorisable as a 'movement', Max Roach and Clifford Brown, Art Blakey and Horace Silver, and a harder-swinging Miles Davis (with partners including trombonist JJ Johnson and saxophonist Lucky Thompson) were all forming groups of a loosely similar character in 1954. The success of hard bop was also aided by the invention of the long-playing micro-groove record and 'high fidelity' reproduction – innovations that enabled the jazz club atmosphere of extended solos and in-person charisma to be more accurately represented on disc.

Hard bop and cool music vied with each other during the Fifties. Some writers described cool as archetypal Cold War music – intellectual, pessimistic, repressed, mistrustful of emotional commitment. But it was undoubtedly the dominant jazz form with the public for a brief period, during which it made bop sound ill-disciplined and excessive. But hard bop regained ground, and cool evaporated. By the end of the Fifties the expressions cool or 'West Coast' had taken on a pejorative ring. Only later was the work of Tristano, Lee Konitz, Chet Baker and Gerry Mulligan to recover its proper due.

But even hard bop didn't lead jazz musicians to smile all the way to the bank. Rock 'n' roll was underway by the mid-Fifties, and to be commercially popular, music needed to possess at least some explicit elements of blues, and the new version of a danceable beat. It was therefore the jazz groups that plainly featured the most pop-oriented material – tunes like Lee Morgan's, 'The Side-winder', and Bobby Timmons' gospelly, 'Moanin', (for Art Blakey) – that made the charts. One of Silver's song titles from the Fifties, 'Opus de Funk', brought a word into common currency that was soon to become an idiom of its own, and 'jazz-funk' was the predominant version of the music from the late Sixties to the beginning of the Eighties.

Miles Davis had continued to develop in his own way through this period. His music had become hotter and more urgent (John Coltrane was in his post-1954 band), but he still felt comfortable with a jazz of more oblique effects. He was also getting bored with the inexorable succession of chord changes underneath orthodox jazz improvisation (the restless Tristano had felt the same way at the end of the Forties) and began instead to explore modes – cycles of scales – as in Indian music. *Kind of Blue*, Davis' most famous exploration of this method, was released in 1960 and became one of the most influential and evocative jazz records of all time.

The modal experiments of Miles Davis and others were leading to a more diffuse and ambiguous jazz. And some newcomers – notably the Los Angeles saxophonist Ornette Coleman, an ex rhythm-and-blues player – were developing methods of thematic improvisation that abandoned chords altogether. These changes led to the controversial 'free-music' scene of the 1960s, a development that substantially broadened the vocabulary of many improvisors but which scared the record industry, and was only a limited success with the wider jazz public. During this time, with a more instrumentally-sophisticated rock music also on the rise, the only commercially successful jazz was that which merged with pop as 'fusion', 'jazz-rock', 'funk' or 'crossover'. Bebop in its original guises was not to return in a big way until the late Seventies. Since that time a revivalist interest in bop by many young musicians (often described as 'jazz postmodernists' or 'neoclassicists') has dominated both jazz playing, and the econom-ics of jazz recording.

Adderley, Julian Edwin 'Cannonball'

(Born Florida, September 15, 1928; died August 8, 1975)
Virtuosic alto and soprano saxophonist, originally an army music instructor. Initially played in a style strongly flavoured with the ideas of CHARLIE PARKER, but also affected by the more raucous and bluesier styles of Eddie Vinson and Louis Jordan too. Adderley's mature method was glossier and more self-conscious than Parker's; the notes more rounded, the accents more predictable and he had a tendency to leave very little space in the music, which is, at times, fatiguing to the ear. But Adderley had infectious swing, and his sensitivity to gospel and blues-influenced music made him a significant figure in the 'soul-jazz' movement of the 1960s that predated funk.

★*Somethin' Else* (Blue Note CDP 746 338–2)

Somethin' Else is one of Adderley's most famous albums, cut in 1958 with the MILES DAVIS rhythm section of the period. Adderley's Charlie Parker allegiances are strongly apparent here, as is his tendency to play all over everything – a torrent of notes that makes the discreet, offhand presence of Miles Davis here seem almost an admonition. Hank Jones is on piano, ART BLAKEY on drums.

★*Them Dirty Blues* (JVC/Fantasy VDJ 1598)

Adderley's most commercially successful session, recorded in February 1960. The material is attractive, with melodies like BOBBY TIMMONS' soul-jazz, 'This Here', plus, 'Work Song', and, 'Easy Living'. Nat Adderley's trumpet is alternately crisp and cantankerous, gliding through the music as if on skis and there's buoyant rhythmic support from Sam Jones, on bass, and Louis Hayes, on drums.

Baker, Chesney H 'Chet'

(Born Oklahoma, December 23, 1929; died May 13, 1988)
One of jazz music's most celebrated romantic figures, but the mythology around him obscured his real gifts. Baker's popular image was as the James Dean of jazz (his combination of

smouldering youthfulness and seductive balladeer's singing voice couldn't miss in the Fifties, when 'cool jazz' was big) but he was both a poignant and obliquely emotional trumpeter/flugelhorn player and, when roused, a fleet and imaginative player of fast bop. Baker came to prominence in 1952, at the age of twenty three when CHARLIE PARKER picked him as a partner for a West Coast session, then formed a groundbreaking piano-less quartet with fellow saxophonist GERRY MULLIGAN.

From the late 1950s to the 1970s Baker was more often than not out of action with drug problems and some of his performances drifted purposelessly, but the last decade of his life saw many performances of bruised and bruising tenderness, often captured on record. Shortly before his death in 1988, Baker featured in a painful documentary by film-maker Bruce Weber called *Let's Get Lost* – a film that ruthlessly pursued his Dorian Gray-like decline from Fifties vocal and jazz idol to dependent, heroin-addicted child-man who could still on occasion produce sublime music. Baker's singing voice is often described as an 'acquired taste', and though its later manifestations obey no known rules of pitching accuracy, its battered sound could be highly communicative and its rhythmic momentum as effective as a drummer. Baker recorded extensively during his last years, with very patchy results – and after his tragic death (he fell from a hotel window in Amsterdam) a Baker industry sprang up, releasing albums regardless of quality.

★*Chet Baker in Paris* (Emarcy 837474/5/6/7-2)

Four volume CD set of Baker in the Fifties, sometimes languid or sentimental to the point of inactivity, but often delicately vivid – notably on the vol 1 tracks with pianist Dick Twardzik, a collection of memorable themes alternately illuminated by Baker's fragile and unsteady lyricism and Twardzik's archetypal cool-style ambiguity and reserve.

★*Chet's Choice* (Criss Cross 1016)

One of the better Baker sessions from his later years (this was 1985), with the excellent guitarist Philip Catherine providing a fluidity that ideally complements the trumpeter's hesitancies and spacey improvising. There's still a cloying quality about some of the ballads (the CD is padded out with more of them than necessary) but generally the music has an urgency and coherence rare for this period of Baker's life.

★*The Italian Sessions* (Bluebird BMG ND 82001)

Baker in unusually bustling mood on a European session from 1962, with an excellent band including guitarist Rene Thomas, and drummer Daniel Humair. This is bop fan's Baker, bristling and bludgeoning over Sonny Rollins' fast 'Pent Up House' (Humair's cymbals rattling relentlessly behind him) and delivering clean, ringing lines over the mid-tempo blues, 'Ballata In Forma Di Blues', over the stalking bass of Benoit Quersin.

Blakey, Arthur 'Art'

(Born Pennsylvania, October 11, 1919; died October 16, 1990)
Originally a pianist, and a bandleader at fifteen – but his own story is that hiring Errol Garner made him redundant on piano and a promoter with a revolver persuaded him to play drums for the first time, unrehearsed, before a live audience. In the 1940s, Blakey worked both with the declining big band of an orchestral jazz pioneer (Fletcher Henderson) and with a vigorous contemporary one (singer Billy Eckstine's). The volatility and drama of his style, based on a steaming cymbal beat and volcanic press-rolls capable of catapulting the most laid-back soloist into space, was soon a hot property.

THELONIOUS MONK, MILES DAVIS, Lucky Millinder and Buddy DeFranco all hired Blakey, but it was a 1954 studio date with the pianist HORACE SILVER that set the pattern for the drummer's career into irrepressible old age. Blakey and Silver (with saxophonist HANK MOBLEY, bassist Doug Watkins and trumpeter KENNY DORHAM) established The Jazz Messengers, a cooperatively-run band, thereby laying the foundation stone of an unfailingly swinging and bluesy 'hard bop' outfit that played on for three and a half decades. As well as being an inspired propellant of established jazz musicians, Blakey was always a remarkable talent scout as well. Many of the finest musicians now at work, for example, JACKIE MCLEAN, Wayne Shorter, Bobby Watson, LEE

MORGAN, FREDDIE HUBBARD, Joanne Brackeen and Wynton Marsalis were Messengers. As a performer and guiding spirit of modern jazz, Blakey continued with unabated commitment right until his recent death.

⋆*A Night in Tunisia* (Blue Note CDP 7465322)

Blakey in 1960, sounding like an express train coming out of a tunnel. The doyen of the bebop renaissance of the 1980s had been introducing the jazz world to powerful newcomers for decades; here it was the trumpeter, Lee Morgan, and the saxophonist, Wayne Shorter, the latter one of the most original Coltrane disciples. The clarity of CDs intensifies Blakey's heated, fervent style. His classic drum intro – galloping uptempo playing, punched through with wild cymbal splashes against a background cymbal beat like rain on an iron roof – which opens the title track here, makes you leap out of your seat convinced that you've been hijacked into the front row of the Village Vanguard, circa 1960. Shorter is succinct and gritty, Morgan closes 'A Night in Tunisia' with some delicious half-valve warped notes and pianist BOBBY TIMMONS sustains the pressure with an endlessly changing backdrop of trills, percussive sounds and sudden, packed arpeggios.

⋆*Night at Birdland, vols 1 & 2. With Clifford Brown.*
(Blue Note, CDP 7456519-2; 7456520-2)

Classic 1954 Blakey, featuring the drummer plus Horace Silver, CLIFFORD BROWN and Lou Donaldson. The playing is constantly on an improvisational razor's-edge and the material is excellent, including pieces that became bebop standbys, like 'Wee Dot', 'Now's the Time' and 'Night In Tunisia'.

Brown, Clifford

(Born Delaware, October 30, 1930; died June 26, 1956)
One of the great jazz trumpeters, whose impact on the music was blunted by his early death, in a road accident, at the age of twenty five. Privately taught jazz theory and the trumpet, piano, vibes

and bass from his mid-teens, Brown was a professional by eighteen, working around Philadelphia with many stars of bop. His style was principally founded on the fleet brass techniques of DIZZY GILLESPIE and FATS NAVARRO, both of whom encouraged him. He worked for a while in a rhythm and blues band (Chris Powell and the Blue Flames), then with arranger Tadd Dameron, with Lionel Hampton, briefly with ART BLAKEY, and then joined drummer MAX ROACH in the quintet – at times including SONNY ROLLINS, SONNY STITT and Harold Land – for which both he and Roach are most fondly remembered.

Bebop trumpeters had to wrestle with the unforgiving nature of the instruments's design to keep up with the mercurial agility of saxophonists in the same style, and the price was often paid in half-formed notes and poor tone. Exceptionally, Brown's sound was polished and full-blooded at any speed, however audacious his improvising, and his influence on contemporary trumpet stars like Freddie Hubbard and Wynton Marsalis is incalculable.

★*At Basin Street* (Emarcy 814 648-2)

Sonny Rollins was twenty six when this record was made, and the partnership between Rollins and Brown (caught here on one of only two studio sets linking them) is close to its briefly incandescent best. Though the Roach/Brown band was always perceived as a hard bop group, Rollins and Brown took it to the limits of the preoccupation with chords. The saxophonist is astonishing on 'Gertrude's Bounce' (with its smoothly descending two-octave opener) and on 'I'll Remember April'. Pianist Richie Powell's arrangements are worth noting too, particularly in the countermelody to 'What Is This Thing Called Love?'.

★*Study In Brown* (Emarcy 814 646-2)

A 1954 recording with the first tenor/trumpet connection in the Max Roach band, that between Brown and West Coast tenorist Harold Land. Land is featured here in some of his best recorded playing, neck and neck, at headlong pace, with Brown on 'Cherokee', attractively furnishing the whistle to Richie Powell's churning traction on 'Take the A Train'. Roach's cymbal work on the same track is a momentous piece of precise, apposite, scene-setting percussion.

Brown, Raymond Matthews 'Ray'

(Born Pennsylvania, October 13, 1926)
A bass player who modelled himself on the young man who founded the modern counter-melodic technique on the instrument – Ellington's prematurely-departed bassist, Jimmy Blanton. Brown began working with DIZZY GILLESPIE in 1945, then married Ella Fitzgerald and formed a band to accompany her two years later. A rhythmically driving bassist with a big, blues-inflected sound, Brown became Oscar Peterson's regular partner in the early Fifties and sustained this role until 1966, when he began increasingly to turn to jazz management. In 1974, Brown became a founder member of the LA 4, a superior lounge-jazz ensemble, featuring guitarist Laurindo Almeida, BUD SHANK on reeds, and Shelley Manne on drums.

★*This One's For Blanton* (Pablo J33J 20010)

Recreation by Duke Ellington and Brown (under Ellington's name) of the 1940 duets between Ellington and Jimmy Blanton. Brown's luxurious sound, immaculate time and phrasing, and calm, unhurried spontaneity conjure fresh figures out of 'Sophisticated Lady', 'Do Nothing Until You Hear From Me' and others.

Burrell, Kenneth Earl 'Kenny'

(Born Detroit, July 31, 1931)
Classy and incisive inheritor of the guitar style of CHARLIE CHRISTIAN and Django Reinhardt, Burrell worked around Detroit in the early 1950s, then moved to New York, and joined the Benny Goodman band in 1957. He recorded extensively under his own name in the Sixties, but was often to be found in the company of partners (such as organist Jimmy Smith and soul saxophonist Grover Washington) who played with a strong and

danceable beat and were never far from the blues. Like Christian before him though, Burrell was as effective with large forces as with small groups, and his big band collaborations with GIL EVANS lost little in drive and enthusiasm.

★*Guitar Forms* (Verve 825 576-2)

One of Burrell's finest albums, with charts arranged by Gil Evans, in 1965. On five of the tracks the guitarist is accompanied by an illustrious big band including LEE KONITZ, Steve Lacy and Johnny Coles, and on 'Lotus Land' the balance between soloing and atmospheric Spanish-flavoured band dynamics is perfect. ELVIN JONES is on drums, and is also the composer of a deft small-group blues, 'Downstairs' – Burrell's stock-in-trade.

★*Togethering* (Blue Note CDP 746 093-2)

Far more earthy Burrell set, interpreting less promising material; but this more recent session on Blue Note does strike some sparks from the pairing of the guitarist with soul and funk saxophonist, Grover Washington. Drummer Jack DeJohnette and bassist Ron Carter, both adept at sidestepping the cliches of fusion, lend sinewy support.

Byrd, Donald

(Born Detroit, December 9, 1932)

College educated musician who hit the headlines with ART BLAKEY's Jazz Messengers in 1955 and 1956, an association that quickly led him into collaborations with leading modernists like SONNY ROLLINS and THELONIOUS MONK. Byrd's sound is hot and full-bodied, and though his primary influences, unsurprisingly, were GILLESPIE, MILES DAVIS and CLIFFORD BROWN, he managed to evolve a genuine lyricism of his own and was capable, in the late Fifties, of composing distinctive tunes. Always preoccupied with the value of education, Byrd has been both a busy educator and self-educator, studying with Nadia Boulanger in Paris, acquiring a string of degrees, and becoming Chair of the Black Music Department at Washington's Howard University for a period in the Seventies. He became a successful crossover artist in this period (using his students to form the band Blackbyrds) and though his music in that vein veered toward the banal, it produced some of the early jazz-funk hits. Byrd's best-selling fusion album *Black Byrd* (Blue Note) is not yet available on CD.

★*Fuego* (Blue Note CDP 746 534-2)

Excellent late Fifties Byrd set, with the title track and 'Lament' owing something to the Miles Davis *Kind of Blue* manner, but with fine soloing from JACKIE MCLEAN on alto.

★*I'm Tryin' To Get Home* (Blue Note CDP 784 188-2)

Complex and sophisticated session using a choir and the arrangements of Byrd and pianist Duke Pearson. Byrd is on flugelhorn much of the time, close to the Miles Davis/GIL EVANS flights in such atmospheric pieces as 'I've Longed and Searched for my Mother'.

Christian, Charles 'Charlie'

(Born Texas, July 29, 1916; died March 2, 1942)
A key member of that coterie of frustrated big-band soloists of the late Thirties who forged the harmonically adventurous bebop out of the standards and standbys of the swing repertoire, Charlie Christian inspired the methods of virtually all bop guitarists until the invasion of jazz guitar-playing by the more elemental sounds of rock. One of the first, in the swing era, to make extensive use of the recently invented electric amplification, Christian had worked with a variety of Oklahoma territory bands and touring bands before the impresario John Hammond smuggled him onstage at a Benny Goodman gig and the guitarist established one of jazz music's indelible legends by improvising ninety minutes-worth of dazzling solos on 'Rose Room'. Christian became a celebrity through work with Goodman's bands, but it was during his after-hours visits to Minton's Playhouse, frequented also by THELONIOUS MONK, CHARLIE PARKER, DIZZY GILLESPIE among others, that his enduring reputation as a bebop pioneer was established. Aside from his work with Goodman, Christian played and

experimented endlessly. By 1940 however, tuberculosis was getting a hold on him, and a reluctance to rein in his fast-lane lifestyle contributed to his death at twenty five. KENNY BURRELL, JIM HALL, WES MONTGOMERY, BARNEY KESSELL and many other guitarists are in his debt.

★*Live at Minton's 1941* (Jazz Anthology/Musidisc France 550012)

Variable in sound quality and with plenty of background ambiance, these recordings made by enthusiast Jerry Newman in the Harlem bebop clubs are nevertheless classic Christian. Driven on by Thelonious Monk and Kenny Clarke on drums, the guitarist is freed of the formalities of a commercial recording session and cuts loose at length with beautifully built guitar solos, notably on the 'Topsy' remould, 'Swing to Bop'. The flow of Christian's ideas recalls Parker in flight, though the guitarist didn't live long enough to completely free himself from the evenness of swing.

★*Genius of the Electric Guitar*. (Giants of Jazz GOJCD 53049)

Christian's Columbia recordings with various Benny Goodman bands. Included is the famous 'Solo Flight', but Christian's blues roots are distinctly audible on the following: 'Blues in B'; the informal jam on 'Waiting for Benny'; the proto-bop phrasing on 'Till Tom Special'; and the movement away from swing-style on-the-beat accenting on 'Air Mail Special'. In these recordings Christian's long, parabolic runs, rhythmic adventurousness and improvisation over modified harmonies prefigure Charlie Parker.

Clark, Conrad Yeatis 'Sonny'

(Born Herminie, Pennsylvania, July 21, 1931; died January 13, 1963)
A regular performer on Blue Note studio sessions of the Fifties (and DEXTER GORDON's favourite accompanist), Clark was a pianist whose directness, percussive style and sympathy for attractive themes, based on crisp rhythmic motifs, made him a natural for the label's no-nonsense house style of the period. He died of a

heart attack after prolonged narcotic and alcohol abuse, but the ten albums he made with Blue Note testify to his consistency and outgoing imagination, as does his ability to inspire and divert the most illustrious company.

★*Cool Struttin'* (Blue Note CDP 746 513-2)

The HORACE SILVER touch, and that of Hampton Hawes, combined with Clark's rigorous logic – and with a first-class band including JACKIE MCLEAN on alto, ART FARMER on flugelhorn, PAUL CHAMBERS on bass and the urgent, hustling Philly Joe Jones on drums.

Coleman, George

(Born Memphis, Tennessee, March 8, 1935)
One of the fastest and most tireless of hard bop saxophonists and a virtual definition of that style – big, beefy tone, blues-steeped intonation, craftily wrought quotation, frequent use of double-time and harmonic inspiration even at the most breakneck tempos. Coleman's deep affection for blues came from early experience in bands devoted to the idiom, notably BB King's in the early Fifties. His all-round technical assurance and penetrative, unsentimental style later won him the tenorist's job with MAX ROACH, Slide Hampton, Wild Bill Davis, Lionel Hampton, ELVIN JONES, MILES DAVIS and many others. In more recent times, Coleman has led a variety of bands of his own, from quartet and quintet showcases for his own instrumental skills to an octet featuring other hard bop players as muscular as him, as well as his grittily appropriate arrangements.

★*Big George* (Charly CDCHARLY 83)

A Coleman octet recording from 1977, including two other excellent Memphis musicians in pianist Harold Mabern and altoist Frank Strozier. It's an object lesson in witty, unostentatious arrangement, tailor-made for the idiom and the methods of the players, with a variety of tempos and ensemble voicings used in 'Body and Soul' (Coleman's fingers are too restless ever to settle for Coleman Hawkins' inexorable gravitas on such a tune) winding up with the Woody Herman 'Four Brothers' group-sax sound, an invitation to sample the extended skills of all the players on a rolling 'Green Dolphin Street', a nod to rock on 'Joggin'' and to the harmonic foundations of 'Giant Steps' on 'Big George' itself, which brings the imperious best out of the leader.

Cowell, Stanley

(Born Toledo, Ohio, May 5, 1941)
Classically-trained pianist and composer who studied both in Europe and the States, and whose early associates in jazz, in the early Sixties, were RAHSAAN ROLAND KIRK and Yusef Lateef. Cowell performed through the latter part of that decade with a variety of powerful modernists including MAX ROACH, BOBBY HUTCHERSON and MILES DAVIS, and became a regular accompanist for Roach and his singer wife Abbey Lincoln. Cowell's range enables him to play in early stride styles, free music, funk, and bebop, with equal conviction.

★*Back to the Beautiful* (Concord CCD 4398)

An excellent recent session for Cowell including the standard 'A Nightingale Sang In Berkeley Square', as well as his own original pieces. He is with Eighties saxophone prodigy Steve Coleman, a man as equally influenced by hip-hop and rock as by bebop.

Davis, Eddie 'Lockjaw'

(Born New York, March 2, 1921; died November 3, 1986)
Immensely attractive blend of the broad, affable style of the swing tenorists and the speedier mannerisms of bebop (Davis worked with the big band of Andy Kirk in the Forties, and then began a long on-off relationship with the Count Basie band in 1952). A powerful, emphatic performer whose early style had a distinct connection with the booming, bluesy authority of Illinois Jacquet, Davis came from a school that believed in raising the temperature as early as possible and keeping it on the boil. As an improvisor, some of his most engaging work was to be heard in partnership

with fellow-tenorist JOHNNY GRIFFIN, an association that ran intermittently for over two decades.

★*Tough Tenors* Milestone/ACE (821 293–2)

Davis and Johnny Griffin together in 1970, with bebop pioneer Kenny Clarke on drums, Jimmy Woode on bass and Belgian pianist Francy Boland. Davis furnishes his customary mixture of admonishing squeals, headlong charges and an attractive contrast of cantankerous wildness and a reassuringly rumbling vibrato, and Griffin's fleet virtuosity fills every chink.

Davis, Miles Dewey

(Born Alton, Illinois, May 26, 1926)
Of Miles Davis, the composer and arranger GIL EVANS once said, 'he is aware of his complete surroundings . . . the quality of a certain chord, its tension or lack of tension, can cause him to create a sound appropriate to it. He can put his own substance, his own flesh, on a note, and then put that note exactly where it belongs'. Alto saxophonist JACKIE MCLEAN said, 'Miles can play three notes and say as much as someone playing thirty'. For his own part, though he's as aware as anybody that he deserves his status as one of the giants of American music, Davis just says 'don't call me legend. Call me Miles Davis'.

Over a career now spanning more than forty years, Davis has not only developed one of the most evocative solo voices in the history of jazz but also made the music sound different to the way it sounded before, on at least five major occasions. His innovations began with the haunting orchestral *Birth of the Cool* recordings of 1949, in collaboration with the gifted Canadian arranger Gil Evans. In the 1950s he ran one of the finest post-bop bands, with John Coltrane as his front-line partner. In 1960, with one of the all time jazz classics, *Kind of Blue*, he explored modal playing on scales rather than chords, and at one stroke removed much of the monotony that accompanied endless improvisation on chord patterns in all but the most inventive hands. Again with Gil Evans (*Sketches of Spain*, *Porgy and Bess*) he used his poignant trumpet sound as the only solo voice against lustrous orchestral textures. In the middle Sixties, when many adventurous jazz players were turning to the tumult of free-form, Davis loosened bebop still further and brought back a collective interplay, reminiscent of the earliest jazz, in one of his finest quintets – with Wayne Shorter, Tony Williams, Ron Carter and Herbie Hancock. The band became the nucleus of Miles' moves into the electronic age and with *In A Silent Way* and *Bitches' Brew* he gave jazz-rock fusion a rare sting and flavour.

Miles Davis was that rare entity in earlier jazz, the offspring of a middle-class black family that paid for a formal musical education. By the time he went to the Juilliard School of Music at eighteen, he had already extensively played trumpet in high-school bands, and soon began playing hookey from the School to hang out on bebop's boulevard, 52nd Street, New York. He joined CHARLIE PARKER in 1945, quickly establishing himself as a bop trumpeter very different from DIZZY GILLESPIE, his very hesitancy imparting a tremulous delicacy to his music. Though Davis maybe didn't have Dizzy Gillespie's furious virtuosity, he had something else that appealed to Parker – an oblique lyricism that, even at twenty, was distinctively his. He was preoccupied with timbre and texture while most of his colleagues were obsessed with speed.

In 1948, Davis began collaborating with arranger Gil Evans and saxophonists GERRY MULLIGAN and LEE KONITZ – three white musicians who had been working in a superior dance-band (Claude Thornhill's) using instrumentation unusual for jazz, including French horn and tuba. The so-called *Birth of the Cool* sessions, which resulted from this collaboration, inspired the 'cool' movement of the Fifties, the hallmarks of which were restraint, dispassionate investigation of form and avoidance of emotional extremes.

The *Birth of the Cool* nine-piece was an artistic success but a commercial failure. Davis' career declined, partly through narcotics problems, but in 1954 he made a startling comeback at the Newport Festival with a new, fully-formed style, mingling minimalism with tightly-edited bursts of boppish bravura, sketching his ideas with incisive brush-strokes. By hanging tantalisingly behind the beat, and giving himself an entirely new palette of trumpet contemplativeness through the use of the metal harmon mute, he was able to open fresh choruses of improvisation with such unexpected phrasing as to repeatedly change the character of the tune. A brilliant quintet followed – including John Coltrane

– and Davis also took up work with Gil Evans again, making ground-breaking orchestral albums (*Sketches of Spain, Porgy and Bess*) in which the orchestra furnished glowing texture for the almost exclusively solo voice of the trumpeter.

On *Kind Of Blue*, a 1960 session featuring Coltrane, pianist BILL EVANS and saxophonist CANNONBALL ADDERLEY, Davis led one of the most inspirational jazz recording sessions ever. It was a rippling, sometimes raga-like exploration of modified blues and cycles of scales that – despite its restraint – still burned with jazz's traditional heat. It was Davis' response to the emerging free-jazz movement.

In the mid-Sixties Miles Davis (always possessed of a Blakey-like shrewdness for spotting new talent) re-formed his quintet with the new generation of post-bop players such as Wayne Shorter (saxophones), Herbie Hancock (piano), Ron Carter (bass) and Tony Williams (drums). This was perhaps Davis's most flexible and improvisationally agile small-group, demonstrating, on a sequence of albums, a one-touch responsiveness and collective ingenuity that remains unsurpassed and is still widely imitated by young players. In the late 1960s, never inclined to rest on his laurels, Davis began to be attracted by the textural and rhythmic possibilities of rock and roll and funk (as well as by the increased audience potential and income) and started to incorporate electronics and rock percussion techniques into his music. But, like everything else he touched, Miles Davis's rock music bore a distinct trademark. (For further developements in Davis' career, see page 271.)

★*Birth of the Cool* (Capitol CDP7 92862-2)

The revolutionary nine-piece that Davis led for two weeks in 1948, but which had an impact out of all proportion to its brief existence. The recordings were made later, after the band had stopped performing live. Evans' and Mulligan's subtle, contemplative scoring is immediately quite distinct from the freneticism of bebop. The originality of the *Birth of the Cool* sessions resulted from the blending of such unconventional ensemble methods with low-key, unhurried bop-based improvisation, inflected with the flowing sounds of the saxophones – particularly the fragile high sounds of Lee Konitz' alto and the plush mid-range of Mulligan. Davis himself sounds less than happy – more tremulous and Gillespie-like, and trying to play too fast. An historic event, nonetheless.

★*Miles Davis Vols 1 & 2* (Blue Note CDP 781 501-2/502-2)

Miles Davis, recording here with MILT JACKSON, Jimmy Heath and others in 1953, delivering some of his best recorded improvising from any era of his playing. The arrangements owe a lot to the graceful, velvety *Birth of the Cool* manner, and help the soloists to be more varied in their approaches. Much of the dynamism of the session is also down to the presence of ART BLAKEY at the drums, who often sounds engagingly like a man in a bad temper doing the washing up in the background. Davis leans intriguingly ahead of the time, starting new choruses with unusual melodic figures that push him toward new resolutions.

★*Workin' and Steamin'* (JVC/Fantasy VDJ 1521/1522)

The band that formed after Miles Davis' 'comeback' performance, in 1954, at the Newport Festival. Nothing to choose between these two discs since the group that made them could have played nursery rhymes and made them swing (Davis even manages to make music both mysterious and vivacious out of 'Surrey with a Fringe on Top'), the rhythm section being RED GARLAND on piano, Paul Chambers on bass and Philly Joe Jones on drums, and the saxophonist – John Coltrane. Coltrane's contrast with Davis, terrifying bursting-dams of sound against the trumpeter's terse restraint, was part of the charm.

★*Kind of Blue* (CDCBS 62066)

Kind of Blue, recorded in the late Fifties, was Miles' second response to bebop (the first was *Birth of the Cool*) and in the company of Coltrane, pianist Bill Evans, altoist Cannonball Adderly, bassist Paul Chambers and drummer Jimmy Cobb, the trumpeter laid down one of the most enduring of all postwar jazz recordings. In its use of sequences of scales rather than chords, *Kind of Blue* found the meditative spaciousness of a structure close to Indian music. Bill Evans' piano, (sharpened and polished by the tempo stability of

CDs) sounds like spring rain, and Davis' trumpet is able to create infectious swing with a handful of notes.

★*CBS Years* (Jam Today Records 463 246-2)

Compilation disc of takes over the CBS period from 1955 to 1985, including 'All Blues' (from *Kind of Blue*), 'Some Day My Prince Will Come', 'Filles de Killimanjaro' (from the post-bop Wayne Shorter/ Herbie Hancock band) and some of the later funk and fusion work. Useful guide to Miles' development, though the complete discs are preferable up to the mid-Sixties. After that, considering that excellent Shorter/Hancock/Tony Williams sessions like *Sorcerer*, *Nefertiti* and *Miles in the Sky* are bizarrely unavailable on CD, the sampler comes into its own.

★*Porgy and Bess* (CBS Import 35DP61)

Miles Davis is the only soloist on this trumpet concerto, for which the brooding arrangements were conceived by Gil Evans. 'Summertime', which is played with a piquant muted sound over an unexpected mid-tempo clip, and a devastating 'Gone', performed fast against shattering Philly Joe Jones drum breaks in the later stages are unforgettable.

★*Sketches of Spain* (CDCBS 62327)

Sketches of Spain is a revelation for CD listeners who have grown used to their battered vinyl copies of this Gil Evans orchestral piece, which uses Spanish folk motifs and Davis' trumpet like a solo singer. The subtlety of Evans writing for the percussion, the brass and the low notes enriches the conventional backing behind Miles as if it was an old painting that had been suddenly restored. An arrangement of Rodrigo's 'Concierto D'Aranjuez' is a major feature of the album (an interpretation which classical listeners sometimes find trite, and the section playing isn't all that steady at times) but Davis' performance on the glowing 'Solea' is hypnotic.

Davis, Walter

(Born Richmond, Virginia, September 2, 1932; died 1990)
A devoted student of BUD POWELL, the pioneering genius of bop

piano, Davis exhibited the characteristic keyboard style of the idiom – clipped, offhand runs against nudging left-hand chords, melodic complexity without over-elaboration, absence of sentiment. Davis' first professional job was in Newark, New Jersey, with Babs Gonzales' bebop-vaudeville hybrid, Three Bips and a Bop, followed by work with drummer MAX ROACH's group in the early Fifties, in partnership with the highly unusual tenor saxophonist HANK MOBLEY. In the late Fifties, Davis was hired by DIZZY GILLESPIE for his big band, then worked with trumpeter DONALD BYRD and recorded with both Byrd and altoist JACKIE MCLEAN for Blue Note. Intermittent work with ART BLAKEY's Jazz Messengers followed (he alternated with the more celebrated BOBBY TIMMONS), but the insecurities of the profession drove Davis to seek an alternative living as a costume designer.

He returned to music at the end of the Sixties. Having travelled to India to play and study, he worked with the iconoclastic ARCHIE SHEPP, and then joined SONNY ROLLINS' band, with whom he appeared on the *Horn Culture* album for Milestone. In, *Bird*, Clint Eastwood's biopic of Charlie Parker, Davis performs on the soundtrack with typically incisive, tightly-sculpted music, forming a new accompaniment to the original recordings of Parker's solos.

★*Illumination* (Denon DC 8553)

A Davis recording from the late Seventies, notably with two brilliant younger musicians in bassist Buster Williams and drummer Tony Williams. Tony Williams, as usual, seethes like a pressure cooker, while the material reflects Davis' bebop past, his awareness of recent fusion and his experiences in India.

Desmond, Paul

(Born San Francisco, November 25, 1924; died May 30, 1977)
Excellent 'cool school' alto saxophonist whose originality was often obscured by his partnership role in various bands led by Dave Brubeck. Desmond began working with Brubeck in 1948 and remained in close association with the pianist until the late 1960s. His most famous contribution to the Brubeck band was the

perenially popular tune 'Take Five', a theme of playful grace and catchiness that has become a modern jazz classic. A dedicated improvisor whose roots were in Lester Young and the variations on that style explored by LEE KONITZ, Desmond's music never hardened into mannerism despite the Brubeck years, and his advanced techniques on the alto even endeared him to an uncompromising *enfant terrible* of free-music, the saxophonist Anthony Braxton.

★*East of the Sun* (Discovery DSCD 840)

Desmond in a mood of unselfconscious ease with highly compatible partners – the guitarist JIM HALL (a musician of comparable sensitivity and delicacy to Desmond), and MODERN JAZZ QUARTET stalwarts, Percy Heath, on bass, and Connie Kay, on drums.

★*Late Lament* (Bluebird BMG ND90207)

Desmond's first non-Brubeck outing for RCA in 1961, originally entitled *Desmond Blue* and featuring the leader's feathery alto style against a non-glutinous, string-section backing on apposite material, such as 'My Funny Valentine'.

Donaldson, Lou

(Born Badin, North Carolina, November 1, 1926)
As with most alto saxophonists forming their style in the early Fifties, Donaldson fell under the influence of CHARLIE PARKER, but his dislike of overt experimentalism and his enthusiasm for the spirited, blues-oriented simplicity of early jazz led him increasingly toward soul-jazz and funk in the Sixties, after brief periods with ART BLAKEY and Charles Mingus. More declamatory and unambiguous in style than Parker, Donaldson brought rhythm 'n' blues ideas to his improvising, and often compounded the effect with the use of an organ in his bands.

★*Blues Walk* (Blue Note CDP 746 525-2)

Classic example of the way that some of the early funk-oriented

Blue Note sessions could swing hard without the dominating presence of major soloists. This is Donaldson's second album as a leader, recorded in 1958, and features the great conga player Ray Barretto in addition to Dave Bailey on drums. This dynamic rhythm section generates irresistible momentum on the title track, 'Play Ray' and 'Callin' All Cats'.

Dorham, McKinley Howard 'Kenny'

(Born Fairfield, Texas, August 30, 1924; died December 5, 1972) Kenny Dorham had a meteoric early career – replacing MILES DAVIS in the CHARLIE PARKER quintet in 1948 after stints with DIZZY GILLESPIE, Billy Eckstine and Lionel Hampton, becoming a founder member of the ART BLAKEY/HORACE SILVER Jazz Messengers in 1954, then replacing CLIFFORD BROWN in the MAX ROACH quintet after Brown's fatal road accident in 1956. Like LEE MORGAN, Dorham has been rediscovered in the hard bop and dance-jazz renaissance of the 1980s, his appeal to the latter audience being related to his enthusiasm for Latin-American music.

★*Round About Midnight At the Cafe, Vols 1 & 2* (Blue Note CDP 746 541-2; 746 542-2)

Two discs featuring the band that Dorham formed immediately after leaving the Jazz Messengers, still carrying a strong flavour of the spirit of that band through the presence of funky pianist BOBBY TIMMONS and assisted by saxophonist JR Monterose. Dorham originals such as 'Monaco', 'Mexico City' and 'Hill's Edge' are featured, as is the guitarist KENNY BURRELL on some tracks.

★*Una Mas* (Blue Note CDP 7465152)

Una Mas ('One More Time') resoundingly confirms Dorham's Latin enthusiasms, as well as including a wispy and gentle version of Lerner and Loewe's 'If Ever I Would Leave You' and Dorham's own punchy, one-note, 'Straight Ahead', tailor-made for jazz-dancers. A superb rhythm section including Herbie Hancock and Tony Williams – in those days Blue Note regulars – enhances it, as does the resourceful presence of tenorist JOE HENDERSON.

Ellis, Mitchell Herbert 'Herb'

(Born McKinley, Texas, August 4, 1921)
Member of the popular touring trio 'Great Guitars' (with BARNEY KESSEL and Charlie Byrd), Herb Ellis is a CHARLIE CHRISTIAN disciple who plays bebop with a distinct percussive twang, well suited to his blues inclinations. After stints with the Casa Loma Orchestra and Jimmy Dorsey in the Forties, Ellis joined the Oscar Peterson trio for much of the next decade, accompanying Ella Fitzgerald and Julie London.

★*Two for the Road* (JVC/Fantasy VDJ 28015)

In ideal contrast to Ellis's urgent, hustling style is Joe Pass's more graceful orchestral one; the two soloists spinning new melody from evergreen jazz material like 'Love for Sale' and 'Cherokee', and grooving on the infectious rhythmic potential of bop guitarists' favourites, such as the catchy 'Seven Come Eleven'.

Ervin, Booker Telleferro, Jr

(Born Denison, Texas, October 31, 1930; died July 31, 1970)
A musician who Charles Mingus described as 'one of the trance players', one of those who inhabit their music totally, Ervin was one of the most distinctive of tenor saxophone voices, as gravelly a sound as Lee Marvin singing. He worked extensively in the midwest in the Fifties until recommended to Mingus, whose band he joined in 1958. Ervin also worked with the pianists Roland Hanna and Randy Weston and led his own small-groups in the Sixties. A player of deliberation and intelligent austerity, Ervin's selective approach in his solos led to a remarkable improvisational appropriateness whatever the tempo or theme. Though he was influenced by the work of DEXTER GORDON and John Coltrane, his tone was harder than either and – unlike either of those voluble performers – he preferred to mould and manipulate a handful of phrases in each solo rather than hurtle feverishly over the chord changes.

★*That's It* (Candid CCD 9014)

Ervin's best session as a leader, largely comprising his own pieces.

Sinuously reflective on spacey ballads like 'Uranus', the saxophonist is, nevertheless, at his strongest over the testing changes of 'Speak Low', accelerating through them to stretches of sustained, surging passion.

Evans, William John 'Bill'

(Born Plainfield, New Jersey, August 16, 1929; died September 15, 1980)

Evans has been one of the most influential pianists in postwar jazz, his methods audible in the music of McCoy Tyner, Herbie Hancock, Keith Jarrett and many others. One of the subtlest piano players in jazz history, Evans possessed the rare gift of being introspective without sacrificing strength. Though he could play hynotically at very low volumes and was a master of ballads, there was a steely core to his improvising that made it commanding whatever the tempo or the mood. And unlike many bop pianists, whose solos were streams of semiquavers rattling over rickety hurdles and bridges of skinny left handed chords, Evans' left hand was perpetually orchestrating what was going on in his right, so that his solos unfolded as immensely subtle stories.

Bill Evans was taught piano, violin and flute as a child, and his first contact with jazz piano was swing. But by the mid-Fifties, having absorbed BUD POWELL's approach to uptempo playing and Lennie Tristano's experiments with breaking the rigid bar-line structures of bop (a characteristic of Evans solos is the long improvised line that sweeps aside the hurdles of the chord changes) and rich harmonic variation in the left hand, Evans had become unique. He joined MILES DAVIS in 1958, a connection that only lasted eight months, but which saw the making of an historic jazz record, *Kind of Blue*. His playing here was mostly reflective and full of drifting, atmospheric arpeggios, and sudden sinewy runs propelled by a startling rhythmic drive. From this point on, Evans began to record and perform almost exclusively as a leader with his own trio. At the beginning of the 1960s, Evans was working with the guitar-style double bass playing of Scott LaFaro, and with the addition of Paul Motian on drums, the band developed an uncanny empathy. Evans' compositions 'Blue In Green' and 'Waltz For Debby' have become jazz standards.

★*Portrait in Jazz* (Fantasy FCD 6301162)

The first trio recording of Evans, LaFaro and Motian, before the collective interplay of these three had reached its peak and therefore still finding Evans displayed in the leader's role. By 1959, when this record was made, Evans had more or less fully absorbed his studies and experiments (notably drawn from Tristano) and formed them into a lyrically-driven whole – his timing was immaculate, his shading of a note taking care of minutiae with an offhand grace. The disc contains a memorable version of 'Autumn Leaves' and an initially thoughtful, then dancing and animated version of *Kind of Blue's* 'Blue In Green'.

★*Sunday At the Village Vanguard* (Riverside VDJ 1519)

A stunning example of the Evans trio's virtues – by 1961 far more reflexive and collectivised – and the pianist's first live recording. The music boils with invention and empathy, with Evans' playing at its most intense synthesis of introspection and impulsiveness. Tracks include Miles Davis', 'Solar', and a sublime interpretation of Gershwin's poignant, 'My Man's Gone Now'. This classic Evans trio was broken up just ten days later – LaFaro was killed in a road crash.

★*Everybody Digs Bill Evans* (Fantasy FCD 6431129)

Evans' second trio album – with Philly Joe Jones on drums, one of the pianist's most suitable partners; punchy and purposeful after Jones' sensational drum intro to, 'Night and Day', with Debussyesque reflectiveness on the beautiful, 'Peace Piece'.

★*At the Montreux Jazz Festival* (Verve 827844-2)

A 1968 live performance, with a very different band (Eddie Gomez on bass and the muscular Jack DeJohnette on drums) that won Evans one of several Grammy Awards. Brilliant Evans extemporisation on 'Nardis', 'Someday My Prince Will Come' and 'Embraceable You', with solo versions, not included on the original vinyl, of 'Quiet Now' and 'I Loves You Porgy'.

Evans, Ian Ernest Gilmore 'Gil'

(Born Toronto, May 13, 1912; died March 20, 1988)
One of the best-loved figures in jazz, a man whose youthfulness, broadmindedness and constant endorsement of living vibrantly in the present won him every kind of accolade from Honorary Doctorates and Fellowships, Grammy Awards and pollwinners' prizes to performance of his work at the White House. He had the lightest touch of any jazz writer, was a genius at harnessing the potentially explosive elements of composition and improvisation for creative use, and could infuse a band with his personality by means that were barely perceptible.

The fourteen year old Evans heard a recording by Louis Armstrong, which led him to take up the piano and then to play in a variety of obscure bands in Canada and later in California. He moved to New York at the beginning of the Forties, initially working in the dance band business and as a staff arranger for the Bob Hope radio show, but he spent as much time as he could in public libraries, poring over classical scores. The art of jazz composition was hardly twenty years old when he arrived, and the most adventurous jazz composer of the day was Duke Ellington, who had disproved the theory that jazz writing was largely a matter of adding texture to the 32-bar song-forms and blues that made up most of the raw material of jazz. Evans concurred, and his rudimentary classical studies led him to consider non-jazz instrumentation as well. With dance-band leader, Claude Thornhill, in the late 1940s, Evans developed a new sound for the jazz line-up. He augmented the usual instrumentation with french horns, tuba and woodwinds. It often sounded poignant and reflective and replaced the superheated quality of both bebop and its predecessor swing, with a light, floating lyricism that explored texture and timbre more than explicit beat and the conversational call-and-response 'riffing' technique common to Thirties swing orchestras. Some dubbed the effect 'clouds of sound'.

The ideas appealed to the young MILES DAVIS, then a bebop trumpeter in CHARLIE PARKER's band but a player neither temperamentally nor technically entirely suited to such a frenetic idiom. In 1949, Davis, pianist John Lewis (later of the MODERN JAZZ QUARTET), and saxophonists GERRY MULLIGAN and LEE KONITZ joined with Gil Evans to form a ground-breaking but short-lived jazz orchestra. Its recordings came to be known as *The Birth of the Cool*.

Evans' collaborations with Miles Davis continued into the 1960s. The arranger's touch enriched the simplest materials with scores that made the most threadbare phrases glow, and imparted new subtleties to already complex work – as he did with Gershwin's *Porgy and Bess* and a remake of Rodrigo's *Concierto D'Aranjuez* for Davis's *Sketches of Spain*. The records became classics, and after these triumphs, Evans resisted the temptation to further elaborate his innovations in jazz, opting instead for refinement and distillation. His raw materials became increasingly skeletal, and he frequently made the arrangements flexible enough in interpretation for the ensemble sections to sound improvised as well as the solos.

Though Evans had, like Ellington, introduced some of the vertical richness of symphonic music to jazz, his open-mindedness frequently led him also to pop music for new ideas. But these were not the self-conscious musical crossovers that so often find their way into the 'orchestral pops' repertoire. They were full-blooded jazz, bursting with improvisational drive and new sounds, but buoyed up by Evans' old mastery of selection and deployment. The inspired rhythm-and-blues guitarist Jimi Hendrix was much admired by Evans, but the younger man died tragically in 1970 only days before a collaboration between the two was due to take place. Evans always kept a place for some of Hendrix's themes in his band's repertoire.

★*Out of the Cool* (MCA MCACD 5653)

A 1960 album that provided an opportunity for Evans – who had reached a wide public with his sumptuous orchestral interplay with Miles Davis – to reveal that his own bands could sound as sensuous, surprising and light on their feet, despite their size, as Miles' horn could on its own. Principal trumpeter here is the underrated Johnny Coles, whose subtlety of inflection is striking on the mood piece 'Sunken Treasure' and whose double-time ingenuity intensifies an already vigorous adaptation of George Russell's 'Stratusphunk'. Trombonist Jimmy Knepper also makes his clean and deliberate mark, grippingly desolate on 'Where Flamingoes Fly'.

★*Priestess* (Antilles ANCD 8717)

A terrific live session from Evans' looser and more pop-oriented phase, including a sensational blues saxophone performance from Dave Sanborn on 'Short Visit', but with horn playing hardly less animated from George Adams and Arthur Blythe. Lew Soloff, Ernie Royal and Hannibal Marvin Peterson blister the paintwork in the trumpet section.

★*Live at Sweet Basil* (King K32Y 6017)

Gil Evans' famous Monday Night Orchestra, which played at Sweet Basil's under Evans' leadership until his death, and continued afterwards as a tribute to him. A typical, exhilarating night's work, featuring tunes by Jimi Hendrix, Charles Mingus ('Orange Was The Colour of Her Dress, Then Blue Silk'), Herbie Hancock and others, and featuring powerful soloists such as tenorist George Adams and the distinctive guitarist Hiram Bullock.

Farlow, Talmage Holt 'Tal'

(Born Greensboro, North Carolina, June 7, 1921)
An excellent guitarist emerging from the CHARLIE CHRISTIAN stable in the 1940s but at times indicating (notably in a trio with the vibist Red Norvo) a lyrical originality that substantially extended the Christian legacy. Farlow's faults could be over-embroidery but he is both a creative ensemble player and a musician aware (as Django Reinhardt was and many beboppers were not) of the most telling nuances and timbral effects of the guitar.

★*The Legendary Tal Farlow* (IMS/Polydor CJ266 390)

Farlow leading a septet including ART FARMER (trumpet), Jimmy Cleveland (trombone) and Harold Mabern (piano). Easy-paced repertoire includes 'I Can't Get Started', 'Prelude to a Kiss' and 'You Stepped out of A Dream'.

Farmer, Arthur Stewart 'Art'

(Born Council Bluffs, Iowa, August 21, 1928)
Trumpeter and flugelhornist Farmer's early career embraced

every current style of the Forties and early Fifties – he worked in the rhythm 'n' blues band of Johnny Otis, the swing band of Benny Carter and the bebop band of Wardell Gray, establishing a reputation for flexibility and accommodation to his surroundings that has blurred perceptions of his individuality. This catholicity extended later to work with composers as different as George Russell and Quincy Jones, but his partnership with saxophonist BENNY GOLSON from 1959 (a band that included the young McCoy Tyner) gave jazz one of its most attractive bop-influenced small groups, The Jazztet. Farmer's playing is often wistful, but his phrasing unusual (he favours wide intervals and behind-the-beat accents) and he exhibits a poise and burnished tone that have given him a notable reputation among fellow musicians, if a more modest one with the public. *Back To The City*, the only Jazztet session released on CD, is now underservedly deleted.

*_Maiden Voyage_ (Denon C38 7071)

Typical warmth and poise on flugelhorn from Farmer, notably on ballads such as Charles Mingus' 'Goodbye Pork Pie Hat' and BILL EVANS' 'Blue In Green'. Farmer is accompanied here by Masahiko Satoh (piano), Ron Carter (bass) and Jack DeJohnette (drums).

Feldman, Victor Stanley

(Born London, April 7, 1934; died May 12, 1987)
Feldman was a child prodigy on the wartime London jazz scene, adept on piano, drums and vibes. By the time he was twenty he had worked with virtually all of the prominent British jazz and dance-band leaders, notably Ronnie Scott, John Dankworth and bandleader Ted Heath. Both Feldman and Scott had formed close contacts with the Woody Herman orchestra in the early Fifties and in 1955 Feldman moved to the States to join the band. The fertility of his ideas and the depth of his knowledge made a lasting impression on front-rank American modernists such as MILES DAVIS and CANNONBALL ADDERLEY. But Feldman worked largely in the West Coast studios, nonetheless writing the jazz standard 'Seven Steps to Heaven', which became a Miles Davis album title.

★*The Artful Dodger* (Concord CCD 4038)

Feldman on keyboards with an oddly balanced quintet of Los Angeles pros, featuring Jack Sheldon on trumpet. Not sensational, but featuring the leader in good form on SONNY ROLLINS' calypso 'St Thomas'.

Ferguson, Maynard

(Born Montreal, May 4, 1928)
Canadian trumpeter, renowned for his stratospheric high notes, which he displayed to spectacular effect with the Stan Kenton Orchestra of 1950–53. Like many technically gifted performers, Ferguson has had difficulty subsuming his skills within a convincing musical structure when working on his own account – and his choice of unremarkable fusion and pop material for his own orchestras, from the early Seventies onwards, has made this transformation all the harder.

★*Birdland Dreamband* (Bluebird/BMG ND 86455)

The young trumpet star in action in 1956 before his style became too muscle-bound, with a cut-down big band strongly flavoured by the Kenton legacy, and showcasing excellent partners like saxophonist Al Cohn and pianist Hank Jones. The band, unsurprisingly, is given to sustained, somewhat frantic intensity and enthusiasm for permanent climax, but Ferguson's own playing reveals a coherence and sensitivity he didn't often display later.

Flanagan, Tommy Lee

(Born Detroit, March 16, 1930)
Flanagan is a deft, upbeat, bop-derived pianist probably best known for his shrewd and sensitive accompanying work for Ella Fitzgerald, and as a musical director for Tony Bennett. He has however pursued a fruitful career as a leader and a creative improvisor in his own right – in the Forties and Fifties with bands led by MILES DAVIS, SONNY ROLLINS, John Coltrane (*Giant Steps*) and Coleman Hawkins, and again since the mid-Seventies. Where the

work of some bop pianists can be fast and intricate to the point of relentlessness, Flanagan always maintains a bounce and brightness – his instant trademark.

★*Tokyo Recital* (JVC/Fantasy VDJ 28013)

Good trio session with typically pearly Flanagan ruminations on 'Caravan', 'Chelsea Bridge', 'Take the A Train' and others.

Freeman, Earl Lavon 'Von'

(Born Chicago, October 3, 1922)

Earl Lavon 'Von' Freeman, the Chicagoan saxophonist, formerly partner to Sun Ra, Andrew Hill and DEXTER GORDON and father of the powerful avant-bop musician, Chico Freeman, is an energetic performer still in his distinctive prime. Freeman Snr sounds as if he has listened to a mixture of Lester Young, Coleman Hawkins, Ornette Coleman and John Coltrane – an unusual combination of influences for a musician of his generation. He has a legendarily curious tone – a querulous, sometimes squawky sound that blends fragments of bebop constructions, thematic variations running a clear line back to Lester Young, scatterings of the booming, fat-toned sound of the Coleman Hawkins school, and unexpected liberties of pitch and tuning that predate Ornette Coleman. Had Von Freeman not chosen to stay with friends and family in Chicago and instead moved to New York, as his son did, it's a certainty that his name would nowadays be much better known that it is.

Freeman's father was a trombone-playing policeman and jazz-lover, his mother had been a church musician, and all the Freeman sons turned pro – Earl Lavon on saxophones, George on guitar, Bruz on drums. They were taught by a famous Chicago tutor, Walter Dyett, and Von was at school with Gene Ammons, later to become one of the fastest and fiercest saxophonists to to work in the territory between swing and bebop. Freeman performed around the Chicago clubs in the years after the war, when the city was full of exciting jazz, and joined the experimental and quirky early bands of pianist/composer Sun Ra. The experience thus made him a different caste of bebop player, able to anticipate the demands of the period between the spawning of bebop and the coming of free form. The Freeman brothers' group employed an illustrious sequence of pianists – AHMAD JAMAL, Andrew Hill and Muhal Richard Abrams. Freeman was open to the influences of fellow musicians and this has remained one of his strengths.

★*Serenade and Blues* (Chief CHIEFCD 3)

A 1975 trio set featuring Von Freeman with John Young, on piano, and Wilbur Campbell, on drums. Those who have heard Von Freeman in his son's band, with a more adventurous rhythm section, might find this relaxed breeze through blues and standard songs a little unassuming. But his appearances on record are rare enough, this is his only CD, and his sound and fluency make striking remoulds of songs such as 'Time after Time'.

Garland, William M 'Red'

(Born Dallas, May 13, 1923; died April 23, 1984)
A much-copied bebop pianist, distinctive for his characteristic percussive two-hand block chord solos, which brought a jangling, bar-piano forthrightness to an idiom sometimes inclined to inscrutability. Having worked in the 1940s with the blues band of Eddie Vinson (including the young John Coltrane), Garland took up his most celebrated employment between 1955 and 1958 as a member of the first, and great, MILES DAVIS Quintet, recording enduring albums like *Workin' and Steamin'*.

★*Soul Junction* (JVC/Fantasy VDJ 1523)

Effectively the Miles Davis band without Miles – trumpeter DONALD BYRD convincingly occupies the chair. John Coltrane is forthright and emotional, and Garland bluesy in a manner that echoes much earlier jazz. His playing throughout is an exuberant delight.

Getz, Stanley 'Stan'

(Born Philadelphia, February 2, 1927)
Stan Getz has been one of the few top-flight jazz artists to have

made an impact in the pop charts (and with wider audiences) and yet never lost the admiration of purists. His celebrated beautiful tone, originally an adaptation of the poignant timbre of Lester Young, made a big impact with the public when Getz was just twenty. His 1947 recording of the ballad 'Early Autumn' (with the Woody Herman band) engaged the ears of a jazz generation with its shy, evaporating sound and concentration on atmosphere over notes. Getz's ability to move mountains with very carefully edited material worked again in the 1960s with his bossa nova recordings. Working with guitarist Charlie Byrd, Joao and Astrud Gilberto and others, Getz produced a string of gliding, sensuous, effortlessly relaxed hits like 'Desafinado', and the ever-enduring 'Girl From Ipanema'.

Yet throughout the years, and despite all the temptations to become merely a special-effects man with a lovely sound, Getz has remained an improvising jazz musician to his fingertips. He began young, playing in bands led by Jack Teagarden, Stan Kenton, Jimmy Dorsey and Benny Goodman whilst still in his teens, and making his first record under his own name at nineteen. Joining Woody Herman, he found himself in the company of a number of young white Lester Young disciples, including ZOOT SIMS, Al Cohn and JIMMY GIUFFRE. During the Fifties and Sixties Getz recorded extensively, many of the sessions being meetings with other imposing jazz figures – with Shelley Manne, DIZZY GILLESPIE (*Diz and Getz*, a session that found the saxophonist in ebullient, very nearly truculent mood), JJ JOHNSON and others.

After the jazz samba period, Getz began forming bands with some of the sharpest upcoming musicians – notably a brilliant quartet with the young Gary Burton, on vibes, Steve Swallow, on bass, and Roy Haynes, on drums. He also went into partnership with Chick Corea, in the late Sixties, making two albums (*Captain Marvel* and *Sweet Rain* – the latter once a CD, but currently deleted) that showed how much even the guru of cool beauty could be moved by the right company, and even glimpses of the idea that some of the more rugged and muscular tenor styles of the 1960s weren't uninteresting to him.

Ill-health has hampered Getz's later career, but a 1988 concert in London showed a delighted audience that, despite some shortening of stamina, the glistening, drifting bubbles of a classic Getz solo come as readily to him as always.

★*At Storyville* (Vogue VG 600 093)

A live Getz date from 1951, with an excellent bebop rhythm section featuring ex-Parker pianist AL HAIG, JIMMY RANEY, on guitar and Tiny Khan, on drums. Getz is in far more dynamic mood here than the image he assumed in *Early Autumn*, charging through fast versions of 'Parker '51', 'The Song Is You', and a stream of varied choruses on 'Thou Swell'.

★*At the Opera House* (Verve/USA 831 272-2)

Six years later, Getz' mid-Fifties quintet in an encounter with an instrumentalist as technically elegant as himself – trombonist JJ JOHNSON. Regarded by many as displaying some of the saxophonist's most challenging, and challenged, improvising; almost fierce on 'Crazy Rhythm' and at his most poetic on 'It Never Entered My Mind'.

★*The Brothers* (Carrere 98426)

Material from Savoy recordings of the 1940s, featuring Stan Getz in company with the other white Lester Young fans of his circle – Al Cohn, Serge Chaloff, Brew Moore and Allan Eager. Getz is most substantially featured on the kind of drifting ballads – 'Indian Summer', 'Wrap Your Troubles in Dreams' – that most reflected the success of *Early Autumn*.

★*Jazz Samba* (Verve 810 061-2)

Probably Stan Getz' most famous record. This was the first album of the Sixties bossa nova boom, and contained the hit record 'Desafinado' and the voice of Astrud Gilberto. Charlie Byrd is rich and orchestral on guitar and Getz' horn floats like a bubble over the shuffle of the rhythm. Fluffy music and no great tribute to improvisation, but only Getz, with his effortless control of dynamics, delicacy and timing, could have done it this way.

Gillespie, John Birks 'Dizzy'

(Born Cheraw, S Carolina, October 21, 1917)
A colossus of modern trumpet playing and crucial component of

the informal group that helped found bebop as an idiom in the late Thirties. A Southerner, Gillespie was the son of a bricklayer and amateur musician, who gave the boy a working knowledge of mandolin, drums and piano. Later Gillespie Jr won a scholarship to Carolina's Laurinburg Institute and by the mid-Thirties, then living in Philadelphia, he began to find regular work as a trumpeter in the style of the thrilling Roy Eldridge, a swing musician of virtuosity and high drama whose music was characterised by sudden eruptions into the upper register, wide leaps of intervals, explosive runs and more scrambled and angular phrasing than even Armstrong's.

In 1937, Gillespie took Eldridge's place in the Teddy Hill Band, establishing himself with an excellent technique and an advanced harmonic knowledge that led him beyond the more basic song-forms of swing. Two years later he joined Cab Calloway, but was soon sacked for a mixture of musical unconventionality and disruptive behaviour. He began sitting in with the band that drummer Kenny Clarke had put together at Minton's Playhouse, with MONK, CHRISTIAN and PARKER.

Like Charlie Parker, Gillespie did not simply use notes harmonically related to the chord of the tune he was playing in, but also momentarily, those derived from another chord a semitone away. He would also play major chord solos over minor key changes, or substitute new chords for those of the standards. During this period, Gillespie was also working extensively on composition, contributing arrangements to big bands he worked with in the early Forties, most notably Billy Eckstine's.

In May 1945 Gillespie participated with Parker in the first full-blooded bebop recording session, making an impact almost as startling as Parker's with his mixture of early-jazz bent notes and blues effects, breathtaking speed and constant variety and powers of surprise. The trumpeter formed a big band at the end of the Forties which – though its overall ensemble sound was not as audaciously new as the impact of a bebop small-group – nevertheless opened a new chapter in the history of jazz orchestration, and Gillespie compositions like 'Night In Tunisia', 'Groovin' High' and 'Salt Peanuts' became modern standards. The trumpeter also revealed an interest in Latin (particularly Cuban) rhythms that has stayed with him for life and of which he has written: 'the people of the calypso, the rhumba, the samba and the rhythms of Haiti all have something in common from the mother of their music. Rhythm. The basic rhythm because Mama Rhythm is Africa.'

Dizzy Gillespie has recorded and toured constantly with small groups and orchestras from the 1950s to the present day, as well as having encouraged promising newcomers (FATS NAVARRO, KENNY DORHAM, MILES DAVIS, CLIFFORD BROWN, LEE MORGAN, Jon Faddis, Arturo Sandoval), been feted by governments and arts foundations in many countries, and received innumerable awards, tributes and honorary doctorates. Close association with the vigorous jazz impresario, Norman Granz, saw many international tours and recording sessions for Granz's label Pablo, and though Gillespie's fire seemed occasionally dimmed on studio work in the Sixties, it re-emerged with a vengeance as the trumpeter approached his sixth decade. In the Eighties he has spectacularly toured with his United Nations orchestra, featuring some of the most illustrious jazz artists to have built their reputations a long way away from New York or Chicago or Kansas City. Latin-American improvisors of the impact of saxophonist, Paquito de Rivera, and trumpeter, Arturo Sandoval, are in the band, as well as the fleet and eloquent hard bop trombonist, Slide Hampton, Brazilian duo Airto Moreira and Flora Purim, and the seventy four year old saxophonist and flautist JAMES MOODY, still one of the wittiest, most musical and farsighted of all the surviving first-wave beboppers. Moody soloed on the 1946 big-band recording of Gillespie's classic 'Emanon', so his place in such a high-profile version of his mentor's orchestra is nothing less than fitting.

Dizzy – *Live at Carnegie Hall 1947* (Pablo/USA CD 20038)

Gillespie's first Carnegie Hall concert, featuring Ella Fitzgerald and James Moody and including 'Salt Peanuts', 'How High The Moon' and George Russell's 'Cubana Be-Cubana Bop'. Not as powerful a selection as 'Emanon', 'Things To Come' and 'Our Delight' from *In The Beginning* (not available on CD), but an indication of the impact of this revolutionary band.

The Champ 1951–52 (Vogue VG 670213)

Material that was originally included on *Dee Gee Days* (Dee Gee

Records was Gillespie's own short-lived attempt to form an independent label) and featuring some spectacular musicians in their young prime, including John Coltrane, WYNTON KELLY, ART BLAKEY and MILT JACKSON. Though some of the music was commercial for the period – Gillespie sings 'Swing Low Sweet Cadillac' – and is infused with pre-bop interpretations of the blues, brilliant trumpet playing constantly rubs shoulders with the marketing ploys. 'The Champ' was the best-selling bebop tune of the early Fifties.

★*The Giant* (Accord/Musidisc 139 217)

A session cut in Europe in the 1960s, finding a scalding Gillespie alongside some equally seat-of-the-pants playing from a virtuoso bop saxophonist, JOHNNY GRIFFIN. Griffin is fast, witty and garrulous as ever, and Gillespie considered and poised on 'Serenity', succinct and effortlessly dealing new ideas on 'Stella By Starlight'.

Giuffre, James Peter 'Jimmy'

(Born Dallas, April 26, 1921)
Reed player and composer Jimmy Giuffre's name is most commonly associated with the two themes he composed – 'Four Brothers' for the Woody Herman Second Herd, and 'The Train And The River', the latter a compelling piece of cool jazz featured in the Newport Festival movie *Jazz On a Summer's Day*. Giuffre worked with eminent white big bands in the Forties (Buddy Rich's, Jimmy Dorsey's, Woody Herman's), and became associated with the West Coast 'cool' school in the next decade, frequently appearing in small combos (in particular with drummer, Shelley Manne, and with trombonist, Bob Brookmeyer) with unconventional instrumentation, primarily devoted to exploring melodic variation. Giuffre continued these investigations with small ensembles (notably with pianist, Paul Bley, and bassist, Steve Swallow) in the Sixties, and has also conceived larger, semi-straight works for bigger groups, as well as pursuing a career as an academic and teacher.

★*Quasar* (Soul Note SNCD 1108)

A discreet but elegantly complex 1985 session by Giuffre. The lineup seems oddly balanced at first – the leader on flutes, clarinet and saxophones, with Pete Levin's electric keyboards and bass. But Giuffre's control over his materials and sense of texture doesn't fail him. Levin is more prominent if anything, but his taste doesn't lapse. Giuffre's version of 'Shadows', on the bass flute, is worth the disc.

Golson, Benny

(Born Philadelphia, January 25, 1929)
Golson's tenor saxophone playing was close to the full, earthy sound of Lucky Thompson, but also incorporated the harmonic audacity of Don Byas. For all that this repertoire made his instrumental contributions useful, Golson's talent was primarily as an inspired composer and arranger, classics such as 'I Remember Clifford' emanating from him. Golson made his first impact with the GILLESPIE big band (1956–58) and then with BLAKEY's Jazz Messengers, which in turn led him to form a closely related outfit called The Jazztet, with ART FARMER on trumpet. Though lucrative studio work took Golson out of sight for much of the Seventies, he returned in the next decade to re-form The Jazztet.

★*Stardust* (Denon CY 1838)

Excellent Eighties Golson session in the imposing company of FREDDIE HUBBARD, on trumpet, and new-generation star sidemen Mulgrew Miller (piano) and Marvin 'Smitty' Smith (drums). Golson's deft arrangements sparkle, inspiring a reciprocal elan in the soloists.

Gordon, Dexter Keith

(Born Los Angeles, February 27, 1923; died August, 1990)
Bertrand Tavernier's 1986 feature film *Round Midnight* brought Dexter Gordon into the movie theatres of the world, but the sheer drama of his performances on the tenor saxophone is ultimately his real epitaph. He was first a clarinettist, then an alto

saxophonist, and a tenorist by the age of seventeen, at which point he joined the Lionel Hampton band (featuring in scorching tenor dialogues with Illinois Jacquet) and not long afterward the influential, bop-oriented Billy Eckstine band. Lester Young was an overwhelming influence on his early playing – Gordon was drawn to Young's storytelling lyrical strength and sense of shape – and Coleman Hawkins, who had founded the principles of tenor improvisation virtually single-handed, was inevitably another. Hawkins was, in terms of the structure of his improvisations, one of the most sophisticated jazz soloists of the 1930s, and the melodic variation that sprang from such rich harmonic awareness fired Gordon too. Then came CHARLIE PARKER, with whom Gordon worked in 1945. Parker's reflexive speed, altered chords, seat-of-the-pants key changes and sheer stamina inspired Gordon to forge a style that had Parker's dynamism, added to Hawkins' gravitas, and Young's delicacy. He explored these qualities further in energetic partnership with another tenorist, Wardell Gray.

By the end of the 1940s, Gordon's skills had grown into a playing style of immense melodic variety, a freedom from cliche and repetition over even the most prolonged extemporisations, and a mischievous enthusiasm for rampant quotation from other tunes. An arsenal of boneshaking special effects – warbles, hoots, honks and hoarse, ascendent cries completed the characteristics of this master. The style awakened the gifts of John Coltrane who was to become far more of a cult figure even than the star of *Round Midnight* and who always acknowledged the depth of his debt to Gordon. The route from Gordon to Coltrane was a connection that profoundly influenced the direction of jazz music from the 1960s onward, and remains everywhere audible in the sound of the 'jazz revival' today.

Dexter Gordon, a jazz colossus in every sense, had to cope with lean years in the business, some because of changes in fashion, like the 1950s enthusiasm for 'cool' jazz, some because of problems with narcotics and drink. He came to feel more at home in Europe than America, and when he became an expatriate in Copenhagen, America often appeared to forget him. But his genius as an improvisor, even when not running at full throttle, always marked Gordon out from the ranks of the formula-followers. Of his recordings after the bountiful Blue Note period of the early 1960s, many of the best (among them *The Panther* with TOMMY

FLANAGAN on piano, *The Apartment* from Europe in the Seventies, and *Silver Blue* with Al Cohn), are not so far available on CD.

★*The Chase* (Giants of Jazz GOJCD 53064)

A bebop album that even outsold Charlie Parker in 1947. Gordon is in tenor partnership with the lighter-toned, but equally quick-thinking, Wardell Gray; unusual for its time in that producer Ross Russell allowed six-and-a-half minutes on the title track to capture much of the gladiatorial, live atmosphere generated in a club. First-generation bebop at its best.

★*Dexter Blows Hot and Cool* (Contemporary CDBOP 006)

One of Gordon's few recordings from the mid Fifties, when he was at a low ebb following a narcotics prison stretch – but nonetheless a vigorous jaunt through the customary hard bop materials in the company of the excellent, shortlived pianist, Carl Perkins, including a slow, trenchant 'Cry Me A River'.

★*Go* (Blue Note CDP 746 094-2)

Gordon's own favourite album, recorded with his most suitable rhythm section of Sonny Clark (piano), Butch Warren (bass) and Billy Higgins (drums) on his return to New York in 1961 after the second prison sentence. *Go* features two sublime examples of Gordon's massive authority at slow tempos as well as fast, with reverberating renditions of 'Guess I'll Hang My Tears Out To Dry' and 'Where Are You?', but also displays the charging, flat-out bop horn king's clout on 'Second Balcony Jump'.

★*Our Man in Paris* (Blue Note CDP 7463942)

Another Blue Note classic, this time from 1963 in Paris, finding Gordon in exactly that tireless, seven-league-stride form that influenced Coltrane. Like ROLLINS, Gordon combines the weight and solidity of the early saxophonists with the alacrity of bebop. Much of his playing here, even on the fast 'Scrapple from the Apple', is the closest you can get to a musical version of a sculpture in granite. An added bonus is the presence of pianist BUD POWELL –

not functioning on all cylinders by this time – but full of unexpected melodic twists.

★*Something Different* (Steeplechase SCCD 31136)

One of Gordon's finest albums made shortly before his celebrated 1976 homecoming from Europe. Gordon, as surefooted and convincing as at any time in his career, finds a surprisingly compatible foil in Philip Catherine's guitar.

Green, Grant

(Born St Louis, Missouri, June 6, 1931; died January 31, 1979)
Always close to the territory between bebop and the beginnings of jazz-funk in the Fifties and early Sixties, Grant Green recorded first with ELVIN JONES (1959) and in the following two years appeared in bluesy organ groups led by Sam Lazar and Jack McDuff. By the mid-Sixties, Green was recording for Blue Note under his own name, in the company of excellent horn players like JOE HENDERSON and HANK MOBLEY. With a mixture of organ-like, punchy chord playing and pure, gliding lead lines Green quickly became a popular sideman, his style looking toward the coming of jazz-fusion rather than being locked in CHARLIE CHRISTIAN-like bop playing. Drug problems led to long layoffs, and when he returned to playing in the early Seventies it was mostly to bland and routine funk sessions. Green's best Blue Note session, *Solid*, is currently unavailable in any format.

★*Idle Moments* (Blue Note CDP 784 154-2)

Some of the best guitar playing of the early Sixties documented here in Green's mixture of strength, confident attack and lyricism, with sustained improvisations that don't evaporate into the neutral repetition of funky licks that the guitarist adopted later. Apart from the title track, Green is thoughtful and inventive in his rendition of John Lewis' 'Django'.

★*Born to be Blue* (Blue Note CDP 784 432-2)

Green's tone in his earlier and stronger records was an unusual combination of delicacy and muscle, bluesy but with a fragile, vibrating edge. That flavour and his ability to construct long and coherent solos make a marked contrast with Ike Quebec's robust tenor on this album, and pianist, SONNY CLARK, makes a moving job of 'If I Should Lose You' as well. Green's playing is at its peak on 'Count Every Star' and the ballad 'My One and Only Love'.

Griffin, John Arnold III 'Johnny'

(Born Chicago, April 24, 1928)
Even in the current era, in which virtuosity in jazz has become commonplace, Johnny 'Little Giant' Griffin still counts as one of the hottest tenor saxophone players in the business, a musician of stunning agility, fertility of ideas and evocative, wailing tone. A hard-bopper to his fingertips, Griffin joined the Lionel Hampton band as a seventeen year-old, began his recording career, for Blue Note, in the company of serious contemporaries John Coltrane and HANK MOBLEY, and was a tailormade member of ART BLAKEY's Jazz Messengers, his style being virtually a saxophone reflection of Blakey's own drumming. When the 'soul-jazz' boom occurred, at the end of the 1950s, Griffin made some of the most distinctive and least formulaic contributions to the genre, notably with the compulsive 'Wade In The Water' from *Big Soul*. He then formed a two-tenor partnership, in the mould of DEXTER GORDON/Wardell Gray, with the gritty swing saxophonist EDDIE 'LOCKJAW' DAVIS. Like his friend Gordon, Griffin moved to Europe in 1962 where he joined the Kenny Clarke/Francy Boland band, as well as recording extensively with local and expat groups. As the years passed, instead of becoming a declining pyrotechnician, as his astonishing speed decreased, Griffin developed into areas that he had previously swept imperiously past, like ballad playing.

★*The Little Giant* (JVC/Fantasy VDJ 1547)

Early Griffin. The material may be eccentric for the saxophonist's usual purposes ('Green Grow the Rushes', 'Black is the Colour of My True Love's Hair'), but the original material is soon left gasping at the start-line by its interpreter's furious virtuosity.

★*Blowin' Session* (Blue Note CDP 781 559-2)

Griffin in breakneck partnership with John Coltrane and Hank Mobley – a situation in which the newcomer generally proved himself ahead for sheer explosive energy and speed.

★*The Man I Love* (Black Lion BLCD 760107)

The tenorist during his fertile European period of the early Sixties, with some of the best material from two albums Griffin cut with expatriate drummers Ed Thigpen and Albert Heath, including the brooding, trenchant, beautifully constructed 'Blues for Harvey'.

Haig, Allan W 'Al'

(Born Newark, New Jersey, July 22, 1924; died November 16, 1982)
Haig was an excellent pianist of the first bebop wave in New York, influenced initially by Nat King Cole and Teddy Wilson and quickly developing a sense of order and logic of his own. Haig was the favourite piano accompanist of both CHARLIE PARKER and STAN GETZ, and was a member of Parker's brilliant 1945 band that recorded for Dial. Haig worked with Parker again between 1948 and 1950 and, with a perfect calm appropriateness, in partnership with Stan Getz in the early Fifties. Throughout the next two decades however, Haig's talents were seriously neglected, though he began recording fruitfully again in the last eight years of his life. Haig's sophisticated piano playing is now extensively documented on vinyl (on Spotlite) but hardly at all on CD.

★*Live in Hollywood* (Xanadu FDC 5162)

Haig in the high-class company of a quartet led by the excellent guitarist JIMMY RANEY, a fellow Getz accompanist from the early Fifties and temperamentally and stylistically a perfect foil.

Hall, James Stanley 'Jim'

(Born Buffalo, New York, December 12, 1930)
Because Jim Hall is a brilliant jazz guitarist who doesn't shower

the listener with notes, his restrained gifts are easy to underestimate. Often dubbed the thinking fan's guitarist, Hall is a master of melodic subtlety and fresh statements delivered with a tightly-edited brevity, cool, plush tone and immense swing. He first came to public notice with the Chico Hamilton group of 1955, then worked with the JIMMY GIUFFRE trio (appearing on the famous *Jazz On A Summer's Day* movie of the Newport Festival), the Ella Fitzgerald trio of 1960–61, and in a duo with saxophonist LEE KONITZ. Hall also worked memorably with pianist BILL EVANS, a musician after his own heart, and in the SONNY ROLLINS band of 1961 (see Rollins, Sonny: *Quartets*). Apart from his unique solo sound and crisp chordwork, Hall is also one of the most ingenious contrapuntal improvisors alive, frequently submerging his music within a group texture.

★*Jazz Guitar* (EMI-Manhattan CDP 746 851-2)

An excellent Hall trio date with Carl Perkins, on piano, and Red Mitchell, on bass. A welcome return to its original format for this recording, after being butchered in the Sixties on a budget-label repackaging job (*The Winner!*) in which Larry Bunker's drums were dubbed on. Though his sound is often hushed to the point of evaporation, Hall's timing is impeccable and he swings furiously through 'Stompin' At The Savoy' and 'Seven Come Eleven', whilst demonstrating his balladeer's romanticism on the gossamer chords of 'Deep In A Dream'.

★*Alone Together* (JVC/Fantasy VDJ 1033)

A 1972 live set with bassist, Ron Carter, another improvisor who shares Hall's grace, melodic resourcefulness and softness of touch. Though untempo work on Sonny Rollins' 'St Thomas' and 'Whose Blues' display the guitarist's relaxed momentum, the atmosphere – inevitably given the instrumentation and the perfectionist gloss of both men – is largely restrained.

★*Concierto* (CTI/Polydor 813 661-2)

A 1975 session with a sizeable and illustrious ensemble – including CHET BAKER, PAUL DESMOND, Roland Hanna and drummer Steve

Gadd – primarily assembled to rerun 'Concierto D'Aranjuez' in an arrangement scored by the usually schmaltzy Don Sebesky. Unexpectedly, the formula just about works on this occasion, with Hall's mellow sound and effortless lyricism neatly counterbalancing the risks of excess.

Henderson, Joseph A 'Joe'

(Born Lima, Ohio, April 24, 1937)

That there should have been nights during jazz's unfashionable period in the 1970s, when a saxophonist of Joe Henderson's qualities could be playing to an almost empty Ronnie Scott's Club, is an enduring mystery. Now, the musical intelligence of a musician so resolutely committed to the search for alternatives to the obvious, is once again getting its just desserts.

Henderson first appeared in a 1962 band of trumpeter KENNY DORHAM, following it with a stretch with HORACE SILVER, then co-leading the Jazz Communicators with FREDDIE HUBBARD, joining Herbie Hancock from 1969–70, and working for four months with the rhythm and blues band Blood, Sweat and Tears. His Blue Note session playing was usually powerful and concise (he appears on LEE MORGAN's classic *Sidewinder* album among many others) but extended explorations of fusion in the Seventies didn't enhance Henderson's initially glowing reputation.

His early and his recent work with tight, boppish groups demonstrates that this is his ideal environment. Henderson is fundamentally a bebopper, his playing extensively founded on SONNY ROLLINS and Coltrane. He is also one of the few practitioners of his instrument to eschew high volume and high register as a means of conveying heightened intensity, preferring to maintain an even, hollow, faintly mournful tone, and develop his improvisations almost entirely by means of new melody. Usually happy with standard jazz forms, Henderson frequently unfolds his thoughts in a mixture of muttering double time, oblique resolutions, and deft, but minimal, use of the modern saxophonist's favourite prop – fast repeated phrases to convey rhythmic energy. He can also be devastating on a blues (much of his youthful listening was to rhythm and blues players like Chuck Berry and Bo Diddley), each fresh idea often seeming to be only of merit to the saxophonist as far as it is a springboard for the next one.

★*One Thing* (Blue Note CDP 784 152-2)

Once again, hard bop on the cusp of freedom, in a band in which the impulses to 'stay inside' or move out of chords are in tension. Henderson barrels through the repertoire with rugged ease, but Andrew Hill is already playing a wider role than that of the conventional bop pianist, creatively linking and expanding on the horns/rhythm relationship and adding discreet dissonance here and there. Kenny Dorham is on trumpet, Pete LaRoca on drums.

★*State of the Tenor – Live at the Village Vanguard, Vols 1 & 2*
(Blue Note CDP 746 296-2; 746-426-2)

Ideal circumstances for listening to Joe Henderson, bristling with ideas on a selection of pieces mingling neo-bop, Latin music and abrasive reconstructions of soft-centre music like, 'All the Things You Are'.

Hubbard, Frederick Dewayne 'Freddie'

(Born Indianapolis, April 7, 1938)
In the 1960s, trumpeter Freddie Hubbard was one of jazz music's most dazzling prodigies. Trumpet heroes of the fast, unsentimental and highly technical movement called hard bop had included CLIFFORD BROWN and FATS NAVARRO, both of whom had died young. Hubbard seemed like their natural inheritor, of Clifford Brown in particular. Hubbard's pitching was almost faultless, his inventiveness limitless, his energy irrepressible. He began working around Indianapolis as a teenager, appearing with local guitar hero WES MONTGOMERY, and strongly influenced by a neighbourhood trumpeter, BOOKER LITTLE. He moved on to New York in 1959, working with SONNY ROLLINS, Quincy Jones and others, and in 1961 – like many of the finest trumpeters in post-Fifties jazz – received his most testing apprenticeship in BLAKEY's Jazz Messengers. In the same year Hubbard won the *Downbeat* magazine New Star award and, after the Blakey stint, he began recording as a freelance for Blue Note, working with DEXTER GORDON, Herbie Hancock, JACKIE MCLEAN and with Wayne Shorter, a former fellow Jazz Messenger. He then began recording as a leader, showing that he was not only adept as a hard bop trumpeter, but sensuous and thoughtful as a

balladeer, often on the softer-toned flugelhorn. Regrettably of his two best records from this period, *Hub Tones* was deleted on CD in 1989 and *Breaking Point* doesn't exist in any format.

In the Sixties, Hubbard was regarded as an adventurer as well as a virtuoso, appearing as part of the double-quartet featured on avant-garde saxophonist Ornette Coleman's famous *Free Jazz* album (not currently on CD) and on Eric Dolphy's *Out To Lunch* session, and Coltrane's *Ascension*. But during the next decade, like many jazz musicians, Freddie Hubbard began to turn toward the developing jazz connections with pop and funk, and recorded a succession of softer and more accessible funk-based albums for the CTI label. Though this material was always immaculately assembled and professionally played, it rarely stretched Hubbard the improvisor anywhere near the limit of his exceptional potential.

The resurgence of interest in the virtues of the earlier periods of jazz, that came toward the end of the Seventies, led to Hubbard reforming some classic partnerships – notably with VSOP, an entire, Davis-less, MILES DAVIS band from the Sixties' era (Herbie Hancock, Wayne Shorter, Tony Williams and Ron Carter).

Hubbard's best work is generally not well served by the record industry – one of his finest Eighties albums, *Sweet Return*, with Roy Haynes, pianist Joanne Brackeen, and others has also been deleted.

★*Best of Freddie Hubbard* (Blue Note CDP 793 202-2)

An assortment of Hubbard's Blue Note work, including the excellent 'Outer Forces' from the *Blue Spirit* album and the title tracks from *Open Sesame* and *Hub-tones* – the latter recorded by one of the trumpeter's most suitable bands, including James Spaulding, on reeds, and a young Herbie Hancock.

★*Ride Like The Wind* (Elektra Musician 960029-2)

Freddie Hubbard in the 1980s, largely returned to form as an improvisor following the previous unproductive decade. This album finds the trumpeter with a sextet augmented by brass, and thus echoing big-band jazz, fusion and bop – most successfully in a dancing version of Joe Zawinul's memorable Weather Report hit 'Birdland'.

Hutcherson, Robert 'Bobby'

(Born Los Angeles, January 27, 1941)
Until the 1960s it was hard for modern vibraharpists to avoid the overwhelmingly influential bluesy swing of the MODERN JAZZ QUARTET'S MILT JACKSON, but Bobby Hutcherson (though it was hearing a Jackson record that set him off) developed a distinctive line of his own. Another member of the Sixties Blue Note stable, Hutcherson worked extensively with the rising musicians of that era – Herbie Hancock, Andrew Hill, Tony Williams – to develop a music exhibiting some of the freedoms of the then avant-garde, but within organised rhythm patterns and sophisticated explorations of counterpoint. He had come to New York from California in 1961 with a boppish group featuring trombonist Al Grey, but his broad-mindedness and distinctive tone led him to work on Eric Dolphy's classic *Out to Lunch* (see page 214) then freelance work with a variety of New York modernists, and then to a series of challenging Blue Note albums under his own leadership. In more recent times Hutcherson's fusion exploits made his sound more anonymous and his impact on jazz has lessened.

★*Dialogue* (Blue Note CDP 746 537-2)

Hutcherson on an early session as leader, exploring what he called 'a fusion of free counterpoint' – tougher music than much of the vibraharpist's later work, frequently involving parallel melody lines and exploration of rhythm and tone-colour rather than conventional bop harmony. Hutcherson's awareness of the avant-garde is apparent in the fierceness of 'Les Noirs Marchent'.

★*Happenings* (Blue Note CDP 746 530-2)

Hutcherson's third Sixties Blue Note session, more orthodox, but featuring some of the most imaginative vibraharp improvisation to have emerged since the high points of Milt Jackson's work. Where Jackson was always happiest when able to bend his thoughts toward the blues, Hutcherson's harmonic knowledge gave him immense range – which he resoundingly displayed in this session on the straight-ahead uptempo 'Aquarian Moon' (a headlong, glittering high-speed display) and the slow, harmonically subtle 'Bouquet'. All the tracks but one – Herbie Hancock's 'Maiden Voyage' – are Hutcherson originals.

Jackson, Milton 'Bags'

(Born Detroit, January 1, 1923)
One of jazz music's greatest vibraharpists and a man who has maintained his standards of technical expertise, deceptive simplicity and powers of sympathetic listening through forty-five years of work. Some of Jackson's earliest outings involved collaborations with DIZZY GILLESPIE, through which he quickly proved himself to have been crucially influenced by the thinking of CHARLIE PARKER rather than by other vibists, like Red Norvo or Lionel Hampton. Jackson's conception of an extemporised line ran longer than the earlier vibists and the phrasing was more reminiscent of a horn than a keyboard instrument. His solos were instantly recognisable for an endlessly varied set of favourite devices – the percussive hammering of a repeated note, the deft double-time breaks between theme and solo, and the use of the vibrato mechanism to extend a prolonged note. He proved himself to be one of the few improvisors capable of exploring and enhancing the compositions of THELONIOUS MONK. Jackson has played with the best, but his most celebrated context is the MODERN JAZZ QUARTET – launched in 1954 and, with minimal personnel changes, one of the longest surviving of all jazz groups – in which he shared the bulk of the solo responsibilities with pianist John Lewis.

Throughout this period, Jackson continued to guest with many other artists (including WES MONTGOMERY, MILES DAVIS and Quincy Jones) and led his own bands. Jackson left the MJQ in 1974 (critics had often observed that his best playing was done outside the band, and he himself was unhappy about financial arrangements within it) but he rejoined it when it reformed in the Eighties.

★*Milt Jackson* (Blue Note CDP 781 509-2)

An early Jackson classic – the 1948 recordings finding the twenty-five year-old vibist in a quartet setting – with Thelonious Monk on 'Mysterioso', 'Evidence', the brilliant 'Criss Cross', and three others, plus five tunes with his future MJQ partner John Lewis, including 'Willow Weep For Me' and a warm and fluid 'What's New'. LOU DONALDSON appears on some tracks, at this point helplessly slipstreaming Charlie Parker.

★*At The Montreux Jazz Festival* (JVC/Fantasy VDJ 28007)

The Milt Jackson Big Four at Montreux in 1975, with material including 'Everything Must Change', 'Stella By Starlight' and 'Mack The Knife'.

Jamal, Ahmad (Fritz Jones)

(Born Pittsburgh, July 2, 1930)

One of the few musicians MILES DAVIS has ever admitted to being an unqualified fan of, Ahmad Jamal is not only a unique piano improvisor but also a composer capable of bridging the normally yawning gap between unconventional and exploratory music and the commercial record business.

A child prodigy, strongly influenced by Art Tatum, he formed his first band in 1949 and had a hit record with the folk-song 'Billy Boy', an early success that may have led to the widely-shared critical view that Jamal is simply an above-average cocktail pianist. However his sustained energy and independence of spirit has rescued him, in this critic's eye's, from inclusion in any school. Fascinated by the resonances and timbres of the piano, he has explored them to subtle and ethereal effect rather than allow himself to be caught in the maze of bop harmonic improvising, and he is an imposing collective performer inasmuch as he often leaves motifs hanging tantalisingly in the air for his partners (predominantly percussionists) to toy with, before collecting them up again in sweeping codas. Since he is a maverick, Jamal is – almost inevitably – poorly represented by currently available recordings. The 1970 *Awakening* (MCA) is deleted on CD, and an excellent 1981 concert with Gary Burton, is unavailable on the format.

★*At The Pershing* (Vogue VGCD 600049)

Live concert by Jamal from Chicago's Pershing Room, where so many of his memorable performances took place. Excellent jazz vehicles get the probing Jamal treatment, including 'Woody 'n' You', and a moving version of one of his most popular compositions, the sedate, atmospheric chamber-piece 'Poinciana'.

Johnson, James Louis 'JJ'

(Born Indianapolis, January 23, 1924)
The first truly convincing bebop trombonist, overcoming what seemed like the insuperable technical obstacles to playing this gruff and bulky instrument fast, accurately and with clean tone. Johnson built a devastating technique to handle bebop eighth-notes at speed, but didn't lose his poise – and he made the older styles, with their smeared notes, comic effects and vague pitching, seem obsolete.

A member of both Benny Carter's and Count Basie's bands when barely past twenty, and an occasional partner of DIZZY GILLESPIE and MILES DAVIS between 1949 and 1953, Johnson began a fruitful partnership with Scandinavian trombonist Kai Winding in 1954 – a practitioner of much the same persuasion, though together the two sometimes became inclined to a fastidious over-perfection. Film-score and studio work occupied Johnson in the 1950s and 1960s, but he made several excellent albums, including appearances with SONNY ROLLINS (*Sonny Rollins Volume 2*, Blue Note CDP 781 558-2) and with STAN GETZ. Johnson's own compositions tend toward the ornate and self-conscious (including semi-classical writings for Gunther Schuller's Third Stream Orchestra) but his improvising skills, particularly in stimulating company, are undimmed.

★*The Eminent JJ Johnson, Volume I* (Blue Note CDP 781 505-2)

Johnson with his own sextet on two dates in 1953 and 1954, the first including trumpeter CLIFFORD BROWN. Johnson virtually writes the book on bebop trombone technique with perfectly-honed, flat-out performances on uptempo pieces like 'Get Happy', and evocative sustained-note displays on 'Lover Man'.

★*Things Are Getting Better All The Time* (Pablo/USA 311 260)

Punchy 1983 collaboration between Johnson and fellow-trombonist Al Grey, including 'Softly As In A Morning Sunrise' and 'Things Ain't What They Used To Be'.

Jones, Elvin Ray

(Born Pontiac, Michigan, September 9, 1927)
Drumming changed for keeps when Elvin Jones arrived. His

ability to sense a basic pulse but realise it through polyrhythmic playing, that constantly seemed to be delaying or dropping crucial accents, was the next giant step not only in developing the jazz drum legacy of MAX ROACH, but also in anticipating the percussive complexities of fusion music.

Jones came from a musical family – his brothers, Thad and Hank, were a celebrated trumpeter and pianist respectively – and his early work included both conventional bop bands like JJ JOHNSON's and swing-tinged ones like trumpeter Harry Edison's. Jones' determination to draw the statement of the beat away from dependence on the ride cymbal was already audible on a dramatic, if not always harmonious, live session with SONNY ROLLINS in 1957. ('Sonnymoon For Two' from *Live At The Village Vanguard, Vol 1*, Blue Note CDP 746 517-2).

The drummer's most famous showcase was the John Coltrane Quartet, for which he furnished an unbroken tumult of cross-rhythms (frequently resembling a constant solo) against which Coltrane would set his fire-sermon odysseys (see page 212). But as Coltrane moved ever further out into free-music during the year of his death (1966), Jones' notions of the ultimate flexibility of jazz metres were tested to breaking point and he left the band in favour of more conventional post-hard bop ensembles featuring excellent early-Coltrane disciples like Joe Farrell and Dave Liebmann. Jones has mostly recorded and toured with small groups of this type ever since, performing a sharp and forthright jazz constantly driven by that big, restless, ambiguous and inimitable beat.

★Polycurrents (Blue Note CDP 784 331-2)

One of Jones' best small-group recordings as a leader, assisted by a saxophone front line almost as rhythmically insistent as he is. The band is at its best on Jones' heaving, disruptive approaches to mid-tempo playing and saxophonists Frank Foster (a direct, sinewy Basie sideman), Joe Farrell (an early-Coltraneist) and Pepper Adams help the album to move as if on wheels.

Jordan, Sheila (Sheila Dawson)

(Born Detroit, November 18, 1929)
Sheila Jordan must be the most skilled and imaginative bebop

vocalist never to have been seriously discovered until she was thirty-four, and then to have remained largely out of public view for most of the last twenty years. She was a student of music theory with the ascetic pianist, Lennie Tristano, in the Forties and a devoted CHARLIE PARKER enthusiast (she even formed a vocal trio to put lyrics to Parker tunes). During the Fifties, in comparative obscurity as far as her career was concerned, she was married to bebop pianist Duke Jordan.

Out of this apprenticeship she has evolved an undemonstrative style without bravura, emotionalism or coyness. She is (unsurprisingly, given the Tristano experience) reliant on cool and careful melodic improvisation, mostly in a kind of quiet mid-register yodel, and very attentive to the meaning of lyrics, and sometimes even spontaneously concocting new ones. She recorded a memorable version of 'You Are My Sunshine' with composer George Russell (to whom goes the credit of discovering her), making her debut LP *Portrait of Sheila* for Blue Note in 1962. She has regularly taught jazz singing, worked with soloists of the calibre of LEE KONITZ and Roswell Rudd, recorded TV commercials, and appeared in Carla Bley's ambitious fusion opera *Escalator over the Hill* (see page 241).

★*Portrait of Sheila* (Blue Note CDP 789 002-2)

Sheila Jordan's best album, made in 1962 and featuring the singer with Barry Galbraith's guitar, Steve Swallow, on bass, and Denzil Best, on drums. Jordan's instrumental technique as applied to the voice is much in evidence here, never remote and always spontaneous, tender on 'If You Could See Me Now', abandoned on 'Let's Face the Music and Dance'. Steve Swallow is a highly sensitive foil.

Kelly, Wynton

(Born New York, December 2, 1931; died April 12, 1971)
Unlike many of the horn players, who often learned in hand-to-mouth ways, bebop pianists more often than not possessed all the technique and harmonic knowledge they needed. These could be counterproductive qualities once BUD POWELL's dominance of the idiom took hold, because Powell's followers frequently used their

skills to produce a claustrophobic and airless piano style in which there was neither space nor delicacy. Wynton Kelly, whose origins were in the blues bands of Cleanhead Vinson and Ray Abrams, was the opposite – a bop player of charm and a genial, twinkling sprightliness that made him highly sought-after in his short career, notably by DIZZY GILLESPIE, Dinah Washington and Lester Young in the early Fifties. Kelly's most famous employer was MILES DAVIS, whose band he joined between 1959 and 1963. Kelly's lightness of touch made him a perfect pianist for a band devoted to loosening the bonds of bop, and he also recorded extensively with a relaxed and bluesy late-bop band of his own, sometimes accompanying other powerful soloists such as guitarist WES MONTGOMERY.

★*Kelly Blue* (Fantasy FCD 6331142)

More or less Miles Davis' classic *Kind of Blue* band, with Paul Chambers, on bass, and Jimmy Cobb, on drums. The soloists include Nat Adderley, on trumpet, Bobby Jaspar, on tenor and, on two tracks, the vigorous BENNY GOLSON.

Kessel, Barney

(Born Muskogee, Oklahoma, October 17, 1923)
One of CHARLIE CHRISTIAN's most adept followers on guitar, Kessel was self-taught and his first notable job was in a big band led by the Marx Brothers' Chico Marx. Big band work with more plausible leaders followed in 1944 and 1945, first with Charlie Barnet, then Artie Shaw, leading to a prosperous career in the West Coast recording studios with intervals for recording with CHARLIE PARKER and performing with the Oscar Peterson trio and in the Jazz At The Philharmonic touring show. Under his own name Kessel recorded for the West Coast's Contemporary label in the Fifties and in recent times has toured worldwide, with HERB ELLIS and Charlie Byrd, as the package 'Great Guitars'.

★*To Swing Or Not To Swing* (JVC/Fantasy VDJ 1554)

Excellent early Kessel session, demonstrating how full the

guitarist's tone is in all tempos but how tough and vigorous he can be in the firmly-struck accents and busily accumulating runs. The band is a septet including trumpeter Harry Edison and saxophonist Georgie Auld, the whole effect reminiscent of a Count Basie small band.

Kirk, Rahsaan Roland

(Born Columbus, Ohio, August 7, 1936; died December 5, 1977) Anyone who ever witnessed a live performance by Rahsaan Roland Kirk is unlikely to have forgetten the experience. The German writer, Joachim Berendt, wrote that Kirk 'had all the wild untutored quality of a street musician coupled with the subtlety of a modern jazz musician'. He was that rare thing, a spirited jazz improvisor who was also a performer in the fullest sense of the word – his gigs were dramatic and theatrical, as well as musical to a degree often underestimated in the light of his imposing visual presence. He looked like a particularly exotic brand of busker, playing several reed instruments and capable of blowing three at once – he also deployed whistles, car-horns, nose-flutes, and other paraphernalia.

Kirk was accidentally blinded as a baby and later described an inner life in which voices and sounds from his imagination and the real world combined, frequently to direct his life choices. He began playing with rhythm and blues bands at the age of eleven, and led his own at fourteen. Two years later, following a dream in which he played three horns at once, Kirk tried out several in a music shop and was driven by economics to buy the firm's cheapest, and therefore most archaic, second-hand saxophones. These included military-band relics such as the stritch and the manzello, instruments related to the modern soprano and alto. The young Kirk developed a way of playing three-part harmony simultaneously.

It was thus easy for Roland Kirk to become a novelty act, but harder to be taken seriously. In 1960 he began to come to public notice, with opinions of him being divided between those who perceived his use of whistles, horns and sirens, as a sideshow, and those who recognised the musician's deep understanding of early jazz, including Jelly Roll Morton who had similarly deployed such effects. Almost inevitably, Kirk began working with Charles Mingus, one of the few modern jazz composers similarly interested in such earthy methods, playing on the *Oh Yeah* album. Through the 1960s and 1970s Kirk led his own band, the Vibration Society, playing what he called 'black classical music', and delivering a repertoire that mingled blues, rock 'n' roll, bebop, New Orleans and the avant-garde, in a manner that made it impossible to categorise the artist as being dominated by any single persuasion. Though he suffered a paralysing stroke in 1975, he continued successfully to play one-handed for the next two years, until a second stroke resulted in his death. CD representation of Kirk is patchy, with no inclusion of his best albums *Kirk's Works*, *Rip Rig and Panic*, *Rahsaan Rahsaan* and *The Inflated Tear*.

★*Soulful Saxes* (Affinity/Charly CDAFF 758)

Roland Kirk's recorded debut in 1956, when he was twenty. This album is shared with two other powerful, if more orthodox, saxophonists in BOOKER ERVIN and ZOOT SIMS – but half of it features the young Kirk exploring his own unique avenues with a piano trio, leaning heavily toward spiky, robust and distinctively abrasive interpretations of the blues. He is already capable of simultaneous three-part harmony (using the technique in a limited way on 'A La Carte', a rhythm & blues-like piece), but overdubs improvised duets between the tenor and manzello on 'Stormy Weather' and 'The Nearness of You'. Little notice was taken of this debut album at the time (Kirk had to wait until 1960 and the patronage of RAMSEY LEWIS) but the artist's independence of mind is powerfully apparent in it.

★*We Free Kings* (Polydor 826-455-2)

Kirk five years later, with partners including the excellent Hank Jones, on piano, and Charlie Persip, on drums. That Kirk could have sustained a reputation as a gifted and tireless tenor saxophonist without any of his other wayward talents is apparent from his work here. The three-part technique (assisted by some overdubbing on *Soulful Saxes* but never resorted to thereafter) is by now in its full raucous prime on what became a Kirk classic 'Three For The Festival'. Kirk's garrulous flute playing (it extensively influenced Seventies rock flautists like Jethro Tull's Ian Anderson) is to be heard on 'You Did It, You Did It'.

★*Live In Paris 1970, Vols 1 & 2* (Concert Catalogue/France FCD 109 & 115)

By 1970 Roland Kirk was at full fearsome stretch, and able not only to perform contrapuntal arrangements on three horns but to improvise one line against another. This French material includes the ubiquitous 'Three For The Festival' but also a venomous version of 'You Did It', a rapturous Charlie Parker medley and the passionate 'Inflated Tear', a 1968 composition devoted to the recollection of his childhood blinding.

Konitz, Lee

(Born Chicago, October 13, 1927)

Lee Konitz is the best-known of those white jazz musicians who emerged concurrently with the rise of bebop in the 1940s, but whose version of it was dominated by the influence of the pianist, teacher and rigorous theoretician, Lennie Tristano, rather than by CHARLIE PARKER. Tristano was a fellow Chicagoan whose impatience with what seemed to him the irrational pursuit of basing a melodically and rhythmically sophisticated improvised music on the materials of Tin Pan Alley standards, led him to develop a linear, low-volume, dynamically narrow but melodically complex music without the bluesy emotionalism of orthodox bop.

Konitz began working around Chicago in the mid-1940s, meeting and studying with Lennie Tristano during this period. He joined the superior dance band led by Claude Thornhill (within the ranks of which the talent of arranger GIL EVANS was beginning to flower) and shortly afterwards MILES DAVIS sufficiently admired the young Lee Konitz' delicate embroidery on alto to hire him for the plush, sumptuously orchestrated *Birth of the Cool* recordings, a sound significantly influenced by Thornhill's ensembles. Konitz' ethereal tone inevitably became more muscular after a stint with the Stan Kenton Orchestra in the early Fifties, and some of his records with GERRY MULLIGAN, and another brilliant Tristano influenced saxophonist, WARNE MARSH, deservedly became classics.

Latterly, Konitz' preoccupation with strictly musical values has been reflected in the tough situations he has put himself into. He has made many improvised duo recordings (an exposed and demanding setting for spontaneous music) and even joined British guitarist Derek Bailey's Company project one year, exposing himself to collaborations with many improvisors who would have been total strangers to him. But a Konitz solo always displays its originator's inimitable trademarks – fast, whirling runs descending into breathy low sounds, flute-like slow ascents vibrating with puffs of air; long, stately notes plumbing the depths of the silence around them. Konitz' widespread reputation has derived from his variations on orthodox lyricism, and his recent recordings have returned to this territory. Much of the best of recorded Konitz is not yet available on CD and some that was – like the *Duets* album, with a variety of high-class partners such as guitarist JIM HALL and tenorist JOE HENDERSON – has been deleted.

★*Motion* (Verve 821 553-2)

Konitz is often thought of as a player of intellectualised refinement, but this 1961 session pitches him against a musician of very different inclinations – the tumultuous drummer, ELVIN JONES. Jones' forcefulness and dynamism (the Tristano-school drummers were supposed to stay out of the way but Jones has no interest in this theory) stings the saxophonist into performances of both grace and intensity on a selection of standards including 'All Of Me', 'You'd Be So Nice To Come Home To' and 'I Remember April'. Konitz' forthrightness on 'Foolin' Myself' reveals how far the saxophonist had come from the shy, evaporating sound of the *Birth of the Cool*.

★*Konitz Meets Mulligan* (Pacific Jazz/EMI CDP 746 847-2)

Lee Konitz' 1952 stint with the Stan Kenton Orchestra did much to assist his projection and forcefulness, and an exuberant session of the following year with baritonist, Gerry Mulligan, demonstrates it. Konitz' long, fluting lines and wry inflections contrast vividly with Mulligan's throaty robustness on baritone, and the electric vitality of their musical repartee and intimacy on 'Too Marvellous For Words' has rightly made it a classic.

Lee Konitz In Rio (MA Music A 737-2)

A 1989 release, Konitz with a Rio de Janeiro band, playing an assortment of samba-like pieces that strongly recall the STAN GETZ forays into Latin music in the 1960s. Inevitably that means a lot of Konitz at his most fragile and wispy, full of slow slurs and purring sounds, drifting luxuriously over a shuffling beat (augmented by a cello) and featuring a lot of rather unmemorable solos from the other sidemen. Once you cut through the soupy arrangements however, Konitz' playing, though more reserved, is as rich in surprises and unexpected switchbacks as ever.

Lambert, Hendricks and Ross

Lambert, 'Dave' (born Boston, June 19, 1917; died October 3, 1966)

Hendricks, 'Jon' (born Newark, Ohio, September 16, 1921)

Ross, 'Annie' (born Surrey, England, July 25, 1930 (see also page 183).

Lambert, Hendricks and Ross were a popular multi-national vocal trio who were among the most effective purveyors of the generally ill-advised art of concocting clever vocal equivalents to jazz instrumentals. They (being the British-born, but California-raised, singer and actress, **Ross**; ex-drummer and participant in the first recorded bebop vocal 'What's This', **Lambert**; and **Hendricks**, a singer-songwriter dissuaded from a law career by the praise of CHARLIE PARKER) came together in 1959 to vocalise Count Basie hits for the album *Sing a Song of Basie*. The group had a short life in its original form, despite the success of the Basie album; Annie Ross left in 1962 to be replaced by Yolande Bevan, and the trio disbanded two years later. The rhythmic audacity and inflectional surprises of jazz are frequently lost in 'vocalese', but LHR preserved a surprising amount of it – not least because of Annie Ross. Her understanding of jazz improvisation is spectacularly audible from her remarkable 1952 hit based on Wardell Gray's 'Twisted' solo, through to her Buck Clayton 'Fiesta In Blue' impressions on *Sing a Song of Basie*.

The Swingers (EMI, Manhattan CDP 746849-2)

The original personnel on an excellent selection including 'Airegin', 'Now's The Time' and 'Little Niles'.

Lewis, Ramsey

(Born Chicago, May 27, 1935)
One of the earliest and most successful of all fusion musicians, pianist Ramsey Lewis' single and album, entitled *The In Crowd* were both million-sellers in 1965. Lewis has a percussive and funky keyboard style, though his original influences were players of much more orchestral techniques, like Art Tatum and Oscar Peterson. His music, since the Sixties, has rarely had much appeal from the improvisational point of view, but has often been catchy and highly accessible.

Lewis is a university trained player, and began working in and around Chicago, with his own trio, in 1958. In the same period he performed with leading improvisors, like SONNY STITT and MAX ROACH. But soul, gospel and funk are his preferred forms of jazz (demonstrably with his hits, 'The In Crowd', and his earlier, gospelly, original, 'Wade in the Water').

★*The In Crowd* (Black Tulip 2636462)

The music that changed Lewis' life; his variations on the 1965 Dobie Gray hit, to which he gave a chiming, crisply-accented charm, perfectly tailored to the middle of the road market of the period. Lewis' music, for all its reliance on a handful of favourite devices, does retain a grass-roots simplicity and bounce that later fusion artists have lacked, but a whole album of his work still tries the patience.

Little, Booker Jnr

(Born Memphis, Tennessee, April 2, 1938; died October 5, 1961)
Another precociously gifted 1950s trumpeter who died young and left the jazz world wondering what he might have achieved. Little's mercurial technique and razor-edged sound were perfectly adapted to the fast-moving idiom of hard bop which he seemed – like his contemporaries FREDDIE HUBBARD and LEE MORGAN – to be a natural exponent of, but he possessed a musical imagination that extended beyond bop and hinted at the audacity of an Ornette Coleman or a MILES DAVIS. Little grew up in the Memphis of the Fifties with other dynamic jazz talents – GEORGE COLEMAN, Charles

Lloyd, PHINEAS NEWBORN. He moved to Chicago in 1957 and joined drummer MAX ROACH, and no more appropriate newcomer could have been found to fill the place left by the accidental death of CLIFFORD BROWN. Little became closely associated with Roach, and the partnership lasted on and off – alongside relationships with Eric Dolphy and John Coltrane – until the trumpeter's death at twenty three from uraemia.

By the time of his death, Little was clearly beginning to chafe at the structural obligations of bop – he was fascinated by the impact of unorthodox compositional methods on improvisation – and his soloistic skills were so advanced in the balancing of dissonance and tonality as to anticipate the sound of Miles Davis' trumpet, but the Miles of several years later.

★*Out Front* (Candid CCD 9027)

One of Little's final studio sessions, and the one that most sharply indicates the gathering potential cut off in 1961. It features two associates always linked with Little – Max Roach and Eric Dolphy – and though the prevailing atmosphere is often reflective and the compositional style ambiguous and gently abrasive, the soloing of Little and Dolphy, in particular, are among their most moving and personal on disc.

McGhee, Howard B

(Born Tulsa, Oklahoma, February 6, 1918; died July 17, 1987)
A fine trumpeter who successfully bridged bebop and swing, working with the Charlie Barnet and Andy Kirk bands in the Forties, then with Coleman Hawkins, and often including CHARLIE PARKER in groups he led in Los Angeles toward the end of that decade. McGhee's work during the 1950s was curtailed by narcotics, but he reappeared in 1960, and worked with the Ellington band in 1965. McGhee's regular occupation of the trumpet section's upper echelons in readers' polls testified to his popularity and ability to cross boundaries of taste. With his crisp phrasing yet casual feel, sensitive use of the mute and intelligent adaptation of ideas drawn from earlier players like Roy Eldridge and modernists like DIZZY GILLESPIE and FATS NAVARRO, he was an

improvisor who could convey excitement without resorting to bluster. Little of McGhee's best work is available on CD.

★*Autumn in New York* (Black Lion BLCD 760130)

McGhee guesting on an album under SONNY STITT's name, but in breezing form on three of his own compositions on this 1962 Birdland session.

McLean, John Lenwood 'Jackie'

(Born New York, May 17, 1932)
Jackie McLean has frequently been regarded as a CHARLIE PARKER clone, an opinion that doesn't stand up to closer listening. McLean is less attentive to the details of harmony than Parker, in some respects more impressionistic and nervous, like a forerunner of the Sixties avant-garde (with which he eventually became involved), and his emotional qualities are starker and more strident. The pianist BUD POWELL was McLean's neighbour in youth and, after the two studied together, Powell recommended McLean to MILES DAVIS. In the Fifties, the rapidly maturing McLean then found work with a succession of inspired leaders, including pianists Paul Bley and George Wallington, then Charles Mingus and ART BLAKEY.

Narcotics difficulties and regular work as an actor in Jack Gelber's play *The Connection* sidetracked McLean in the Sixties, and in the following decade he was often kept from playing by commitments to counselling work with drug abusers and by academic pursuits – though he had an unexpected, small-scale disco hit with a 1979 single 'Dr Jackyll and Mister Funk'. But despite his otherwise low profile on the performing and recording scene over the last twenty years, McLean has actively promoted the interests of promising new players, from drummer Tony Williams and trombonist GRACHAN MONCUR in the Sixties, to Christopher Hollyday, a young altoist in his own image, today.

★*Let Freedom Ring* (Blue Note CDP 746 527-2)

Widely hailed as McLean's breakthrough to independence, 'Let

Freedom Ring' from 1963 represented the saxophonist's inspiration, through the new music of Ornette Coleman, to loosen bebop's fetters.

★*One Step Beyond* (Blue Note CDP 746 821-2)

McLean's concept of the sax-led piano trio developed into an augmented band featuring Grachan Moncur, on trombone, and BOBBY HUTCHERSON, on vibes. This is also the recording debut of one of the most thrilling drummers of recent times – Tony Williams, then seventeen and soon to become a dominant force in one of Miles Davis' finest bands.

★*New York Calling* (Steeplechase SCCD 31023)

Early Seventies McLean, leading the Cosmic Brotherhood, the young band that included his son Rene, on tenor and soprano.

Marmarosa, Michael 'Dodo'

(Born Pittsburgh, December 12, 1925)
An excellent first-wave bebop pianist whose accomplishments are barely known outside the coterie of pioneer bebop collectors. Improvisation is irresistible to Marmarosa – he is always embellishing and refining, in theme statements as well as in solos, and he possesses a joyous, singing tone and a distinctive capacity to make each chorus of a solo take on its own rounded character. Marmarosa's sense of improvisational shape was registered as early as 1943, in a beautiful extended solo on Charlie Barnet's 'The Moose', and after a stretch with Artie Shaw, Marmarosa moved to the West Coast and was busy there as a freelance, working with CHARLIE PARKER (Dial recordings in 1946–47, including 'Moose the Mooche' and 'Ornithology') and Lester Young (1945 recordings of 'These Foolish Things' and 'DB Blues') among others. In poor health for much of the Fifties, he cut three albums in the early Sixties (of which the CD listed below was one), then returned to obscurity. Among jazz musicians entitled to regard themselves as under-recorded, Dodo Marmarosa could with justice include himself.

143

★*Chicago Sessions* (Affinity/Charly CDAFF 755)

Originally issued as *Dodo's Back*, this 1961 trio album with Richard Evans, on bass, and Marshall Thompson, on drums, was one of Marmarosa's few later recordings to stand serious comparison with the punch and elation of his Forties playing. The soloing crackles with surprises – the unexpected mixture of bustling chords suddenly entering, the single-note ripples on 'Why Do I Love You?', the brief stride-piano entrance on 'Green Dolphin Street' – and Marmarosa throughout gives the impression of playing nothing that isn't governed by his unerring sense of proportion.

Marsh, Warne Marion

(Born Los Angeles, October 26, 1927; died December 18, 1987) A saxophonist member, as was LEE KONITZ, of the Lennie Tristano cool coterie, but a man with a much slighter reputation than Konitz, due partly to lack of encouragement, and partly to a life lived only peripherally to performing jazz, since the ultra purist position of the Tristanoites, which he epitomised, was a rejection of the commercial compromises of club life. Yet had Marsh played as much as the other Tristano adherents, he might easily have gained the status in jazz that an improvisational flair, at times close to genius, entitled him to.

Marsh played with Hoagy Carmichael in 1944, and after army service, with Buddy Rich and then Lennie Tristano following a move to New York in 1948. His debt to Tristano is probably more audible than for any other saxophone player, his improvisations consisting of complex linear variations of great rhythmic subtlety, mostly delivered fast in a pale, glancing tone adapted from Lester Young. Marsh's tone, in fact, is one of the oddest in jazz saxophone playing, cool to the point of chilliness in the mid-register, but turning into a wry, squawky sound on high notes. He recorded with Lee Konitz and with ART PEPPER in the Fifties (*Art Pepper with Warne Marsh*, Contemporary, VDJ 1577) and there were reunions with Tristano until the mid-Sixties. In 1966, Marsh returned to California and worked as a music teacher and swimming instructor. Reawakening of interest in Marsh's glacial shrewdness brought him back into partnership with Lee Konitz for two tours of Europe in 1975 and 1976. His best recorded work is hard to find and CD availability is so far poor.

★*Lennie Tristano Quintet/Live at Birdland 1949* (Jazz Records JR 1CD) *Live In Toronto 1952* (Jazz Records JR 5CD)

Fascinating, though erratically recorded material from the early days of Warne Marsh's collaboration with Lennie Tristano in the 1949 set, with both musicians ready to stretch the structures even this early on. The 1952 session sounds better, and Marsh's even, deliberate lyricism and melodic audacity is pitched against the related virtues of altoist Lee Konitz.

Mitchell, Richard Allen 'Blue'

(Born Miami, March 13, 1930; died May 21, 1979)
A bluesy, but thoughtful, trumpet soloist, strongly associated with rhythm and blues through early work with such groups as Earl Bostic's in the Fifties. Mitchell's down to earth style was perfectly suited to the gospelly bop of the HORACE SILVER group and the trumpeter remained with Silver between 1958 and 1964, his style becoming more vigorous and heated during this tenure. After this Mitchell became a leader for the first time, leading a fine band including Chick Corea, on piano. Blues affiliations stayed with him, and he toured with Ray Charles in the late Sixties and with bluesman John Mayall in the early Seventies.

★*The Thing To Do* (Blue Note CDP 784 178-2)

Mitchell's debut as leader, on a 1964 session featuring the Horace Silver group but with the twenty three year-old Chick Corea in Silver's place on piano, plus Junior Cook, on tenor, Gene Taylor, on bass, and Al Foster, on drums. Mitchell's only CD so far, and a little muted; the ballad 'Mona's Mood' though, shows off his clear, ringing tone and balanced construction.

Mobley, Henry 'Hank'

(Born Eastman, Georgia, July 7, 1930; died May 30, 1986)

One of the Blue Note stable who was neither a legendary pioneer nor a fierce iconoclast, but a saxophonist of delicacy and poise who – in his own reflective and sidelong way – did much to soften the barrelling attack of hard bop with the bluesy poignancy of Lester Young. Unlike many jazz improvisors of more robust resources, Mobley's method depended on a combination of unpredictable departure from the beat, with a minimum of tonal bravura or special effects. The result was that his undemonstrative audacity could easily be thrown off balance, and the right accompanists were crucial to him, particularly on drums.

Another tenorist who cut his teeth in blues bands (with Paul Gayten's rhythm and blues band in Newark in 1950), Mobley worked with Tadd Dameron and DIZZY GILLESPIE before joining the HORACE SILVER group in 1954, which was soon to become the Jazz Messengers, and his intelligence and unconventionality are already obvious in several solos on the band's debut session (*Horace Silver and the Jazz Messengers*, Blue Note CDP 746 140-2).

Mobley's talents, constantly hampered by ill-health, then brought him a flood of illustrious jobs, and between 1957 and 1962 he was a member of bands led by MAX ROACH, ART BLAKEY, his unusual rhythmic ideas meshing with Blakey's drumming, and MILES DAVIS, delivering a beautiful version of 'I Thought About You' on the latter's *Some Day My Prince Will Come* (Mobile Fidelity/USA MFCD 828). Narcotics problems dogged him through the Sixties and Seventies, though he worked for two years with pianist Cedar Walton. By 1975 he had virtually retired, eventually dying of pneumonia at fifty-five. A player of restrained fire, with a sense of melodic shape and quirkiness rivalling that of SONNY ROLLINS – though with none of Rollins' bullish theatricality.

★*Soul Station* (Blue Note CDP 746 528-2)

One of the best, and best-known, of Mobley's high-quality Blue Note recordings, this 1960 session featured the saxophonist with WYNTON KELLY, on piano, Paul Chambers, on bass, and Art Blakey, on drums. Inaccurately named, to appeal to the soul-jazz fad of the time, it is far from a honking, gospelly session and instead reveals Mobley at his most ingenious. The plausibility of comparisons with Rollins are justified by the two labyrinthine unaccompanied choruses on the bluesy 'Dig Dis', and the eloquent interplay with Blakey on 'This I Dig Of You' is masterful. All Mobley's partners here complemented him perfectly.

★*Roll Call* (Blue Note CDP 746 823-2)

The follow-up to *Soul Station* and very nearly as good, featuring an open-handed, almost aggressive Mobley on the title track (though still mobilised by subtly camouflaged rhythmic disruptions) but now in near-perfect balance with his ambivalent, shadowy lyricism on 'The More I See of You'.

Modern Jazz Quartet

Lewis, John Aaron (born La Grange, Illinois, May 3, 1920)
Jackson, Milt (born Detroit, January 1, 1923)
Heath, Percy (born N Carolina, April 30, 1923)
Kay, Conrad Henry 'Connie' (born New York, April 27, 1927).
One of the best-loved and longest-lived of all modern jazz groups, the Modern Jazz Quartet has attracted mixed opinions from critics, but its accessibility, melodic simplicity and fastidious romanticism has won it a big audience not restricted to jazz fans alone. It started life as DIZZY GILLESPIE's 1946 rhythm section, at that time featuring pianist John Lewis and vibraharpist Milt Jackson, with RAY BROWN, on bass, and bebop pioneer Kenny Clarke, on drums. In 1952 the quartet became an autonomous band, with Percy Heath having replaced Brown. Already the elements that were to make the MJQ so popular were audible in the repertoire. There was a strong allegiance to subtle, needling blues (Jackson was a genius at it and Lewis, though his style was deceptively simple, showed a much more skeletal flair for the same thing), occasionally ravishing displays on ballads, and considerable dependence on European classical forms (even on orthodox material the band frequently used sophisticated counterpoint) reflecting Lewis's classical training.

In 1955 the subdued and empathetic Connie Kay replaced Clarke and one of the most famous lineups of all time was completed, Kay's presence giving the band its characteristic tiptoeing atmosphere as well as helping to speed up its transformation into the kind of chamber-jazz emsemble that attracted audiences otherwise alienated by the raucousness of a good deal of jazz. The years 1956 to 1960 were high points for the MJQ, with the criticism from some quarters that their music was anaemic and a waste of the talents of Jackson, in particular, being effectively countered by their intensity (despite low volumes) in collective improvisation, the uncanny sensitivity of Kay to just the right percussive effect, and a number of enduring compositions from Lewis including 'Django' and the vibrant 'Golden Striker'. After this period, John Lewis' attempts at blending jazz and formal elements from European music became more self-conscious, and the remainder of the Sixties, and the years until Milt Jackson's resignation in 1974, produced increasingly colourless reworkings of past formulae, an elegant decline nevertheless rivettingly reversed on the urgent *Last Concert* album (not available on CD). Lucrative offers led to the reforming of the band for concert tours in the early Eighties, but recordings of substance did not emerge from these reunions. Much of the most valuable and engaging MJQ material (notably the Prestige *Modern Jazz Quartet* and Atlantic *Art of the Modern Jazz Quartet* dealing with the early years) isn't issued on CD.

★*Concorde* (Carrere CA 98 427)

An excellent insight into early MJQ, Connie Kay's debut with the band recorded in New York in 1956. 'Concorde' itself is a fugue, glowingly displaying the conversational counterpoint between Lewis and Jackson, and there is a medley of four Gershwin tunes that has the same impact, possessed of both mutual improvisational glee and an abiding sense of form and order. Jackson is by now in his most relaxed prime, his playing a mixture of hairsbreadth accelerations and delays against the beat, his phrasing fluent and responsive to the overwhelming sense of collective responsibility within the band.

★*Immortal Concerts* (Giants of Jazz/Hasmick GOJCD 0234)

Beautiful MJQ set recorded live in Europe in 1960. Not only are all the musicians in their most persuasive groove of quiet, nudging authority, but the repertoire is an anthology of high-class jazz raw materials – 'Django', 'Bluesology', 'I Remember Clifford', 'Round Midnight', 'I'll Remember April' and nine others. Scintillating swing, and none of the distant, treading-water episodes the band was later inclined toward.

★*No Sun In Venice* (Atlantic/WEA K781 340-2)

John Lewis' evocative film-score for Roger Vadim's *Sait On Jamais*, with Connie Kay at his fastidious best (notably in the cymbal work behind Lewis' sober harmonic statement on 'The Cortege') and a glistening rendition of an all-time MJQ favourite, 'The Golden Striker'.

Moncur, Grachan III

(Born New York, 1937)
Trombonist son of Grachan Moncur II, bassist with the original Savoy Sultans. A major figure on the Sixties and Seventies American avant-garde, Moncur is notable for having adapted to the musical upheavals and rejection of formalism of the period, without sacrificing the organised, boppish JJ JOHNSON-derived technique that marked him out through earlier work with Ray Charles and with the ART FARMER/BENNY GOLSON group. After a period as one of the up-and-coming Blue Note house musicians of the Sixties, along with Herbie Hancock and Tony Williams, Moncur was associated with prominent avantists such as ARCHIE SHEPP (1967–69) and the Jazz Composers' Orchestra Association, but in the Eighties reverted to more traditional pursuits with the blues organist John Patton and with the hard bop-based Paris Reunion Band. The Blue Note is his only CD, but his evocative requiem for civil rights leaders *Echoes of Prayer*, originally on the Jazz Composers' Orchestra's label, deserves reconsideration.

★*Evolution* (Blue Note CDP 784 153-2)

Moncur on the cusp of post-bop and semi-free music, performing a set of his own pieces in glittering company including trumpeter LEE MORGAN, saxophonist JACKIE MCLEAN and drummer Tony

Williams. At times an uneasily blended programme, veering from
the loose and sprawling title track, to the tight 'Monk in
Wonderland', but constantly lifted by the enterprise of the soloists
and Moncur's brisk and booming trombone.

Monk, Thelonious Sphere

(Born Rocky Mount, N Carolina, October 11, 1917; died February
17, 1982)
Few jazz musicians can ever have expressed their disinterest in
inessentials with more vinegary determination than the late
Thelonious Monk. In the 1940s he and DIZZY GILLESPIE virtually
embodied the bebop life – the behavioural eccentricities, the
bizarre headgear – but Monk especially embodied it in music.
Critics argue about whether or not he was actually a bebopper
because much of his style revolved around a dismantled and
dissonant stride piano technique (he was originally an admirer of
Teddy Wilson, a surprisingly urbane and rational model), but in
his thinking about harmony and in the constant surprises of his
phrasing and timing he still sounds contemporary today. It has
been written of Monk that he is the 'purest' jazz composer –
drawing only on the music's own past for materials and never
preoccupied with European borrowings, programmatic music or
any of the fashionable jazz cults that appeared during his lifetime.
Asked to account for some of the apparent oddities in his work,
Monk always reacted with incomprehension, claiming that he
only played what made sense to him.

As a child, Monk adapted early piano lessons to accompanying
his mother's singing in church, and the music of evangelism
played a big part in the formation of his unique approach. In New
York in the Forties, Monk played with a wide variety of musicians,
including after-hours playing with Kenny Clarke at Minton's
Playhouse, where many of the first experiments in bebop were
shared. In 1943 he joined Coleman Hawkins – always a discrimi-
nating leader with an ear for originality – and made his recording
debut with the saxophonist. By 1947 he was leading his own
bands in some brilliant recordings, but false imprisonment on a
drug offence and a subsequent ban from New York clubs kept
him out of public circulation until the mid Fifties. In any case his

acerbic and uncompromising style was not universally popular either with his fellow bebop musicians (many of whom adopted an even, multi-noted legato approach that foundered among the pianist's dissonant chords, sudden prolonged silences and hopping runs) or with the public, for whom his playing sometimes seemed too weird even by hipster standards. The year 1957 represented Monk's ascent to the stature he deserved, and a residency at the Five Spot Club, with the young John Coltrane, led to the blossoming of his career through invitations to festivals and to European tours. There were associations with many prominent horn players (most of them too orthodox for him), but in tenorist CHARLES ROUSE and sopranoist Steve Lacy, Monk found two men prepared to savour and investigate his irregular methods, and both of them remained audibly influenced by Monk throughout their careers. Jolting, exclamatory tunes like 'Well You Needn't' and 'Straight No Chaser' began to enter the repertoires of many bands, even American and European improvisors and avantists, like the Dutch ICP and adventurous saxophonist Anthony Braxton, played his work, and the uncharacteristically mellow 'Round Midnight' became a classic.

★*Genius of Modern Music, Vols 1 & 2* (Blue Note CDP 781 510-2 & 781 511-2)

Thelonious Monk's Blue Note sessions of the late Forties and early Fifties are, for sheer improvisational wilfulness, among the most compelling jazz ever to find its way on to that august label. They also contain (apart from early versions of his sharpest tunes like 'Straight No Chaser', 'Well You Needn't' and 'Round Midnight') solo passages that provide a more comprehensive picture of all Monk's skills than simply the stabbing dissonance and long-pause style for which he's renowned. On 'Thelonious', for example, a repeated one-note pattern against glowering, restless chords, Monk begins his solo with an offhand banging on the most cursory of tunes, follows it with a churning low-register figure, lurches into some bouncing stride playing, then quotes from 'Salt Peanuts'. The second volume is later, better recorded, and features the more urbane though equally blues-derived influence of MILT JACKSON, a man who understood Monk's uniqueness well enough to play creatively with him.

BEBOP

★*Thelonious Monk and John Coltrane* (JVC/Fantasy VDJ 1510)

The only tracks to have been recorded by one of the most famous and shortlived of postwar jazz bands, the 1957 quartet with Monk, John Coltrane, Wilbur Ware, on bass, and Shadow Wilson, on drums. Apart from Monk classics like 'Ruby My Dear', 'Nutty' and 'Crepuscule with Nellie' the sessions are remarkable revelations of Monk's impact on even the most loquacious and ambitious of soloists. Coltrane is forced to explore space and delays in Monk's company, and the result is some of the saxophonist's quirkiest playing.

★*Brilliant Corners* (JVC/Fantasy VDJ 1526)

A session with SONNY ROLLINS and MAX ROACH, and the beginnings of one of the most suitable regular Monk bands, that with tenorist Charlie Rouse. Rollins and Monk weren't a perfect partnership, despite some temperamental similarities, and the saxophonist's mild unease led him to simplify his soloing to a point that underused him, but cornettist Thad Jones turned out to be unexpectedly galvanised by Monk, responding vigorously to this music of gaping intervals and convoluted phrasing. The album is a fascinating display of the attempts of gifted improvisors to come to terms with Monk's utterly personal compositions.

★*Misterioso* (Carrere 98915)

Live recording of the 1958 Monk bank that featured tenorist JOHNNY GRIFFIN, with Ahmed Abdul Malik on bass, and Roy Haynes, drums. Griffin was less inclined to humour Monk than either Rollins or Coltrane, and roared through the repertoire largely oblivious to the leader's prickly nuances – but the band shouldn't be underrated for this alone because Griffin conveys a furious excitement that can be an attractive counterweight to Monk's proddings and needlings, and Roy Haynes balances suspense and inevitability with a poise worthy of the leader.

★*Alone in San Francisco* (JVC/Fantasy VDJ 1549)

Because he was so hard to partner, and because his use of dynamics is so personal, solo performances by Monk represent some of his most satisfying work. A more ruminative Monk is to be heard here, but the pianist's pared-down lyricism brings vim and muscle to 'Remember', and one of his best blues performances is to be heard in this version of the famous 'Blue Monk'.

Montgomery, John Leslie 'Wes'

(Born Indianapolis, March 6, 1925; died June 15, 1968)
A powerful influence on the playing of contemporary guitar stars Pat Metheny (who took up the guitar in the year Montgomery died) and George Benson, Wes Montgomery had become a victim of the middle of the road market by the end of his life, which wanted his easy swing and soft, luxuriant sound but had no use for his sensational improvising skills. But the fact that Montgomery found spontaneous composition of streams of joyous melody as easy as falling off a log is detectable on his early recordings for the Riverside label.

Montgomery didn't start on the guitar until his late teens, but six months later he was busy on the Indianapolis jazz scene. A fan of CHARLIE CHRISTIAN, he learned Christian's solos note for note, and borrowed Django Reinhardt's technique of soloing in octaves too, developing the latter to a fluency belying its awkward fingering and creating a trademark relentlessly used by George Benson, in the latter's funk career. Two years with the Lionel Hampton Band from 1948 to 1950 might have launched Montgomery's career, but he never liked straying far from Indianapolis and returned home to a day job and a punishing series of nightclub playing assignments throughout the Fifties. At the end of that decade he was discovered by CANNONBALL ADDERLEY (by this time Montgomery was thirty four) and began recording extensively – with his brothers Monk and Buddy, as the Mastersounds, and later the Montgomery Brothers, with his own organ trio with Mel Rhyne, and eventually with established jazz stars such as JOHNNY GRIFFIN, FREDDIE HUBBARD and Jimmy Smith.

Montgomery's music was not portentous or self-consciously weighty – he was a free-swinging bebopper with a rich vocabulary of soft, nudging chords, gliding octave figures and single note runs that at their best sprang euphorically from the harmonies rather than simply filling them in. In addition to his lyricism and rhythmic momentum, he had a texture all his own because he plucked the strings with his thumb and never used a pick. In the most suitable settings these virtues conveyed a music of genial, athletic beauty – but they were also the qualities that the record business perceived as ideal raw material for the MOR market. Most of Montgomery's later recordings featured sugary orchestration and a lacklustre roll through the guitarist's special effects, though as the 1965 Paris CD reveals, he never quite lost his magic touch, despite his soft-pop output from 1964 on. Montgomery died of a heart attack at the age of forty three.

★*Far Wes* (Pacific CDP7 94475-2)

Some excellent early Montgomery West Coast sessions including the reliable, if unremarkable, skills of brothers Monk, on bass, and Buddy, on piano, but with a distinguished and undervalued guest in the watchful, dry-toned Harold Land, on tenor. The guitarist confounds occasional allegations of emotional shallowness with a shapely and moving performance on Carson Robinson's 'Old Folks', and 'Leila' (with altoist Pony Poindexter) it also includes some of Montgomery's most explicit tributes to the romanticism of Django Reinhardt. Unlike an earlier vinyl, *The Montgomery Story*, however, this doesn't include the bluesy 'Bock to Bock' or the Chicago recordings that featured Freddie Hubbard.

★*Incredible Jazz Guitar of Wes Montgomery* (Riverside VDJ 1538)

This album was one of Montgomery's best, an uncluttered and direct 1960 session that found him in excellent company with pianist TOMMY FLANAGAN, bassist Percy Heath and drummer Albert Heath. Despite softening into some rather meandering tunes in the end, the uptempo bop of Sonny Rollins' 'Airegin' and Montgomery's walking-riff theme 'Four On Six' finds the guitarist in full unquenchable flood, and Tommy Flanagan provides appropriately pearly, buoyant solos of his own.

★*Full House* (JVC/Fantasy VDJ 1508)

Delightful, fast-moving session with Montgomery in the company of tenorist Johnny Griffin and the WYNTON KELLY trio. This album, coming after Montgomery's move toward MOR had begun, was proof to his admirers that in a club he was still the most joyous and freewheeling of improvisors.

★*Round Midnight* (Charly CDCHARLY 13)

Recorded in Paris with the band that Montgomery brought to Europe in 1965, including Harold Mabern, on piano. The repertoire includes Coltrane's 'Impressions' (Montgomery had worked with the saxophonist on the West Coast five years before), a driving 'Mister Walker' and a gentle 'Round Midnight', soon toughened by the unscheduled arrival of Johnny Griffin.

Moody, James

(Born Savannah, Georgia, March 26, 1925)
A much-loved jazz club artist of continuing inventiveness on saxophones and flute, and irrepressible surrealism that sometimes finds its way out in song. Moody's delightful melodic unpredictability and fondness for mingling hard bop complexities with earthy blues and gospelly sounds have served him well since the 1940s, when he was a member of DIZZY GILLESPIE's first big band. Moody's connection with Gillespie continued on and off through the Fifties and Sixties, and he also played briefly with MILES DAVIS, and with Gene Ammons and SONNY STITT. Moody's tenor sound is indebted to DEXTER GORDON, though without Gordon's sledgehammer weight, and he builds his solos from a rich palette of deftly chosen devices – wriggling slurred sounds, end-of-line accents like exclamation marks, constant tonal changes, and a gradual widening of the intervals in his phrasing. Moody was active on the Las Vegas session scene through most of the Seventies but has latterly returned to touring and is popular with audiences everywhere.

★*Something Special* (BMG/RCA PD 83008)

Well, it wasn't as special as all that, not really being comparable to the irrepressible Moody in person, but it remains the best of his Novus recordings so far and features an excellent band including

Kirk Lightsey, on piano, and Idris Muhammad, on drums. The leader is in amiable form on 'Moody's In The Mood For Love'.

Morgan, Lee

(Born Philadelphia, July 10, 1938; died February 19, 1972)
Trumpeter Lee Morgan was one of the early stars of the first wave of jazz-funk – but his involvement in a more commercial jazz didn't require him to alter a technique that was already deeply inflected with earthiness, blues and funky phrasing. Morgan displayed much of the robustness of the earliest jazz trumpeters, his solos peppered with half-valve slurs and bent notes, his tone bright and brassy, and such directness appealed to DIZZY GILLESPIE, one of the best judges of a trumpeter, who hired Morgan at eighteen in 1956. He played in an alert and confident Clifford Brown-ish manner on John Coltrane's 1957 Blue Train, and was later a member of the 1958 Jazz Messengers with ART BLAKEY, his blazing solos on BENNY GOLSON's 'Blues March' regularly raising the roof.

In the early Sixties Morgan withdrew to Philadelphia but a commercial hit, with a danceable blues, called 'The Sidewinder', brought him greater accolades than before. Morgan continued to develop as a colourful and often moving performer until he was shot outside the New York nightclub Slug's, following an argument with a woman friend. CD representation of Morgan's output, predominantly on Blue Note, is good, but an issue of the furious Live at the Lighthouse album with reed player Bennie Maupin and pianist Harold Mabern would be welcome.

★The Sidewinder (Blue Note CDP 746 137-2)

A hit in the Sixtiess, and a hit all over again, since 'The Sidewinder' became popular with the dance-jazz audience of the Eighties. The title track is a mid-tempo swinger with a driving beat, but so is the much brisker 'Boy What A Night', which bristles with Billy Higgins' buzzy cymbal sound and has a long, curling melody line ending in a tantalising break before a characteristically blurted, throaty tenor solo by JOE HENDERSON. Morgan's solo on 'Totem Pole' is one of his finest, and the presence of Higgins is a big plus for the disc, a man in Ed Blackwell's mould of furiously swinging moderation. Morgan's trumpet effects – in other settings inclined to the over-ornate – are both under tighter control and expressed through a more abrasive, and distinctive, tone.

★*Search for the New Land* (Blue Note CDP 784 169-2)

Morgan could have sat back and replayed the formula of 'Sidewinder' for the rest of the 1960s (and Blue Note did get him back to repeat the mixture with the same band on *The Rumproller*) but his subsequent work demonstrated that his talents went beyond exciting soloing and catchy compositions. This album was altogether musically richer, the intense and complex extended title piece being atmospherically complemented by the work of Wayne Shorter, on reeds, and Herbie Hancock, on piano.

★*Cornbread* (Blue Note CDP 784 222-2)

Straight hard-bop, once again given the Billy Higgins effervescence, and this time pitching the wailing alto of JACKIE MCLEAN and the delicate tracery of HANK MOBLEY's tenor against Morgan's crackling trumpet work. More down-the-line, but irresistible.

Mulligan, Gerald Joseph 'Gerry'

(Born New York, April 6, 1927)
Just twenty one when he worked in the august company of MILES DAVIS, LEE KONITZ and GIL EVANS on the pathfinding 1948 *Birth of the Cool* sessions, Gerry Mulligan contributed some timeless tunes like 'Jeru', 'Rocker' and 'Venus De Milo' to the band's roster, establishing an atmosphere of relaxed lyricism that has stayed with him to the present day. Mulligan had been a rapid developer, contributing arrangements to the dance-bands of Claude Thornhill and Gene Krupa while still a teenager. Thornhill's principal arranger was Gil Evans who recruited Mulligan to the *Birth of the Cool* project, as the extended voicings of the scores required a baritone saxophonist sensitive to the softer, more reflective atmosphere of the cool style. Mulligan – attracted, like his baritone model Serge Chaloff, to the graceful, airier saxophone sound of Lester Young – developed a technique that combined speed and smoothness.

Gerry Mulligan was constantly searching for new forms and timbres for jazz, but balanced this curiosity with his attraction to the 'classicism' of the Basie-Young mainstream. In 1952 he formed a famous piano-less quartet with the late CHET BAKER, on trumpet, a group that became famous for delicate traceries of counterpoint that set the tone for much that came to be dubbed the 'West Coast' style. From time to time Mulligan expanded the group, adding Lee Konitz, and even odder instrumentations for a jazz band, such as two baritones, tuba and French horn. As his reputation grew, Mulligan contributed to film scores (the music from the 1958 movie *I Want To Live* has recently been reissued and the crew-cut-and-shades image virtually defines the late-Fifties cool jazz style). Yet he was also capable of relaxed participation in jam sessions, with musicians as different as STAN GETZ and THELONIOUS MONK. In the 1980s Mulligan frequently led a cut-down jazz orchestra playing his own subtle and elegant work. Mulligan's extraordinarily empathetic meeting with altoist PAUL DESMOND in 1957 (*Blue in Time*), would be an attractive addition to the Mulligan CD roster.

★*California Concerts, Vols 1 & 2* (EMI/Manhattan CDP 746 860-2, 864-2)

The pianoless quartet in the early Fifties with Mulligan deft and assured, Chet Baker less so, though always at home, in a querulous kind of way, on a sizeable scattering of blues and ballads.

★*Fabulous Gerry Mulligan Quartet* (Vogue VGCD 600028)

The quartet live at the Salle Pleyel in Paris in 1954, with trombonist Bob Brookmeyer having replaced Baker, and imparting to the band a more grounded and purposeful feel, if sacrificing a little in poignancy. Powerfully propelled by Red Mitchell, on bass, and Frank Isola, on drums, the band delightfully remakes standards like 'Walkin' Shoes' and 'Lullaby of the Leaves'.

★*Age of Steam* (A &M CDA 0804)

Mulligan's effective combination of breezy, laid-back swing, dynamic evenness and subtle harmonic mobility, at work on a set of pieces devoted to the leader's enthusiasm for steam railways and bearing appropriate titles. The recording revitalised material he had written in the early Seventies for 14-piece ensemble, and featured a young band that expertly polished his already meticulous pieces.

Navarro, Theodore 'Fats'

(Born Key West, Florida, September 24, 1923; died July 7, 1950) A trumpeter who would unquestionably have been a major influence on the evolution of bebop in the 1950s (what influence he did have came through the line of trumpeters who admired him, like CLIFFORD BROWN and LEE MORGAN) if narcotics addiction hadn't led to tuberculosis and his early death. Like CHARLIE PARKER, Navarro was intelligent, articulate and restless about the possibilities of the new jazz. Unlike either Parker or DIZZY GILLESPIE, he was not attracted by unbroken fusillades of uptempo playing but maintained an utterly distinctive poise and shapeliness in all his work, balancing a spontaneous bite against the impression that his solos had been written out beforehand. After early swing work with Andy Kirk, Navarro replaced Gillespie in the Billy Eckstine band in 1945 (no CDs of this hothouse of bebop so far exist), then recording with Coleman Hawkins, EDDIE 'LOCKJAW' DAVIS, Illinois Jacquet and others before commencing a close association with composer Tadd Dameron, whose notions of larger-scale bebop were more spacious and suited to Navarro's style. Later Navarro/Dameron collaborations, like *Good Bait*, deserve reissue.

★*The Fabulous Fats Navarro, Vols 1 & 2* (Blue Note CDP 781 531-2 and 532-2)

Essential Navarro, featuring a string of dazzling themes illuminated by the trumpeter's glowing tone. A fascinating contrast of brass styles are to be heard in Navarro's alternating choruses with the more heated Howard McGhee on 'Boperation' and 'The Skunk' (vol 2) and Navarro's harmonic imagination on 'The Chase' and 'Lady Bird' at times rivals Parker's. Some key tracks from this period, involving pianist BUD POWELL and the young SONNY ROLLINS ('Wail', 'Bouncing with Bud', '52nd Street Theme' and 'Dance of the Infidels') are unfortunately missing from the CD, but what's here provides more than a flavour of an unfulfilled jazz genius.

Nelson, Oliver Edward

(Born St Louis, June 4, 1932; died 1975)
A gifted composer and arranger and a forceful alto saxophonist, Nelson's contribution to jazz development has been limited only by his choice of a life in the Hollywood studios, writing music for films and TV ('Ironside', 'The Six Million Dollar Man'), rather than on bandstands. In the 1960s, Nelson's most fruitful collaboration was with the adventurous saxophonist Eric Dolphy – a good match, since Dolphy's wide leaps of intervals and devious phrasing ideally balanced Nelson's pure sound, straighter conception and clean articulation in the upper register. Apart from his famous *Blues and the Abstract Truth* and a sophisticated seven-part suite (*Afro-American Sketches*) using a richly augmented big band, Nelson made the beautiful *Images* with Dolphy, part of which is available as Fantasy's *Straight Ahead*, but not on CD.

★*Black Brown and Beautiful* (Bluebird/BMG ND 86993)

A 1970 Nelson dedication to Ellington, augmented by the lustrous alto saxophone of a veteran Johnny Hodges, on the leader's own 'Yearnin'' and on Ellington originals 'Creole Love Call' and 'Rockin' In Rhythm'. Vocalist Leon Thomas, a forceful singer who seemed a rising star in the Seventies but faded, appears briefly.

Newborn, Phineas Jr

(Born Whiteville, Tennessee, December 14, 1931)
An imposingly well-equipped pianist, convincing in the styles of BUD POWELL, Art Tatum or the earlier stride players, who was virtually ignored by jazz observers and the public after the 1960s.

Newborn made his debut in New York in the mid-Fifties, and was heralded as a giant, but erratic involvement with the jazz scene over the next decade led to his faultless articulation and easy improvisational flow being overlooked and many of his records went out of print. What remains available reveals a jazz talent of great stature, leaning heavily toward blues, but made distinctive by a grasp of many styles united through idiosyncrasy rather than theatricality.

★*Harlem Blues* (JVC/Fantasy VDJ 1558)

Ideal context for Newborn, the emphatic and muscular blues artist, with Newborn, the glossy lyricist, at work not far beneath. This Sixties Contemporary session finds the pianist with players matching his own drive and enveloping command of an instrument, RAY BROWN, on bass, and ELVIN JONES, on drums.

Nichols, Herbert Horatio 'Herbie'

(Born New York, January 3, 1919; died April 12, 1963)
Herbie Nichols, like Phineas Newborn, was a piano original whose insights were matched by the neglect he experienced, and he didn't live long enough for belated recognition despite the fact that some members of the Sixties avant-garde were beginning to draw attention to him, at the time of his death from leukaemia. He was an uncategorisable performer, like THELONIOUS MONK, who also suffered from the baffled neglect of the jazz world – but unlike Monk, he was never welcomed back. Nichols' unfashionable preference – the avantists, notably Ornette Coleman were adopting it after Nichols had stopped recording – was for paraphrase and restatement of themes rather than a preoccupation with streams of new melody on the chords. But though he grew up around the bop pioneers, Herbie Nichols was never accepted as part of that culture and was an outcast all his life, virtually never performing his extraordinary originals – including 'Lady Sings the Blues' for Billie Holiday – in public, condemned to a supporting career in rhythm & blues and Dixieland bands. Nichols led only six recording sessions in his lifetime, and his brilliant early Blue Note work (with MAX ROACH and ART BLAKEY sharing the drum duties) is unfortunately not on CD.

★*Bethelehem Sessions* (Affinity/Charly CDAFF 759)

Nichols' last recordings, made in 1957 – far more mixed and uncertain than his earlier work, but full of insights into a remarkable stylist nonetheless. This set – which might have suffered from some pressure to make Nichols more palatable to the public – includes the only two ballads the pianist ever recorded. There's a bland account of 'All the Way', and a disembodied treatment of Nichols' only love song 'Infatuation Eyes'. But Nichols' most personal quality, the ability to evoke the particularity of places and emotional events, is still audible on the ironic 'Love Gloom Cash Love' and the grotesque, ricocheting 'S'Crazy Pad'.

Parker, Charles Christopher 'Charlie' (also 'Bird')

(Born Kansas City, August 29, 1920; died March 12, 1955)
Miles Davis said that the history of jazz could be told in four words: 'Louis Armstrong, Charlie Parker'. Most assessments would tip the hat to a few more artists than that, notably to Davis himself, but Parker's genius – despite the undoubted influence of other key musicians of the bebop era, and the pressure of history on it – wrenched jazz into modernism and changed the way all subsequent players conceive of it. In the mid-1940s when he was at his creative peak, Parker constantly rewrote the rules of saxophone improvisation, riding over the natural starting points and pauses suggested by the bar-lines to produce phrases of quirky lengths and unexpectedly-placed resolutions, interspersing long-note passages with flurries of sixteenths, constantly rising and falling in volume. It was a rebuilding of saxophone law incorporating Lester Young's lightness and storytelling skill with Coleman Hawkins' attack; but within a modern harmonic framework incompatible with a swing-band repertoire.

Charlie Parker was the son of a Kansas song-and-dance man and a devoted mother, Addie Parker, who gave the boy his first saxophone. His early familiarity with it came through a little teaching and a lot of eccentric self-education, during which the young Parker learned the instrument in all the keys, innocent that the information was largely redundant to jazz-playing in the Thirties. The knowledge was invaluable later and helped with his remarkable spontaneous facility for drifting in and out of key without losing his place. The boy began to work with local Kansas bands and eventually joined the Jay McShann Orchestra in New York. Parker's first recordings reflect Lester Young, Johnny Hodges and Benny Carter, but the harmonic departures – augmenting the basic chords with higher related notes and using these as the materials of a new melody line – were already audible.

Parker left McShann in 1942, and began sharing his ideas with other radical musicians including DIZZY GILLESPIE, THELONIOUS MONK and the other habitues of the after-hours Minton's Playhouse. Though he took up jobs with the Earl Hines and then Billy Eckstine bands, Parker's addiction to narcotics and alcohol made him an unreliable sideman, and in any event his musical sympathies were elsewhere. In 1944, he began recording with his own groups, initially in a territory somewhere between modernism and swing (though on early recordings with McShann it's clear that his preparations were virtually complete by 1942) and with unsuitable partners. Then a year later he recorded with the formidable prototype bebop band drawn from Dizzy Gillespie and MILES DAVIS (trumpets) with MAX ROACH, on drums, Curley Russell, on bass, and Argonne Thornton, on piano, the latter a hasty substitute for the absent Thelonious Monk. Classics of the bebop idiom emerged from these performances, like 'Now's the Time' (a bristling blues containing three devastating Parker choruses, to which a mystified *Downbeat* magazine awarded a no-star rating), 'Billie's Bounce' and 'Koko'.

Parker's music stunned the jazz world – infuriating its traditionalists, astonishing its adventurers. It was without sentiment or even much reflectiveness, steeped in the blues, alternately cajoling and imperious, scathing and desperate, an avalanche of music in which ricocheting melodies, impetuousness and delayed payoffs and a scalding level of emotional energy had the same impact, on more perceptive listeners, that the King Oliver/Louis Armstrong band had had on its arrival in Chicago over twenty years before. Many other classics including 'Cheryl', 'Buzzy' and 'Parker's Mood' were recorded by Savoy over the next three years, as well as the brilliant 'Ornithology', 'Yardbird Suite' and 'Night In Tunisia' (with Miles Davis, tenorist Lucky Thompson and pianist DODO MARMAROSA) and later 'Cool Blues' for the West Coast's, Dial label, between 1946 and 1948. The Savoy takes of

1944–48 and the Dial recordings are generally taken to represent Parker's finest work.

New opportunities brought Parker a wider public, notably through the Jazz At the Philharmonic roadshow organised by liberal promoter Norman Granz, but his personal habits were making him hard to work with and when Roach and Davis left, RED RODNEY, a young white trumpeter, joined the band, with AL HAIG, on piano. From this point until Parker's death, Granz and others were frequently looking for new settings for the saxophonist's talents, and Parker himself was preoccupied with producing work along what he perceived as the more sophisticated and enduring lines of, recent arrivals in California, Igor Stravinsky and Edgard Varese. Parker worked on Granz-organised recording sessions until his death in 1955, some of them inappropriate, some excellent.

★*The Savoy Recordings, Vols 1 & 2* (Vogue VG 655 650107)

A more extended representation of the 1944–1947 Savoy material than formerly available on CD, and with crisp reproduction. The material comes from the 1944 Tiny Grimes session that produced 'Red Cross', 'Billie's Bounce' and 'Ko-Ko' from a 1945 session including Miles Davis, and work featuring Bud Powell, John Lewis and Max Roach.

★*Legendary Dial Masters, Vols 1 & 2* (Stash STCD 23/25)

Parker's celebrated Dial material in compilation form, much of it featuring the saxophonist at his devastating creative peak, and some of it imperfect performances that nevertheless retain an agonising beauty of their own – like the famous tortured 'Loverman' when Parker was barely able to stand, let alone to play, but on which his searing tone slashed through the uncertainties of form and the blurted flurries of notes were as expressive as anything he recorded. Dial also recorded some scorching Parker blues, notably 'Cool Blues' (from a February 1947 session after Parker's six month stretch in the Camarillo mental hospital, with a surprisingly accommodating Errol Garner on piano) and a breezing, lyrical and supremely confident 'Relaxin' at Camarillo' with more appropriate partners a week later.

★*Rare Bird* (Rare 04/05)

Parker broadcasts (including the soundtrack of the only known movie of the saxophonist in action on 'Hot House') between 1947 and 1954. A collector's item, because the sound quality is about as good as current technology can make Forties airshots, but featuring Parker with trumpeters Dizzy Gillespie, KENNY DORHAM and FATS NAVARRO, and various ensembles augmented by strings and woodwind. Five tracks are from the 1950 gig at New York's Birdland in which Fats Navarro – on his last public appearance a week before the end of his life at twenty seven – breezes through characteristically effortless solos on such tunes as 'Ornithology' and 'Out of Nowhere'.

★*Bird – The Complete Charlie Parker on Verve* (Verve 837 141-2. Ten-disc set)

A no-stone-unturned package of 137 selections featuring more or less everything from Parker's years with Norman Granz. They thus include items recalling the tours with Granz's travelling Jazz At the Philharmonic roadshow (sometimes musical, but frequently pyrotechnical), the recordings with classical string sections and with Machito's Latin orchestra, the intriguing oddities like the session with Monk, Dizzy and an ill-matched Buddy Rich on drums, and the floundering exploration with a GIL EVANS woodwind jazz ensemble and assorted vocalists that Granz himself pulled the plug on after four takes. All this material, endless retakes, false starts, studio banter and all, has been repackaged with a helpful booklet, and includes the piquant 1946 occasion when Parker encountered his old (and by this time langourous-sounding) hero Lester Young onstage and produced a raw, slashing masterpiece of a solo on 'Love for Sale'. The 1949 Carnegie Hall concert includes an exuberantly scatting Ella Fitzgerald ('How High the Moon'), the famous June 1952 'alto summit' for Bird, Benny Carter and Johnny Hodges, the inexorable and unrelenting 'Funky Blues', and the meeting with Machito delivers a smooth, warm Parker on 'Mango Mangue'.

Parlan, Horace Louis

(Born Pittsburgh, January 19, 1931)

A distinctive pianist who has made equally distinctive musical relationships – with uncategorisable jazz personalities like Charles Mingus and ROLAND KIRK, and with gritty, no-nonsense soloists such as tenorists BOOKER ERVIN and EDDIE LOCKJAW DAVIS. Parlan's piano playing avoids bravura and breakneck pyrotechnics, concentrating on the atmosphere of the work in hand through a mixture of exclamatory left-hand chords and stinging right-hand phrasing, the overall impact predominantly bluesy. In the Sixties he made seven trio albums for Blue Note and also recorded extensively with stars like DEXTER GORDON and STANLEY TURRENTINE – having served an apprenticeship in rhythm and blues music, with the demanding Parkerish saxophonist SONNY STITT, and then with the even more demanding Mingus. It was Parlan who introduced Booker Ervin to Mingus, and the pianist's earthiness clearly drew him to soloists of Ervin's rough, bustling manner – like Eddie 'Lockjaw' Davis in 1962 and Roland Kirk from 1963 to 1966. Parlan moved to Copenhagen in 1973 and has continued to record and play there.

★*Happy Frame of Mind* (Blue Note CDP 784 134-2)

Parlan's only CD release, but a good example of his independence and musicality, being a session with a distinct identity. Drawn from the early Sixties Blue Note period, it features the pianist with Booker Ervin in firebreathing pursuit, and guitarist GRANT GREEN lending his soulful drive to some very distinctive material including Sun Ra sideman Ronnie Boykins' 'Home is Africa' and Randy Weston's 'Kucheza Blues'.

Pedersen, Neils-Henning Oersted

(Born Orsted, Denmark, May 27, 1946)
One of the great bass virtuosi of recent times, Oersted Pedersen is accomplished in virtually any feasible achievement on the instrument – his tone is rich and sonorous, his articulation crystal-clear, his melodic ideas buoyant and song-like, he swings hard and he is both commanding as a soloist and sympathetic as an accompanist. Unsurprisingly, all thses skills endeared him to the best jazz artists very early in his career. His mother was a church organist and the boy studied piano at first, though quickly emerged as a prodigy on bass. At fourteen he was playing with

local jazz bands, and was asked to join Count Basie's band at seventeen – though he turned it down. Oersted Pedersen became house bassist at the Club Montmartre, in Copenhagen, in the Sixties (playing with visitors like SONNY ROLLINS and BILL EVANS), and after a fruitful partnership with expatriate pianist Kenny Drew, he joined Oscar Peterson's trio. Oersted Pedersen has recorded extensively, with Peterson, with guests on festivals (notably DIZZY GILLESPIE at Montreux 1975) and in several compellingly conversational duos.

★*The Viking* (Pablo CD 231 0894)

One of Oersted Pedersen's best duo recordings, this time with the graceful Belgian guitarist, Philip Catherine. The atmosphere is predominantly mellow, but the two intertwine with immense charm and understanding and their shared dislike of coarseness or ostentation glowingly reactivates 'My Funny Valentine', 'Stella by Starlight' and Django Reinhardt's beautiful 'Nuages'.

Pepper, Arthur Edward 'Art'

(Born Gardenia, California, September 1, 1925; died June 15, 1982)

A devoted admirer of CHARLIE PARKER, but also influenced by the white West Coast 'cool school' scene of the 1950s, Los Angeles altoist Pepper was a fascinating mixture of bebop speediness and a kind of fragile, wounded introversion that made his solos recognisable from the first few notes. Pepper often began solos, particularly later in his troubled life, as if the notes were being wrung out of him – and throughout his career an audacious use of space, fondness for remoulding a single phrase or fragment of a melody, and sudden bursts of raw emotion gave his music an unpredictability that suggested, in method, THELONIOUS MONK. Pepper's music possessed a blend of tenderness, anger and pragmatism that was genuinely moving – though the saxophonist was also a virtuoso to a degree that CHET BAKER, for instance, was not, and he could play with furious elan in the right circumstances.

Pepper was a brisk starter in music, playing around the Los

Angeles clubs by the age of seventeen. In the early Forties he briefly joined the bands of Benny Carter (whose alto playing exerted a powerful influence on him) and Stan Kenton, and he was an early admirer of Charlie Parker. Pepper played a second stint with Kenton from 1947–52 and then began a series of prison sentences for drug offences that interrupted his career until the late Sixties, when he was rehabilitated and made a dramatic comeback. Pepper began recording again, played with Don Ellis and at the Newport Jazz Festival, and began touring the world. He was extensively recorded in his last years, and his music and his turbulent life became more widely known through the film *Notes from a Jazz Survivor*, and his blunt and often spinechilling autobiography *Straight Life*. Pepper's own sense of surprise at actually being alive during his last years strongly colours his later emotional and self-revealing music.

★*Meets the Rhythm Section* (Contemporary CDCOP 004)

This album was a hastily arranged session to take advantage of the presence in Los Angeles of the MILES DAVIS rhythm section of 1957. The saxophonist hadn't played for six months, was badly strung out and exhausted, but the drive of Philly Joe Jones, on drums, brought to life the man who wanted to be the best white jazz musician ever. The rapport between the players is obvious, notably on the new Orleans standby 'Jazz Me Blues' and impassioned 'Star Eyes'.

★*Plus Eleven* (Contemporary CDCOP 007)

Arranger Marty Paich's reworkings of jazz standards with Pepper featured on alto, tenor and clarinet. A sublimely realised session, Paich's settings economical and unfussy but full of vitality and Pepper storming his way through a blistering tenor account of 'Walkin'' and a sensational clarinet version of 'Anthropology' moving from murmuring low-pitched reserve to wild high-register exhilaration.

★*Living Legend* (JVC/Fantasy VDJ 1582)

A 1975 session with Pepper's ideal form of accompaniment, the piano trio – and a highly compatible one with Hampton Hawes at the keys (the dynamic and bluesy pianist making his last recording) the darkly dramatic Charlie Haden, on bass, and Shelly Manne, on drums. This is Pepper after a long layoff from recording and powerfully affected by a relatively recent influence – John Coltrane. The Californian demonstrates here, as in several examples from the late Seventies to his death, that he could at times be as spinechilling as Coltrane – and he can be heard at his most fraught, heartfelt and brooding on the slow and sorrowful 'Lost Life', one of his great recorded performances.

★*Blues for the Fisherman* (Mole Jazz MOLECD 1)

A session under the nominal leadership of pianist Milcho Leviev, recorded, in June 1980, at Ronnie Scott's in London. Not featuring as wired and alert a rhythm section as Miles Davis', nor as urgent and atmospheric as that on *Living Legend*, but the disc is a fine example of Pepper in later live performance, when his anxieties, hesitancies and sudden swirls of melody seemed more explicit and affecting, than when he was forcing himself to be the commanding studio pro. The springy, sharply accented 'Make a List, Make a Wish' also confirms the talents of Pepper the composer.

Pettiford, Oscar

(Born Okmulgee, Oklahoma, September 30, 1922; died September 8, 1960)
Duke Ellington's short-lived but revolutionary partner Jimmy Blanton changed the course of jazz bass playing, and at first in the 1940s there were few musicians who could take up where he left off. The man eventually heralded as the keeper of Blanton's flame and his natural successor was Oscar Pettiford, who continued Blanton's guitar-like counter-melodic accompaniment and fast pizzicato solo technique – not only on bass but cello as well. His tone boomed and his time-playing was an irresistible driving thump that propelled the most laggardly soloists.

Pettiford had been a pianist as a child, taking up bass at fourteen, touring with a band led by his father. He briefly joined the bands of Charlie Barnet and Roy Eldridge in the Forties, then recorded with Coleman Hawkins, Earl Hines and Ben Webster between 1943 and 1944, in the latter year co-leading a band with DIZZY GILLESPIE. Following this, Pettiford began a three-year stint with Duke Ellington, then Woody Herman, in between leading his own occasional orchestra and recording with THELONIOUS MONK. He settled in Copenhagen in 1958, working there with STAN GETZ and BUD POWELL, before dying of a virus in 1960. Pettiford's big band is available on vinyl on Spotlite (SPJ 153).

★*Vienna Blues – the Complete Session* (Black Lion BLCD 760104)

Pettiford's best work isn't available on CD – both *Blues Brothers* and *Bohemia After Dark* deserve to be – and most of his recorded work with European musicians doesn't match earlier American sessions. This episode with locals, including the fine Austrian tenorist Hans Koller, was cut in Vienna in 1959 and nevertheless displays the bassist's mellow sound, driving beat and gracefulness on slow pieces, notably the caressing 'Gentle Art of Love'.

Pike, David Samuel 'Dave'

(Born Detroit, March 23, 1938)
Good modern vibraharpist who pioneered the amplified vibes around 1960. Pike began as a drummer, and taught himself vibes later. He moved from Detroit to Los Angeles as a teenager and worked with some of the finest West Coast players, including pianists Carl Perkins and Curtis Counce, and tenorist James Clay. In 1960 he moved to New York and began a partnership with the flautist Herbie Mann, touring the globe with Mann's popular fusion band. Pike played the Berlin Jazz Festival in 1968 and elected to settle there, working with front-rank local players such as guitarist Volker Kriegel and bassist Eberhard Weber, as the Dave Pike Set. Pike returned to California in 1973 and has recorded occasionally since, notably with pianist Cedar Walton.

★*Dave Pike with Charles McPherson* (Timeless CDSJP 302)

A 1988 recording with a Dutch rhythm section, on much jazzier material than the fusion-oriented Pike had gone in for in earlier years – Parker's 'Scrapple from the Apple' gets a sharp account from McPherson, one of the most inventive altoists to have taken his lead from Bird. Robust and unpretentious, with Monk's 'Off Minor' appropriate material for Pike's clangy, percussive attack. This is currently McPherson's only CD too, and the saxophonist deserves far more exposure for his provocative bop remoulds, featuring his own personal mixture of jaggedness and mellowness.

Powell, Earl 'Bud'

(Born New York, September 27, 1924; died July 31, 1966)
The most influential pianist of the bebop era and one of the most influential in all jazz, his sound still audible in the work of many young practitioners for whom his music is a subconscious or second-generation influence. Powell went as far as he could to give the piano the vocalised horn sound of CHARLIE PARKER – but not through primitivism, special-effects dissonances or any kind of gimmickry, rather by developing an equivalent to the harmonic complexity and ecstatic energy of Parker. Powell at his best never settles for long on any single idea, prodding at everything he thinks of with restless counterpoint or punchy left-hand chords, swerves into other keys, and brief Tatumesque embroidery.

Powell was taught classically, but in his late teens, fascinated by jazz, began hanging out on the New York bebop scene. His jazz piano inspirations were initially the dapper, dancing sound of Teddy Wilson, the fluency of Nat 'King' Cole and the Wilsonesque (but punchier) manner of John Kirby's pianist Billy Kyle. But the genial manner of these players had an emotional timbre unsuitable for bebop, particularly in its first wave, and Powell set about providing a piano equivalent for Parker's headlong flights – Powell's harmonic knowledge and faultless technique (notes ring out with the clarity of hammers on flint even at the fastest tempos) giving him something close to the resources of Art Tatum. Powell worked with Parker on 52nd Street and recorded on some of the early Savoy sides, but his early recordings as a leader were for piano trio, in which setting he was devastating.

Later in his life Powell became prone to periods of mental disturbance, but much of his work during the 1950s remains compelling and, on the 1953 Massey Hall concert with Charlie Parker, Charles Mingus, DIZZY GILLESPIE and MAX ROACH, he is both his usual propulsive accompanying self and harmonically highly audacious in solo performance – this is, incidentally, a crucial jazz document demanding CD release, as is Verve's *The Genius of Bud Powell*. Powell played whilst tranquillised for much of the 1950s, and moved to Paris at the end of the decade where he appeared – adequately, and sometimes upliftingly – on the albums of other expats like DEXTER GORDON. Invited to work in New York once again in 1964, he never returned to Paris, and died in the States two years later. Five thousand people turned out in Harlem for his funeral.

★*The Bud Powell Trio Plays* (Roulette/EMI CDP 793 902-2)

Early Bud Powell can be heard on tracks like 'Floogie Boo' with the Cootie Williams band in 1944, but not on CD – this recording from 1947, is the first Powell-led session with Curley Russell, on bass, and Max Roach, on drums, plus nine tunes from a 1953 encounter between Powell, George Duvivier, on bass, and Art Taylor, on drums. The six-year gap between the artist at his most dynamic and at the beginnings of decline, is audible in the difference between the rhythmic complexity and alternately delicate and savage left-hand playing on 'Bud's Bubble' (1947) and the less ordered thoughts and darker colours of 'Embraceable You' or 'My Heart Stood Still'.

★*The Amazing Bud Powell, Vols 2 & 3* (Blue Note CDP 781 504-2, 571-2)

A CD of Volume 1, with its takes of the classic 'Un Poco Loco', is now deleted, but these are two fine Blue Note sessions; volume 2 featuring a variety of sidemen, and volume 3 the trio of Art Taylor on drums, and Paul Chambers, on bass. Volume 2 is notable for a sensational Powell original, 'Glass Enclosure' – a piece of constantly changing mood, from the vivacious to the sinister – and a typhoon of exultant bebop on 'Ornithology'. Powell the peerless blues artist is in magnificent shape on volume 3's 'Some Soul' (showing his cavalier disregard for the niceties of form by chopping the fifth chorus from twelve to ten bars) and 'Keepin' in the Groove'.

Raney, James Elbert 'Jimmy'

(Born Louisville, Kentucky, August 20, 1927)
Bebop led many guitar players to pretend they weren't playing
guitars – the textures the instrument was capable of were lost in
the rush to play speedy single-note lines and support other
musicians with the sketchiest latticework of chords. Jimmy Raney
is an electric guitarist whose melodic ear and empathy with the
instrument helped bop to sound like a natural idiom on it, his
methods lying somewhere between the song-like relaxation of
Lester Young and the chunky drive of CHARLIE CHRISTIAN. Raney
worked around Chicago and New York as a teenager, joining
Woody Herman in 1948, then playing in small groups with
excellent white beboppers like pianist AL HAIG before joining STAN
GETZ in 1951 (playing beautiful counterpoint with the tenorist on
the *Getz At Storyville* CD on Vogue VGCD 600093) and replacing
TAL FARLOW in the Red Norvo group a year later. The later Fifties
found Raney in low-key supper-club jobs, rejoining Getz in
1962–3, then dropping out for much of the Sixties. He returned to
touring in partnership with his guitarist son, Doug, from 1972 on.

Two Jims and a Zoot (Mobile Fidelity MFCD 833)

Raney in partnership with another fine guitarist, JIM HALL, in a
1964 studio session that also involved the unfailingly swinging
ZOOT SIMS, on tenor. Raney and Hall intertwine neatly on the
contrapuntal theme statements of several Latin-tinged pieces (the
bossa nova craze was still in evidence at the time), but the urge of
all these improvisors is toward a straight bop 4/4 and they turn
most of the material into this loping pulse as early as decently
possible.

Complete . . . In Tokyo (Xanadu FDC 5157)

Excellent Raney live set with the guitarist in breezing form on
some bebop classics, with fizzing support from Sam Jones, on
bass, and Billy Higgins, on drums.

Roach, Maxwell 'Max'

(Born New Lane, N Carolina, January 10, 1924)
Max Roach is the quintessential modern jazz drummer, the most

complex of all the percussionists to have emerged from the first wave of bebop and the first drum partner of CHARLIE PARKER not simply to stay afloat around him but actively push him to new heights. But he has almost as substantial a reputation as a campaigner, a teacher, and what Gary Giddins called 'a monitor of the music's best instincts', avoiding artistic compromise throughout his long career. Roach took his lead from Kenny Clarke, who built the first bridges between swing and bop and who advanced the then subversive notion of wilfully superimposing on-beat and off-beat accents on the basic pulse instead of maintaining swing's even four. Creating this ebb and flow of accent against a steady legato cymbal beat, brought more ambiguity and sense of organic flow into the music and it also elevated the creative role of the drummer. Max Roach went as far as to say that he wanted 'to do with rhythm what Bach did with melody'. Roach's playing often sounded like several drummers at work at the same time.

Roach was born in Carolina but was moved to New York at four. He rapidly took to music as a child and received his first drumkit at twelve, eventually studying theory and composition at the Manhattan School of Music. Like most of the rising generation of jazz musicians, he was drawn to the informal 'bebop workshops' at Minton's Playhouse and Monroe's Uptown House, meeting the leading bop pioneers. He was good enough to replace Kenny Clarke in Coleman Hawkins' band at nineteen, then working with DIZZY GILLESPIE, Benny Carter and STAN GETZ before becoming Charlie Parker's regular drummer from 1947 to 1949. Roach then became associated with Charles Mingus, recorded the celebrated 1953 Massey Hall concert with Mingus, BUD POWELL, Dizzy Gillespie and Parker, before forming one of the finest small groups of the mature phase of bop with trumpeter CLIFFORD BROWN. Brown's death in a road crash affected Roach badly, but he continued with a variety of fine brass players (DONALD BYRD, BOOKER LITTLE, FREDDIE HUBBARD and others), partnered SONNY ROLLINS on some of Rollins' strongest records, and in more recent times has experimented with choirs, with solo singers (including his wife Abbey Lincoln) string quartets and all-percussion ensembles with strong African connections. In the Sixties, Roach's vociferous civil rights campaigning had him blacklisted from studio work, and also produced one of his most striking records,

We Insist – Freedom Now Suite. Roach – who was the single most dynamic influence on Coltrane's partner ELVIN JONES – has remained open to post-bop developments in jazz, and performed in highly conversational duos with formidable avantists such as reed player Anthony Braxton and pianist Cecil Taylor. In his mid-sixties, he still plays with his old methodical fire, and is also Professor of Music at the University of Massachusetts.

Early work by Roach can be heard on much of the Savoy, and some of the Dial, recordings of Charlie Parker's in the 1940s. A good selection of his later work is available on CD, although his exciting 1979 percussion ensemble M'Boom unfortunately isn't.

★*Max Roach in Concert* (Vogue VG 600 032)

Live recordings from two concerts in the early days of the Brown/Roach unit, with guest performers Teddy Edwards, on saxophone and the percussive, metallic Carl Perkins, on piano, on four of the tracks. One of the best representations of the group at work just the same, with a thrilling extended version of Duke Jordan's 'Jordu', Bud Powell's 'Parisian Thoroughfare' and some memorable Clifford Brown trumpet on 'Tenderly'.

★*We Insist! Freedom Now Suite* (Candid CCD 9002)

Max Roach was joined by trumpeter Booker Little in 1958, who quickly proved himself the only fitting inheritor of the place in Roach's band formerly occupied by Clifford Brown, and developed one of his most telling bands by dispensing with a pianist and featuring himself, Little, the fleet and inventive saxophonist GEORGE COLEMAN and Ray Draper, on tuba. *Freedom Now* was conceived in collaboration with the singer Oscar Brown Junior (it also features Abbey Lincoln), and apart from sensational trumpet performances from Booker Little on the furious 'Freedom Day' and 'Tears for Johannesburg', draws a rugged, magisterial performance from a veteran Coleman Hawkins over the whiplash of Roach's drums, on 'Driva' Man'.

★*Birth and Rebirth* (Black Saint BSR 0024)

A duet between Roach and avant-garde saxophonist Anthony

Braxton from 1978. Braxton is a multi-instrumentalist of super-lative technique and theoretical interests that take in both jazz and contemporary straight music, thus frequently filtering the jazz tradition through very unexpected rhythmic and harmonic materials – but he exhibits a profound and at times subversive understanding of bop. Despite all their differences, Roach and Braxton struck up a spectacular rapport, the drummer's poly-rhythmic mastery complementing, pushing and echoing the saxophonist's labyrinthine runs and blurted, sharply accented dissonances at every turn.

★*Pictures in a Frame* (Soul Note SNCD 1003)

Roach's working hard-bop band with Odean Pope, on reeds, and Cecil Bridgewater, on trumpet, in a session that for once reverses the usual pattern of jazz groups sounding better in live perfor-mance than on disc. The band breaks down into sub-groups for much of the record, with Pope meshing thrillingly with Calvin Hill's bass on 'Japanese Dream', and Roach's solo drums trium-phantly confirming all the old virtues of melody-in-rhythm, on the dazzling 'Reflections'.

Rodney, Red (Robert Chudnick)

(Born Philadelphia, October 27, 1927)
Busy in the Forties big bands (Jimmy Dorsey, Gene Krupa, Woody Herman) before his meeting with CHARLIE PARKER, Rodney disco-vered bebop whilst in the trumpet section of Woody Herman's Second Herd, and his admiration for Parker's music led him to follow the altoist around until he eventually won a coveted place in the quintet when MILES DAVIS left. Rodney worked effectively with Parker through 1949, and in the mid-Fifties cut a memorable album displaying his vigorous and bustling style in partnership with multi-instrumentalist Ira Sullivan – *Modern Music from Chicago* (Fantasy, vinyl only). A combination of narcotics difficulties and busy studio work then kept Rodney out of circulation, but he resurfaced in the mid-Seventies with the renewal of interest in bop, recording good albums in Britain, Scandinavia and the States. A more recent collaboration with Ira Sullivan resulted in a

captivating album *Sprint!* (1982) which is currently, and surprisingly, unavailable in any format.

*Red Giant (Steeplechase/USA SCCD 31233)

Ten tunes from a Copenhagen session in 1988, in which Rodney is teamed up with a trio of two hard-bitten local beboppers and an expatriate American pianist, Butch Lacey. As a group performance it's variable, but Rodney's own playing is expressive, witty and thoughtful – over a wide-ranging repertoire that includes 'Greensleeves', Coltrane's 'Giant Steps' (rather unwisely, but maybe inevitably, taken at a dragging mid-tempo), and Waller's 'Jitterbug Waltz'. Rodney displays a nice bruised optimism on ballads.

Rogers, Shorty (Milton Michael Rajonsky)

(Born Lee, Massachusetts, April 14, 1924)
Always identified with the 'cool' West Coast jazz scene of the 1950s, Shorty Rogers was a punchy boppish trumpeter whose reputation in jazz was made as an arranger. Rogers' big-band work of the 1950s has stood up well, through a combination of careful craftmanship and determination to ensure that the cool style, however restrained, always swung. Rogers was raised in New York, attended the High School of Music and Arts (setting of TV series, 'Fame') and began working with vibraharpist Red Norvo in his late teens. He began to try his hand at arranging in the army, and when he joined WOODY HERMAN's trumpet section in 1945 he quickly made telling contributions to the repertoire of Herman's band-within-a-band, The Woodchoppers. But it was the second Herman Herd of 1947 that expanded Rogers' horizons and he began producing effervescent large-scale charts like 'Lemon Drop', 'More Moon' and 'Keeper of the Flame', including audaciously scoring a chunk of CHARLIE PARKER's 'Dark Shadows' saxophone solo as an ensemble figure for 'I've Got News'. Rogers left Herman for Stan Kenton's band in 1948 and though its unwieldy size and disinclination to swing were alien to him, he gained valuable experience scoring for Kenton's exotic instrumentations and formed a rich creative relationship with saxophonist ART PEPPER.

Rogers recorded first as a leader in 1951, but his finest album of the Fifties was *Cool and Crazy* for RCA two years later, original 10" versions of which now trade for astronomical sums. Rogers also recorded some rhythm & blues sides with local musicians (including GERRY MULLIGAN under a pseudonym) with a band called Boots Brown and his Blockbusters in 1952, but spent much of his time thereafter in the Hollywood studios. The Eighties saw him return to playing (often in partnership with saxophonist Bud Shank) and he has toured Britain, fronting the National Youth Jazz Orchestra.

★*Short Stops* (BMG/Bluebird ND 90209)

The essential compilation for Rogers fans. This set merges material from three recording sessions for RCA in the early Fifties, including the one that produced the *Cool and Crazy* material, and a set dedicated to Count Basie. The bands Rogers assembled for these encounters – including ART PEPPER, Hampton Hawes and MAYNARD FERGUSON – were the pick of the West Coast. Pepper is at his most rhapsodic on the ballad 'Buccy', Hawes is brisk and pearly on 'Diablo's Dance', while the Herman 'Four Brothers' saxophone sound is recalled by 'Boar-Jibu', and 'Short Stop' is a blues. The buoyancy of much of this music firmly counters the common contention that the 'cool school' was subdued, unemotional and never used driving rhythm sections.

Rollins, Theodore Walter 'Sonny'

(Born New York, September 7, 1930)
For four decades the irrespressible, garrulous and often subversive music of Sonny Rollins has dominated 'modern' jazz, and now that most of his powerful contemporaries have died he has become the most imposing survivor of the bebop era still fully functioning on the saxophone. Rollins' trademark from the mid-Fifties was a muscular, vibrato-less, frequently ironic (rather than proclamatory) style that in the course of a single unrehearsed solo could embrace blues, West Indian calypso (his parents came from the Virgin Islands), bleak, pebbly minimalism, alternated with mischievous manipulations of Tin Pan Alley doggerel, and

episodes of broad, rolling swing, highly reminiscent of Coleman Hawkins. Much of Rollins' entitlement to his lofty position in jazz lore is, however, due to the remarkable manner in which he makes all these odd bedfellows sound, for a few brief hours, as if they were made for each other.

Theodore Walter, or Sonny, was the only one of several musically-inclined Rollins children to display a preference for jazz over classical music. A saxophone-playing uncle introduced him to the blues, and by the end of the 1940s he was able to hold his own with some of the music's major artists. Rollins arrived in jazz at a time when the saxophone (which had only emerged from its rather mawkish and sentimental adolescence barely 20 years before) was dominated by three colossi – Coleman Hawkins, Lester Young and CHARLIE PARKER. By the end of the Twenties, Hawkins had shifted the subject of improvisations from the theme to the underlying chords and had toughened the instrument's usually plaintive sound with his craggy, booming tone. Lester Young preferred the earlier method, and had a soft, poignant sound, but his thematic improvising was inspired. The youngest of the three, Parker, borrowed methodology from Hawkins and phrasing from Young, but applied a completely different rhythmic sense to it that energised the music and created bebop, jazz's new form.

Rollins witnessed all this, but also espoused the popular, proto-rock 'jump' music of the 1940s; an early manifested enthusiasm for popular and dance music that remains with him. By 1951 he was forging a unique saxophone style that had Hawkins' Rodin-like weight, Parker's intensity and Young's melodic inventiveness – with more than a dash of the abrasive drive of DEXTER GORDON. The confection appealed to MILES DAVIS, who hired him. By the mid-Fifties, Rollins had encountered another major influence – perhaps his greatest – in the idiosyncratic pianist THELONIOUS MONK. Under Monk's influence Rollins' lines became more restless, his inclination to change direction in mid-solo more marked, and his appetite for fresh, uncliched material (however unwieldy) stronger. A penchant for developing improvisations from repeated melodic fragments frequently led him to take favourite standbys of jazz soloists and stand them on their heads.

In 1956, Rollins began working in the definitive hard bop group, that led by CLIFFORD BROWN and MAX ROACH, and it was with the latter (a drummer with as much musical curiosity as Rollins, and the technique to handle Rollins' cavalier displacements of the beat) that he recorded some of his most lasting work. But Rollins was buzzing so hard in the late 1950s that almost any setting would strike sparks off him – he recorded then with Monk, with drummers Philly Joe Jones and ELVIN JONES, and together with Roach and the great bassist OSCAR PETTIFORD, on the 1958 civil-rights dedicated, *The Freedom Suite*.

The rise of the avant-garde led to a two-year sabbatical from 1959 to 1961, while Rollins worked out his own solutions to the problems of form, and he returned with a sound even further away from orthodox bop, more wayward in construction and dependent on unconventional timbre and tonal distortion than ever. Though disinclined to rethink formalities as comprehensively as Ornette Coleman, Rollins nevertheless began working with two key Coleman sidemen (trumpeter Don Cherry and drummer Billy Higgins). Then finding himself still unconvinced that he had arrived at the method he was seeking, in 1966 he took a second and longer layoff, this time for five years.

Rollins in more recent times has become less intractable. Some of his recorded work of the past dozen years or so has veered toward the commercial (funk, more gentle ballad-playing than formerly, soul), but his mercurial musical mind has rarely slowed in live performance, constantly drawing on his encyclopaedic store of melodies and applying to them that personal chemistry that enables him constantly to re-synthisise the material.

★*Collectors Items* (Carrere 98406)

A showcase for Miles Davis and a moonlighting Charlie Parker (here 'Charlie Chan'), but featuring the Rollins of 1954 with the beginnings of his post-Parker development in evidence, already playing with a gravelly tone, with a growing rhythmic adventurousness and a fondness for amplifying sketchy motifs. Rollins dramatically demonstrates the latter tendency (prefiguring a later classic, 'Blue Seven') in the baleful, deliberate 'Veird Blues'.

★*Sonny Rollins Plus Four* (JVC/Fantasy VDJ 1524)

Actually the Clifford Brown/Max Roach band in March 1956, but with Rollins taking the leadership credits for contractual reasons. Brown's last recording, and the young trumpeter is in scorching form on Rollins' bebop original 'Pent-up House'. Rollins and Roach demonstrate their almost arrogant comfort with rhythmic adventures on the waltz-time 'Valse Hot'.

★*Saxophone Colossus/Tenor Madness* (Prestige CDJ ZD 002)

Probably Rollins' most famous album, *Saxophone Colossus*, of 1956, is the apogee of achievement in his work with Max Roach and a masterpiece of spontaneous composition. In addition to the energetic, elbowing calypso 'St Thomas' and an imperious version of 'Mack the Knife' ('Moritat') there is the prolonged improvisation on the bleak, mid-tempo 'Blue Seven', an assembly of brooding, staccato variations that Rollins' musical intelligence and control of shape turns into one of the greatest episodes of recorded jazz. *Tenor Madness* features Miles Davis' rhythm section of 1956, who find themselves appearing behind both Rollins and John Coltrane. The gig was a Rollins date, but Rollins asked a spectating Coltrane to participate in the two-tenor blues chase of the title. The session is fascinating both for Rollins' collaboration with a band that, like him, was moving away from strictly bop harmony, and for the catalyst of a drummer who imparts a nervous, precarious edge to most proceedings, the fiery Philly Joe Jones. Coltrane's music is still unsettled at this stage, and his dense, harmonically complex style is much more symmetrical than Rollins' – but as the only recorded encounter of the two tenor stars, a special session.

This two-for-one CD is an opportune combination of two of the finest sessions in modern jazz in one neat package, and a chance to compare Rollins at the height of his powers on recordings only a month apart.

★*Way Out West* (Contemporary CDCOP 006)

An example of Rollins' ability, during the late Fifties, to pull even musicians unfamiliar with his methods into his own erratic orbit. In this case, it is at a meeting with West Coast players in 1957. The two versions of the blistering uptempo 'Come Gone' – the first of which opens with Rollins swaying and curling over only RAY BROWN's bass, then accelerating to a mixture of boppish chord-running, blazing double-time and a preoccupied toying with perplexing phrases – are a tour de force, and a close second to 'Blue Seven', in which an initially stiff and tentative Shelly Manne is fired by Rollins' intuitive percussive sense to become twice the drummer he was at the start of the set. There are also generous helpings of the famous Rollins' fondness for transforming naff pop tunes, like 'Wagon Wheels' and 'I'm an old Cowhand'.

★*Night at the Village Vanguard, Vols 1 & 2* (EMI/Manhattan CDP 746 517-2, 518-2)

Experienced connoisseurs tend to agree that Rollins' most transported moments in live performance beat most of his studio work, extensive as the latter is, and this is an occasion from 1957 that supports the view. Freed by the absence of a piano from the inexorable march of the chords, Rollins is in roaring form with Wilbur Ware, on bass, and drummer ELVIN JONES – rhythmically unruly like Rollins, though restraining himself here. Rollins' brand of muscular whimsy is fully unfurled for 'Old Devil Moon' and 'Softly as in a Morning Sunrise'. The outstanding debut of 'Sonnymoon for Two' is on vol 2.

★*The Freedom Suite* (JVC/Fantasy VDJ 1520)

Another trio album, this time from 1958, with Max Roach back on drums and Oscar Pettiford on bass. The title is a dedication to black rights and the album is a mixture of a concentrated and committed Rollins – magisterial on the 19-minute title piece, his farsightedness about the development and architecture of a spontaneous composition rarely so controlled – and a detached and ironic Rollins, on the doodling 'Shadow Waltz'. Rollins is so much in charge of his materials on *The Freedom Suite* that he repeatedly creates tension by playing the notes of chords yet to arrive in the next bar, an audacity facilitated by a pianist's absence. A nervous Riverside producer bizarrely made *Shadow Waltz* the title of the session, in the Sixties, when the civil rights struggle was at its most heated.

★*Newk's Time* (Blue Note CDP 784 001-2)

Another session from the golden Rollins year of 1957, featuring

Philly Joe Jones, on drums, with WYNTON KELLY, on piano – but once again most notable for a piano-less episode, the extraordinary tenor/drums duet on 'Surrey with a Fringe on Top'. Rollins introduces the theme straightfacedly enough, then slows it to an indolent gait winding up as two bleary low notes oscillating diffidently, improvises in a mood between this lazy one and a barrelling double time (Jones' cymbals hustling furiously), travelling home calypso-style with the theme returning in a skewed, one-eyed manner. It's a magnificently wilful performance.

★*Quartets* (Bluebird/BMG ND 85643)

Rollins recorded six albums for RCA in the three years after his first comeback in 1961, *The Bridge* being one of the best known for its associated anecdote about Rollins being given to practising on the catwalk of the Williamsburg Bridge during his sabbatical. This CD includes 'Quartets', the bustling and convoluted 'John S' and a quirkily considered 'God Bless the Child' – all in the company of the gently lyrical guitarist JIM HALL. Good music, though the temperature is down compared to the 1957–58 work.

★*Sunny Days, Starry Nights* (Carrere 98152)

Rollins from the mid-Eighties, after the saxophonist had modified the frequency of his furious improvisatory flights to suit his more mature years, and expanded the amount of pop and funk in his work, in pursuit of a non-purist audience. Though most of his records since the Seventies have had their moments, none of them have had his Fifties and Sixties panache – but *Sunny Days* gets close. The rhythm section (including Mark Soskin, on keyboards and Tommy Campbell, on drums) is, not surprisingly, less flexible than Roach et al, but 'Mava Mava' is a vintage Rollins calypso full of erratically bending and straightening notes and 'I'm Old Fashioned' is a delightful gutting and dissecting of the Jerome Kern standard.

Ross, Annie (Annabelle Short Lynch)
(See also Lambert, Hendricks and Ross.)

(Born Surrey, England, July 25, 1930)
One of the few British born jazz artists, with careers beginning in

the early postwar period, to make an impact worldwide, Annie Ross certainly shared the then overwhelming (and inevitable) pressure on British musicians to replicate American music. But she possessed several qualities that were then uncommon among European jazz vocalists which made possible her transition to a wider stage. She understood instrumental improvisation, she could be spontaneous and swinging yet faithful to the spirit of a song, and she had immense confidence, often expressed as a coolness to the point of diffidence. With the Lambert/Hendricks/Ross vocal trio, she made a lasting, if minor, contribution to jazz history and the group spawned several imitators, most notably the 'vocalese' ensemble Manhattan Transfer.

Though born in England, Annie Ross was raised in Los Angeles, eventually studying to be an actress in New York. She came to prominence in the States in 1952 with a set of lyrics of her own to accompany the lines of Wardell Gray's tenor improvisations on 'Twisted'. Through the Fifties, she worked in France, the UK (with Jack Parnell and Tony Crombie) and America; forming Lambert, Hendricks and Ross at the end of the decade for a Basie-dedicated project and eventually touring the world's festivals with the group and winning international readers' polls on her own account. She left in 1962, freelanced and worked in TV (notably on the early 'That Was The Week That Was' satire shows for BBC), opened her own nightclub (Annie's Room'), acted and sang in productions of Brecht, and returned to New York in 1985, primarily as a singer.

★*A Gasser* (Pacific/EMI CDP 746 854-2)

One of only two Ross-led CDs currently available (the other is a rather lethargic set with GERRY MULLIGAN), this 1959 album finds the singer in both her trademark mood of knowing resignation on an illuminating version of Ellington's 'I Didn't Know About You' and in a less familiar mode of blazing directness on the aptly-titled 'Everything I've Got'. Saxophonist ZOOT SIMS, always an inspiration, plus driving drummer Mel Lewis help to give this excellent session its sparkle.

Rouse, Charles 'Charlie'

(Born Washington, DC, April 6, 1924; died November 30, 1988)

A tenor saxophonist of unusual tone and considerable rhythmic flexibility who managed to do what some more eminent saxophone players (including SONNY ROLLINS and John Coltrane) had struggled with – to successfully play with THELONIOUS MONK. Rouse and the wayward, uncompromising pianist performed together in a quartet from 1959 to 1970. Though pundits frequently questioned Monk's judgement in hiring Rouse, with hindsight the saxophonist proved to have been more skilful at creatively meshing with him than anyone else.

Like many talented bebop players of his generation, Rouse performed briefly in the saxophone sections of the Billy Eckstine and DIZZY GILLESPIE orchestras in the Forties, and followed that with employment by Tadd Dameron, Duke Ellington and Count Basie. Freelance work led to Rouse's partnership with Monk in 1959, and whilst, in the 1960s, Monk introduced far fewer new themes than he had in the previous decade, his quartets were often energetic and creative, and Rouse became an increasingly astute interpreter of some of the most pungent material in jazz. In the Seventies Rouse played with a quintet led by MAL WALDRON, another forcefully independent pianist, and then in the group Sphere, which dedicated its activities to Monk (Sphere was Monk's middle name) when the originator had retired from playing. In his last years Rouse sometimes performed in England with the local pianist Stan Tracey, a union that resulted in an excellent vinyl album *Playin' in the Yard* (Steam Records), and, as Rouse claimed, some of his most fruitful work since the years with Monk.

★*Epistrophy* (Landmark/USA LCD 15212)

Rouse in action a month before his death. This October 1988 session was a birthday tribute to Monk, and Rouse's rugged, unembroidered style, less forceful, of course, than in his Monk-inspired prime, is displayed on five classic compositions including 'Nutty', 'Blue Monk' and 'Round Midnight'. It's an oddly balanced band (Buddy Montgomery's vibes are a feature) and the acerbic quality of the originals fades a bit, but Don Cherry on trumpet is a musician whose structural quirkiness rivals Monk's own.

Rowles, James George 'Jimmy'

(Born Spokane, Washington, August 19, 1918)
One of the principal regrets a jazz-loving European might have for not paying extensive visits to New York over the past decade and a half is missing the opportunity to hear the pianist Jimmy Rowles unfurling jazz history in his favourite location, a night-club. Rowles is a walking encyclopaedia of jazz and American popular song, ingenious as an improvisor (remaking the most familiar materials in his own image whilst retaining their original piquancy) and all but unfathomable in the depths of his knowledge and recall of Tin Pan Alley's most dignified and durable achievements. Rowles' sparkling, Tatumesque, offhand dominance of the keyboard ought to place him, if not alongside jazz music's great immortals, certainly not far behind.

Rowles was living on the West Coast in the Forties, where he worked with Lester Young, Benny Goodman and Woody Herman and later Tommy Dorsey. A photographic memory for song-parts made him an inspired and buoyant accompanist, for example on later recordings by Billie Holiday, but this talent largely kept him in the studios and it wasn't until his move to New York in 1973 that he began to perform publicly with more frequency. In that year Rowles made an excellent album with STAN GETZ (*Peacock*, CBS, vinyl only), made trio albums for the Choice and Xanadu labels and recorded separately and with success with the great bassist RAY BROWN, with ZOOT SIMS, LEE KONITZ, and Stephane Grappelli. Rowles' daughter Stacy, a trumpeter, has also appeared with him on record.

★*We Could Make Such Beautiful Music* (Xanadu FDC 5152)

Jimmy Rowles, in the late Seventies, with a trio comprising George Mraz, on bass, and Leroy Williams, on drums. Some unremarkable tracks, 'I Can't Get Started' and 'In the Still of the Night', but Rowles' wit, full-bodied technique and Lester Young-like sense of thematic improvisation are at their jaunty best on a bossa nova version of 'Stars and Stripes Forever', Errol Garner's 'Shake it Don't Break It' and a tangential version of 'Here's that Rainy Day'.

Shank, Clifford Everett 'Bud', Jnr

(Born Dayton, Ohio, May 27, 1926)
One of many saxophonists who initially performed such a refined and seamless version of CHARLIE PARKER as to be written off as an insignificant imitator, reedman Bud Shank later toughened his style into a distinctive sound and became one of the most graceful and adept exponents of the difficult art of bebop flute as well. A clarinettist originally, Shank worked in the gargantuan, forty piece, big band of Stan Kenton in 1950, and became closely associated with the work of those Kenton alumni and others involved with the white 'West Coast' school. Shank appeared on early recordings led by trumpeter/arranger SHORTY ROGERS and also appeared in the Lighthouse Allstars band; like Rogers, he too disappeared into studio work for long periods to resurface, again with Rogers, for joint tours in the Eighties. Shank's music often veers toward pop (his pop album *Michelle*, with CHET BAKER on trumpet, was a chart hit) but he remains capable of stylish playing in the right company. He was a founder member of the LA Four in 1974, a group devoted to smooth, commercial bop.

★*At Jazz Alley* (JVC/Fantasy VDJ 1120)
Bud Shank's alto in its rougher, tougher 1980s guise on a live quartet set from a Seattle club. Not a revelation about this complex, underrated performer, but a fitful display of his bop roots and an occasionally successful struggle to throw off the habitual restraint of those studio years.

Shaw, Woody

(Born Laurinburg, N Carolina, December 24, 1944; died May 10, 1989)
Though he worked with most of the bandleaders of consequence in modern jazz, it is with a cooperative group commemorating a departed jazz scene – the Paris Reunion Band – that Woody Shaw is probably best remembered in Britain. Like many Afro-Americans devoted to bebop, Shaw worked in Paris in the Sixties with one of the idiom's founders, the inspiring drummer Kenny Clarke. The Reunion band was a frequently incandescent tribute to those days.

Not a first-generation bebopper however, Shaw was eleven

and just taking up the trumpet when CHARLIE PARKER died, and the hard bop cult – a version of Parker and Gillespie's ideas tinged with gospel and blues, and characterised by a brusque, unsentimental virtuosity – had already come to maturity by the time he was a teenager. (Shaw's father was a member of a Newark gospel group, the Jubilee Singers.) By then he had played extensively in high school bands and begun working with a local Newark musician, organist Larry Young – whose interests lay in a territory between jazz, funk and rhythm 'n' blues. The young Shaw worked around New York (at one point in a band led by Willie Bobo featuring Chick Corea) and then reed inspiration Eric Dolphy's until the latter's death on a Charles Mingus tour in 1964. The same year, Larry Young and Shaw went to look for work in Paris – finding it with Clarke, BUD POWELL and saxophonist JOHNNY GRIFFIN – and the next year the trumpeter's fondness for blues, of which he was a young master, took him into the band of a pioneering spirit of jazz funk, pianist HORACE SILVER.

But though Shaw was developing into a quintessential hard bop musician, his imagination repeatedly drew him beyond it. Like his contemporary FREDDIE HUBBARD, with whom he is often compared, Shaw possessed a glistening technique, a warm, enveloping tone, and the improvisatory foresight to make many choruses of variations on a theme sound like a developing entity rather than a series of alternative stabs at embellishments. Unlike Hubbard, Shaw was not transfixed by the commercial music industry, with the result that his work did not diminish into pyrotechnics played over MOR backdrops but genuinely sought to find new treasures in a much-plundered seam. Though steeped in the possibilities of improvisation on conventional chord patterns, Shaw had been influenced enough by the Sixties free scene to be convinced that judicious experiments with atonality could reveal new colours to songs, rather than simply negate or dismiss them. This curiosity didn't keep him in employment as steadily as Hubbard, however. Shaw even went into hibernation in San Francisco at the beginning of the Seventies, when jazz-rock's downgrading of improvisation in favour of rhythmic impact and electronics seemed to be at its most overwhelming – but when the public interest in bop revived in the late Seventies so did Shaw, and his subtle blend of bop harmonic technique and free-music borrowings gave his music considerable bite.

★*Imagination* (Vogue VG 651 600603)

Not a perfect representation of Woody Shaw's gifts, because the session is longer on expertise than atmosphere and it doesn't display much of the trumpeter's wilder side – but as a piece of neo-bop it's a good deal better than many of the recordings of the recently-graduated practitioners in the idiom. Shaw is accompanied by an excellent band (including the dramatic Steve Turre on trombone and Kirk Lightsey on piano) and on such bop trumpeter's classics as 'If I Were A Bell' he intriguingly handles the tune with a mixture of its faintly coy delicacy and sudden rocketing double-time ascents – giving it an ambiguity that's pure Shaw.

Shepp, Archie

(Born Fort Lauderdale, Florida, May 24, 1937)

Even twenty five years after the most intense activity on the black American jazz avant-garde, the reputation of *enfant terrible* still lingers around tenor saxophonist Archie Shepp. But at the time, Shepp's radicalism was more political and verbal than musical. He was both famous for his denunciations of the white-dominated establishment (one of his polemics in the jazz magazine *Downbeat*, elicited a storm of protest that was later reflected in a large reduction of subscribers) and for his solidarity with the civil rights movement, but his tenor playing had always been a rich mixture of forcefulness and romanticism. Shepp's influences included Ben Webster and Coleman Hawkins, as well as PARKER, ROLLINS, Coltrane and Ornette Coleman and he is a gentle and sensuous ballad player as often as he is a guttural and muscular exponent of what – in recent times particularly – has frequently been a particularly earthy and bluesy version of a hard bop repertoire.

Shepp was raised in Philadelphia, and began playing in the town's rhythm & blues bands as a teenager – meeting John Coltrane and LEE MORGAN in the process. In the late Fifties he studied drama, not music, and performed in *The Connection*, a celebrated play about jazz and narcotics. A partnership with the pianist Cecil Taylor occupied the early Sixties (Shepp clearly indebted to both Rollins and Coltrane in his solos on the now unavailable *Air* and *Into the Hot*), as did the formation of the New York Contemporary Five, with trumpeter Don Cherry among others. From 1965 Shepp began working with an increasingly restless and experimental John Coltrane, and the association with a musician of such eminence put Shepp indelibly on the map. Shepp's music and Coltrane's were jointly released on a 1965 album *New Thing at Newport* which, far from representing the furies of the avant-garde, actually consisted of an accessible blend of jazz, rock music, careful composition and spoken passages by the leader. A more celebrated collaboration was *Ascension*, Coltrane's expansion of his quartet by seven extra players in an attempt to find suitable compositional materials within which to house free collective improvisation. Shepp, more than all the others, deployed the most traditional materials of early jazz through his use of vibrato, vocalised sounds, and hoarse evocations of the blues, and he continued to develop these materials as a composer as well as a player (sometimes using the sound of street marches as well as rhythm & blues and free sections) with the subsequent *Fire Music* and *Mama Too Tight*.

Shepp worked successfully in France from 1969–1970, returned to the States and brought Motown into his music in collaborations with the singer Joe Lee Wilson. He also began a fruitful partnership with the trumpeter and composer Cal Massey on various projects that included a patchy attempt to blend jazz and African traditional music at a Pan-African festival and a theatre event dedicated to Billie Holiday. Through the Seventies, Shepp taught as much as he played (drama as well as music) and in the Eighties he has successfully toured with his own bands, increasingly committing himself to a rugged, sometimes savage bebop – except that Shepp doesn't use the term, preferring 'the baroque period of Afro-American music'.

Archie Shepp's most powerful and influential records *Four for Trane*, *Mama Too Tight* and *On this Night* are not currently available on CD, though another, *Fire Music*, is. (See below.)

★*Fire Music* (MCA MCAD 39121)

Extended works by Shepp in interesting company (trumpeter Ted Curson and saxophonist Marion Brown are featured) including two impressive testimonies, from 1965, to his developing powers as a composer – 'Hambone' and 'Les Olvidados' (The Forgotten Ones). The former piece uses folk songs, the buoyancy and simplicity of which are repeatedly badgered and bustled by the harshness of the soloists and complex shifts of metre; the latter (a reflection of Shepp's work with inner-city delinquents) conveys a powerful sense of urban dead-end existence through the leader's own passionate playing and Marion Brown's troubled alto sound.

★*Blase* (Affinity/Charly CDCHARLY 77)

A session from Shepp's year in France, this one recorded for the BYG label in late 1969. It finds Shepp, without his regular partners, united here with an assortment of those American avantists who happened to be in Paris at the time. This informality has mixed results – the collaboration with blues harmonica players Chicago Beau and Julio Finn is unsteady to say the least – but the gentle, unembroidered account of 'There is a Balm in Gilead' by Jeanne Lee's vocals, Shepp's caressing horn and Lester Bowie's trumpet is worth the disc. Drummer Philly Joe Jones connects surprisingly well, with Shepp and the Art Ensemble bassist Malachi Favors, on the formidable free-blow 'Touareg'.

★*Goin' Home* (Steeplechase SCCD 31079)

Archie Shepp and pianist HORACE PARLAN in duet from 1977 – the saxophonist's collaborations with this sensitive keyboard artist being frequently fruitful, *Goin' Home* more than most. The session is devoted to spirituals, performed in a selfless and unvirtuosic manner that keeps the original simplicity intact. 'Steal Away to Jesus', 'Amazing Grace' and 'Go Down Moses' are pure Shepp, but personalised by no more than judicious quirks of intonation and phrase.

Silver, Horace Ward Martin Tavares

(Born Norwalk, Connecticut, September 2, 1928)
'Funk' seems to have been part of the language of music for a long time, but fans of the notion might be surprised to discover that

one of its first uses in a song title was pianist Horace Silver's doing, as far back as the mid-Fifties, with the tune 'Opus de Funk'. Silver is a classic example of an artist who energised a new way of playing jazz by astute rearrangement rather than subversion of existing methods. Though a devotee of the work of BUD POWELL, as well as of THELONIOUS MONK, he avoided the streams of notes characteristic of bebop, linking Monk's percussiveness to those more forthright relatives of jazz – rhythm 'n' blues and gospel music – and also featured infectiously simplified theme statements that were more like swing than bop. Silver's development is closely related to that of ART BLAKEY (they were partners in the original Jazz Messengers), a musician similarly devoted to a brisk, blues-based music – and unsurprisingly, both men have become popular with the recent dance-jazz movement.

Silver's first high-profile work was with STAN GETZ in 1950, and the opportunity brought more prestigious accompanying jobs with Coleman Hawkins and Lester Young, then with MILES DAVIS and Art Blakey. In 1954, Silver's first recording band (with Blakey on drums) became the first Jazz Messengers, and the departure of tenorist HANK MOBLEY and trumpeter DONALD BYRD for the MAX ROACH/CLIFFORD BROWN band, encouraged Silver to form a new permanent quintet with Louis Hayes replacing Blakey on drums. Silver wrote prodigiously for the original Messengers and its successors, contributing to the jazz repertoire innumerable catchy blues ('Home Cookin', 'Filthy McNasty', 'Senor Blues'), ballads ('Calcutta Cutie', from *Song for My Father* is one of his best) and emphatic soul pieces like 'The Preacher'. Having featured many distinctive younger players in his bands over the years (including popular saxophonist Eddie Harris and the Brecker brothers) Silver still tours and performs, and has latterly formed his own record label, Silveto.

★*Horace Silver Trio* (Blue Note CDP 781 520-2)

Silver's 1952 and 1953 sessions for Blue Note, and intriguing examples of his evolution from Bud Powell. Already Silver was turning away from the onward rush of Powell's music, preferring to lag slightly behind the beat creating an air of laconic expectancy, hitting brusque single-note solos assembled out of short phrases against lazily banging chords in his left hand. Silver's fertility with fresh melodic ideas, drawing on the simple figures of blues and gospel music, was nourished by a method so dependent on the succinct phrase. 'Opus de Funk', is one of the disc's standout tracks.

★*Horace Silver and the Jazz Messengers* (Blue Note CDP 746 140-2)

The first edition of the Jazz Messengers in 1954, with the high-octane fuel provided by Silver's piano and Blakey's drums blasting an already vigorous band into space. 'Doodlin', a Silver original whose rythm & blues drive was given even greater emphasis on a Ray Charles recording, is featured here, as is the soulful, backbeat-driven Silver classic 'The Preacher'. KENNY DORHAM is on trumpet and Doug Watkins on bass.

★*Finger Poppin'* (Blue Note CDP 784 008-2)

A 1959 recording by what's widely regarded as Sivler's finest and most joyous band, featuring BLUE MITCHELL, on trumpet, and Junior Cook, on tenor, with Gene Taylor, on bass, and Louis Hayes, on drums. Mitchell and Cook meshed perfectly with Silver, their performances models of crackling economy and an awareness of when not to get in the way of the beat, and in addition to 'Juicy Lucy' and 'Finger Poppin', the fast blues 'Cookin' at the Continental' is one of the leader's most exciting performances.

★*Song for my Father* (Blue Note CDP 784 185-2)

One of Silver's best-known works, springing from a mid-Sixties session that (though less taut and insistent than the earlier recordings) produced the blues of the title, and the evocative ballad 'Calcutta Cutie'.

Sims, John Haley 'Zoot'

(Born Inglewood, California, October 29, 1925; died March 23, 1985)
Of all the saxophonists to have taken their lead from the poetry and persuasive diffidence of Lester Young's tenor, Zoot Sims was one of the most respected and affectionately regarded. He could

virtually swing in his sleep, his delivery was sleek and husky, and he conveyed an impression of both optimism and tenderness. Though overshadowed by the reputation of STAN GETZ, a white tenorist whose early career took much the same turns, Sims' loping, indefatigable style and wit was for many an attractive alternative to Getz' more fragile lyricism.

Sims was one of seven siblings born into a West Coast vaudeville family. He took up clarinet to join a school band when he was ten, and taught himself jazz by listening to the recordings of Coleman Hawkins, Chu Berry, Lester Young, Ben Webster and Don Byas. Sims acquired the nickname 'Zoot' when he joined an LA band led by Ken Baker and happened to be occupying a music stand with 'Zoot' written on it; after a succession of local gigs he joined Benny Goodman, and then Woody Herman after army service. It was in the saxophone section of the Herman band that Sims met a group of like-minded young reed players, Stan Getz, JIMMY GIUFFRE, AL COHN, Serge Chaloff and others, With Getz, Herbie Steward and Chaloff, Sims was part of the famous 'Four Brothers' ensemble sound – a popularised form of bop, since it blended the idiom's busy lyricism with the smoothness and more even accents of swing.

Bandleaders always wanted Sims, and he worked with Artie Shaw, Benny Goodman again, Stan Kenton and GERRY MULLIGAN (as well as taking part in Woody Herman reunions) before spending the later years of his life as an international freelance, often in partnership with a similar stylist, Al Cohn. He recorded the Prestige label's first LP in the Fifties (*Zootcase*, currently deleted in all formats), made many delightful records with Cohn, one with violinist Joe Venuti (*Joe and Zoot*, vinyl only), and recorded extensively for Norman Granz' Pablo label from the Sixties on. Sims also took up the soprano saxophone in the Seventies, avoiding its main drawbacks of unpredictable pitch and sour tone. Two ebullient collaborations with the great JIMMY ROWLES on piano (*Warm Tenor* and *If I'm Lucky*) are not so far available on CD, and neither is the excellent Count Basie collaboration *Basie with Zoot*.

★*Down Home* (Charly CDCHARLY 59)

Zoot Sims in 1960 with an excellent quartet, including Mingus sideman Danny Richmond, on drums, rolling through a selection of standards and blues on what's often taken to be one of the saxophonist's best sessions. His beat is insistent, his phrasing inventive and the general atmosphere exuberant from the opening 'Jive at Five' to the last note.

★*Motoring Along* (Sonet SNTCD 684)

Sims lyrically enmeshed with a frequent tenor partner, Al Cohn, on one of their most svelte and luxurious of sessions.

★*Somebody Loves Me* (Denon DC 8514)

Formerly *Nirvana*, a session featuring guitarist Bucky Pizzarelli and drummer Buddy Rich. Sims duets delicately with Pizzarelli on four tracks, Rich is surprisingly restrained, and the resourceful-ness of the leader's tone and phrasing – including the unexpected high register opening of 'Gee Baby Ain't I Good To You' and the shimmering romanticism of 'A Summer Thing' – is in full flow.

Solal, Martial

(Born Algiers, August 23, 1927)
An explosive French pianist whose style can reflect the orchestral pianistics of Art Tatum, the boppish monologues of BUD POWELL, and, at times, the trio methods (though rarely the meticulous contemplativeness) of BILL EVANS. Solal's performances are vigorous and muscular, witty and clear-headed, and he has been one of the foremost jazz pianists in Europe since his emergence in the 1950s, with a technique, harmonic knowledge and dislike of cheap effects and well-worn licks that entitle him to a bigger reputation than he has.

Solal was born of French parents in Algiers and moved to Paris in the Forties. In the following decade, he worked with the illustrious expatriate Americans living there, including drummer Kenny Clarke and the veteran genius Sidney Bechet – he also worked on Django Reinhardt's final recording session. In the Sixties, Solal's reputation took him to America, and he played the 1963 Newport Festival – a debut that led to further US trips and other international tours. The pianist also occasionally ran a big band, and has written much film music, for Jean-Luc Godard and others.

★*Live 59/85* (Accord/Musidisc 239 963)

Wide selection of Solal live performances, including work with his most forceful and suitable percussion partner, Daniel Humair. Uneven material, but a formidable display of Solal's firework-shows of whirling arpeggios, thunderous left-hand rhythms and admonishing block-chord playing.

Stitt, Edward 'Sonny'

(Born Boston, February 2, 1924; died July 22, 1982)
A brilliant saxophonist, unfairly burdened with the reputation of being a CHARLIE PARKER imitator, Sonny Stitt was one of the fastest and most accomplished of all bebop saxophonists; an independent explorer of bop's intricacies who, at times, turned his remarkable facility into something in the nature of competitiveness. An altoist at first, he switched to tenor at the end of the Forties to downplay the Parker comparisons, and for three decades proceeded to tour the jazz haunts of the globe firing fusillades of blistering improvisation at all comers. Stitt's virtuosity could border on the impassive and his performances could be unfaltering whether he was inspired or not. His life epitomised the headlong existence of the itinerant jazz soloist – moving from town to town, playing with unfamiliar rhythm sections, participating in hasty and sometimes characterless recording sessions. But on form he could be as good as anybody, his inventiveness boundless.

Stitt served his apprenticeship in the Forties big bands (Tiny Bradshaw's, Billy Eckstine's, DIZZY GILLESPIE's) and began leading his own groups at the end of that decade, recording with BUD POWELL, JOHN LEWIS, MAX ROACH, ART BLAKEY and many others. Between 1950 and 1952, after he had taken up the tenor, he co-led a band with fellow-tenorist Gene Ammons, and the two played with a demonstrative, conjuror-like virtuosity that was frequently hypnotic. Such skills brought Stitt on to the Jazz at the Philharmonic tours, showcases for such gunslinging music, and later Stitt came to work in bands formed specifically as tributes to the achievements of beboppers, the various Charlie Parker memorial bands, and the Giants of Jazz.

One of the most recorded jazz musicians of all time, Stitt was still working at full stretch (despite a good deal of discomfort from the cancer that eventually killed him) until a few weeks before his death. Frustratingly, Stitt's best work is not currently preserved in the catalogues, and virtually none of it is on CD. The best, absent, material includes the Prestige recordings he made in the early Fifties, the recordings with Gene Ammons, and the early Seventies *Tune Up* album with Barry Harris on piano.

★*In Walked Sonny* (Sonet SNTCD 691)

Stitt liked nothing better than stoking up the heat and on this Sixties get-together with Art Blakey's Jazz Messengers the pairing couldn't be more apt. Blakey is gleeful and relentless at the drums, and Stitt's horn soars. The repertoire includes a thumping 'Blues March' and a restless 'I Can't Get Started'.

Taylor, Martin

(Born Harlow, England, 1956)

One of the few British jazz guitarists to have won an international reputation, Martin Taylor specialises in a warm, relaxed blend of the swing players and the post-Charlie Christian beboppers. Taylor's solos develop with logic and clarity and his sound (he favours an acoustic guitar with a floating pickup) has an inviting glow that has made him a surprise commercial success in the United States.

Taylor took up the guitar at the age of four (his father was a dance-band musician) and he made his professional debut at eight. By his mid-teens he was working the cruise ships as an entertainer, at sixteen even sharing a QE2 voyage with the Count Basie band and sitting in with them. He formed close associations with the drummer Lennie Hastings, with bassist Peter Ind and guitarist Ike Isaacs, performing in London venues with all of them. But Taylor's big break came when he was invited to join the veteran violinist Stephane Grappelli, accompanying him on numerous American trips and demonstrating as sensitive an understanding of Grappelli as any partner he had had in thirty years. Taylor also appeared with many mainstream jazz musicians including clarinettist Buddy de Franco and cornettist Ruby Braff, and with non-jazz figures such as Yehudi Menuhin and Nelson Riddle. Taylor won the 'Artist Most Deserving of Wider Recognition' and 'Jazz Guitarist of the Year' categories of *Downbeat* magazine readers' polls in 1987 and 1988.

★*Sarabanda* (Gaia/USA 139018-2)

Taylor's only CD so far, and a major jazz hit in the States. Graceful, lyrical music bridging swing, jazz and soft pop, with John Pattitucci, on bass, Paulinho da Costa, on percussion, and a guest appearance, for one track, by Stephane Grappelli.

Terry, Clark

(Born St Louis, Missouri, December 14, 1920)
Enormously influential trumpeter, whose sound considerably affected the development of a St Louis brassman six years younger than him – MILES DAVIS. Terry brought the flugelhorn into jazz (it became a Davis trademark) and his playing is a colourful mixture of half-valve slurs, muted effects, whimsical bebop and immense rhythmic bounce, with the voices of those idiosyncratic trumpeters Charlie Shavers, Rex Stewart and DIZZY GILLESPIE at work on his style.

Terry came up in local St Louis bands but after World War II collected a string of illustrious employers including Lionel Hampton, Charlie Barnet, Count Basie, Duke Ellington (for eight years) and Quincy Jones. During the Ellington period (1951–59) Terry made several memorable contributions, notably to 'Up and Down' and 'Lady Mac' from *Such Sweet Thunder*. He was later employed as a staff musician by NBC for the 'Johnny Carson Show' (one of the first blacks to be hired for a TV house band) and occasionally featured on the show, with his blues-scatting nonsense song 'Mumbles'. Terry has worked extensively as a jazz teacher since, though periodically he has also partnered JOHNNY GRIFFIN, THELONIOUS MONK, Ben Webster, Oscar Peterson and others in a series of effervescent encounters, and has occasionally run his own big band. Terry is not well represented in terms of available CDs. A recommendable album by his own band, *Live on 57th Street*, is currently out of print, and a collaboration with Ben Webster *Happy Horns of Clark Terry* isn't on CD.

★*Oscar Peterson Trio Plus One* (Emarcy 818 840-2)

One of the trumpeter's best-ever records, though not under his own name. Terry saved many of his best recorded performances for other people's gigs, and he's outstanding on this 1964 Peterson date, with the pianist accompanied by RAY BROWN, on bass, and Ed Thigpen, on drums. It features Terry's celebrated technique of alternating phrases between the flugelhorn and the trumpet, here on 'Jim', some bristling instrumental solos and Terry's hilarious form of vocal blues gibberish 'Mumbles'.

Thielemans, Jean Baptiste 'Toots'

(Born Brussels, April 29, 1922)
Toots Thielemans is a musician too easily sidelined as a vaudeville act (he developed a bebop style for the harmonica and features a good deal of whistling in his performances as well) whose work is underpinned by an effervescent musicianship. His career has been a considerable commercial success since a world-wide hit with his own composition 'Bluesette' a lilting, lyrical and unjazzy theme, played on the soundtracks to many TV shows and movies (notably *Midnight Cowboy*, *Sugarland Express*, *The Wiz* and the childrens' programme *Sesame Street*). Aside from his excursions into mass popularity, Thielemans has an intimate understanding of bop, and a feeling for the harmonic intensity and fierce emotionalism of John Coltrane too. He is an unclassifiable performer.

Thielemans began his musical life on accordion, and took up harmonica when he was seventeen – but hearing Django Reinhardt turned him on to the guitar, and playing on American bases in Europe after the war brought an awareness of the new bop movement. Thielemans sat in on 52nd Street on a visit to America in 1947 and two years later met CHARLIE PARKER during the saxophonist's celebrated visit to the Paris Jazz Festival. He toured Europe with Benny Goodman in 1950, then went to the

States to work with Dinah Washington and George Shearing as a guitarist. After 'Bluesette', constant studio and movie-score work competed with his continuing desire to tour as a jazz performer. Nevertheless he did and his work with the late bassist Jaco Pastorius, on the currently deleted *Word of Mouth* album, contains a harmonica tour de force, 'Blackbird'.

★*Live in the Netherlands* (Pablo CD 20040)

Thielemans in top gear in 1980 in collaboration with a relaxed and elegant foil to his animated manner, guitarist Joe Pass. A jazzy set with, a strong dash of blues, a bebop workhorse 'Thriving on a Riff' and 'Autumn Leaves'.

Timmons, Robert Henry 'Bobby'

(Born Philadephia, December 19, 1935; died March 1, 1974)
Originally a BUD POWELL disciple, Bobby Timmons made his reputation by borrowing from both the clattering attack of HORACE SILVER and the pounding chordal style of Red Garland; a blend that he rarely seemed to forge into an entirely successful whole. But as a combination of urbanity and earthiness it was popular, its roots lying explicitly in black church experience. Timmons did go down in jazz history for the creation of a number of archetypal hard-bop classics, suffused with gospel motifs – like the insistent, playful 'Dat Dere' (to which Oscar Brown Jr put words) and the famous gospel-jazz theme 'Moanin', written while Timmons was with ART BLAKEY, in 1958.

Timmons came to fame with Blakey (having worked with KENNY DORHAM, CHET BAKER, SONNY STITT and CANNONBALL ADDERLEY previously) and recorded his particular brand of hard-driving and rather unsubtle music sporadically through the Sixties. His preference was for the trio – the setup he played with, in Greenwich Village bars, for most of the later years of his short life.

★*This Here's Bobby Timmons* (Carrere 98953)

A 1960 trio recording, the best of the pianist's albums from the

Sixties, and notable for a heated rendition of his trademark theme 'Moanin'.

Turrentine, Stanley William

(Born Pittsburgh, Pennsylvania, April 5, 1934)
A soul-jazz saxophonist who could also be an imaginative improvisor, Stanley Turrentine has mostly occupied the musical territory his bluesy sound mapped out for him. His father was Thomas Turrentine, a swing saxophonist with the original Savoy Sultans, and Turrentine Jnr served his apprenticeship with rhythm and blues and soul bands, working in the early Fifties with a Lowell Fulson group that included Ray Charles on piano. Turrentine worked with MAX ROACH in the late Fities, but during the next decade he moved increasingly toward more popular music, playing extensively with organist Jimmy Smith, ground that he has continued to inhabit since.

Straight Ahead (Blue Note CDP 746 110-2)

Exactly what the title suggests, a flat-out soul-jazz burn-up with Turrentine teamed with a remarkable lineup of like-minded performers in 1984 – Jimmy Smith on organ, George Benson on guitar amongst others.

Wonderland (Blue Note CDP 746 762-2)

The pop side of Turrentine, in which the saxophonist devoted himself to the music of Stevie Wonder, and even features Wonder himself in a harmonica solo on 'Boogie On, Reggae Woman'. It's more a display of Turrentine's soulful sound than an exploration of jazz improvisation, but the former gets plenty of air on the ballad 'You and I' and Wonder's own comprehension of the essence of jazz is intelligently emphasised on the session.

Waldron, Malcolm Earl 'Mal'

(Born New York, August 16, 1926)
Excellent and highly original pianist, with an instantly recognisa-

ble style. Waldron favours block-chord playing and a percussive technique, as well as being devoted to repeated, trance-like effects – all of which amounted to an interesting diversion from the mercurial qualities of bebop. For some years Waldron has operated as a bandleader and a solo artist, but his most illustrious employer was Billie Holiday, for whom he worked in the last two years of the singer's life.

Waldron was formally trained, specialising in composition for ballet. But in the early Fifties he performed mostly with blues groups, before joining Charles Mingus. Waldron became John Coltrane's pianist in the period after the saxophonist left MILES DAVIS, and he became closely involved with the Sixties avant-garde, performing with Eric Dolphy as well. Waldron settled in Europe, in the mid-Sixties, and has been busy as a film-score writer as well as a recording and performing artist.

★*Alone '86* (Paddlewheel/King K32Y 6167)

Good Waldron session bringing together the rugged purposefulness of Waldron with the volatile qualities of JACKIE MCLEAN's alto saxophone, on an excellent repertoire featuring four Waldron originals, and tunes closely associated with Billie Holiday.

★*The Super Quartet Live At Sweet Basil* (King K32Y 6208)

Where McLean is direct and fiery, saxophonist Steve Lacy is circuitous and crafty, and these qualities in Lacy are if anything a more appropriate foil for Waldron. They're also just right for another excellent choice of material, this time featuring pieces by both Waldron and Thelonious Monk.

Woods, Philip Wells 'Phil'

(Born Springfield, Massachusetts, November 2, 1931)
Woods was invariably labelled a Charlie Parker clone in the Fifties, but he has always been an intelligent and sensitive one, modifying the pure style with the atmospherics of earlier jazz in vocalised growls and bent notes. In recent years he has devoted himself to fresh and thoughtful variation on acoustic bebop (even to the

extent of turning the microphones off in many live situations), avoiding technical displays and bravura. Woods played with guitarist JIMMY RANEY in the mid-Fifties and then joined DIZZY GILLESPIE's big band, following that up with a key role as a founder of the Quincy Jones orchestra. Woods moved to Europe and broadened his original bop specialism with a looser and more accessible band, the European Rhythm Machine, but when he returned to the States in the early Seventies it was to return to more straight-ahead bop with a fine quartet with Hal Galper on piano. Though the excellent trumpeter Tom Harrell augmented the band from 1984, the original bite of the quartet was diffused. Woods nevertheless continues to be an energetic recording artist, as well as an active educationalist.

★*Birds of A Feather* (Polystar J33D 20003)

Fine Woods quartet session from the early Eighties, revealing the extent to which the altoist's tone had deepened and strengthened since his early associations with the CANNONBALL ADDERLEY school of Parker variation. 'Star Eyes' is a measure of the intensity and collective momentum of the band. 'Goodbye Mr Evans' a ravishing ballad display.

★*Gratitude* (Denon CY 1316)

An augmented 1986 band, less exciting and confident, but nevertheless sustaining a strong group feeling. Hal Galper is on piano, Tom Harrell on trumpet and flugelhorn, and the album supports a frequent reservation about Woods' recordings, that the balance of solos against ensemble sound and group momentum veered too sharply in favour of the former as the Eighties went on.

4

TURNING POINT:
THE SIXTIES AVANT-GARDE
AND BEYOND

AT THE BEGINNING of the 1960s 'free-jazz' sent a shock-wave through Afro-American music, which reverberated for most of the decade. For many of the players reared on bebop and its mutations, the idiom had become a treadmill of predictable chords and a devaluation of themes to mere decorations, hung on the beginnings and endings of a ritual procession of solos. Parallel to the development of the civil rights movement in America and a growing liberalisation of personal politics, the free-jazz movement prized collective, collaborative improvisation, perhaps with several horns intertwined to produce a 'group solo' not exclusively dependent on the inclinations of any one participant.

These weren't entirely new departures in jazz. Jazz music's early antecedents – like the shouts and field hollers of the railroads and plantations – were free, in their own way, because their practitioners had never known what their formal structures should be. And since the majority of New Orleans musicians were self-taught, their choice of notes and intonation followed few rules. The Sixties radicals pursued some similar courses. In many cases they attempted to behave as if bebop intonation already existed, but the harmonic structures it was founded on did not.

Jazz, in this period, was thus loosening its connections with harmonic principles inherited from Europe. The musics of other cultures were dependent on different intervals between notes, different perceptions of rhythm, different instrumentation, and this wider perception of how improvisation might be organised was influential in the work of several key avantists of the era.

Saxophonists John Coltrane and Ornette Coleman were the two most prominent figures of the movement, though multi-reed player Eric Dolphy, composer/bassist Charles Mingus and pianist

Cecil Taylor, were highly influential too. Both Coltrane and Coleman had played in rhythm and blues bands in their youth, but while Coltrane – an obsessive student of the mechanics of music and a powerful technician – quickly gained credibility as a virtuoso, Coleman spent much of the Fifties being accused of incompetence. The erratic and personal apprenticeship that Coleman imposed on himself gave him a highly distinctive vocalised tone, and a conviction that, as he once put it, the ultimate logic of improvising on a predetermined chord pattern is that a musician might just as well write the solo out and learn it note for note.

In 1960 Coleman recorded the album *Free Jazz*, and established its modernist credentials by placing a reproduction of Jackson Pollock's 'White Light', on the cover. A largely free exchange for two jazz quartets working simultaneously (one, Coleman's regular group, the other, a more boppish ensemble including trumpeter Freddie Hubbard), the disc inspired a generation, not just in America but across the globe.

In England, the West Indian alto saxophonist, Joe Harriott, was simultaneously working in a similar territory, the British Spontaneous Music Ensemble (galvanised by drummer John Stevens and altoist Trevor Watts) pursued forms of free-jazz inspired by Coleman, and similar angles were explored in Holland and Germany. And by the mid-Sixties a form of free-jazz, more dependent on explicit emotionalism, began to grip the sophisticated new rock audience in a way that Coleman's quirky lyricism had not. John Coltrane recorded *A Love Supreme*, variations on a simple, repetitive, chant-like spiritual theme, that sold a quarter of a million copies after its release in 1965. Coltrane later embraced free jazz more uncompromisingly, to the point where members of his own quartet began to be uneasy with the music, and he died in 1966, with his work only half done.

Many of the achievements of the Sixties avant-garde seem to have disappeared with the current postmodernist enthusiasm for the classic forms of jazz, and a prevailing distrust of 'self-expression' as inevitably indulgent. But this volatile period in jazz, though it produced much erratic and ill-considered music, generated a great deal of new vocabulary for improvisors and it's audible in the work of some of the most respectable classicists of today.

Ayler, Albert

(Born Ohio, July 13, 1936; died November 25, 1970)
No-one in such a short but intense musical career stirred things like Albert Ayler. Appearing on a scene already split over the merits of ORNETTE COLEMAN and CECIL TAYLOR, Ayler, with his honks and cries, seemed even more unnerving than they were. Just as the jazz public came to terms with this, his music became more formal, short solos being framed by passages of collective interweaving reminiscent at times of a New Orleans band. Then he changed again, aiming it seemed for the rhythm 'n' blues market he had once tackled, as a young saxophonist, with the blues artist, Little Walter.

A factor unifying all these changes was that Ayler never took the obvious route. From New Orleans dirges and marches to unfettered noise and then to Johnny Hodges-style balladeering, he found inspiration in areas of black music neglected by mainstream jazz musicians. He seems, in any case, to have been somewhat other-worldly. Titles from his early albums like *Ghosts*, *Spirits*, *Witches And Devils* and *The Wizard* suggest a leaning towards the occult (he was frequently an interpreter of spirituals as well). Even at his wildest, Ayler always paraded the virtues of a good tune, the catchy folk-melody of *Ghosts* being a prime example. On the other hand, his most celebrated quote about music was, 'it's not about notes any more. It's about feelings.'

Ayler, in uncompromising early form, can be heard on various albums from 1964, notably on, *Spiritual Unity*, with bassist Gary Peacock and drummer Sunny Murray, and on *Vibrations*, which is available on CD. Murray, Peacock and trumpeter Don Cherry, were in the quartet Ayler brought to Europe that year, believing he would get a more positive response for his music away from the States. He had already built something of a European reputation, while stationed with the US army in France, where he is reported to have been much taken with the military bands.

The collective style in its various guises lights up a host of exhilarating albums from the mid-1960s, including, *Bells*, *Spirits Rejoice*, and the Greenwich Village sides. The highly spiced 'Prophet', from, *Spirits Rejoice* – jazz meets the Posthorn Gallop – is a striking example of pure energy channelled through musical form.

Ayler's legacy survives today in the playing of David Murray and others, but his was never a way of playing readily copied. Rather, he encouraged saxophone players, by example, to develop power and stamina and to work on their own sounds rather than take those that come with the horn.

★*Vibrations* (Freedom FCD 41000)

The quartet with Cherry, Peacock and Murray, recorded in Denmark. Ayler sounds uncannily like an old-time New Orleans saxophonist, his tone rough around the edges and with an agitated, quivering vibrato. Bass and drums are faultlessly and unprecedently free in this context, Murray's rat-a-tat with undulating volume ('Ghosts') – his version of the Art Blakey press-roll – and shimmering cymbals ('Mothers') being patented trademarks. 'Mothers', is a beautiful and typical Ayler dirge, and even those whose tolerance level for honking and squealing is limited will find there is a great deal more detail worth savouring.

★*Live in Grenwich Village* (MCA/Impulse MCAD 39123)

Material from two live performances by the Ayler band in New York in 1967. The quartet is a showcase for Ayler himself, and Beaver Harris is splashily energetic on drums. While it's a fierce session at times, Ayler's ability to express a wide emotional range with simple materials, and his immensely rich tonal palette make his musicality clear with the benefit of over twenty years hindsight.

Coleman, Ornette

(Born Forth Worth, Texas, March 19, 1930)
Coleman had begun playing saxophone professionally in his teens, mostly in the blues bands popular in the black neighbourhoods of Fort Worth. Fascinated by the timbre of the horn, he would frequently practise tone colours on the same note all day, and developed in a local musical environment that didn't encourage distinctions between genres such as bebop, dance music, pop or rhythm-and-blues. The young Coleman thus developed an earthy, vocalised sound that had much in common

with the early blues musicians, a strong, danceable beat, and a good deal of the complex solo style of Charlie Parker, but cut loose from its chords.

Unlike most of the beboppers, Coleman was interested – as the earliest jazz musicians had been – in the song, not the song-form. He was composing attractive tunes with obvious roots in bop intonation and phrasing early on in his career, but saw no reason why improvisation on them should not compress or extend the melody, change its key, elect to make it exhilarated where it had been poignant, reflective where it had been purposeful – and suspend, into the bargain, the beginning-middle-and-end logic that even the most adventurous jazz musicians accepted as 'Natural'. The problem lay in making this reactive method useful to an ensemble without descending into chaos.

In the company of a number of like-minded players, including bassist Charlie Haden, trumpeter Don Cherry and drummer Billy Higgins, Coleman began to find the confidence to play small-group jazz in a more flexible manner, in which departures of line, rhythm and mood evolved organically, one performer picking up the ideas of another. After developing these techniques in the unlikely rehearsal space of a Los Angeles garage, Coleman suddenly shot to prominence as a result of two records made on the West Coast – *Something Else!* and, *Tomorrow is the Question*. He also attracted the attention of a number of non-jazz composers, including Gunther Schuller and Leonard Bernstein, since artists in both jazz and formal music were at the time looking for bridgeheads between the two territories – a fitfully successful collaboration sometimes known as the 'Third Stream'.

Coleman's artistry had grown out of his own peculiar self-generated apprenticeship, into a unique musical voice. But though he would play a blues, whilst abandoning the usual twelve-bar shape in favour of irregular lengths, or a Gershwin ballad, with its elegance rattled by dissonant squawks, tremulous sounds and impulsive runs, Coleman's variations on themes were not formless or random. They expressed the overlapping, contradictory ambiguities of life, with elation, desperation and the shades between constantly jostling with each other. Moreover, Coleman seemed to be saying, the episodes of a life have tidy endings only in fiction.

Coleman became a prophet of the 1960s movement known as

'free-jazz', some of which successfully interpreted his methods of ensemble improvisation, some of which was an incommunicative din. Coleman himself performed only sporadically over the coming decade, rejecting many concert and club offers as a one-man protest against what he saw as the higher economic and professional status accorded to his contemporaries in modern classical music. Coleman had long felt that the barriers between musical idioms were mostly erected by critics and social and racial caste systems, and had been happy to cross the tracks even in the early Sixties. His string quartet, 'Dedication To Poets and Writers', was performed in 1962, followed by the 1965 woodwind quintet, 'Sounds and Forms', and two years later Coleman won the first ever Guggenheim Fellowship for jazz composition. Moving in the other direction, toward dance music and the soul-derived funk idiom that became popular in the early 1970s, Coleman also managed to marry his spontaneous ensemble ideas (later dubbed his 'harmolodic theory') with this method of music-making too, deploying it in his electric band, Prime Time. All of these strands of Ornette Coleman's work are still audible in his, nowadays infrequent, public appearances. Many still regard him as one of the greatest, and most unpredictable, geniuses of the blues.

★*At the Golden Circle Vols 1 & 2* (Blue Note CDP 784 224-2, 225-2)

Ornette Coleman's brilliant trio – with David Izenzon on bass, and Charles Moffett on drums – on its European tour in 1966. Some of the finest Coleman soloing, and the best examples of his concept of how a contemporary jazz group should function, are apparent in these sessions. Though Moffett is an odd choice, Izenzon's bass playing is remarkable. Coleman's own creativity is displayed in most of its variations, atmospheric and evocative on 'Snowflakes and Sunshine', contemplative on 'Morning Song'.

★*Tomorrow is the Question!* (JVC/Fantasy VDJ 1364)

One of the early sessions that woke the jazz world up to Ornette Coleman. 'Tomorrow' represents Coleman's playing the way he originally envisaged it (his first recording, *Something Else* features a pianist) and the first authentic Coleman quartet displays the power unleashed by Don Cherry (trumpet), Charlie Haden (bass) and Billy Higgins (drums). Coleman's beautiful tone is at its most affecting on the intense 'Tears Inside'.

★*Song* X (Geffen 924096-2)

The mid-Eighties record that perplexed both Coleman fans and admirers of the guitarist Pat Metheny, though probably more of the latter than the former. Metheny had long been an admirer of Coleman's themes, and the two came together, not for a respectful skirting around their particular preoccupations, but a flat-out jam that didn't cramp Coleman and revealed the profound improvisational insights that Metheny's commercial pursuits often camouflage.

Coltrane, John

(Born North Carolina, September 23, 1926; died July 17, 1967)
With Coleman Hawkins and Lester Young, John Coltrane was the tenor saxophonist everyone sought to copy. He set new standards of technical excellence, and every switch in his style seemed to inspire a fresh wave of emulation. As the meticulous harmonic exploration, played with a vitreous sound hovering between Dexter Gordon and Stan Getz, gave way to a more billowy attack, it was as if the state of the art of saxophone playing changed overnight. When his music grew more abstract and he lent support to a new generation of improviser, free jazz became instantly more acceptable. After he took up the soprano saxophone, an instrument hitherto ignored suddenly found hundreds of takers.

Coltrane was a late developer. Three years older than Sonny Rollins, he did not make the same immediate impact on the scene. Growing up in Philadelphia, he was one of several local musicians who joined Dizzy Gillespie's orchestra in 1949. When Gillespie cut down to a sextet, Coltrane remained as the saxophone player and took the odd solo that found its way on record. Yet still he was barely noticed until he joined Miles Davis' 'comeback band' in 1954, and the increased fluency of his recorded work over the next two years justified fully the respect, bordering on adulation, he began to attract. After a year with Thelonious Monk and a further stint with Davis, he was the most talked-about saxophone player in modern jazz.

The later recordings with Davis, notably the *Kind Of Blue* album and some live recordings, set the seal on the first stage of his maturity. Once established as leader of his own quartet from about 1960, Coltrane was inspired by the powerhouse yet loose-limbed drumming of Elvin Jones, towards a freer approach, with no loss of intensity. The modal vamping exemplified by his version of 'My Favourite Things', a big seller on record and the first important example of his style on the soprano saxophone, and the supercharged, semi-abstract blues, 'Chasin' The Trane', signalled new avenues of exploration that converged on his major composition for the quartet, 'A Love Supreme'.

Restless at the prospect of capitalising on his achievements, Coltrane gradually broke up his group. He championed musicians like Archie Shepp and Pharoah Sanders, and most of his work subsequently paid more than lip-service to the cause of free improvisation. Twenty years on, many would agree he died before this part of his career was fully resolved. Certainly, there are few individual moments, from this final period, to number among his greatest solos, and an overall sense of direction is hard to discern. But whatever the verdict, there can be no dispute over 'Flamenco Sketches', 'Blues Minor', 'I Want To Talk About You', and all the other masterpieces from earlier times.

★*Giant Steps* (Atlantic/WEA 7813372)

Recorded in 1959, this album set the seal on the first stage of Coltrane's career. Tunes like the blues 'Mr PC', and the ballad 'Naima', have become standards (the latter one of many Coltrane ballads that chill the spine when caressed at slow tempo) and the melodies of 'Spiral', and 'Syeeda's Flute Song' are unforgettable. *Giant Steps* (and its more aggressive blood-relative, *Countdown*) provides the historical significance. Hurtling through an ever-shifting harmonic background, Coltrane laid down the kind of challenge that few could match at the time.

★*Africa Brass 1 & 2* (Blue Note MCA MCAD 42001)

A 1961 performance by a Coltrane group augmented to fourteen pieces, including trumpeter Freddie Hubbard and reed player ERIC DOLPHY in addition to the regular lineup. Dolphy did much of the orchestration work for this powerful session, but Coltrane's own performances here are often regarded as being amongst his most powerful. One of the Coltrane band's most familiar devices, the repeated rhythmic figure, is the compulsive heatbeat of 'Africa', and underpins some sensational percussion work from Elvin Jones. An early outing for Coltrane's soprano saxophone is featured on 'Greensleeves'.

★*Blue Train* (Blue Note CDP 746 095-2)

One that Coltrane, for a while at least, counted as personal favourite – and it featured the side of Trane also audible on his work with Miles Davis around the same time (see Miles Davis), namely an attempt to break the stranglehold of measured bop solos over cycles of chord patterns that was stifling development, by packing the harmonies with ever more concentrated doses of musical high-explosive until they burst, showering listeners with blazing cinders of notes. *Blue Train* features Lee Morgan, on trumpet, and one of the most swinging of all drummers, Philly Joe Jones.

★*A Love Supreme* (MCA DMCL 1505)

A Love Supreme, is the album that most remember Coltrane for – a four-part devotional work featuring his finest band (with Elvin Jones, McCoy Tyner and Jimmy Garrison). On CD, in particular, Jones' drum sound – a wild and elemental display of astonishing polyrhythmic playing that embraces soloists and bears them aloft – washes all over you, and its appropriateness to the mood of Coltrane at the time, a kind of manic trance, becomes more apparent than ever.

Dolphy, Eric

(Born California, June 20, 1928; died June 29, 1964)
Eric Dolphy remains the only jazz musician to stand out as a soloist on no less than three instruments. Even today, anyone

who plays bass-clarinet has Dolphy's legacy to reckon with. Flautists of the calibre of James Newton dedicate compositions to him. The wide intervals, carried off through his exceptional fluency on the alto saxophone (what English saxophone virtuoso Evan Parker describes as having 'instant access to any part of an extended range at any moment') live on in the work of Anthony Braxton and Bennie Wallace. Above all, time has taken nothing from the vivid expressiveness that imbued everything he touched.

Brought up in Los Angeles, Dolphy played lead alto and recorded with the Roy Porter big band in 1949. He made his first impact, outside California, when he joined Chico Hamilton's quintet, in 1958, in time to appear in the film, *Jazz on A Summer's Day*. The first recording under his own name, *Outward Bound* (1960), was packaged in a futuristic style as if Prestige Records were setting him up as a rival to ORNETTE COLEMAN, then very much the talk of the jazz world. Dolphy did record with Coleman and contribute to the spread of free jazz, but he was never exclusively identified with it.

As a sideman, Dolphy will forever be linked with CHARLES MINGUS, touring with him several times in the early 1960s and taking a leading role on the seminal recording of *Mingus Presents Mingus*. He also added an extra voice to John Coltrane's quartet (the one with McCoy Tyner, Jimmy Garrison and Elvin Jones), while also finding time to appear on important recordings of the period by George Russell (*Ezz-thetics*), Max Roach (*Percussion Bitter Sweet*) and Oliver Nelson (*Blues And The Abstract Truth*). He also joined with Ornette Coleman on John Lewis's *Jazz Abstractions* album: at a concert in 1963, he even performed the featured saxophone part on 'Abstraction', a piece that straight composer Gunther Schuller had designed with Coleman in mind.

Recordings of several concerts, mainly European, have been issued since Dolphy's death and add to the general perception of the qualities of one of the great jazz soloists of the past thirty years. With his bird calls on flute, galumphing squawks on bass-clarinet – once described as the sound of someone trying to swallow the instrument – and impossible intervals expertly negotiated on the saxophone, Dolphy, by all accounts gentle and unassuming away from the stand or the recording studio, comes across in music as being very much larger than life.

★*At The Five Spot 1 & 2* (JVC/Fantasy 1504/1525)

A partnership that achieved much in a very short time was the pairing of Eric Dolphy and trumpeter Booker Little. Both highly advanced in the ways of music and both consummate technicians, they complemented the other to perfection because each inhabited a different emotional terrain. Where Dolphy was all fire and brimstone, Little coaxed an exceptionally plangent sound from the trumpet that was unique (echoes of it persist today in the playing of Canadian expatriate Kenny Wheeler). 'Fire Waltz', and the delightfully relaxed, 'The Prophet', stand out on this live recording from 1961, which also includes Mal Waldron on piano, Richard Davis on bass and Ed Blackwell at the drums.

★*Out To Lunch* (Blue Note CDP 746 524-2)

Out to Lunch came top in *Wire* jazz magazine's recent readers' polls, maybe surprisingly – and perhaps a reflection of the cachet that Blue Note records now have as an emblem of designer hipness, which is no bad thing. *Out to Lunch*, was Dolphy's last recording, and the sound of his flute here – particularly on 'Gazelloni', is a graceful reminder of how much his playing on the lighter instrument differed from his rather guttural, jagged investigations of the bass-clarinet.

Mingus, Charles

(Born Arizona, March 22, 1922; died January 5, 1979)
Outstanding both as composer and instrumentalist, Charles Mingus was a big man with character to match. Often bracketed alongside Duke Ellington, who was once briefly his employer, and with a host of orchestral works to his credit, his genius was perhaps realised more consistently in smaller groups. Melodies unfolded in self-generating spirals while Mingus controlled the performance through his own playing, bolstered at times by shouts and gestures that could by turns encourage or threaten. As a bass player, he set new levels of solo virtuosity. Younger musicians can match him for speed and technique, but few impose such an overwhelming personality upon their music.

Mingus was brought up in Los Angeles, where he played at

different times with the bands of Louis Armstrong and Kid Ory. An unusual beginning for an alleged iconoclast, but it explains his strong sense of tradition and the way his mature music largely bypassed the modernistic tendencies of the 1940s. After making his reputation with Lionel Hampton and Red Norvo, he dropped out, in the early 1950s, when jazz was hit by a slump. Legend has him working for the Post Office, from which he is rescued by the encouragement of Charlie Parker.

Various experiments reached mature fulfilment in his 1956 recording, *Pithecanthropus Erectus*. From this point, Mingus produced those albums – among them, *East Coasting*, *Blues And Roots*, *Tijuana Moods*, *Mingus Presents Mingus*, and, *Black Saint And The Sinner Lady*, – on which his reputation will stand. The moods ranged from the satirical to the gently brooding; from unabashed gospel to unconcealed violence.

Inactivity and apparent decline was followed, in the 1970s, by a comeback sufficiently pronounced to suggest Mingus had climbed new peaks. Unfortunately, illness eventually stopped him playing and restricted him to orchestral work and to writing pieces for a group led by his long-time drummer, Dannie Richmond. Since his death, a mammoth big-band score called, 'Epitaph', fragments of which he had recorded in 1962, was discovered and literally pieced together by Gunther Schuller: a public performance in 1989 was preserved for television and ultimately released as an album.

★*New Tijuana Moods* (Bluebird/BMG ND 85644)

This disc contains both the original, *Tijuana Moods*, and material not issued before. It seems that, at the time, either Mingus or the record company spliced contrasting bits and put them together for the original release. The results are included here alongside the unedited and unissued versions, which not surprisingly are longer and contain expanded solos. These 'Mark Two' pieces compare, on the whole, very favourably: the leeway given to each individual more than compensates for any loss of drama. For instance, 'Los Mariachos', the most elaborate composition, benefits from an extra slice of Jimmy Knepper's impassioned trombone, always worth hearing at length.

★*Black Saint And The Sinner Lady* (MCA MCAD 5649)

Mingus's major orchestral work, certainly up to that time.

Recorded in 1963 with an eleven-piece band and using overdubbing in ways almost unheard of for jazz albums, *Black Saint* exorcises the debt to Ellington. The flashing brass, the gruff rumblings of the saxophones and Quentin Jackson's growling on trombone are all Ducal standbys, as are Charlie Mariano's echoes of Johnny Hodges. Against this the thematic material, such as the Mexican fanfares on, 'Mode D', and the convoluted rhapsodising on, 'Mode E', could come only from Mingus, while the feverishly up-front emotional cast provides another indelible link. *Black Saint*, very loosely, is a suite with themes and motifs from the first three movements being developed in the final three. Mariano, who takes a leading role throughout, gives a tremendous performance.

★*Pithecanthropus Erectus* (WEA/Atlantic K781 456-2)

A high-spot of Charles Mingus' recorded output, made in the mid-50s and featuring the altoist, Jackie McLean. All of the medium-to-big jazz bands that have opted for the organic interweaving of semi-improvised lines rather than the military precision of tight section playing (later Gil Evans, most recently Loose Tubes) owe a great deal to the wayward genius of Mingus, who combined a rough-hewn soulfulness and gospel-like drive with the speedy eccentricities of excellent bebop soloists. McLean is pushed almost to distraction by the heaving, surging blurs and smears of sound that Mingus draws from his band and – though the stops and starts and restless changes of time have come, over the years, to convey more indecisiveness than 'modern-times' sound effects – the vigour, anger and independence of Mingus' music still blares uncompromisingly at you.

Taylor, Cecil Percival

(Born New York, March 25, 1932)
Pianist Cecil Taylor's apprenticeship in the 1950s took in Stravinsky, Bartok and Elliott Carter inside the prestigious New England Conservatory, and Monk, Bud Powell and Duke Ellington outside it. He now belatedly receives an enthusiastic response from the academic music establishment, but it's no more than what might have been his due a quarter-century ago. Mikhail

Baryshnikov, who danced to Taylor's music on a series of concerts in the States at the end of the Seventies, spoke glowingly of the pianist revealing to him 'another dimension about dancing to music'. He has also been called 'the Art Tatum of the avant-garde'.

Taylor is of the generation of JOHN COLTRANE, ORNETTE COLEMAN, CHARLES MINGUS and ALBERT AYLER, the musicians who treated bebop as a starting point rather than a destination, and who reforged jazz history with a boldness that has not been repeated by any movement since. In some respects, because of his scalding speed, melodic density and the relentlessly high pressure of his attack, Taylor came to be regarded as the hottest potato of the lot. This status meant that, for years, his principal employment was as a dishwasher, ironically enough in the very New York jazz clubs that wouldn't let him on the bandstand. For a while, it seemed only the fulfilment of the inevitable. Though he had been able to play difficult classics at seven, and his mother was a devoted Duke Ellington fan, Taylor had always been told at home that a career in music was no life for a favoured son.

Despite the setbacks of his early musical career, Taylor never lost the conviction that what he was doing (modifying the notion of swing, improvising without chord patterns, spontaneously composing with the timbres and intonations of jazz, but with some of the devices of conservatoire music as well) was right no matter what. As well as his classical influences, early Taylor reveals recognisable elements of Bud Powell, Horace Silver and Duke Ellington, and the pianist himself acknowledges a debt to Dave Brubeck too. After appearing with small groups featuring swing and bebop players in the early Fifties, Taylor quickly set to building the more dense, multi-layered and multi-cultural sound his mixed training had enabled him to hear in his head, and he involved an ex-New Orleans soprano player, Steve Lacy, in the pursuit. By the end of the Fifties, Taylor had something of a reputation as a fascinating curiosity, but the arrival of Ornette Coleman eclipsed him and he spent most of the Sixties in obscurity, occasionally playing – more often in Europe – with other avantgardists such as Archie Shepp and Albert Ayler.

In the later Sixties, Taylor became a powerful force in New York's Jazz Composers Guild, later working spectacularly on a Jazz Composers' Orchestra recording of Mike Mantler's 'Communications'. Working more regularly with a sensitive and perceptive altoist, Jimmy Lyons, Taylor's opportunities increased as his early achievements seemed clearer with hindsight. He also became active in jazz education, and worked extensively with ballet dancers.

★*Unit Structures* (Blue Note CDP 784 237-2)

Some of Taylor's richest and most engaging music, as well as some of his most personal and oblique. These 1966 recordings featured Alan Silva on bass and Jimmy Lyons on alto, and the title of the album was an accurate reflection of Taylor's methods, organising his thematic material in overlapping blocks. Jimmy Lyons' alto melodies in the best track on this disc – 'Enter Evening' – highlight the empathy and intensity of the group.

★*Conquistador* (Blue Note CDP 746 535-2)

This album was made in 1966 when Taylor was already a musical typhoon, but with the passage of the years, much of what drove some listeners to put their hands over their ears now seems logical, bursting with energy and some of the most constructive collective interplay of the entire movement. Hardly anybody could work with Taylor – his stamina has always floored most partners, his hailstorms of notes unmatchable with complementary solos and his concept almost a personal secret – but his partners here number those who did find a way in, like Jimmy Lyons, on alto, Alan Silva, on bass and Andrew Cyrille, on drums.

★*In Berlin '88* (FMP CD 11 discs)

Strictly for Taylor nuts, and rich ones at that, but for those with the wherewithal, an extraordinary display of the riches and potential of free improvisation. The German label recorded Taylor with a variety of European improvisors including guitarist Derek Bailey, drummer Han Bennink (an inspired collaboration), cellist Tristan Honsinger and saxophonist Evan Parker. Taylor's receptiveness and his encouragement of his varied partners defies much of his reputation for intransigence.

5

THE JAZZ RENAISSANCE:
FROM FUSION TO WORLDBEAT

THE AVANT-GARDE badly frightened the music industry. Even former admirers of jazz were concerned that the demands of such unorthodox music were bewildering, or downright alienating, to a substantial slice of potential audiences. And in the Sixties, there was certainly no lack of alternatives to jazz. The new breed of virtuoso rock guitarists, including Jimi Hendrix, Eric Clapton, Carlos Santana and Jimmy Page, appeared to offer plenty of improvisational thrills and technical fireworks, and they were fashionable as well. Bands like Steely Dan and Blood Sweat and Tears used explicit jazz materials. In the face of all conquering rock and pop, older notions of what jazz was didn't seem relevant any more. Though the 'mainstream' of rejuvenated or preserved earlier styles (now including hard bop) did continue, and free jazz protected itself and continued to develop in isolated pockets around the world, the version of jazz that made the biggest impact in the late Sixties and early Seventies was the one that linked itself to rock music, or, as it became known, 'fusion'.

Exponents of this hybrid explained the new arrival with a good deal of reference to expressions like 'communication' and 'body music' – recalling earlier forms of jazz that had unquestionably reached much wider audiences than either bebop or free music. Jazz appeared, at first, to be recovering its health and vigour, by rejecting introspection, and by seeming to recapture the era of the 'jiving' and 'jump' bands that had grown out of swing. But the reforged music of the Sixties and Seventies *was* a different story. It made use of new electronic instrumentation, particularly electric double-basses, amplified drums, and, for Miles Davis, an electronic trumpet. It also attempted to create a new kind of jazz that blended extensive improvisation with highly decorative versions of rock and funk rhythm playing.

In 1970, Davis released a key fusion record – *Bitches' Brew*. A fusion band called Weather Report was formed from a nucleus of some ex-Davis sidemen. British guitarist John McLaughlin (who had also played with Davis) formed a more conventionally melodic and less electronic band called the Mahavishnu Orchestra. Following these, George Benson, a brilliant jazz guitarist, became a soul singer-guitarist and had massive hit records. Fine instrumentalists like pianists Chick Corea, Herbie Hancock and George Duke, guitarists McLaughlin and Larry Coryell, drummer Billy Cobham, even the great saxophonist Sonny Rollins, began playing funk. As had frequently been declared in the music press throughout the idiom's history, jazz appeared to have passed away. But the reign of this kind of fusion hasn't lasted. Though 'crossover' music, as it is sometimes known, still flourishes (some record labels, like GRP, are devoted to it) even its vaunted danceability and funkiness has frequently come to seem dated and corpulent, by comparison with the urgent crackle of a contemporary dance form, like rap. As for jazz, salvation came with a wave of young, but tradition conscious, performers who worshipped the heroes of the bebop era and yet were able to communicate directly with a new, unprejudiced jazz audience in the Eighties.

The Jazz Renaissance

In autumn 1990, *Time* magazine put a picture of trumpeter Wynton Marsalis on its cover and heralded 'The New Jazz Age'. Record companies are now reissuing their jazz back-catalogues as fast as they can blow dust off the tapes and convert the contents into digits. New venues surface in the jazz listings weekly. After years of relegation to an audience of consenting adults in private, or absorption into anonymous fusion idioms, full-blooded jazz has become acceptable public entertainment again. Closet-enthusiast film-directors (Bertrand Tavernier with *Round Midnight*, Clint Eastwood with *Bird*, Bruce Weber with *Let's Get Lost*) have even risked serious money on it, though reducing the odds by making their key characters the oldest of jazz clichés, the self-destructive intuitive genius. The word 'jazz' might now be applied – in any week in London – to salsa bands, hip hop bands, bebop bands, blues bands, standards-singers, free improvisers in back rooms, dub poets, New Orleans revivalists. Free music, at one time having avoided recognisable tunes or tempos as if they were viruses, now quotes them, if sometimes ironically. Bebop and its forerunners are revered as classical forms. Young New Orleans trumpeter Marsalis has dedicated himself to preserving and championing and uprating some of the earliest traditions of jazz. Some outfits – like the British, Loose Tubes, and the black American one, Art Ensemble of Chicago – even combine large chunks of the music's history and contemporary forms, in the course of a single show.

Some inexorable creative forces of the Afro-American strand continued to flower. Miles Davis recorded a good deal during the Eighties despite illness, starting patchily with half-hearted disco music, but displaying occasional flares of his old lyricism against the breathless, restless rhythmic counterpoint of funk-based rhythm players. And the dominance of rhythmic invention as the driving force in much new jazz is confirmed by one of the brightest stars of the era, New York altoist Steve Coleman, who recorded a good deal of his own street-corner music for funkers and rappers to considerable impact, though most clearly audible as an orthodox jazz soloist in his work with bassist Dave Holland's neo-bop band. Coleman is part of a New York group of musicians (M-Base) including pianist, Geri Allen, and singer, Cassandra Wilson, who are certain to make a big impression on the developing jazz of the Nineties, and they've already made a big impression on many of the players of their own age currently emerging in Europe.

In Britain, the Jazz Renaissance began with black youth with time on their hands, in a period of high unemployment, developing styles of dancing that fitted even the fastest tempos of bebop. A film, *Absolute Beginners*, made in Britain, featured some of these dancers and with a score composed by Gil Evans. A young London tenor saxophonist, Courtney Pine, had a bestselling album with a mixture of the hard, incantatory style of the classic John Coltrane quartet and elements of hard bop. Contemporary with Pine came another young black saxophonist, Steve Williamson, a musician of dedication, broadmindedness, curiosity and technique. A skilled Asian composer and trombonist, Fayez Virji, also appeared in London – a dominant member of an exciting, largely black, big band called Jazz Warriors. A West Country saxophonist who had cut his teeth in fusion bands and music theatre, Andy Sheppard, not only made a mark on his own account but began to be hired on prestigious orchestral assignments with major American composers Carla Bley and George Russell.

The older notion of 'fusion' still survives. It remained dominant through stars like the highly inventive tenorist Mike Brecker and guitarist Pat Metheny until the early Eighties; and even now Miles Davis continues to lead powerful fusion groups and make memorable records. But bebop has come back in the neo-classical revival of the current era, symbol of a kind of polished, techno-cratic elegance. Less formalised jazz continues to be heard – free-improvised music still has a small but increasingly knowledgeable audience all over the planet, with musicians as diverse as the still dazzling, veteran pianist Cecil Taylor and British pianist Alex Maguire, imposingly delivering it. And the 1990s will certainly see a continuing, international strengthening of indigenous (some-times jazz-flavoured, sometimes not) improvising styles, through the work of the resourceful new musicians beginning to be heard from both familiar homes of jazz and less familiar ones like Russia, Bulgaria, India.

Abercrombie, John L

(Born Portchester, New York, December 16, 1944)
Abercrombie is in the front-rank of post-bop jazz guitarists, the ones whose styles were formed from a combination of the clean, swinging sound of Charlie Christian-derived bop and the gravelly bluesiness emerging from the Sixties rhythm & blues boom via Jimi Hendrix, Eric Clapton and others. Unlike his contemporary John Scofield however, Abercrombie has devoted a lot of time to impressionistic playing – in which respect he is closer to PAT METHENY, but with little of Metheny's folksiness and with a stronger exploratory urge.

John Abercrombie began on guitar at fourteen, played in rock bands whilst still at school, went to the Berklee School of Music and remained in Boston in 1967 working with blues organist Johnny 'Hammond' Smith. In 1969 he played in Mike and Randy BRECKER's jazz-rock group Dreams, then with Chico Hamilton, Gil Evans, saxophonist DAVE LIEBMAN and fusion drummer BILLY

COBHAM. But in the mid-Seventies when he began recording for the German label ECM, Abercrombie flowered as an original soloist and a writer. His subtle strengths were to be heard on many excellent ECM sessions (both live and in the studio) and in partnership with the acoustic guitarist Ralph Towner. Unfortunately an imaginative early Abercrombie trio session *Friends* isn't available now, and nor is the atmospheric *Gateway*, with Dave Holland on bass.

★*Getting There* (ECM 833 494-2)

A live session quite explicitly made from Metheny materials. It opens with a smooth piece of mid-tempo funk that features the luxurious cat-stretches of Mike Brecker's tenor, finds the saxophonist sounding wistful and JAN GARBAREK-like, on the slow 'Remember Hymn', and at his assertive best on a fast, playful funk melody called 'Furs on Ice', with a tune like a child's song. Attractive, though insufficiently illuminating Abercrombie's own talents.

★*John Abercrombie Trio* (ECM 837 756-2)

Tangy, energetic live Abercrombie, recorded in Boston in 1988 with Marc Johnson, on bass, and Peter Erskine, on drums. Much more representative of the sound of an Abercrombie band at full pressure, with the attractive 'Furs on Ice' getting harder treatment and several glowing reworkings of Bill Evans' vehicles – the guitarist's fondness for Evans' approach being one of his most attractive features.

★*Timeless* (ECM 829 114-2)

Abercrombie's first ECM recording from 1974, with JACK DEJOHNETTE, on drums, and Jan Hammer, on organ, synthesiser and piano. Wilder and rougher than Abercrombie's later work but full of his deft, economical phrasing and punchy chordwork, plus a substantial bonus in some remarkable organ-playing from Hammer, something of a special-effects player in the later fusion period, but in scalding form here.

Abrams, Muhal Richard

(Born Chicago, September 19, 1930)

An influential musician in a highly influential scene – Sixties Chicago. Abrams would be exceptional on piano alone – he is at home with a variety of styles, from ragtime and boogie, to bebop and free music. As a free player, he is looser and more open than Cecil Taylor, less inclined to phrase in assertive bursts. His early *Young at Heart* album displayed styles from James P Johnson all the way up to Taylor, but it isn't yet on CD.

But Abrams has been many other things in jazz music besides a pianist, not least a leading light of the Association for the Advancement of Creative Musicians, a Chicago self-help group from which the ART ENSEMBLE OF CHICAGO – its best-known offspring – was spawned, in the late Sixties. The AACM was set up to help local black players promote the kind of music that was frightening off the record companies, and it organised teaching too. Abrams had a guru-like relationship with the AACM, exerting a moral authority that made a profound impression on many young players.

Abrams, a product of the Chicago Music College, originally worked on the city's regular jazz scene, backing visiting soloists. But by the end of the Fifties, bebop was frustrating him. He formed The Experimental Band, with Eddie Harris, ROSCOE MITCHELL and others in 1961, and it was from this nucleus that the AACM emerged – a community of musicians all living in the black districts of the South Side. Without Muhal Richard Abrams there might not have been an Art Ensemble of Chicago, or an organisation to corral the city's jazz energies in the Sixties.

Abrams' blend of the Harlem stride he loved in childhood, bebop's rigour and free music's impressionism has engendered a breadth of view he has taken into composition. But his Sixties disc *Levels and Degrees of Light* was preoccupied with not getting in the soloists' way and keeping the composition to pointers and atmospheric motifs, including some eventually exasperating birdsong. The session thus relied heavily on ANTHONY BRAXTON's fierce alto, Maurice McIntrye's more lissome tenor and Abrams' liquid piano figures. In the Seventies, Abrams led a successful sextet (including saxophonist Henry Threadgill), the AACM big band, and appeared on several Chicago-based recordings including sessions with the Art Ensemble, CHICO FREEMAN and Anthony Braxton.

The Hearinga Suite (Black Saint 120 103-2)

Abrams' seven-part *Hearinga Suite* doesn't mix as much contemplation and ferocity as his earlier orchestra recordings, but he continues to deploy atmospheric linking-devices drawing together some powerful solo contributions, all regrettably unattributed in the CD insert. It's a mixture of tramping, on-the-beat themes, bebop, the sounds of human conversation and Ellington-ish ensemble devices. Andrew Cyrille's drumming is as loose and buoyant as ever, and Abrams furnishes chords of probing dissonance on piano. A lot of the writing sounds like music waiting, in the middle of a more extended piece, for ideas that don't actually appear – long, slow, swaying chords, seductive washes of tone colour, snatches of exuberant jazz. It sounds a little like a retrospective that has come too early and surveyed too benignly, but it's intelligent and open music for all that.

Adams, George Rufus

(Born Covington, Georgia, April 29, 1940)
A raw and raucous saxophonist, influenced primarily by Coltrane, and further by Parker, Ben Webster and Coleman Hawkins – his hoarse, vocalised tone and broad-brush effects connect contemporary music powerfully to the jazz past. Adams has most frequently been seen in company with the pianist DON PULLEN, as well as in work with two great composer/arrangers, Charles Mingus and Gil Evans. All Adams' partners have been impressed by his ability to suit his style to the requirements of others, and he exhibits enough of the explosive energy of the Sixties avant-garde to abruptly raise the temperature, whilst retaining sufficient of a contemplative side to cool it.

Like many players with a feeling for the blues, Adams played in rhythm & blues and blues bands shortly after taking up the saxophone at school, and spent the summer of 1961 (after becoming a music graduate) touring with singer Sam Cooke. In the mid-Sixties Adams worked with blues and soul-jazz organ groups, then moved to New York in 1968 and began to appear with Gil Evans and Art Blakey. In the early years of the next decade he spent three educational years with Charles Mingus, and after that joined a Mingus pianist – DON PULLEN – in a powerful quartet working a territory between high energy free music and bop. With Pullen, and on his own, Adams continues to be an exciting and dramatic soloist. On occasion, and not wholly successfully, he will even launch into an abrasive vocal blues. The Adams/Pullen quartet is almost exclusively recorded on small European labels, with Blue Note taking a recent interest in Adams solo albums, with mixed results.

★*Don't Lose Control* (Soul Note SNCD 1004)

One of the first Adams/Pullen recordings, made in 1979 in Milan. This is the studio session (there were two live shows recorded around the same time) and it emphasises the interdependence of such a balanced quartet. Cameron Brown, on bass, and Dannie Richmond, on drums, sustain the temperature unrelentingly, while Pullen's combination of stormy abstraction and hard-boppishness energetically complements Adams' ruggedness.

Alexander, Monty

(Born Kingston, Jamaica, June 6, 1944)
An entertaining pianist with roots in swing, Alexander possesses a considerable two-hand technique and his closest links are with Oscar Peterson – but he moderates the frequently pounding, rather stubbornly exhibitionistic qualities of Peterson, with a reflective lyricism, the warmth of Caribbean music and sensitive accompaniment, often from a hand-drummer. Alexander become popular in the States in the Sixties, frequently working with bassist Ray Brown and sometimes vibist Milt Jackson. The quantity of records he has made as a leader is somewhat out of proportion to his ability to vary his output, and there have been a number of recorded reunions of his Triple Treat band, with guitarist Herb Ellis and Ray Brown.

★*Jamboree* (Concord CCD 4359)

A return to roots by Alexander, a little different to his usual Peterson-esque fluency. On a mixture of Jamaican folk songs, calypso and reggae, the pianist appears with two steel drummers, plus his regular hand drummer Robert Thomas and the crackling Marvin 'Smitty' Smith on orthodox drums.

★*Saturday Night* (Timeless MCD 024)

The disc for Alexander fans converted by hearing him live. This is a more conventional set by the pianist, with Ed Thigpen on drums, plus bass and hand drums. Engaging concert material from 1985, with the leader on breezy form exploring material by Johnny Mandel, Milt Jackson and Cedar Walton among others.

Art Ensemble of Chicago

Lester Bowie (born Frederick, Maryland, October 11, 1941)
Joseph Jarman (born Pine Bluff, Arkansas, September 14, 1937)
Roscoe Mitchell (born Chicago, August 3, 1940)
Malachi Favors (born Chicago, August 22, 1937)
Don Moye (born Rochester, New York, May 23, 1946).
A product of the 1960s Chicago free scene, that always displayed more inclination toward organisation than the New York one (in the Ensemble's case through theatricality and irony as much as musical structure) the band first appeared as Roscoe Mitchell's Art Ensemble in 1967, with Mitchell on alto, Lester Bowie on trumpet and Malachi Favors on bass. Joseph Jarman joined two years later, with Don Moye following in 1970. The band performs on many instruments, using a range of tone colour rare for any group of its size, and it has always drawn on jazz history – incorporating snatches of marches, blues, field hollers and bebop as well as the expressionism of free music. In recent years the Ensemble's original impulsiveness and desire to disrupt hardening styles has lessened. But it remains a triumph of chemistry uniting improvisation, music theatre, jazz history and composition.

However, CD issue principally represents late Art Ensemble. None of the Paris material is so far available in the format. Unfortunately neither is *Urban Bushmen*, the most complete representation of the variety of the band's styles, nor *Les Stances à Sophie* (with soul singer Fontella Bass), *Message to Our Folks* (featuring some sparkling bebop playing as well as free music) and *People in Sorrow* – all either deleted or only on vinyl.

★*Full Force* (ECM 829 197-2)

More overtly sophisticated and smooth Art Ensemble, but a good indication of the band's powers. 'Magg Zelma' is a rich, colourful and collaborative piece of extended impressionism, and the blues 'Charlie M' (dedicated to Mingus) is a striking example of how strongly the Ensemble can play conventionally, with Moye's drums underpinning dynamic shifts from the stealthy to the fanfare-like, and a trumpet solo from Bowie characteristically full of slurs, growls and wriggling runs.

★*Third Decade* (ECM 823 213-2)

Recorded in Germany in 1984, the Art Ensemble's celebration of its remarkable longevity. It's a less purposeful and clearsighted set than several not on CD, but still displays much of the old mischief – the way the frisky 'Funky AECO' pursues the contemplative 'Prayer for Jimbo Kwesi'. Patches of glittering detail, patches of roaring free-jazz, and – though less of an imposing whole – still a session of character and energy from one of the most inventive of post-Sixties jazz groups.

Ballamy, Iain Mark

(Born Guildford, England, February 20, 1964)
One of the new generation of distinctive British jazz musicians to have risen with the success of the big band LOOSE TUBES. Saxophonist Iain Ballamy, however, is a rarity among a throng of Coltrane devotees in that he isn't preoccupied with unleashing showers of notes and is at his best with the almost lost art of ballad playing. As well as making his mark over the past six years with Loose Tubes, Ballamy has also performed a good deal with Earthworks – the unique fusion quartet led by ex-Yes drummer BILL BRUFORD. He can be unsettled by fast tempos (resorting to a mixture of perfunctory blurts, corkscrewing runs and long pauses) but is often sublime on the less fashionable territory of slow and mid-tempo tunes. His sound, which embraces a softly scurrying double-time low register murmur that suggests an overheard conversation, a lissome, cello-like mid-range and a blend of very sparing Coltraneish high-pitched split notes and an

engaging squawkiness reminiscent of the late Warne Marsh, is a confection of genuine distinctiveness.

Ballamy has now formed his own band, Balloon Man – a captivating blend of grace and humour, lyricism and abrasiveness and above all spontaneity and structure. It is the culmination of a process of self-education that has followed few rules. Ballamy's father Mark is a jazz pianist, and Ballamy Jnr took classical piano lessons from the age of six – but intensified his efforts when he discovered Fats Waller and Scott Joplin in his early teens. He then heard a saxophone player rehearsing with a band his father was playing in, and changed instruments at once. Within two years Iain Ballamy was working with the mainstream players of the British jazz scene, mostly playing American bop and standards.

In 1983, Ballamy met pianist DJANGO BATES, and the partnership flowered – the two discovered in each other, and in their contemporaries on the British scene, an independent slant on jazz that didn't require rote-learning the devices of American stars. In partnership with Bates, and in Loose Tubes, Ballamy absorbed African ideas, gamelan, pop, brass band sounds and free music. Ballamy is now in demand for many British groups, and continues to develop his own music.

*_Balloon Man_ (Editions EG EEGCD 63)

Excellent debut by the quirky Ballamy, with Django Bates at his formidable best on piano, like a more rugged Keith Jarrett. Ballamy's fast fluency is displayed on the vigorous 'Mode for Bode' (full of fizzing contrapuntal conversations between keyboards and tenor), his genre-jumping on the accordion tango 'Rahsaan' and his lyricism on 'Remember' and the poignant 'All I Ask Of You', a rearrangement of a hymn.

Bang, Billy

(Born Mobile, Alabama, September 20, 1947)
No received wisdom about the jazz violin applies to Billy Bang. He is by generation and background disinclined to the amiable, jaunty raffishness of a Stephane Grappelli. But those who wince at his associations with the post-Coltrane avant-garde and anticipate an

evening of screechings and scratchings need have no fear either. Bang plays with the packed and tumbling intensity of a Coltraneish saxophonist, but his tunes are succinct and direct, and his variations on them pull no punches, being a constant, churning torrent of wriggling high-register sounds; curt, exclamatory chords; long, expostulatory phrases and plucked passages that bounce around the walls like squash-balls. He began with bassist John Lindberg and guitarist James Emery in the String Trio of New York, and from his earliest work it was clear that the more abrasive, fidgety and dissonant manner of free-jazz violin playing instigated by Ornette Coleman (closer to that of his original mentor, Leroy Jenkins) didn't exclusively appeal to him. Bang made several solo and duo albums of fitful inventiveness, but his work with larger groups reveals his strength as both a soloist and a composer.

★*Live at Carlos* (Soul Note SNCD 21136-2)

A 1986 session for Billy Bang's sextet, recorded in New York and featuring six originals by the violinist. It's a highly unusual instrumentation – violin, trumpet, bass, electric guitar, marimba (Thurman Barker) and drums. But Bang wanted harmonic support that was looser than a piano's, and combines those freedoms with rhythmic variety that takes in jazz, African music, reggae and the Middle East. Fresh, uncompromising, rhythmically vigorous contemporary music.

Barbieri, Leandro J 'Gato'

(Born Rosario, Argentina, November 28, 1934)
Barbieri is a tenor saxophonist who came to general notice in the 1960s – but unlike many players influenced by the 'sheets of sound' approach pioneered by Coltrane, he placed considerable emphasis on timbre rather than speed. As a result, the Argentinian's sound is easily recognisable in most of the contexts he has appeared in – a hot, tumultuous, desert-storm of a tone.

Barbieri took up the saxophone at six, after hearing a recording of Charlie Parker's 'Now's The Time'. When he developed into a professional, he quickly became Argentina's leading jazz musician, and turned his back on the country's indigenous musics to work in jazz and jazz-influenced popular music, notably with Lalo Schifrin. He moved to Italy in the Sixties looking for musical challenges, and met DON CHERRY, cutting two impressive and successful albums with him (*Complete Communion* and *Symphony for Improvisors*), following these with sessions with STEVE LACY (*Nuovi Sentimenti*) and ABDULLAH IBRAHIM (*Confluence*). From the early Seventies, Barbieri rediscovered his Latin American origins and mostly abandoned free jazz, except in the edge that it had given to his sound. A series of records, for the Impulse label in the U.S., devoted to Latin American dance rhythms and percussion followed. Over it all Barbieri's throaty, somewhat macho style rolls on, and his qualities of manic passion were appropriate for the soundtrack to Bertolucci's 1972 film *Last Tango in Paris*, for which the saxophonist won a Grammy. Later Barbieri has moved further away from his more creative jazz roots and has become something of a Latin-jazz MOR specialist, making *Caliente* for A & M, with Herb Alpert as producer.

★*Chapter One Latin America* (MCA MCAD 39124)

The best of Barbieri's 'Chapters' series of albums, with the saxophonist flamethrowing his way across a landscape clattering with South American percussion effects and the delightful bandoneon playing of Dino Saluzzi. Recorded in Rio de Janeiro, 1973.

★*Hamba Khale* (Charly CD CHARLY 79)

Barbieri with South African pianist Abdullah Ibrahim (Dollar Brand). One of the Argentinian's most successful partnerships musically, since the contrast of Barbieri's flailing impulsiveness and Ibrahim's dignified, hymnal piano is so startling.

Bates, Leon 'Django'

(Born Beckenham, England, October 2, 1960)
Django Bates, the pianist and composer from Beckenham, goes on proving that the unruly energies, that made him a jazz celebrity with LOOSE TUBES, have not sobered down; by the end of the

Eighties he had become one of the most powerful forces in new British jazz. Bates is apparently immune to desultoriness and prolixity, the enemies of so much improvisation, and his playing is a constant redefinition of jazz possibilities.

Bates studied music early; learning piano, trumpet and violin. He went to Morley College as an aspiring trumpeter, and then to the Royal College of Music, in 1978. He dropped out of the latter, after a fortnight, to go on the road and formed a band, Humans, that later evolved into Human Chain. Work with saxophonists Tim Whitehead and DUDA PUKWANA and with FIRST HOUSE and Loose Tubes led, in 1986, to his selection (alongside ANDY SHEPPARD) for the prestigious GEORGE RUSSELL UK tour. As the decade ended, Bates' strengths became increasingly insistent. His work is highly accomplished and musically erudite, it burnishes rather than obscures its references. Yet it is also capable of being whimsical and anarchic, at times, and as likely to found a scorching improvisationally dynamic performance on a tango, a calypso or a vintage music-hall ditty, as on what is usually called 'straight-ahead jazz'. With compositions such as 'Sweet William' (dedicated to his father, a devoted record collector who gave Bates his start) and the hymnal 'Sad Afrika', Django Bates is also shaping as a big-band composer of real vision.

*Human Chain 'Cashin In' (Editions EG EEGCD57)

Bates' offbeat trio, which might begin with a sound like guitarists with very slack strings playing over neat, supper-club drumming and then shift into tango-like tempos, coloured with accordion effects from the leader's synthesiser. This eclecticism will then clear away and a jazz pulse will find the pianist playing a thumping solo in a manner somewhere between the urbane folksiness of KEITH JARRETT and the faintly baleful loquacity of PAUL BLEY. Human Chain depends equally on the cleanness and precision of drummer Steve Arguelles and the quirky multi-instrumentalisms of Stuart Hall, but the keyboard player is its lynchpin and its constant source of surprise. The intelligence and incisiveness with which Bates deploys the treacherous opulence of the synthesiser, makes Human Chain sound a much bigger outfit than it is.

*Powder Room Collapse Orchestra – Music for the Third Policeman
(AH UM 003)

Thirteen movements by Bates intended to reflect characters and events from Flann O'Brien's surreal novel, *The Third Policeman*. The session opens with prancing folksy flute figures; followed by graceful Bates piano, marching tuba sounds and meandering reeds accelerating to sinister climaxes. Fast bebop represents the character 'John Divney', with Bates soloing adroitly on tenor horn, and jaunty Irish flute themes drifting in and out. Odd samba patterns appear, backed by gurgling reeds and jangling banjos, and the theme gets its most graphic imagery in the sound of a bicycle backpedalling, turning into erratic funk and then Ellingtonish sultriness.

Beckett, Harold Winston 'Harry'

(Born Barbados, May 30, 1935)
Harry Beckett is one of Britain's great flugelhorn exponents. He is a delightfully expressive and convivial sounding improvisor, his phrasing constantly light and buoyant, his playing alert to the contributions of partners, his sound glowing. He has consistently displayed these qualities since his arrival in Britain in 1954 (in 1961 they won him a place in a British band, led by Charles Mingus, for the film *All Night Long*) and the continuing exuberance of his playing made him, for a time in the Eighties, a staple member of the JAZZ WARRIORS, for most of whom he was an elder statesman, older by some thirty years. A Beckett solo might be a latticework of softly squealed high notes that are momentarily held, before wriggling out of earshot; short, drumlike accents; and a scattering of sidelong, knowing growls that he rarely uses unless truly relaxed. His favourite materials are child-like melodies that resemble uptempo lullabies set to jazz rhythms, riff-based tunes and repeated rhythm section figures, over which his horn skips and pirouettes. Beckett has played with just about every jazz band of any consequence in the last thirty years in Britain under leaders such as Graham Collier, MIKE WESTBROOK, STAN TRACEY, MIKE GIBBS, Ronnie Scott and many others.

★*Put It Right Mr Smoothie* (Splasch Records CD H 313-2)

A fine recent display of Beckett's inimitably open-handed repertoire, both as an improvisor and a composer – and with a
contemporary now at the height of his powers in saxophonist
Elton Dean. The band is the Anglo-Italian quartet, formed three
years ago to play Nineties freebop.

Benson, George

(Born Pittsburgh, March 22, 1943)
Like Nat King Cole before him, George Benson is the consum-
mate jazz instrumentalist whose singing voice brought him fame.
In 1976, his recording of 'Breezin'' made him a pop star and there
are few opportunities now (they amount to finding yourself in a
New York club on whatever night Benson decides to come and
jam with old friends) to hear a guitarist whose stature in the
Sixties rivalled Wes Montgomery's.

Benson sang and played ukelele as a child, and by the age of
nineteen was touring with organist Jack McDuff. He formed his
own organ group in the mid Sixties, playing in the hard-driving
jazz-funk manner popular in the period, but he also appeared on
albums by other leaders (notably Miles Davis' *Miles in the Sky*)
playing in a manner that was both highly rhythmic and which
took unexpected lyrical twists. But Benson's loyalties lay with a
version of jazz that was danceable and highly communicative, and
'Breezin'' was the high point of that enthusiasm, breaking
previous records for sales of an instrumental track. But Benson
has never entirely left jazz behind, even when it was clear that his
audiences and the record companies were primarily interested in
his elegantly soulful voice – he frequently plays guitar lines in
unison with his singing, and sometimes displays considerable bite
with them. Latterly, as jazz has grown more popular again,
Benson has featured it more explicitly in his work.

★*Breezin'* (WEA K2 56199)

The 1976 jazz-funk record that made Benson's name, the
infectious title track shifting him resoundingly into the pop
market. But Benson's hard-driving, warm-toned guitar sound is

complemented here by the Stevie Wonder-like vocal technique (on Leon Russell's 'This Masquerade') which put Benson into the top spot of the US pop single chart at the same time.

Berg, Bob

(Born New York, April 7, 1951)
Berg, who has confirmed his reputation in Britain as one of the most effective Coltrane disciples through appearances with the Miles Davis band, is a player of effortless technical command and harmonic sophistication, and the resurgence of bop-influenced music has emphasised these qualities. Berg has run against most prevailing orthodoxies. He resisted the fusion music of the Seventies and continued to develop his techniques as a bebop player during that idiom's low ebb, and combined these studies with methods he had explored as a Coltraneish free-jazz enthusiast in the previous decade. The result was that Berg evolved as a tough, precise player with a voice of his own.

From the mid Seventies to the early Eighties he worked with fine jazz pianists, including Horace Silver and Cedar Walton. In 1984 he joined the Miles Davis band and, though fusion still irked him, found that Davis' conception for the style left generous space for a player of his independence. Berg developed a successful relationship with guitarist Mike Stern through the Davis connection.

★Short Stories (Denon CY 1768)

Berg's first album after leaving Miles Davis. 'Short Stories' displays both Berg's brisk linear style and Mike Stern's catchy compositional manner, notably on the driving 'Friday Night At The Cadillac Club'. Backbeats are much in evidence, but the music isn't formulaic – and the presence of David Sanborn's alto is a bonus.

Berne, Tim

(Born 1955)
A highly original alto saxophonist, strongly associated with the

New York free scene – both the earlier black-influenced jazz-based one, and the newer and more eclectic version of which JOHN ZORN is a leading figure. Berne is both an inventive instrumentalist and a composer with an independent view of combining musical materials that will almost certainly give him a catalytic role in the music of the Nineties.

Berne has dedicated himself to finding new structures in music and developing improvisation that is intimately a part of the piece it develops, rather than a random addition. He draws on themes reminiscent of Ornette Coleman, and of bebop and the sounds of contemporary urban streetlife.

★*Sanctified Dreams* (CBS 460676-2)

A departure from the music Berne was making up to 1987, since it features an acoustic band including trombonist Ray Anderson and John Zorn's drummer Joey Baron. A fascinatingly varied session demonstrating Berne's class and curiosity, peppered with bebop, wild ensemble flourishes, careful engineering of dynamic changes and mood, and great rhythmic variety.

Berry, Stephen

(Born 1957)
Originally a guitarist, Steve Berry switched to the upright bass in 1980. During the early Eighties playing a good deal with rehearsal bands and repertoire bands, specialising in older jazz, he grew frustrated with what seemed to him a mainstream music world that had little to interest a younger British audience, ready to listen to a mixture of funk, pop, dance music and jazz, without being distressed by such overlaps. Berry was involved with the workshop band that bassist/composer Graham Collier had orga-nised in 1984 – and, as the nucleus of those players evolved a sound of their own, and the basis of the group that became LOOSE TUBES, he turned increasingly to writing.

★*Trio* (Loose Tubes LTCD 007)

Berry's trio, with Mark Lockheart, on saxophones, and Peter

Fairclough, on drums, on the most conversational of sessions, expressed in Lockheart's, Ornette Coleman-like, sense of solo construction – long, wailing notes, followed by fragmented phrases, then sudden gushing runs – and Berry's firm bass playing, a ringing, resonant presence in which timbre is as important as melodic line, in a manner suggestive of CHARLIE HADEN. The ballad (in spirit, rather than in conventional form) is rehabilitated on the glowing 'My Father's Eyes', and Lockheart demonstrates his mischievous adaptability by ranging from Coltrane/Coleman to Sonny Rollins calypso style, in the midst of a brusque blurted uptempo excursion, 'Bip Bap Dubaddlia'. Fresh, urgent, and always in control.

Blackwell, Edward Joseph

(Born New Orleans, October 10, 1929)
When jazz drummers are discussed, in anything other than specialised circles, the names of Buddy Rich, Art Blakey, Elvin Jones and, maybe in recent years, JACK DEJOHNETTE and TONY WILLIAMS might be expected to come up. Edward Blackwell, far less likely to be referred to, is a drummer entitled to at least as much consideration. An inspired explorer of the timbre of drums and a master of perfectly placed (and tightly edited) accents across the main pulse, Blackwell is a sophisticated innovator of post-bop drumming. But his style is high in musicality and low in theatricality, which – along with sporadic absences from playing due to dependence on a kidney machine – helps account for his relative obscurity.

Blackwell performed around his native New Orleans in the late Forties, with Marsalis Snr (pianist Ellis Marsalis) among others. He met the saxophonist Ornette Coleman there, and by the Fifties both men were getting work in rhythm & blues and blues bands. Blackwell eventually joined Coleman in Los Angeles where they rehearsed extensively together. Coleman's interest in a harmonically looser music than bop, wide ranging melodically but anchored by a steady yet vital pulse, suited Blackwell. The drummer liked the old New Orleans percussionists and the thematic improvising style of the earliest jazz – the hustling, short-volley clatter of his left-hand accents adds a stentorian street-band quality to the hiss and flow of a straight-ahead cymbal beat, and Blackwell also exhibits a speech-like conciseness that reflects his interest in the African drum.

Blackwell didn't appear on Ornette Coleman's first records (having returned to New Orleans before the saxophonist hit the headlines) but rejoined him in New York in 1960, working thereafter with Coltrane, DON CHERRY and for a while Thelonious Monk, and also appearing with Eric Dolphy on the famous 'Live at the Five Spot' session. Blackwell has taught since 1972, when his health has permitted. In addition to working in trumpeter Don Cherry's groups, Blackwell has also participated with Cherry in Old and New Dreams, the quartet (including saxophonist Don Redman) devoted to Ornette Coleman's compositions. Some of Blackwell's most fruitful work with Cherry is on the two parts of *Mu* (Affinity), not so far released on CD.

★*El Corazon* (ECM 829 199-2)

Don Cherry visited Morocco in the mid-Sixties, at the beginning of his world-music explorations – Ed Blackwell joined him there for a year. The intensity of that musical relationship was best expressed on *Mu*, but is still reflected in this session of ten years later, using unadorned and folksy acoustic melodies, wooden flutes and assorted percussion. Cherry is bubbling, whimsical, at times plaintive – Blackwell as light and springy as a dancer.

★*Old and New Dreams* (Black Saint BSR 0013)

The second of two recorded celebrations of Ornette Coleman's compositions (the first was for ECM) with Cherry, Blackwell, bassist CHARLIE HADEN and tenorist Dewey Redman. All four Coleman alumni were by this stage of their careers immersed in global musical enthusiasms of their own – so the disc ranges over musical exotica, strong originals like Charlie Haden's 'Chairman Mao' and Coleman classics.

Blanchard, Terence

(Born New Orleans, March 13, 1962)
Blanchard is another famous graduate of the Art Blakey Jazz

Messengers school, but also a native of New Orleans – and
therefore in danger of eclipse by that city's most famous new jazz
son, fellow-trumpeter WYNTON MARSALIS. Blanchard does not
command (and neither do most other trumpeters) the furthest
reaches of technique as explored by Marsalis, but his understanding of the instrument is very nearly as rich and at times his
uncluttered determination to pursue a new melody line, without
pyrotechnics or exercise-like phrasing, is refreshing.

Blanchard took up the trumpet at eight, joined a New Orleans
classical orchestra as a teenager, and was turned on to jazz as a
result of teaching by pianist Ellis Marsalis (Wynton Marsalis'
father) at the New Orleans Centre for Creative Arts. Blanchard
went to New York to finish studying in 1980, learning classical
music and jazz simultaneously – developing fast enough to be
hired by Art Blakey when Marsalis left him in 1981.

New York Second Line (Concord CCD 430-02)

Blanchard's debut in 1983, recorded with a brilliant assortment of
players on the rise at the start of the 1980s – the distinctive and
unorthodox Donald 'Duck' Harrison, on alto, MULGREW MILLER, on
piano, Lonnie Plaxico, on bass, and Marvin 'Smitty' Smith, on
drums. The repertoire mingles new material with earlier work
(such as 'I Can't Get Started') and is the kind of crackling,
businesslike, straight-between-the-eyes nouveau-bop that makes
these musicians almost as highly regarded as the Marsalises.

Life at Sweet Basil's (Paddlewheel K32Y 6145)

A representation of the music of those departed, late-bop virtuosi
Booker Little and Eric Dolphy, celebrated by Blanchard and
Harrison, with ED BLACKWELL on drums, Richard Davis, on bass,
and Mal Waldron, on piano. Harrison reveals his New Orleans-
derived 'dirty' style here (he is a generally funkier player than
many of his more elegant contemporaries), his work seething
with off-pitch sounds and impassioned cries. At the drums, the
old master Ed Blackwell is as delicate, yet involved, as if he were
spontaneously sketching a background with a soft pencil. Not as
zingy as *New York Second Line*, but strong and heartfelt.

Bley, Carla

(Born Oakland, California, May 11, 1938)
Like Gil Evans and GEORGE RUSSELL, Carla Bley is an innovative jazz composer and orchestrator who, by a mixture of intention and accident, avoided the obvious. She has quoted Erik Satie and the Beatles as significant influences, and pianist PAUL BLEY, composer Charles Mingus and George Russell have left their mark too. In recent years Ms Bley, who still tours extensively with bands of varying sizes, has maintained her energetic output of original work for improvisors, as well as fully-composed works with conservatoire musicians.

Carla Bley (originally Carla Borg), the daughter of a Swedish immigrant living in California, studied piano as a child, and grew up in intimate contact with church music. She dropped out of school at fifteen, worked with a folk singer and played the piano in bars. Growing interested in jazz, she went to New York at nineteen, worked as a cigarette girl at Birdland, and met (and soon married) the Canadian pianist Paul Bley. She began to write jazz music, with her husband's guidance on technicalities. Her melodic sense was quirky, not in slavery to bop melody – it recaptured a lyricism steamrollered by bop's more perfunctory tunefulness, and her songs were personal, quite distinct from Tin Pan Alley cadences, and soon sought-after. Paul Bley began to record her, as did Jimmy Giuffre, George Russell and trumpeter Art Farmer. Carla Bley stopped being a coffee-house pianist and joined drummer Charles Moffett's group with PHAROAH SANDERS. She was then involved in the volatile Jazz Composers' Guild (an attempt by avant-garde New York musicians to control their own work) and when that collapsed helped salvage the Jazz Composers' Orchestra from the ashes. She continued working as a pianist – with DON CHERRY, Clifford Thornton and trombonist Grachan Moncur – but it was her extended suite *A Genuine Tong Funeral* for vibraharpist GARY BURTON, followed by work on bassist CHARLIE HADEN's Spanish-flavoured *Liberation Music Orchestra* album and then *Escalator over the Hill* for the Jazz Composers' Orchestra that secured her reputation. *Escalator*, with a libretto by poet Paul Haines, was an opera, for which few of the star-studded cast (Jack Bruce, Linda Ronstadt, Don Cherry, JOHN McLAUGHLIN) were in the same studio at the same time, and it won prizes everywhere.

Carla Bley now had a second husband and musical partner in trumpeter MIKE MANTLER, and the two formed Watt Records, with Ms Bley continuing to compose jazz-derived work (the first Watt disc, *Tropic Appetites* featured tenorist GATO BARBIERI and British singer Julie Tippetts, formerly Julie Driscoll) and Mantler exploring theatre and literary-related music in *No Answer* (from Samuel Beckett). Carla Bley moved toward composed music plus a single soloist (*3/4* with a classical orchestra and KEITH JARRETT on piano). In the late Seventies and early Eighties Carla Bley's own music took turns both toward a vaudevillian presentation and pop, plus her taste for tango and Kurt Weill, but in more recent times jazz has resurfaced, her bigger bands at times reminiscent of Charles Mingus. She has also recorded and performed in a duo with bassist Steve Swallow.

★*Escalator over the Hill* (ECM 839 310-2)

Carla Bley's landmark of the Seventies, the jazz/pop opera *Escalator Over The Hill*. This CD set even has the original box and accompanying photographs. Bley's odyssey, based on the poetry of Paul Haines, is clearly of its time. But her writing, particularly in the sumptuous and dramatic overture, in which Roswell Rudd's trombone winds up drifting over the evaporating chords of the orchestra with a gleam like a moon over snow, is consistently rich and the improvising of a raft of star guests, including trumpeter Don Cherry and John McLaughlin, demonstrates Ms Bley's capacity for pulling that extra percentage from musicians who've heard it all.

★*Social Studies* (ECM 831 831 2)

Early Eighties Bley, with a low-key but often affecting performance embodying many of her virtues. The standout track, and one of her finest compositions, is the mid-tempo 'Reactionary Tango', a memorable melody that also vibrates with Bley's typical mingling of kitsch, a casually sinister quality, and richly sleazy ensemble writing for the horns.

★*Night-Glo* (ECM 827 640-2)

Carla Bley tightened her grip on improvisors through the

Eighties, moving instead toward more carefully controlled pieces that achieved their effects through jazz intonation rather than lyrical spontaneity. But since electric bassist Steve Swallow has evolved a sound that is the closest thing to the human voice this frequently incommunicative instrument has come, extended soloing from others isn't essential. The mood is reflective, even melancholic, but the themes have all Bley's characteristic skewed charm. Apart from Bley's keyboards and Swallow on bass, this sextet includes the excellent Hiram Bullock on guitar.

Bley, Paul

(Born Montreal, November 10, 1932)

Pianist Paul Bley has never sounded happy inhabiting a well-defined idiom. Though he had demonstrated early on that he had the technique and grasp of regular jazz materials to be a straight-ahead player (he inherited Oscar Peterson's drummer and bassist when his fellow-countryman went to the States in 1949) Bley has rarely strayed far from experimental situations. It was possibly his tendency to explore in a muted rather than ferocious manner, that made him less of a *cause celebre* in the avant-garde upheavals of the Sixties. But it was a band led by Bley that put Ornette Coleman on record for the first time, and the pianist has been drawn to improvisation without the regular tramlines of harmony ever since.

Bley went to New York to study in the early Fifties, and by 1954 was playing at Birdland. He went to the West Coast later in the decade, and Ornette Coleman and DON CHERRY began to work with him in 1958. Bley then collaborated with composer GEORGE RUSSELL (in partnership with Bill Evans on *Jazz in the Space Age*), with Jimmy Giuffre and Sonny Rollins. A series of albums by Paul Bley trios followed through the Sixties (often interpreting the distinctive tunes of his first wife Carla) and in the next decade Bley turned to the emerging electronics revolution. His new partner, singer and keyboardist ANNETTE PEACOCK, was working with the first Moog synthesisers, and together they developed a brooding, sometimes baleful music embracing jazz and art-pop. But Bley quickly returned to the acoustic instrument on which his melodic originality, subtlety in shifting harmonies and clipped, nervous

242

timing (he occasionally suggests what Bill Evans might have sounded like as an avantist) continued to map out his own personal territory. Very little of Bley's unusual early work remains available, especially on CD.

★*Open, to Love* (ECM 827 751-2)

Beautiful unaccompanied Bley, displaying the pianist's cool and candid touch, spacious sense of design and rich left-hand work on a series of compositions perfectly suited to him – including CARLA BLEY's hypnotic and unsettling 'Ida Lupino'.

★*Fragments* (ECM 829 280-2)

The first of two CDs of Bley's mid-Eighties band, including JOHN SURMAN, on reeds, BILL FRISELL, on guitar, and PAUL MOTIAN, on drums. Predominantly restrained in mood, but the material (furnished by all the players and thus embracing Frisell's warped-rock leanings, Surman's faintly rural wistfulness as well as the leader's rainy-streets poignancy) is needling and compulsive.

Brackeen, Joanne

(Born Ventura, California, July 26, 1938)
Joanne Brackeen is a steely, dynamic pianist of great melodic imagination who at times performs like a less ruminative Bill Evans, but whose style has also been associated with CHICK COREA's. She is capable of performing with a compulsive, foot-tapping energy (qualities essential to sustaining a three-year tenure with Art Blakey's Messengers) but her own material is personal, devoid of cliche and whimsical without preciousness.

California born, and largely self taught, Brackeen moved to New York in the mid-Sixties having enjoyed an active career in West Coast bop from 1958, with leaders like Dexter Gordon and Harold Land. She had married saxophonist Charles Brackeen in 1960, and stayed out of music raising their children until the New York move in 1965, after which she resumed occasional appearances. In 1970 she joined one of the most famous bands in jazz – Art Blakey's Jazz Messengers – and followed a two-year stint with employment by two of the music's finest saxophonists, Joe Henderson and Stan Getz. Now Ms Brackeen mostly performs her own material. A brilliant 1982 album *Special Identity* (on Antilles, with JACK DEJOHNETTE and Eddie Gomez) deserves CD release.

★*Fi-Fi Goes to Heaven* (Concord CCD 4316)

Terrific Brackeen record made in 1986 with TERENCE BLANCHARD, on trumpet, BRANFORD MARSALIS, on reeds, Cecil McBee, on bass, and Al Foster, on drums. Despite such illustrious partners, Brackeen painlessly dominates from the keyboard, and is at her graceful best on 'Stardust' and her springiest and most eloquent on the title track.

★*Havin Fun* (Concord CCD 4280)

Less characteristic Brackeen album, devoted more to standard songs and even including George Michael's 'Everything She Wants', but attractive nonetheless for the pianist's focussed energy, and her mixture of intensity and playfulness, notably on 'I've Got the World on a String'.

Braxton, Anthony

(Born Chicago, June 4, 1945)
In a period in which experimentation in jazz is in eclipse, Anthony Braxton remains unshakeably devoted to change. An awesome technician on a multiplicity of instruments (he plays most of the saxophone and clarinet family), he acknowledges an unparalleled breadth of influences: John Coltrane, Ornette Coleman, Eric Dolphy, Karlheinz Stockhausen, John Cage, unfashionable jazz geniuses like the late Warne Marsh and Paul Desmond, Egyptian mysticism, physics and astrology. Some of his pieces suggest Albert Ayler, some Lee Konitz, some an attempt to condense Charlie Parker's legacy into a single breakneck solo. In other parts of Braxton's work, jazz content is shrunk to the point where it is simply irrelevant to look for it or be distressed by its absence. But all through his career Braxton has cherished jazz, and one of his

recent bands (with bassist Adelhard Roidinger and British drummer Tony Oxley) is a jazz band all the way through, albeit without a conventional lick in earshot. Braxton has also written some 300 compositions over twenty years.

Anthony Braxton went to school with two other prominent Chicago jazz artists – ROSCOE MITCHELL and Joseph Jarman, who later came to prominence through the ART ENSEMBLE OF CHICAGO.

He began recording in 1968, with a succession of challenging sessions exploring collective interplay. Braxton's compositions are often given titles in mathematical formulae and the notation is diagrammatic, describing movement and dynamic change. On an early solo saxophone set ('For Alto'), he played with quite different materials according to the nature of the piece – long, sinewy legato lines on some; short, furious squally passages on others, themes dedicated to Cage. Like other members of Chicago's Association for the Advancement of Creative Musicians (AACM, see page 224). Braxton decamped to Paris for a period at the end of the Sixties, but not before he had already formed an adventurous band devoted to stretching jazz orthodoxies and exploring free music in collaboration with the pianist CHICK COREA, plus bassist DAVE HOLLAND and drummer Barry Altschul. The group, called Circle, was shortlived (and Corea was to regret free music vehemently thereafter) but it represented a vibrant musical give-and-take and it was often freshly melodic.

Braxton's work has continued in astonishing variety since. His reworkings of bebop (*In the Tradition*) demonstrate how past triumphs can be celebrated without treating the materials like bone china. He has written for chamber orchestras, for ballets, for electronics, performed in sensational duet with one of bebop's founding fathers, drummer Max Roach (see page 000) and received numerous awards and citations for his work. In 1985, Braxton became Professor of Composition at Mills College, Oakland, California, and he continues to tour and perform with his own band.

★*In the Tradition Vol 2* (Steeplechase SCCD 31045)

The second of Braxton's 1974 Copenhagen sessions devoted primarily to mutated bebop. Reforging classic materials with such panache as to make most of the neotraditionalist movement sound somnambulent, Braxton rattles his way through Parker's 'Donna Lee', Miles Davis' 'Half Nelson', as well as 'Body and Soul' and 'My Funny Valentine'.

★*Six Monk Compositions* (Black Saint 120116-2)

Most interpreters of Monk try to find an equivalent to his crabby ambiguity, but Braxton typically takes the opposite stance and swarms all over the music. Moreover his Monk choices are particularly tough ones, which the saxophonist mostly decides to play at hair-raising speed. It's Mal Waldron, the pianist, who retains Monk's canny, flinty percussiveness. The set includes 'Brilliant Corners', played alternately like a ghostly tea dance and in a flying double-time high register, oddly reminiscent of Art Pepper. The final, 'Skippy', is the most manically fast piece of all, which Braxton negotiates with a hurricane of sound, rattling with tinkling trebly downward runs, dark, heated scurrying, trumpet-like emphatic low tones, and thumping descents of the chords as he occasionally opts to make a point of the harmony.

★*Seven Compositions (Trio) 1989* (Hat ART CD 6025)

Recorded in France, in 1989, this represents the Braxton trio of Adelhard Roidinger (bass) and Tony Oxley (drums), that also visited Britain on the tour. It is almost indecently well-endowed, avoiding melodic or rhythmic cliche, displaying intelligent articulacy even at the craziest tempos, a sense of an evolving jazz tradition in reworking both regular themes and swing, sizzling group empathy, and shrewd deployment of structure as a supportive shape and mood that doesn't ruthlessly dictate the pattern of events. This disc features five pieces by Braxton (bearing his usual formulaic titles) plus Kern and Hammerstein's 'All The Things You Are' and Tony Oxley's 'Angular Apron', a work that goes back to the pioneering days of British free music in the early 1970s. Roidinger's bass playing exhibits both the accuracy and glossy sound of Dave Holland and Oxley's famous surging cymbal beat pushes Braxton's horn through the brisk and almost-straight opening to 'All The Things You Are'.

★*Creative Orchestra* (BMG ND 86579)

Brilliant Braxton achievement from 1976, featuring big-band swing, disrupted march-music, free improvisation and bop. MUHAL RICHARD ABRAMS plays on it, as do Dave Holland, on bass, George Lewis, on trombone, and Roscoe Mitchell, on reeds. A high point of Braxton's sophistication with tone colour and compositional shape.

Brecker, Mike

(Born Philadelphia, March 29, 1949)
Asked who they admire, most fledgling saxophone players won't take long to get to the name of Mike Brecker. A discreetly virtuosic amalgam of the styles of John Coltrane and the rounder, more embracing sound of the soul-saxophonists and southern blues players, Brecker is also the most extensively recorded, since he has performed with John Lennon, Yoko Ono, Eric Clapton and James Taylor. If there is a secret to Brecker's success it is that he has found a polished and sophisticated equivalent for every innovation; a softened abrasiveness from the Sixties avant-garde, a blues-sax raunchiness without coarseness, and an extensive awareness of the jazz past. But Brecker is far from being a brilliant and tasteful mimic. He understands the nuances, nudging inflections, slurs and tonal changes, that lubricate jazz improvisation, and prevent it from being merely fusillades of chromatic scales.

Brecker comes from a musical family – his father was a skilled jazz pianist, though he became an attorney eventually. His older brother, Randy, is a trumpeter who made an early success of his career with the fusion band Blood Sweat and Tears. Bands at summer camps triggered their musical ambitions. Mike Brecker made his debut with a fusion band, Birdsong, then the two brothers formed an influential jazz-rock band called Dreams, with drummer BILLY COBHAM. It was with the success of other Cobham groups that the saxophonist became widely noticed. With vibraharpist, Mike Mainieri, he formed Steps Ahead, in 1978, an intelligent fusion band that featured memorable original compositions and held Brecker's interest for nearly ten years.

*Michael Brecker (MCA MCAD 5980)

Brecker's debut album, which took him until 1987 to get around to. It was one of the strongest albums of that year, confounding expectations that the chameleon Brecker would have nothing to say on a session of his own, and featured a sensational band including CHARLIE HADEN, on bass, JACK DEJOHNETTE, on drums, Kenny Kirkland, on piano, and PAT METHENY, on guitar. The disc opens like a languid Pat Metheny session on 'Sea Glass', but its theme echoes the dignified poise of Abdullah Ibrahim, before Brecker's storming Coltraneish solo. On an unaccompanied duet with DeJohnette, Brecker delivers a saxophone soliloquy that confirms all his mastery of the delicate details of the horn.

Bruford, Bill (William Scott)

(Born Sevenoaks, England, May 17, 1949)
Bill Bruford is an original and broadminded drummer who emerged in the late 1960s and made his reputation in the art-rock movement, with bands like Yes and King Crimson. He grew interested in jazz at school, being out of step by preferring Mingus to the Rolling Stones or the Beatles; he initially tried to push Yes toward jazz.

Since 1986, Bruford has been working extensively with his fusion quartet Earthworks, featuring two prominent Loose Tubes voices in DJANGO BATES (keyboards) and IAIN BALLAMY (saxophone). During King Crimson's comeback period of 1980–84, Bruford experimented with the electronic drums, and the expanded range of sound effects available encouraged his enthusiasm for musical travelogues, recreating the melodic sound of West African drums or the guttural drone of a didgeridoo.

*Dig! (EG EEGCD 60)

Bruford in powerful partnership with Django Bates and Iaim Ballamy. Bates' musical restlessness and impatience with recycled formulae suits Bruford's own, and the repertoire on Dig! shifts from calypso, to a bizarre, melancholy, Nordic version of the Petula Clark hit 'Downtown', to a melange of New Orleans and Coltrane-like music on Bates', 'Dancing on Frith Street'.

Burton, Gary

(Born Indiana, January 23, 1943)

In the 1960s the vibraharpist Gary Burton seemed to have solved many of the problems confronted by practitioners of the instrument. He avoided the clipped, hollow tone of many vibists, colouring his sound through a remarkable chordal technique (using several mallets at once) and a slurred, bent-note effect that had previously seemed beyond the instrument's scope.

Burton surfaced as a seventeen year old, on an early Sixties recording featuring Hank Garland, a country and western session guitarist, on a bebop outing. The young musician's skills attracted tenorist Stan Getz, who hired him in 1964, but later in the decade Burton moved closer to jazz-rock and worked extensively with guitarists – initially LARRY CORYELL, then a variety of others, including PAT METHENY.

Burton's sublime sound and song-like thematic constructions in his solos (as well as an attractive hillbilly quality about his tunes) always made him distinctive, and in some respects his talents were similar to pianist KEITH JARRETT's. But it was with the challenge of unexpected company or of unfamiliar compositions that he often played at his best – most notably on CARLA BLEY's suite, 'A Genuine Tong Funeral', which was composed for him. Burton has remained interested in jazz education, preserving his connection with his old college (Berklee, in Boston) and his career has been variable after that impressive start. He has successfully recorded duets with pianists Jarrett and CHICK COREA, relaunched his quartet life in partnership with an excellent guitarist Mick Goodrick, in 1973, explored semi-classical ventures (once again with Corea) and continued to give promising Berklee musicians exposure in his band – notably pianist Makoto Ozone, and Scottish saxophonist TOMMY SMITH.

★The New Quartet (ECM 835 002-2)

The 1973 Burton quartet with Mick Goodrick, on guitar, Abe Laboriel, on bass, and Harry Blazer, on drums. Though all these players were little known at the time, Burton returned to form with them, discovering an impetus he had lost, through bustling group give-and-take on pieces by Carla Bley, Keith Jarrett, MICHAEL GIBBS and others.

★*Artists Choice* (Bluebird/BMG ND 86280)

A 1963–68 compilation of Burton's music for RCA, during his first, and most energetic phase. There are tracks from his work with George Shearing and Stan Getz, as well as the quirkier presence of saxophonists STEVE LACY and GATO BARBIERI, from the Jazz Composers' Orchestra, introduced to Burton by Carla Bley for 'A Genuine Tong Funeral', two tracks of which are represented here. Burton, the pop-influenced romantic, is in evidence on the multi-tracked 'Norwegian Wood', but generally the music has a youthful buzz about it, that the vibraharpist has found hard to recapture.

B Shops for the Poor

Jon Dobie (guitar, alto), David Petts (tenor), Louise Petts (alto), Steve Blake (tenor, soprano, piano), John Edwards (bass), Sarra Tyler (vocals).

A British band in the tradition of jazz/art-rock hybrids with an explicit political streak, like the now defunct band, Henry Cow. Moving in a resolutely opposite course to the 'fusion' school (which has sought to blend what appear to be compatible elements of jazz and pop), B Shops have merged different musical persuasions in order to emphasise the incompatibility. Their music has been drawn from post-Cage contemporary straight music, European and American free improvisation, and electro-pop, with a clattering industrial impressionism of their own.

★*The Iceberg Principle* (No Wave CD1)

Fourteen originals and a Brecht-Eisler song. The band's first CD is a determined march of dense, obsessive saxophone ensemble patterns, impassively declamatory female singing and episodes of free-jazz collectively improvised – crisply played, melodically audacious, drawing in many strands of music, but stark and severe and not for devotees of orthodox lyricism.

Carr, Ian

(Born Dumfries, Scotland, April 21, 1933)
Scottish-born trumpeter Ian Carr is not only one of the most

distinctive British inheritors of MILES DAVIS' trumpet sound, a pioneer of jazz-rock fusion from the earliest days of the idiom and a prolific composer, he is also a journalist and a jazz academic – the latter a rare breed in Britain, though more common in the States. A biographer of both Miles Davis and KEITH JARRETT, Carr has been fascinated by versions of jazz that are both sophisticated and yet border on pop success, since his first fusion explorations with his own jazz-rock ensemble, Nucleus. Prior to which he worked with his organist brother, Mike, in a Tyneside bebop group called the Emcee Five, which occasionally featured the then undiscovered guitarist, JOHN McLAUGHLIN.

Carr left the north in 1962, coming to London to form a bebop group with saxophonist Don Rendell, that became one of the most highly-regarded British jazz bands of the mid-Sixties. During the decade he worked with many significant bop and post-bop Britons, including saxophonists Joe Harriott and Barbara Thompson, pianist Michael Garrick, and composers Neil Ardley and MIKE WESTBROOK. In 1969, he launched Nucleus (inspired by the mid Sixties work of both HERBIE HANCOCK and Miles Davis) which performed on the 1970 Newport Jazz Festival and, through the next decade, all over the world. In 1986, Carr began developing extended pieces for jazz instruments and string orchestra, the genesis of his full length piece, 'Old Heartland'.

★*Old Heartland* (MMC CDMMC 1016)

An album from Carr of fusion of a different kind – that between his Nucleus-based jazz musicians and the Kreisler String Orchestra, in a programmatic piece based on the notion of walks in the Northumbrian countryside, where he was raised. It blends contemplative (bordering on New Age) lyricism with punchy bass-lines and unexpectedly intricate ensemble writing for the strings. Not a wholly successful session (the ensemble parts aren't consistently tight, nor some of the themes much more than routine) but it's a bold sally by Carr into unfamiliar territory.

Camilo, Michel

(Born Santa Domingo, Dominican Republic, 1954)
A one-man street-party of a pianist, whose dancing, colourful,

Caribbean-dominated music puts him in the same category for pianistic resourcefulness and rhythm-driven accessibility as CHICK COREA, in the Seventies, but without the affectation.

Camilo began as a conservatoire musician, and played in a symphony orchestra in his mid-teens. But as his interest in jazz grew, he took up studies in New York, at the beginning of the Eighties, and began to perform with prominent New York jazz musicians. From 1983 to 1985, Camilo performed breathless salsa music with the Paquito D'Rivera group, contributing an original composition, 'Why Not?', which became the title of a D'Rivera album, and was subsequently recorded by other artists. In the late Eighties Camilo began working around New York on his own account, and his shows began to take off with the press. A pianist of unselfconscious exuberance with a drummer-like forcefulness, who is never far from fiesta-like displays of pounding chordal variations, Camilo is still a resourceful improvisor, whose skills are likely to deepen and widen into the Nineties.

★*Why Not?* (King K32Y 6031)

Why Not? is a 1986 recording featuring Camilo with excellent support, including the charismatic Lew Soloff, on trumpet, and British-born saxophonist Chris Hunter. The title track is the most successful cut, displaying some delightful bravura Soloff, but the trumpeter delivers a lot of blistering street-festival trumpet, on other attractively buoyant themes, throughout the session. Hunter sounds a little as if he's trying to squeeze too much bebop alto into what ought to be spacious, open-handed music, but generally it's a delightful session, invaluable for a party or for an evening in the armchair.

Carter, Betty

(Born Flint, Michigan, May 16, 1930)
A supreme jazz singer capable of reinventing songs in ways that both enhance the already precious ones and wickedly caricature the worst, particularly of Tin Pan Alley. Alternating between sounding unfinished, skidding away from notes half-formed, and a rhythmic bounce as infectious as a drummer ('What A Little

Moonlight Can Do'), Betty Carter can also develop a kind of
sensuous assertiveness, when she stops running, as on the
brooding 'Make It Last'.

Carter comes from Michigan originally, and was born Ella Mae
Jones. She appeared onstage with Charlie Parker, in Detroit, in
the Forties (playing hookey from school and altering her birth
certificate to avoid the club's 'No Juveniles' rule); a period in which
she was hypnotised by bop music and its lifestyle. She maintained
a stormy relationship with the Lionel Hampton band for a couple
of years, being fired seven times by the boss and rehired seven
times by Hampton's wife Gladys, who was a Carter fan. Hampton
wanted her to improvise all the time – he dubbed her 'Betty
Bebop', which she hated – but his pressure helped Carter to
become one of the first jazz singers to get the hang of the new
idiom, and develop ways of using the voice that could genuinely
interact with the horns, rather than conventionally delivering a
clothes-horse vocal line that the others would then busily fall to
stitching their complicated seams on.

But though she was a fine big-band singer, and later an inspired
and inspiring collaborator, with artists like MILES DAVIS and Ray
Charles, it has always been in small groups that she has been at
her most inventive. In such situations she can wind together and
pick apart a tapestry of vocal invention that is quite unlike both
the wide-screen, heart-on-the-sleeve emotionalism of the torchy
jazz singers, or the metallic, disembodied scatting of bop vocalists,
who pretend to be instruments – a practice she nowadays actively
dislikes. Like the late Art Blakey, Betty Carter relishes working
with musicians much younger than herself, and up-and-coming
young musicians, like pianist Benny Green and drummer Winard
Harper, have been dynamic additions to her group in recent years.

Finally – Betty Carter (Roulette/EMI CDP 795333-2)

Despite winning a Grammy in 1989, the exciting *Look What I Got*
was nevertheless bizarrely deleted by Verve. This session, from
1969, is a worthy CD addition however, a live performance of ten
pieces (including two medleys combining 'Body and Soul', 'I Didn't
Know What Time It Was' and 'All the Things You Are')
performed in New York. Carter's ability not only to reforge the
most familiar materials, in her own image, but even to reforge

them several different ways in the same account, is on brilliant display here – skidding, diving and sliding through 'Seems Like Old Times', tantalisingly drawn-out on 'I Remember You', glowing on 'Blue Moon'.

Chase, Thomas 'Tommy'

(Born Manchester, England, March 22, 1947)
Drummer Tommy Chase has been, since the British rebirth of bop through the energies of jazz-loving club DJs like Paul Murphy, a major hit with dance audiences. Chase won Best Group and Best Album awards, from the readers of Britain's *Wire* magazine in 1986. His albums have punchy, bullish titles like *Hard!* and *Drive!*, and he is devoted to hard bop, particularly to the backbeat-driven bop-funk popular with organ-led goups in the Sixties. Chase's current band strongly features an organist.

Chase's own playing, which acknowledges both Art Blakey and Max Roach, but most explicitly displays the boiling cymbal beat and incandescent snare-drum flurries of the former, is an excellent representation of the vigour, and occasional relentlessness, of the hard bop movement. His bands swing so hard, and the riffs on which the music depends (much of the repertoire consisting of the classic originals, or the band's own closely-moulded remakes) echo so infectiously in the mind, that it isn't surprising that Chase became such a favourite of the new bop wave.

Chase was raised in Worsley, on the outskirts of Manchester. Like many school-age jazz fans, in the early Sixties, his enthusiasm for jazz was an oddity to be shared only with one or two other converts. He was turned on to jazz by hearing trumpeter Clifford Brown on record (the fact that the local fish-shop was run by a man called Charlie Parker, and the local optician was Clifford Brown, could only be a source of private amusement for Chase). A professional drummer at seventeen, playing summer shows and cruises, he began forming his own bands in the mid-Seventies in London, supported visiting Americans, and dedicated himself to a salty danceable jazz repertoire, though still with considerable space for improvisors.

★*Rebel Fire* (Mole Records MRTC 002)

A 1990 Chase album, mostly a celebration of effects like raucous soul saxophone, churning organ and whiplash backbeat. More of a club DJ's disc than a feet-up-at-home session, it belts through its material with infectious elan and features a fine organist in Gary Baldwin (an adherent of the Jimmy Smith style) and a powerful up-and-coming talent in altoist Ben Waghorn, strikingly impassioned on 'I Have A Dream'.

Cherry, Donald E 'Don'

(Born Oklahoma City, November 18, 1936)
Trumpeter Don Cherry is an indisputable one-off in jazz. Originally a bebop trumpeter, he is nowadays as likely to perform a John Lee Hooker blues, on a Malinese hunting guitar (the *doussn'gourni*), as a post-bop trumpet variation on an Ornette Coleman theme. He favours a Pakistani pocket trumpet to produce a high, slightly closeted sound, phrasing in bubbling clusters of notes, and he avoids conventionally structured runs in favour of exclamatory and interrogatory sounds, double-take silences, and sudden incandescent ascents from the mid to the upper range of the horn. Cherry's independence has led him to work with some of the best of contemporary musicians, including Ornette Coleman, Sonny Rollins, GATO BARBIERI, CARLA BLEY and Lou Reed. He has also worked onstage with his pop-star step-daughter Neneh Cherry, whom he claims as a significant influence.

Cherry's arrival on the world's jazz stage began in the winter of 1958, when the Ornette Coleman quartet rehearsed for its impending revolution in Cherry's mother's garage in Watts. A revolution that was greeted effusively the next year by enlightened establishment authorities, like the late Leonard Bernstein and Gunther Schuller. Cherry, who is of both Afro-American and Indian-American descent (his grandmother was a Choctaw) has a simple definition of world music – 'the music of people who have been listening and travelling'.

Cherry has been a deserving recipient of the (nowadays almost obligatory) title 'world-musician' since around 1966. It was then that he left the States for Stockholm (having met his second wife Moki, a painter and mother of Neneh, whilst on a European tour with Sonny Rollins) and spent the early months of his new life in the city's Ethnographic Museum, studying ethnic instruments. Cherry then took his new family in a camper through Africa, the Middle East and India. Sitting in with village musicians on three continents led Cherry to perceive his jazz background in a new light, as providing a set of improvisational inflections and timbres that could be introduced into spaces within an overall sound quite different from jazz.

Though before he left the States Cherry had achieved what the *New York Times* called 'the respectful obscurity reserved for important jazz players who didn't die young and who aren't Miles Davis', lack of interest in his expressionistic style didn't hold him up. He had formed an audacious small-group with Argentianian tenorist Gato Barbieri, producing classic albums such as *Complete Communion* and *Symphony for Improvisors*, worked with ethereal ingenuity with Carla Bley and the Jazz Composers' Orchestra on the Indian-influenced *Escalator Over The Hill*, and explored Tibetan and Japanese music, with sitarist Collin Wallcott, in the band Cordona.

Latterly Cherry has signed up with a major record label again (A & M) and recorded the Ornettish jazz album *Art Deco*, and more recently the eclectic *Multi Kulti*. He has returned to the States and even found himself invited to compose a mass, incorporating motifs from all the world's religions, which he performed, with the Brazilian percussionist NANA VASCONCELOS, at a San Francisco festival.

★*Brown Rice* (A&M CDA 0809)

Performed in 1976, in the company of bassist CHARLIE HADEN, drummer Billy Higgins and others, *Brown Rice* begins with a mantra and ends with African music – the session is a more than usually successful attempt to unite Eastern music with jazz, and the cymbal beat of the remarkable Billy Higgins glistens like snowflakes. Cherry's singing is heard a good deal on it, an acquired taste, as may be the raw and ungentle sound of Frank Lowe's saxophone.

★*Art Deco* (A&M 395 258-2)

A distinctly jazzy recording, with two of Cherry's most creative partners – bassist Charlie Haden and drummer Billy Higgins – plus Texan saxophonist James Clay, an early collaborator with Ornette Coleman, but who missed out on Coleman's revolution and spent much of his life as a sideman in the Ray Charles band. Clay has some of the broad tone of Sonny Rollins, and some of the unfinished, squawky quality of the late Warne Marsh. A striking example of the sort of retrospective that gets the process a good name.

★*Multi Kulti* (A&M 395 323)

A strongly ethnic-flavoured 1990 session, finding the trumpeter with a variety of interesting associates (including the soulful altoist, Carlos Ward, and the West Coast multi-genre Hieroglyphics Ensemble) who together perform a repertoire that draws on Western pop, free jazz, Middle-Eastern and African music, and many of the other ingredients that Cherry has been absorbing since the 1960s. Open melodious music, nodding to salsa, funk and hard bop, but without ever giving off that inconsequential quality that much idiom-sampling jazz does.

Cobham, William 'Billy'

(Born Panama, May 16, 1944)
Until the late 1960s, drumkits used in both jazz and rock music hadn't changed much in thirty years. But as rock shows became more spectacular and virtuosic, drum equipment expanded to the point where players sat surrounded by batteries of tom-toms and forests of cymbals. One of the most popular Seventies exponents of a jazz style mutated into fusion, who based his playing on constant stormy rolls around just such a collection of hardware, was Billy Cobham. But Cobham, who came to international prominence through his stint with JOHN MCLAUGHLIN's Mahavishnu Orchestra, wasn't merely a purveyor of party tricks and high volume, but a manipulator of rhythmic tension and release, whose methods were studied by jazz-rock drummers all over the world.

Cobham's skills were first noticed during his employment by pianist Horace Silver in 1968 (though he had begun with funk outfits, such as Grover Washington's) and he moved further into fusion territory when he formed Dreams, with the BRECKER brothers, and worked on several MILES DAVIS albums, including *Bitches' Brew*. He was the first of several drummers with the Mahavishnu Orchestra, a band that brought new sophistication to fusion, by blending strains of jazz, Indian music, rock and country music. Later in the Seventies Cobham formed his own bands, as well as being a highly regarded teacher, both in the States and in Europe, where he lived from the mid-Eighties.

★*The Best of Billy Cobham* (WEA K 781 558-2)

Compilation of Cobham sessions in the Seventies, from albums such as *Crosswinds*, *Spectrum* and *Total Eclipse*. It's a bit of a sprawl, and Cobham's lightning playing, brilliant though it is, becomes inexorable after a time. *Spectrum*, however, was one of the better jazz-rock albums of the period and the best track from it here, 'Quadrant 4', features the soaring, wailing, rock guitar of Tommy Bolin.

Coe, Anthony George 'Tony'

(Born Canterbury, England, November 29, 1934)
It's become commonplace today for jazz musicians to build a reputation on the ability to play in many styles. But some musicians have been displaying this talent for years, and without a hint of pastiche. One such is the great English reed player, Tony Coe. In a career that began in the mid-Fifties, Coe has performed mainstream jazz, bebop, classical music, free improvisation – even been offered a job by Count Basie. He is a brilliant clarinettist, a luxuriant tenorist, and a thoughtful composer, able to draw materials from music as diverse as Debussy's and Louis Armstrong's.

Coe's father was a clarinettist, and the boy learned the instrument formally, but taught himself the saxophone. He studied composition, including, for a time, with Richard Rodney Bennett; and performed, in the early Sixties, with Humphrey

Lyttelton's mainstream band and then with JOHN DANKWORTH. As well as playing with the European/American Kenny Clarke-Francy Boland band, during the Seventies, he extended his experience in the direction of free improvisation, with guitarist Derek Bailey's COMPANY. In addition to jazz work with composer, MICHAEL GIBBS, and other illustrious English players, such as drummer Tony Oxley, and trumpeter Ken Wheeler, Coe also performed with Alan Hacker, clarinettist in the classical and contemporary-conservatoire chamber group, Matrix. In another guise, his is the famous tenor part, with Henry Mancini's band, on the *Pink Panther* soundtracks.

Coe's tone hints at the influence of Ellington's Johnny Hodges, and a more recent one, Paul Gonsalves. His overall musicianship is notable for broadmindedness and a knowledge of modern straight composers (Alban Berg and Pierre Boulez in particular) which have made him an unusually adaptable and resourceful artist.

★*Canterbury Song* (Hot House HHCD 1005)

Attractive and unassuming set by the lustrous Coe, in collaboration with American members of the Paris Reunion band – Benny Bailey, on trumpet, Horace Parlan, on piano, Jimmy Woode, on bass, and Idris Muhammad, on drums. The group wreathes effortlessly through a selection of classy compositions, including the MILES DAVIS vehicle, 'Blue in Green', 'I Guess I'll Hang My Tears Out to Dry' and *Return to Forever*'s sensuous, 'Sometime Ago'.

Coleman, Steve

(Born Chicago, 1956)
Among the new generation of jazz musicians now in their twenties and early thirties, saxophonist Steve Coleman has become something of a guru. He comes in several incarnations. He can be a neo-bop altoist of a force, fluency and freedom that reveals an indebtedness (discerning rather than adulatory) to Charlie Parker and to his namesake, Ornette Coleman. But he is

also a musician raised with the street-beat of the Eighties. A confirmed combatant against the new classicism who dislikes the idea of remaking bebop's triumphs with modern technology, and instead makes a music clearly wide open to the influence of the more adventurous black pop of the present period.

Coleman was born on Chicago's South Side, and grew up listening to funk and rock. His father, a Charlie Parker fan, introduced him to bebop, but it wasn't until he was a student at Wesleyan University that he rediscovered Parker for himself, as the route to learning to improvise, after some years of playing alto with house and funk outfits. Once bitten, Coleman started to absorb experience from some Chicago veterans – notably one of jazz's greatest, underrated, saxophonists, Von Freeman. In 1978, Steve Coleman moved to New York, joined the Thad Jones/Mel Lewis big band, and, later, ensembles led by Slide Hampton, Cecil Taylor and Sam Rivers. These were all associations that helped build Coleman's, currently remarkable, facility with several jazz and pop vocabularies; but regular sessions with the drummer, Doug Hammond – a musician alert to Coleman's emerging inventiveness – were the most useful experiences for the saxophonist.

For his playing alone, Coleman deserves a place in the first rank of modern saxophonists, but he sought a wider influence in modern jazz through his own ambitions. He wanted nothing less than to find a contemporary equivalent for the breakthrough Charlie Parker had made in the Forties. For this purpose he chose hip-hop and rap and other black-derived materials of the Eighties, as elements to combine with bop – and to combine them in ways that stretched the potential of all the forms rather than finding a lowest-common-denominator blend, acceptable to the fusion market. With that in mind, Coleman started the band, Five Elements, whilst working for a highly virtuosic, but more down-the-line jazz band led by bassist, DAVE HOLLAND. His work has become part of the output of a group of like-minded, young, New York players operating under the collective title of M-Base – not only to pursue similar musical ends, but also to take financial and logistical control of their own products. So far, Coleman's work with his own band has been erratic, and admirers of his straight-jazz sound can hear it better displayed on Dave Holland records, such as *Triplicate*.

★*World Expansion* (JMT 872010)

Featuring Coleman with an early New York busking associate, Mark Johnson, on drums, plus the excellent ROBIN EUBANKS and Geri Allen, on trombone and piano respectively, and Cassandra Wilson (a more abstract version of BETTY CARTER) on vocals. This was a 1986 outing for the Five Elements band, enterprisingly developing a group sound of fertile overlaps, dancing rhythms and collective spontaneity – but it's still troubled by the contradictions of working in the same territory as a flat-out grooving band, like Defunkt, and, at the same time, trying to improvise. Coleman's efforts at a brisk impressionism of the world's music cultures disrupt the focus too.

★*Rhythm People – the Resurrection of Creative Black Civilisation* (RCA/Novus PD 83092)

Coleman's 1990 output with Five Elements, this time with the added clout of Dave Holland, on bass, and Marvin 'Smitty' Smith, on drums, but again not quite hitting the mix of creative audacity and airplay funk that he's after. Dave Gilmore's guitar is fierce and bluesy, Coleman's alto is fleet and assertive, and Cassandra Wilson's vocal aerobatics strengthen the set, but an hour of choppy funk rhythms (Reggie Washington, on bass, and Smith, on drums, clatter and skid relentlessly) probably become less wearing to listen to on a DJ's turntable, in a club, than on the CD player at home. Coleman has yet to focus his revolution.

Company

Twelve years ago Derek Bailey first thought of the idea of forming a loosely-knit group for improvising musicians, dedicated to no one particular style of jazz. It was the opinion of this spirited British guitarist (born Sheffield, January 29, 1930) that bands were interesting up to the point that they 'discovered their music', after which they hardened into a style, and became less interesting improvisationally. Since the late 1960s, Bailey, in the development of his career, had been largely true to these principles himself. Originally a nightclub and session performer in the north of England (his father was a professional musician)

Bailey came, via work with British dance-band stars like Kathy Kirby and Lita Roza, to a free-jazz group, along Coltrane lines, in Sheffield. From that point the guitarist and his contemporaries moved further away from mainstream, abandoning fixed rhythms, harmonic structures or tunes.

Bailey conceived of Company in an attempt to combat the tyranny of style. It became a unique association of musicians that was differentiated by geography, language, musical training and personal tastes, and united only by an interest in occasionally making an unpremeditated and unrehearsed music in the company of irregular partners or even total strangers. Musicians as different as the brilliant, modern classical trombonist, Vinko Globakar and, one of the most piquant and distinctive voices of the Cool Jazz movement of the 1950s, Lee Konitz, have taken part.

Over the years, Company – unable to entirely ignore the return to older structural principles elsewhere in jazz – has grown more virtuosic and accommodating to audiences, and less revealing of the expressionist inclinations of players. Furthermore, though Derek Bailey's original enthusiasm was for a music that depended on no shared language or anticipated behaviour, this proved hard to sustain since there was a growing international enthusiasm for precisely this way of playing; a fact that was bound to evolve a shared language. Company's performances, though they would never grace the 'easy listening' racks, continue to provide stimulating experiences at the more ascetic end of free jazz.

★*Once* (Incus CD04)

'Cool school' sax star, Lee Konitz, in 1987, among other things, straightfacedly draping 'It Ain't Necessarily So', over the drifting cello and arco bass (Tristan Honsinger and Barre Phillips). The unfamiliarity of larger free ensembles makes Konitz hesitant at times, and it doesn't sound like a situation he would spend the rest of his life trying to repeat. But *Once* is, nevertheless, an empathetic set of musical conversations, with a high level of dynamic variety. Guitarist Bailey's frosty, gleaming harmonics and skittering runs, and virtuoso bassist Barre Phillips's restless sonorities are powerful features.

Corea, Armando Anthony 'Chick'
(Born Massachusetts, June 12, 1941)
Of all the genuinely gifted musicians to have emerged in jazz over the past thirty years, pianist Chick Corea has been one of the most inconsistent. By the end of the 1960s it seemed clear that he, KEITH JARRETT and HERBIE HANCOCK, were not only the leading pianists of their generation but were sufficiently visionary and artistically ambitious to positively redirect the course of jazz. But though Corea has often played beautifully and contributed several catchy compositions to the music, his work has, equally, often been crude and repetitious.

Corea had an early headstart, classically trained and playing piano and drums before he was ten. In the early Sixties he worked with jazz-funk and jazz-dance bands, led by Mongo Santamaria and HERBIE MANN, and he gained a reputation as a crisp, lyrical acoustic pianist with an infectious feel for Latin music. Later in the decade Corea worked with the saxophonist Stan Getz, as both a composer and a sensitive accompanist, and then joined MILES DAVIS as the trumpeter's fusion involvement intensified. But unlike many jazz-rock bands, Davis's was loose enough to encourage abstraction among the melody players, as long as the pulse was secure. This taste of freer music led Corea and the band's British bassist, DAVE HOLLAND, to leave and form a semi-free band, Circle, which was closer to the European improvising scene than the Afro-American tradition; although Corea left after a year, complaining that the music was leaving audiences behind.

He then formed one of the most vivacious of Seventies fusion bands, the Latin-influenced, Return to Forever (including singer FLORA PURIM), which in its early incarnations was light and flexible, but which became harder and noisier with personnel changes, eventually breaking up in 1980. Since then, Corea has returned to acoustic playing with a jazz trio, and with partners such as pianist Herbie Hancock and vibraharpist GARY BURTON, as well as recording classical music and writing his own piano concerto. In 1986, he resurrected his interest in electric music, which dated from Return to Forever, with his Elektric Band, featuring drummer, Dave Weckl.

★*Now He Sings Now He Sobs* (Blue Note CDP 790 055-2)
Corea's 1968 acoustic piano trio album with drumer, Roy Haynes,

and bassist, Miroslav Vitous, and the best early indication of the sophistication and richness of his resources, drawn from Horace Silver, Bud Powell and Bill Evans. The CD includes the delightful waltz, 'Windows', which Corea originally wrote for Stan Getz' *Sweet Rain* album, but there is enough stretching and twisting of conventional materials to suggest the pianist's coming fascination with the avant-garde.

★*ARC* (ECM 833 678-2)

Corea with, Circle partners, Dave Holland (bass) and Barry Altschul (drums). Fascinating insight into how far (the subsequently conservative) Corea was prepared to go, and how taut and inventive the Holland/Altschul team was. Pieces include the band's uniquely deconstructivist version of the WAYNE SHORTER/ Miles Davis vehicle, 'Nefertiti'.

★*Return To Forever* (ECM 811978-2)

The first *Return to Forever* album, from 1972, and the best by miles. The songs featuring Flora Purim (notably 'What Game Shall We Play Today' and 'Sometime Ago') have a feathery, playful quality that is never coy. Corea's electric piano is delicate, propulsive and as yet devoid of electric-keyboard cliches, while STANLEY CLARKE's bass is springy and agile and the late Joe Farrell's grainy tenor lends a necessary grit.

★*Elektric Band* (GRPD 9535)

Headbanging jazz-rock for fans of Corea's later work. Sometimes possessed of an infectious pulse, and there are bursts of invention from John Patitucci, on guitar; but largely disappointing, and confirmation of Corea's (probably subconscious) drive toward patronising his audiences.

Coryell, Larry

(Born Galveston, Texas, April 2, 1943)
Larry Coryell is a magnificently equipped guitarist uncertain of

what to do with his abilities, but he did deliver (notably with his band, Eleventh House) some of the more convincing displays of fusion guitar playing, as well as working more discreetly in inventive low-volume partnerships, notably with the late EMILY REMLER, a fellow guitarist.

Coryell studied journalism, but as a rock player, influenced by the country style of Chet Atkins and later by Jimi Hendrix, he had performed in amateur bands as a teenager. Formal guitar lessons, after he graduated, led him to turn to a musical career, and he worked with some Latin-influenced and rock-slanted bands, including those led by percussionist Chico Hamilton, flautist HERBIE MANN (on the influential jazz-rock catalyst *Memphis Underground*) and vibist GARY BURTON.

Coryell's feverish, but often exciting, Eleventh House band (including a tempestuous drummer, Al Mouzon, and trumpeter Randy Brecker) toured the world. After its demise Coryell turned to acoustic and, in some cases, classical music. *Introducing the Eleventh House*, would be a welcome addition to the CD listing.

★*Spaces* (Start Records VMCD 7305)

Excellent Seventies session, teaming Coryell with fellow guitarist JOHN MCLAUGHLIN, plus CHICK COREA (piano), Miroslav Vitous (bass) and BILLY COBHAM (drums). Fluent, conversational and undemonstrative exchanges between McLaughlin and Coryell run throughout the disc with a sensitivity that neither man was unequivocally displaying elsewhere at the time.

★*Together* (Concord CCD 4289)

Graceful and selfless exchange between Coryell and Emily Remler, the Wes Montgomery-influenced bop guitarist who died of a heart attack at thirty two. Coryell's style has been through more batterings (from blues and rhythm & blues influences) than Remler's, and the contrast of his punchiness with her balletic fluency brings the set (guitar duos not always being the most dynamic of collaborations) to life. Remler's acceleration of Clifford Brown's, 'Joyspring', into purring double-time, and her discreet encouragement, as an accompanist, are a reminder of what a loss her early death was.

Crispell, Marilyn

(Born Philadelphia, 1947)

Since the whirlwind arrival of Cecil Taylor on the jazz scene at the beginning of the 1960s, there have been few other pianists who have taken on the avant-garde's challenges to jazz structure, tonality and phrasing, with comparable ferocity. Marilyn Crispell is one, a fitting inheritor of Taylor's mantle, and though she has latterly been developing a voice distinct from his, her mixture of disruptive energy, precise articulation and wide range of raw materials continually recalls Taylor's immense contribution to new music. She is most like Taylor on zipping ascents and descents, rippling, atonal arpeggios and banging, dissonant chords; but has a tendency to be less declamatory and unforgiving than him, giving the sometimes brutal Taylor legacy a communicative, conversational air. Unlike Taylor, however, who has usually dominated any situation he appears in, Crispell has been an inspired collaborator, most commonly with multi-instrumentalist and composer, ANTHONY BRAXTON – who has called her, Taylor excepted, 'the strongest pianist I know of'.

Crispell took up the piano at seven, and studied piano and composition at Boston's New England Conservatory. But she switched her studies to medicine, only returning to music six years later – as a blues singer. Coltrane's, 'A Love Supreme', and the piano playing of Thelonious Monk and Taylor, drew her to jazz. She studied the music from then on, mostly at the Creative Music Studio in Woodstock, meeting many inventive musicians, Braxton among them. As with Taylor, many contrasting lines converge and collide, like atomic particles, in her music, and she enjoys ensemble playing partly in order that the particles should be approaching from angles she least expects.

★*Gaia* (Leo Records CDLR 152)

A trio album, featuring Reggie Workman, on bass, and Doug James, on drums. It is Crispell's most balanced recording, intense and shapely improvisation without a formal structure (nor with much recourse to jazz time on the part of Workman or James) yet it is the most compelling and orderly of free sessions. Crispell's Taylorisms are clearly audible, yet these are about the only elements that qualify as 'references' in a taut, selfless, and powerful three-way dialogue.

Crombie, Anthony John 'Tony'

(Born London, August 27, 1925)

A relaxed and propulsive drummer with a style embracing both swing and bop techniques, who emerged in the first British bebop wave of the late 1940s. Crombie continues to appear on club dates with his inimitable blend of cool diffidence and rhythmic punch, and, until recent years, he was also a prolific composer, both for other jazz musicians and for film scores.

Crombie's mother was a cinema pianist in the silent era, and her son was self-taught as a drummer. After working on the London nightclub scene of the war years, Crombie was a driving force in the London bebop circle, that also included JOHN DANKWORTH and Ronnie Scott. He was also an early fusion artist, using a group of jazz musicians to form a rock and roll band called The Rockets, in the mid-Fifties.

Crombie has accompanied innumerable visiting stars including Tony Bennett, Lena Horne and Jack Jones, and backed Coleman Hawkins, Ben Webster and others, at Ronnie Scott's club. His tunes have been recorded by MILES DAVIS, Paul Gonsalves, Stephane Grappelli and others.

Atmosphere (Renaissance CDREN 002)

It may be a small audience that's likely to be fascinated by a short-lived British fusion experiment of the 1950s, but this collection is an intriguing compilation of the work of Tony Crombie's Rockets, in 1958; a band designed to cash in on the rock and roll boom, but which couldn't disguise its jazzy sophistication. Crombie, a sharp, witty arranger, put together all the charts, which mingle bebop and bluesy groovers like, 'St James' Infirmary'. The great Tubby Hayes is to be heard on vibes and saxophones (powerful on baritone, on 'I'll Close My Eyes') and Crombie's cruising swing drives the eight-piece delightfully.

Tony Crombie and Friends (Renaissance CDREN 001)

A recent Crombie session, featuring the thoughtfully swinging tenor of Ronnie Scott (partnered by the dazzling newcomer, Nigel Hitchcock) and a substantial amount of Crombie's tightly edited and, at times Ellington-influenced, piano playing. The Latin pieces on this disc only just escape the humdrum, but elsewhere Crombie's warmth, intelligence and originality shine on.

Crusaders

The Crusaders predated the jazz-rock fusion boom of the Seventies by a considerable number of years. The central figures in the band were, pianist, **Joe Sample** (born Houston, February 1, 1939) saxophonist, **Wilton Felder** (born Houston, August 31, 1940) and drummer, **Nesbert 'Stix' Hooper** (born Houston, August 15, 1938); other players, on sax, trombone and bass came and went. Emerging as the Modern Jazz Sextet, in Texas, in 1958, the outfit then moved to the West Coast, having changed their name to the Nighthawks, and eventually released a first album, in 1961, after a third, and final, change of name to the Crusaders. The band's sound was more plush and relaxed than the more metallic styles that were to surface in jazz-rock. It was created from compelling bass riffs, warm-toned ensembles and, in particular, Wilton Felder's steamy, wide-screen tenor sound. As they became more popular, their work was appropriated by others – notably, with several Crusader-derived hit records, the Average White Band.

The best Crusaders records were made in the Seventies, during the period when the graceful guitarist, Larry Carlton, was a band member, and very little of it is so far on CD. The band didn't recover musically from the eclipse of jazz-rock, despite having been one of the most satisfying group representations of it. Some steps toward more commercial success were made through partnerships with hit singers, like Randy Crawford and Bobby Womack. Stix Hooper left in 1983, and though he was replaced by Leon Chancler, the Crusaders have never returned to prominence. The glossy, driving, highly varied, *Southern Comfort*, deserves reissue.

★*Streetlife* (MCAD 31024)

A Crusaders session from 1979, when the band tried to expand its appeal by adding a vocal line; in which respect it was one of the most ideally suited of all jazz-based groups of the period. Notable for a terrific communion between the band and singer, Randy Crawford, on the title track, which provided the Crusaders with its only pop-chart hit.

Dankworth, John Philip William

(Born Essex, England, September 20, 1927)

John Dankworth is probably the best known of all British jazz musicians who have remained based in the UK – even including Ronnie Scott – because Dankworth has been successful in America, written music for films, and collaborated, in light-classics and pops repertoires, with symphony orchestras all over the world. Dankworth's singer wife, Cleo Laine, more internationally celebrated than he is, has completed the picture.

Dankworth's skills always lay in composition and arrangement, and a mischievous sense of what could be borrowed and adapted from other idioms. Though he is a fluent alto saxophonist, his contemporary Ronnie Scott – who has concentrated on the saxophone almost exclusively – is a more rhythmically loose and lyrically inventive player. Dankworth wrote arrangements for his school dance band, and within fifteen months of taking up the clarinet he had won the individualist's award in a *Melody Maker* dance band championship. He began to run small jazz bands of his own – with something of a debt to Benny Goodman – graduated from the Royal Academy of Music, and discovered Charlie Parker. Along with Ronnie Scott, drummers TONY CROMBIE and Laurie Morgan, Dankworth took to visiting New York, by performing in dance bands on the transatlantic liners, and became a new star in the London clubs. He had always wanted to be a leader and the Johnny Dankworth Seven, strongly influenced by the MILES DAVIS *Birth of the Cool* band, debuted in March 1950 and made him a successful one. The band had hit records with such themes as, 'Experiments with Mice', in 1956, and, in 1959, his big band was a hit in the home of jazz, at the Newport Jazz Festival. Dankworth's success as a jazz musician and composer led to commissions for film scores – notably Karel Reisz's *We Are the Lambeth Boys* and *Saturday Night and Sunday Morning*.

★*Symphonic Fusions* (Pickwick PCD 842)

The Johnny Dankworth Seven, either in its old or current form, would be a better CD choice. This disc represents Dankworth's favourite pursuit, mutations of jazz and the devices of romantic classical music, and finds him in partnership with the London Symphony Orchestra. Some tracks, like 'Fantasia Enigma', are fussy and overwrought, but the version of Harry James' pounding, 'Sing Sing Sing', has a curious over-the-top appeal.

Davis, Anthony

(Born Paterson, New Jersey, February 20, 1951)
Immensely talented pianist whose roots lay in Duke Ellington, Thelonious Monk and Cecil Taylor, but whose contribution has been largely to a contemporary music occupying a territory between jazz and the chamber group. Davis was a classical piano student who went to Yale and, whilst there, met many of the most adventurous jazz avantists of the Seventies, including trombonist George Lewis. In 1974, Davis joined trumpeter Leo Smith's band and a year later ran his own quartet, with Jay Hoggard (vibes) Mark Helias (bass) and ED BLACKWELL on drums. Work with ANTHONY BRAXTON and CHICO FREEMAN followed, and, in 1978, Davis recorded his first album as a leader, *Song For The Old World*.

During the 1980s, Anthony Davis began appearing regularly with the flautist JAMES NEWTON, and the pianist's music increasingly turned to composition. With his octet, Epicene, Davis further explored ensemble writing, and the arrangement of other composers' work. In 1985, Davis' opera X, based on the life of Malcolm X, was performed in the States.

★*Middle Passage* (Gramavision GRCD 8401)

Davis displaying most of his post-Seventies virtues singlehanded. This solo piano set finds him in persuasive instrumental form, working with materials largely from outside orthodox jazz. The title piece was written for the pianist by the contemporary straight composer Ursula Oppens, and 'Particle W' is a piece by Earl Howard, for piano and electronics.

Davis, Miles

(See page 95, for earlier biography.)

Despite his 'My Way' image and a reputation for volatile aloofness, Miles Davis is one of the music's most accommodating collaborators, and it's been his ear for inspirational partners, as much as that haunting trumpet sound, that has shaped what's thought of as music unique to him. With Gil Evans and John Coltrane, through the Fifties and Sixties, and with the dazzling HERBIE HANCOCK-Ron Carter-TONY WILLIAMS rhythm section of 1965–67, Davis has revealed that he's always open for persuasion.

After his comeback to playing, following illness in the early Eighties, there didn't seem to be anybody half as good in his life, although, in Marcus Miller, he clearly had a funk bassist of catalytic bounce. It was the growing influence of Miller, who turned out to be good on just about any instrument, that took the trumpeter through a painful stage of rebuilding his confidence and technique, via the comparatively relaxed re-entry of *You're Under Arrest* (featuring, among other things, the work of Cyndy Lauper) and then, coinciding with a break from CBS (to WEA), the electronically orchestral, *Tutu*. Though Davis seemed to have shrunk in his compelling solo power, the latter disc demonstrated that he and Miller were a substantial force. Miller, in particular, reawakened Davis' talents as a lyrical accompanist providing (with his animated bass lines) something of the rhythmic pattern that had inspired Davis in his earlier, electric bands. Miller also wrote and arranged a repertoire of jazz and funk that had a contrapuntal variety as demanding as anything the trumpeter has worked on. Davis, the dazzling lyrical soloist, is rarely heard today, but his bands continue to be highly rhythmic, and exhibit a freshness in handling electronics that testifies to the trumpeter's continuing taste.

★*Amandla* (WEA K925873-2)

Amandla splices the lazy mid-tempo funk groove, that Davis is so fond of, with a feel for the raw materials of the instrumentation that makes the set full of sudden splashes of colour (guitars are several times used simply as explosive sound effects), and a graceful melodic strength. There is an infectious energy to the pulse on 'Big Time', a characteristic recent Davis piece – dark, monosyllabic riffs snaking out of nowhere between the smacks of the afterbeat and vanishing again, the trumpeter flaring intermittently against them.

Steel drum-like synth effects echo through the lyrical, 'Hannibal', a tune that winds up to an ecstatic collective blast. Reminiscences of Weather Report emerge in the gently dancing 'Jo-Jo'. The influence of the best of Weather Report also leaps from the convoluted bass-and-synths riff that underpins the seething, 'Jilli', and for those who are always wishing the Miles of thirty years ago would reappear, there's a hint of it, with the trumpet unmuted and sounding almost bashfully ruminative, on the tribute to Jaco Pastorius, played in a gentle jazz time. The disc is dedicated to the memory of Gil Evans.

★*Aura* (CBS 463 351-2)

A completely unexpected orchestral session featuring Danish musicians, plus Davis, JOHN MCLAUGHLIN, on guitar, and Vince Wilburn, on drums. This is Scandinavian trumpeter Palle Mikkelborg's concerto for his hero, recorded in Copenhagen to accompany Miles' receipt of the Sonning Music Prize, a prestigious tribute whose earlier recipients have included Stravinsky, Leonard Bernstein and Isaac Stern.

CBS delayed its release, probably troubled by its slow, contemplative, out-of-metre sections, and distinctly un-streetwise exotic instrumentation. Harps echo John McLaughlin's scalding guitar figures, synthesisers unleash cascading peals of sound like church-bells, sustained low trombone notes throb beneath the horn and guitar like sensations from a distant engine-room. Over it all, in nine parts named after colours that Mikkelborg associates with Davis, the trumpet curls, wriggles and lashes out. On the last side's, 'Violet', a reworked blues with references to Messiaen, some of Miles Davis's most exquisite slow playing is to be heard over slurred, sliding chords and the kind of empty space that you hardly ever hear him loose in these days.

Defries, David Colin Walter 'Dave'

(Born London, May 24, 1952)
A fine trumpeter and flugelhorn player who has continued to play

a vigorous part in the crossing of musical boundaries – appearing with the South African-based jazz group, Brotherhood of Breath, the jazz-influenced pop bands, Rip, Rig and Panic, and the pop-influenced jazz band, Sunwind. Defries has also played with two of the most imaginative London-based big bands of the 1980s, LOOSE TUBES and the JAZZ WARRIORS.

Defries began his playing life in the Surrey County School Orchestra and was briefly a formal music student. In the Seventies he worked with London jazz groups, including the African bands of drummer, Julian Bahula, and, the late altoist, DUDU PUKWANA. Defries is an inventive improvisor and a creative thinker about the current jazz scene who is not cramped by categories, and his contribution to the present variety of British jazz has been considerable.

★*Secret City* (MMC CDP 790 001-2)

A 1985 session by a Defries-led band, featuring fellow-trumpeter HARRY BECKETT, singer Maggie Nicols, and a raft of percussionists. It's an evocative programme music, effective in both the wide sweeps of its ensemble and vocal sound and in its engaging details; the trumpet interplay of Defries and Beckett, on the conversational, 'Le Marche', is a high point.

DeJohnette, Jack

(Born Chicago, August 9, 1942)
A one-time pianist turned drummer, Jack DeJohnette has become a highly sought-after musician, with a direct, insistent style and boundless energy in accompaniment. His sensitivity to the requirements of his partners has endeared him to a succession of celebrated leaders – CHARLES LLOYD, Bill Evans, Stan Getz, and eventually MILES DAVIS. Davis and DeJohnette worked together during the most dynamic period of the trumpeter's patchy relationship with jazz-rock fusion, and DeJohnette's crackling accents (as emphatic as a ringmaster's whip), furious one-footed rolls, on the bass drum, and boiling cymbal work, was a crucial contribution to sidestepping the rhythmic predictability of so much fusion music.

DeJohnette studied classical music initially, which established his piano technique, and attended the American Conservatory of Music, in Chicago, where he began playing drums – inspired by the volcanic and intricate bebop drummer, Max Roach. After graduating, DeJohnette threw himself into every kind of music that could conceivably require a drummer – practising intensely, opening his ears to rhythm and blues, bebop, and the free scene of the day. He moved to New York, in the mid-Sixties, joined organist John Patton, then altoist Jackie McLean, and singer BETTY CARTER. But it was DeJohnette's membership of saxophonist CHARLES LLOYD's group, that established his reputation (as it did for KEITH JARRETT). Lloyd's popularity meant that DeJohnette had a passport to perform with many of jazz music's luminaries – John Coltrane, Thelonious Monk, Freddie Hubbard, Stan Getz. The flexibility, open-mindedness and sheer firepower, that won these coveted opportunities, also appealed to Miles Davis, for whom DeJohnette worked between 1970 and 1971, appearing on one of the most influential albums of jazz-rock fusion, *Bitches' Brew*.

In more recent times DeJohnette has worked extensively in Europe, appearing on numerous sessions for the ECM label, with a variety of leaders, and on projects of his own. He has pursued a creative duo partnership with the English multi-instrumentalist, JOHN SURMAN, with whom he made an excellent, all-electronics, album, *The Amazing Adventures of Simon Simon*, in 1984, which confounded conventionally held notions that synthesisers were bad improvising tools. DeJohnette's other ventures have included an erratic fusion band, Compost, and a much more wide-ranging and inventive multi-idiomatic outfit, Special Edition, the vehicle for a string of successful albums for ECM. Latterly DeJohnette has continued to distinguish himself as a straight jazz time-player, mixing uncanny empathy with driving force, notably in Jarrett's Standards Trio.

★*Special Edition* (ECM 827 694-2)

DeJohnette's debut with the Special Edition band, in 1979; the searing Arthur Blythe, on alto, and the equally heated DAVID MURRAY, on tenor. A triumph, due to DeJohnette's ability to create a context for his musicians through engineering the unexpected both in his arrangements, and from his percussion. Blythe and

Murray struck sparks, and the session wound up as one of DeJohnette's finest.

★*Piano Album* (Polygram LCD 1504)

Largely successful display of DeJohnette's less celebrated talents as a pianist, recorded in 1985, with Eddie Gomez, on bass, and Freddie Waits, on drums. Tracks include Cyndi Lauper's, 'Time After Time' (something of a pop-jazz standby in the Eighties) and John Coltrane's, 'Countdown'. An unjustly castigated record when it emerged, because, on the piano, DeJohnette displays all the propulsive energy and abrupt switches of direction that he does as a drummer.

★*Irresistible Forces* (MCA MCAD 5992)

A 1987 Special Edition, this time with two excellent upcoming saxophonists in GREG OSBY (alto) and Gary Thomas (tenor), with the ever-creative Mick Goodrick, on guitar. Alert to the new synthesis of bop and rap-influenced funk (as practised by musicians such as STEVE COLEMAN) DeJohnette successfully widened his own view, and though the session isn't as consistently strong as Special Edition in 1979, it successfully splices bumpy street-funk and the leader's more considered, and sometimes downright boppish, side.

Dennerlein, Barbara

(Born Munich, 1964)
In the 1960s, accompanying the enthusiasm for soul and blues flavoured small-group jazz, the Hammond organ enjoyed a boom in the hands of Jack Macduff, Jimmy Smith, Wild Bill Davis and others. At the beginning of the Nineties, the Hammond looks like making its comeback within groups of a very similar type, producing a music of pumping bass riffs, tidal chords and manic, repetitive trills. One of the most sophisticated practitioners of this earthy music-making is the young German organist, Barbara Dennerlein. Not only is she a vigorous exponent of organ blues,

she is also a writer of attractive compositions that use funky elements to stretch the melodic materials.

Dennerlein was a fast learner. She was given her first organ when she was eleven, and two years later she was playing in public, appearing at the Munich Jazz Festival, when she was fifteen. She has accompanied many visiting stars in Germany and played with Jimmy Smith, when he toured that country. Dennerlein's albums have been prizewinners, and she has appeared extensively at German jazz festivals, often with the drummer Andreas Witte. She is certain to be a prominent figure in European music during the 1990s.

★*Hot Stuff* (Enja 6050-2)

A 1990 recording by a Dennerlein quartet, featuring Britain's ANDY SHEPPARD and Mark Mondesir, on tenor and drums, with Mitch Watkins, on guitar. The tunes are mostly originals and not all of them are memorable, but the rolling groove of the title track and the irresistible mid-tempo, bluesy feel of 'Wow', amount to delightful music for both long-time organ buffs and jazz newcomers. 'Wow' alternates a lazy, insinuating swing with hard-hit accents on top of the beat (Mark Mondesir crackles compellingly throughout the disc) and Andy Sheppard fleshes out the music with a mixture of the offbeat logic of Sonny Rollins, and his own warm, garrulous tone. Dennerlein appeals to the organ fraternity with a deceptively restrained version of a tune tailor-made for the instrument, Benny Golson's 'Killer Joe'.

Eubanks, Kevin Tyrone

(Born Philadelphia, November 15, 1957)
A guitarist of wide-ranging interests, most regularly associated with fusion, but capable of fluent work as a bebop player, and even in free improvisation.

Like many jazz players now in their thirties, Eubanks had a fully-fledged jazz education – but he was also encouraged by family connections, his uncle being the excellent bop pianist, Ray Bryant, and his mother a music graduate. As a teenager, Eubanks was turned on to fusion guitar by the sound of JOHN MCLAUGHLIN, with the Mahavishnu Orchestra, but later he grew interested in bebop. Graduating from the Berklee Conservatory, he played, in succession, with Art Blakey's Jazz Messengers, drummer Roy Haynes, and trombonist Slide Hampton; before discovering less structured music with saxophonist Sam Rivers. In the late Eighties Eubanks signed with the GRP label and released many highly technical and elaborately produced funk albums, not entirely doing justice to his skills.

★*Face to Face* (GRP GRPD 9539)

A Eubanks session, from 1986, with classy support from ex-Miles Davis bassists, Marcus Miller and Ron Carter, plus extensive drums and percussion. It's the kind of lineup that makes most material sound the same, but Eubanks does discover some fresh phrasing here and there. The repertoire is varied enough to include Charlie Parker's, 'Relaxin' At Camarillo', Jobim's, 'Wave', and a headlong, zigzagging Wes Montgomery favourite, 'Trick Bag'.

First House

An inventive British small-group of the 1980s, that has made a series of sophisticated and musically varied recordings for the ECM label. Founded in 1984, in Manchester, the band's young members quickly showed themselves to be working along related lines to a band formed at the same time, LOOSE TUBES, both bands pursuing a creative eclecticism that sought unifying elements in dissimilar musics, rather than one that was simply a selfconscious display of broadmindedness. The mixture won First House the International Jazz Federation's European Young Jazz Artists award, and by 1985 they were touring Europe and making their first recording for ECM. Latin-American music, a lyrical brand of free-improvisation and jazz variations on non-jazz materials, are all part of the First House repertoire and they favour a quiet, pushing rhythm-section sound, not unlike the ECM label's Scandinavian bands. First House's alto player, Ken Stubbs, is a highly varied performer. He can sound almost Getzian, in his rhapsodic playing, and sometimes as self-contained as JAN GARBAREK, or like the offbeat animation of Ornette Coleman.

★*Cantilena* (ECM 1393)

First House's second album, in 1989, with a quartet of Ken Stubbs (alto), DJANGO BATES (keyboards), Mick Hutton (bass) and Martin France (drums). The writing is shared by Stubbs and Bates (plus one track from Loose Tubes', Eddie Parker) and includes the sleazy, softly wailing quality and snakey melodic twists of Bates' 'Underfelt', and Stubbs' 'Low Down', which winds up like an impassioned episode from KEITH JARRETT's Standards band with Bates elbowing and jostling over threshing France drums. There is a good deal of north European contemporary jazz romanticism too (echoing sax parabolas over trickling arpeggios and trance-like percussion) which slightly takes the edge off the group's vitality.

Freeman, Earl 'Chico' Jnr

(Born Chicago, July 17, 1949)
Chico Freeman is the son of one of the world's great underrated saxophone eccentrics, Von Freeman; and though Chico plays with the all-encompassing virtuosity and harmonic awareness of a musician raised in the Coltrane era, he has frequently just missed establishing the sense of individuality that his father consistently does. Sometimes Chico Freeman toys with electronics and funk, in ways that can obscure his music. But he has also led bands (usually with the most distinctive partners, such as fellow saxophonist, Arthur Blythe, and pianist, John Hicks) of considerable creativity, in which the themes attractively pass from orthodox post-bop through corridors of ghostly dissonance, while a weird tonality seems to tug at the sleeves of the tunes.

   Like most modern Chicago musicians, Freeman was influenced by Chicagoan composer/pianist, MUHAL RICHARD ABRAMS, and also by offbeat bandleader, SUN RA. From the mid-Seventies he began working in New York – though, by reputation, he was still associated with the Sixties avant-garde, and in particular as an inheritor of the intense and impassioned music of Coltrane. Freeman has worked with the brilliant drummer, Elvin Jones, and led many bands of his own – but a sustained independence, worthy of his skills, has so far eluded him.

★*Groovin' Late* (Essential Records ESMCD 018)

Since Freeman's best early records (from the period 1979–1982) aren't available on CD, the music of his consolidation of free music and the mainstream predominates and it isn't representative of his first impact on the jazz scene. This session was recorded live at Ronnie Scott's, and though it begins with a disconcertingly anonymous-sounding electronic funk piece, 'Goin' Places' (it doesn't), the disc warms up to some powerful straight-ahead playing in a variety of styles.

Frisell, William Richard 'Bill'

(Born Baltimore, Maryland, March 18, 1951)
Bill Frisell's reputation for playing the guitar for everybody, from PAUL BLEY to Marianne Faithfull, his spectacular thrash-meets-bop concerts with energetic New Yorker, JOHN ZORN, and record company promises of 'a radical guitar hero for the nineties', have all helped build what is now substantial recognition. And inasmuch as Frisell's remarkable sound is not classifiable with that of any current mainstream guitarist in pop or jazz, he deserves his reputation for radicalism – he has the softness of a cerebral bop guitarist, like Jim Hall, but couples it with the sudden fire of Hendrix. The material performed at his concerts can be a patchwork of doctored country intros, lopsided blues, Fifties rock, and film music.

Frisell was a reed player originally, and became a full-time music student. He took up guitar and had private lessons with Jim Hall, as well as developing an interest in Jimi Hendrix. By the time he graduated from the Berklee School, Boston, in 1977, he was good enough on guitar to be winning awards, and the presence of MIKE GIBBS, composer/trombonist and sometime record producer, among the Berklee staff, ignited Frisell's recording career. He worked with Europeans EBERHARD WEBER and JAN GARBAREK, and eventually the groundbreaking ex-Bill Evans drummer, PAUL MOTIAN. By this time Frisell was taking his sound effects even further out, relishing company that opened spaces up in music – particularly John Zorn, who ransacks all available materials with merciless wilfulness.

★*Rambler* (ECM 825 234-2)

Frisell in 1984, with Paul Motian, British-based trumpeter, KEN WHEELER, and others. Frisell's various influences, curiously inter-woven, are more clearly audible here that in later recordings, and this was the session that secured his status as a guitar revolution-ary – the level of organisation is high, thanks largely to the leader's improvisational skills.

★*Lookout for Hope* (ECM 833 495-2)

Two years later, and the impact of Zorn and his cohorts is obvious, not least through the presence of Zorn sidemen, Joey Baron (drums) and Kermit Driscoll (bass). The music has moved away from the faintly wistful abstractions of Frisell's earlier work to a more bitingly sardonic flavour, indebted to Zorn's incorporation of elements of postwar popular culture into his music. There is, therefore, a raucous and nervy account of 'Hard Plains Drifter', with Frisell's warped country sound irresistibly stitching it together.

Ganelin Trio

Ganelin, Vyacheslav (born Kraskov, USSR, 1944)
Chekasin, Vladimir (born Sverdlovsk, USSR, 1947)
Tarasov, Vladimir (born Archangelsk, USSR, 1947).
The Ganelin trio consists of three classically-trained musicians who developed a part-free, part-composed, music out of a combination of the influences of western jazz records (notably Cecil Taylor, Ornette Coleman, John Coltrane) and their own experiences as film-music writers, orchestral players and teachers. When the trio performed at the 1980 Berlin Jazz Festival, they astonished many of their listeners with their forceful independence, and the German critic Joachim Berendt, in an influential quote, called the session 'the wildest and yet the best organised and most professional free jazz I've heard in years'. Thereafter the Soviet label, Melodiya, began slowly to release Ganelin records, and with the thawing of the political atmos-phere, the band was permitted to tour abroad – including Britain and the USA.

Leader, Vyacheslav Ganelin, is a graduate of the Vilnius Conservatory, and a writer of operas and film scores. Vladimir Chekasin, an improvising saxophonist who at times recalls both Rahsaan Roland Kirk and Albert Ayler, began as a violinist, moved to saxophone at eighteen, and has latterly been both a teacher and the director of a conservatory orchestra. Vladimir Tarasov, a drummer, also performs with the Lithuanian State Symphony Orchestra.

The Ganelin Trio is a composer's band, however explosive and reflexive its performances seem. Their shows contain parodies of programme music, early jazz forms, and children's songs. Their underground status, endured for years, inspired a compulsive surrealism that borders on performance art, and which the Trio have preserved in more open times. They display both the folk roots of their own locality and the discipline of a classical training; blending these with jazz influences gleaned from Voice of America radio broadcasts and precious, imported discs.

★The Eighties Document – New Music from Russia (Leo Records, 8 discs)

The Ganelin trio feature – separately, and together – on the final disc of this massive collection of improvised and abstract Russian music of the 1980s. The trio performance is a feverish, sometimes crabbily swinging, sometimes lyrical, sometimes outlandish version of *Old Bottles, New Wine*, recorded on their tour of Britain in 1984. The other discs include vocalist Valentina Ponomareva, Russia's equivalent of Cecil Taylor in pianist Sergei Kuryokhin, and many others. It's a costly investment, the sleeve notes need a microscope, and for those unfamiliar with free music some of it sounds dolorous and tentative. But Russian improvisation has become a powerful force in developing jazz, and these are the musicians providing the impetus.

Garbarek, Jan

(Born Norway, March 4, 1947)
The Norwegian saxophonist, Jan Garbarek, is a unique performer of meditative, introverted hymns to romantic repression, with the

poignant and, sometimes, desolate sound of John Coltrane always audible within them. But for all his initial inspiration from Coltrane, Garbarek is one of Europe's few undisputed jazz originals, once described by the eminent American orchestra-leader, GEORGE RUSSELL, as 'just about the most uniquely talented jazz musician Europe has produced since Django Reinhardt.'

Garbarek took up the saxophone at fourteen, after hearing Coltrane on the radio but knowing nothing of jazz. Even after he had progressed with the instrument, he still knew little about the traditions from which Coltrane's music had come, merely that he desperately wanted to make that alternately defiant and beseeching sound himself. Nearly thirty years later, Garbarek is internationally known in jazz, has worked with its leading artists (notably KEITH JARRETT), and is a celebrity in his native country. Absorbing the Afro-American line of jazz into a music strongly suggestive of northern Europe, Garbarek has composed and improvised using materials intimately meaningful to himself; including setting the works of poet Tomas Transtromer to music and composing for Norwegian productions of Ibsen's dramas, *Brand* and *Peer Gynt*. But Garbarek's ear for musical material extends well beyond the cattle-calls of Norway to include the incantatory music of Bali, native Indian music of North America and the work of sitarist, Ravi Shankar, with whom he performed on the album, *Song For Everyone*.

★*Works* (ECM 823266-2)

A wide ranging display of Garbarek's atmospheric exploits, dating from the beginning of his recording career with ECM in 1970. The saxophonist's involvement with the more urgent side of his Afro-American inspirations is audible in his vocalised sound and busier delivery on 'Beast of Kammodo'. While the delicate upper reaches of his tenor sound are haunting on 'Skrikyl', as is his use of space on 'Passing'. Garbarek also displays his interests in Eastern music, with the Indian flavour of 'Saije'.

★*All Those Born with Wings* (ECM 831394-2)

Unaccompanied Garbarek in a suite of six pieces. It represents the saxophonist as contemporary nomad in twilit landscape, with elongated, echoing phrases reverberating through space, north European folk borrowings reworked, intense multi-tracked tone-poems. Not an album to buttonhole the casual listener, and with its monotonous moments, like most Garbarek-led sessions, but compelling in the right circumstances.

★*Wayfarer* (ECM 811968-2)

One of the most distinguished of all Garbarek groups, in rather more animated action, in 1982, with the resourceful BILL FRISELL, on guitar, an empathetic EBERHARD WEBER, on bass, and Michael Di Pasqua, on drums.

Gibbs, Michael Clement Irving 'Mike'

(Born Salisbury, Zimbabwe (then Rhodesia) September 25, 1937) Michael Gibbs' background, education and subsequent career touched too many places to make it useful to pigeonhole him, in terms of a single nationality. He grew up in pre-independence Zimbabwe, pursued his musical education in the U.S.A., flourished as a composer in Britain, then returned to America. But wherever he belongs, Gibbs is a composer and arranger to rival CARLA BLEY, and even the late Gil Evans, in glowing sonority, open-mindedness, and power to surprise with a thematic ambiguity rare in jazz. Gibbs' writing for brass particularly is an ever-recognisable rising fanfare. His melodies can be brooding or jubilant, and his materials are most explicitly drawn from Gil Evans, MILES DAVIS and Olivier Messiaen.

Gibbs learned piano from the age of seven, then the trombone as a teenager. At Berklee where he went in 1959, Gibbs met the vibraharpist, GARY BURTON, and the two began a musical association that lasted many years. He studied with Gunther Schuller and GEORGE RUSSELL, at the Lenox School, then explored classical composition with teachers such as Aaron Copland, Iannis Xenakis and Lukas Foss. From 1965–1974, Gibbs worked in London, initially as a session trombonist (for JOHN DANKWORTH and Graham Collier among others) then as an arranger. He eventually formed a big band to perform his own arrangements of songs he had written for both Gary Burton and Stan Getz, and this move led to similar work with radio big bands in Scandinavia and Germany. Typically Gibbs uses dense and complex structural ideas in his writing (he mostly avoids the use of big-band riffs or orchestral sections, simply as a source of rhythmic emphasis) yet maintains an infectious and popular appeal, through dance rhythms, electric guitars and keyboards, and frequently clamouring, joyous ensemble sounds.

Gibbs went back to the States, in 1974, as Composer in Residence at Berklee, and through the rest of the decade continued to teach, sporadically tour, and occasionally act as producer or musical director for other artists. In the Eighties, he began working exclusively as a freelance, operating in America and Europe, with artists including Peter Gabriel, Joni Mitchell, Carla Bley, MIKE MANTLER and John Dankworth, also orchestrating a film score by PAT METHENY, a guitar concerto by JOHN MCLAUGHLIN, and a number of ballet scores of his own. Gibbs' early recordings are probably too little known for CD release, but his first Decca/ Deram album *Michael Gibbs* deserves to be considered, despite a few moments of unconvincing ensemble playing.

★Big Music (Virgin/Venture CDVE 27)

Mike Gibbs' first album as a leader in over a decade, but still revealing the alertness to the contemporary scene that first marked him out as a composer. Like Gil Evans, Gibbs has always been prepared to borrow such recent innovations as suit his purposes, and in a substantial big band (recorded in both New York and London in 1988) he has made use of such devices as electronic drums and drum-synths but preserved a good deal of his old, spacious atmospherics. Miles Davis and Gil Evans influences are strong in it, there is excellent guitar work from a trio of JOHN SCOFIELD, BILL FRISELL and KEVIN EUBANKS, and the integration of soloists with texture is more successful than on any Gibbs album, apart from *In the Public Interest*.

Gilberto, Astrud

(Born Bahia, Brazil, 1940)
Astrud Gilberto is synonymous with one song – the haunting

'Girl From Ipanema', which hit the headlines in 1963, and has never really gone away. Gilberto is not a powerful, or even an animated singer, but her sense of time and space is founded on an understanding of how the samba beat creates a flow that the singer can undulate around rather than seek to dominate, her voice rarely rising above a confidential whisper. She has devoted herself to the softly sensuous, and the effortless placing of minimal effects that, working against the insistent shuffle of the rhythm, creates an impression of infectious swing.

Astrud Gilberto comes from Bahia, but was raised in Rio. She married Brazil's bossa nova king, Joao Gilberto, whilst still a teenager, and, as legend tells, when Joao was collaborating with Stan Getz in the making of some jazz-samba recordings, Astrud came in on the cutting of 'Girl From Ipanema', as her first professional engagement, and had a number one hit in many countries with it, followed by movie appearances and world tours.

During the Eighties, after a long semi-retirement, Astrud Gilberto returned to live performance, this time more assertively, and latterly including the songs of Michael Franks, or a jazz classic like 'Caravan', as well as the statutary Jobim. But if anything the come-back only pointed up how uniquely the delicate sway of the early material had been a music that seemed to exist in her bones, and that a wider scope over-stretched her.

Gilberto/Getz (Verve 810 048-2)

The old slinky mixture, Gilberto's fluttering sighs and Getz's feathery tenor sound blending seamlessly (after three or four tracks, perhaps a little too seamlessly) on famous samba hits such as 'Girl from Ipanema' and 'Desafinado'.

Gismonti, Egberto

(Born Carrio, Rio de Janeiro, December 5, 1947)
A virtuoso exponent of many musics, including jazz, Brazilian and African, Gismonti now belongs firmly in the wider 'world-music' frame. He has, nevertheless, continued to perform at jazz festivals and to work with contemporary jazz artists, such as bassist

CHARLIE HADEN and saxophonist JAN GARBAREK. Gismonti's resources, as a musician, have been extended by his experimentation with an eight-string guitar and alternative tunings.

Originally a student of classical music (he studied in Paris with
Nadia Boulanger) Gismonti worked in Brazil as a freelance
arranger, and then developed an interest in a form of funky
Brazilian pop (*choro*), which he followed with an investigation of
jazz and rock guitar, inspired by Jimi Hendrix, Wes Montgomery
and JOHN MCLAUGHLIN. Gismonti spent a period, in the Amazon
jungle, working with Indian musicians to gather material for what
became his first album on ECM, *Danca Das Cabecas*. He continues
to tour extensively, and has composed and performed the music
for several films.

★*Duas Vozes* (ECM 823640-2)

A brilliantly inventive duo session between Gismonti on guitar
and piano and percussionist, NANA VASCONCELOS. In merging
Brazilian percussion effects (Vasconcelos can produce an entire
rain-forest of background noises on his own) with jazz piano, on
'O Dia, A Noite', and with jazz/flamenco, on 'Dancando', Gismonti effected a fusion that cheapened none of the ingredients.
The session becomes emotive, without cloying, on the Amazon
Indian song 'Tamarepeba'; delicate overdubbing of voices and
percussion still sustaining the disc's lyrical simplicity.

Guy, Barry John

(Born London, April 22, 1947)
British bassist Barry Guy, a dedicated, intense and manically
active artist, has chosen to perform the works of a Xenakis or
Berio (or even early English music) in chamber orchestras as much
as he has jazz-derived free music. Guy became enthusiastic about
jazz as a teenager and, after training as an architect, eventually
studied the bass and composition at London's Guildhall School of
Music. Though he quickly grew to appreciate the orthodox jazz
bassist's virtues of strong tempo and big sound, looser improvisation appealed to him more, and he began working with the leading
players of London's 1960s avant-garde, including drummer John

Stevens and saxophonist Trevor Watts, in the Spontaneous Music Ensemble. But by the Seventies, Guy was moving away from a form of free music based solely on jazz. His composition studies at the Guildhall had convinced him that some of the raw materials of contemporary straight composers too could be effectively extended by jazz improvisors. At the same time he emerged as one of the country's great bass virtuosi, in any idiom. Composers of the calibre of Boulez wrote works for him, and, as an improvisor, he performed with a furious, boiling intensity.

In 1970, in association with a self-help organisation, the Musicians' Cooperative, Guy formed a twenty one piece orchestra, the London Jazz Composers' Orchestra (LJCO), and composed an extended piece, *Ode*, for its first appearance. In those early days, the LJCO seemed at times to labour under the weight of its responsibilities to forge new structures from the 20th century languages of jazz tonality, atonality and aleatoric methods, and its sound could be oppressively thick. In recent times, the orchestra's collective interplay has become crisper, clearer and more genuinely conversational, though perhaps with an enhancement of the 'jazzy' element, with new soloists more rooted in the jazz tradition. Now the writing is less crowded, released of the compulsion to say everything that could be said in the space of a single work.

Guy regards the current period as the 'third phase' of the LJCO's life. A life that has seen it moving from the initial point of complex and highly detailed ensemble writing (increasingly involving non-improvising players), through a stage of restoration of responsibilities to the interpreting musicians, and then back again to more firm direction from Guy himself, though with the addition of distinctly jazz-based horn-players, in Simon Picard, Paul Dunmall and Pete McPhail. The Zurich-based Intakt label has helped the orchestra considerably by committing LJCO development to disc, even releasing a double-album of concert work in Switzerland in 1988.

★*Harmos* (Intakt CD 013)

The LCJO's second venture for Intakt, revealing Guy's 'third phase' in a tighter dependence on organisation and structural methods and in raising the profile of exuberant jazz elements above the more preoccupied conservatoire experimentalism the band has exhibited in the past. More harmonically elegant and considered than the earlier, *Polyhymnia*, as if the improvisors and the writer have collaborated to beat a fiery, white-hot metal into a sculpture of poise and resolution.

★*Double Trouble* (Intakt CD 019)

Originally a double concerto for two of the most formidable pianists of the European avant-garde, Briton Howard Riley and German Alex Schlippenbach. In the event, Riley carries the piano role himself here, with a blazing solo early in this fifty-minute piece, which sets the pace. A variety of solos and sub-groupings follows, pulled together by all seventeen members, supplying ensemble parts that superficially sound like free squalls but have been written by Guy to the last detail. Rugged, dissonant, demanding and adventurous orchestral music, within which a ferocious improvising trio (saxophonist Evan Parker, drummer Paul Lytton and Guy himself) reveals how powerful the momentum of the Seventies-derived European free scene still is.

Haden, Charles Edward

(Born Shenandoah, Iowa, August 6, 1937)
One of the indisputably great jazz bassists of the past three decades, Charlie Haden has avoided the attempts of many of his fellow practitioners to sound like a low-register guitar, and delivers instead a rich and sonorous tone, with phrasing at times reminiscent of flamenco music. He emerged in association with the revolutionary saxophonist Ornette Coleman, and learned, through Coleman's music, to unfold counter-melodies related to the tonal centres and the pulse of the piece, but without dependence on a progression of chords.

As a boy, Charlie Haden sang on his parents' radio show. He began working with West Coast jazz musicians in the 1950s, playing with Art Pepper, Elmo Hope, Hampton Hawes and with the adventurous Canadian pianist, PAUL BLEY in 1957. It was Bley's band that first recorded Ornette Coleman and Haden was thereafter a cornerstone of the Sixties Coleman small-groups, which played some of the saxophonist's most vital music.

Late in the Sixties, Haden began an involvement with the New York Jazz Composers Orchestra Association, and it was from the membership of this organisation, and in partnership with a co-founder, CARLA BLEY, that Haden put together his Liberation Music Orchestra, using the songs of the Spanish Civil War to reflect liberation movements of the Sixties. Subsequently Haden has appeared with pianist Alice Coltrane, with KEITH JARRETT, and later with the Old and New Dreams band, dedicated to preserving the best compositions of Ornette Coleman. Haden resurrected the Liberation Music Orchestra in 1982, and has also lent his brooding, dramatic sound to the music of JAN GARBAREK and EGBERTO GISMONTI.

★*Liberation Music Orchestra* (MCAD 39125)

Heated, declamatory orchestral music, arranged by Carla Bley and extensively using Republican songs of the Spanish Civil War, which the tenor saxophone of GATO BARBIERI perfectly complements in its searing intensity. Though this album was a hit with critics when it came out, and it contains one of Haden's most moving compositions, 'Song For Che', it hasn't worn as well as Haden's work with Ornette Coleman from the same period.

★*Ballad of the Fallen* (ECM 811 546-2)

The Liberation Music Orchestra comeback of 1982. Though it was verbose and ill-controlled in live performance, the concise-ness required by the recording brought the best out of a more varied and idiosyncratic set of themes (Spanish Civil War again, plus pieces from Nicaragua and El Salvador) and Carla Bley's arrangements once again burst with life. DON CHERRY was present, plus Dewey Redman on saxophones, and the booming Gary Valente on trombone.

★*Quartet West* (Verve 831 673-2)

Much more modest, small-group, jazz album dedicated to Haden's adopted Los Angeles, performing standards, two originals, and pieces by PAT METHENY and Ornette Coleman. A little low-key by comparison with Haden's more impassioned activities, but intelligent and subtle music, with a bass solo on the leader's dedication to his parents, 'Taney County', displaying his remarkable ability to make the bass sing with a mixture of rich tone colour, time changes and long-range phrasing worthy of a saxophonist.

Hancock, Herbert Jeffrey 'Herbie'

(Born Chicago, April 12, 1940)

Hancock, a MILES DAVIS sideman from 1963 to 1968, already had an illustrious career behind him when he joined the great trumpeter at the age of twenty three. He had performed Mozart's D Major piano concerto, with the Chicago Symphony Orchestra as an eleven year old, had virtually become house pianist of the Blue Note record label, and had written a pop hit – 'Watermelon Man' – which has since been recorded by more than two hundred artists. Hancock's playing with the Davis group combined exactly the agility of bebop and the harmonic inventiveness that the trumpeter wanted, in a period in which hard bop and free-form were both pulling at the loyalties of jazz fans. As a pianist his touch was light and deft, his timing perfect, his themes mostly catchy enough to register after one hearing.

After leaving Davis, Hancock explored further some of the compositional territory he had investigated in his Blue Note days, but with more of the electro-funk technological arsenal to help him. Then came a period of out-and-out commercial work which brought him considerable material success, notably with the funk band, Headhunters, whose first album became the best-selling jazz record ever. He followed this by a return to the 1963–64 Davis group sound, with the VSOP band in the 1970s.

Herbie Hancock now successfully operates in many fields – as a fusion artist, a devastating jazz piano improvisor with a still-torrential stream of fresh ideas, and as a composer. Collaborating with the rock band, Material, he worked on the best-selling album, *Future Shock*, and he was also recently seen, as the nightclub pianist accompanying the late Dexter Gordon, in the Bertrand Tavernier movie, *Round Midnight*. CBS has recently deleted several Hancock discs, from his commercial period, including *Headhunters*.

★Takin Off (Blue Note CDP 746 506-2)

Hancock's impressive 1963 debut as leader, heralded, although he was only twenty three, as one of the most mature beginnings to a recording career in all jazz. The album was a near-perfect blend of Hancock's clean, dancing piano sound, funk/bop construction, and classy pop-oriented composition, with ideal assistance from Dexter Gordon, on tenor, and Freddie Hubbard, on trumpet. It was also the debut of Hancock's funk hit, 'Watermelon Man'.

★Maiden Voyage (Blue Note CDP 746 339-2)

One of the most influential, and compositionally sophisticated, Hancock records, with sidemen who later formed one of the best Miles Davis bands – Ron Carter, on bass, and TONY WILLIAMS, on drums. The title track and 'Dolphin Dance' are among Hancock's most enduring originals – warm, sliding, harmonies, giving new depth to the traditional modern-jazz front line; sharp, rhythmic changes, insistent, riffing piano backdrops and deft fills, that propel the soloists and keep them on the course of the theme.

Hanrahan, Kip

(Born New York)

Hanrahan is primarily a record producer, like BILL LASWELL, whose creativity in the studio, using a good deal of jazz-based resources, has been his contribution to the music. He uses players from jazz, Latin and pop backgrounds for his projects, but requires them to be able to improvise – and not simply on given structures, but to also rework material from the genres they regularly play in. Hanrahan has no use for musicians repeating formulae.

Originally a film student, Hanrahan applies the procedures of film making to record production – perceiving a record as the culmination of the efforts of many people, not simply the most visible artists. In that respect he has been described as an auteur of new music. He worked with one of the most celebrated of all jazz record producers, Teo Macero, in the late Seventies, and with CARLA BLEY, before starting to release his own records – and the five sessions, under his own name, have included musicians as diverse as soul singer Bobby Womack, adventurous jazz artists

DAVID MURRAY, Lester Bowie and DON PULLEN, and 'no-wave' or 'punk-jazz' artists, Arto Lindsay and Anton Fier. Hanrahan's records are not joyous affairs, on the whole, and his manipulation of conventional structures can be taxing – but his antipathy to hardened style is refreshing in the postmodernist era.

★*Days and Nights of Blue Luck Inverted* (Pangaea 461158-2)

Intense and brooding autobiographical session, one of the most personal of Hanrahan recordings – the titles all describe aspects of his upbringing, and of his emotional life, and cover funk, Mingus-like ensembles, and vocals alternately intimate and defiant.

Hargrove, Roy

(Born Chicago, 1971)

One of several very young performers to have hit the headlines in recent years, Hargrove is a trumpeter who is already finding his name mentioned in the same breath as WYNTON MARSALIS. Unlike many of the technocratic newcomers however, Hargrove is interested in shape and design more than blazing virtuosity. But within the spectrum of current musical styles, he is rooted in the neo-bop movement, a situation in which personal development is difficult.

Hargrove was only sixteen, when he won a prestigious music scholarship, and with the prize-money he was making from competition successes, he financed studies at Berklee. Recently Hargrove has appeared on stage with Marsalis, with resurrected West Coast bop altoist, Frank Morgan, and with the dynamic ex-Blakey saxophonist, BOBBY WATSON.

★*Diamond in the Rough* (RCA/Novus PD 90471)

Hargrove's (probably premature) debut, six of the tunes featuring a considerable quintet including John Hicks (piano) and Al Foster (drums). The other five pieces are performed by a sextet. The first band is looser and lighter on its feet, the second is choppier in its rhythmic devices and more funk-inclined – rather than imparting attractive variety to the set, this sextet often sounds mesmerised by its materials and consequently resembles a great deal of other work in postmodernist jazz. Though Hargrove's own hard-bop playing exhibits the surefooted and jaunty bluesiness of Freddie Hubbard (notably on the effortless mid-tempo swing and ingenious tone changes, on Benny Golson's, 'Whisper Not'), and he also reveals flashes of the earlier era's bravura, (as on his fitfully Eldridge-like, sassy, mid-register playing on Monk's, 'Ruby My Dear') the set rarely achieves relaxation.

Harper Brothers

Winard Harper (born 1962); Philip Harper (born 1965)

The Harper brothers have together run their own band since 1985, and the brothers are generally referred to as a single unit in the current accolades greeting the new generation of jazz players (*Time* magazine accorded them a prominent place in its autumn 1990 feature, 'The New Jazz Age'). But Winard – a drummer of precocious poise and sense of dynamics – had been seen on the circuit a good deal before the brothers worked together, notably in bands led by singer BETTY CARTER and tenorist Dexter Gordon. Trumpeter, Philip Harper, had worked with jazz-blues organist Jimmy McGriff and with Art Blakey's Jazz Messengers. Both men have studied with an older-generation altoist devoted to inspiring new talent, the great Jackie McLean.

   The brothers joined forces to form a band noticeably inspired by the hard-bop sound of Art Blakey, and caused a stir with their first album *The Harper Brothers*, not least for their willingness to sound tousled and unruly (a Blakey inheritance), when many of their contemporaries were exhibiting a solemn classicism.

★*Remembrance* (Verve 841 723-2)

Partly aided by the encouragement of live performance, and partly by an unambiguous commitment to a feverish Blakeyesque manner almost all through, the Harper Brothers' second disc does get close, if not to eloquence, then certainly to infectious enthusiasm. Eleven out of the twelve tunes were written, either by members of the band, or specifically for them (a bustling Clifford Brown tribute was contributed by Scotland's Bobby Wellins), which helps the band establish both the idiomatic and dynamic resemblance to the Messengers approach it favours, and yet sound as if it's doing much more than genuflecting. Philip Harper prowls laconically around the backbeat, on Horace Silver's, 'Kiss Me Right', intensifying his statements simply by the occasional blistering high note, after several bars of hushed muttering, quickly falling away to slighter sounds and building to his climax by this accumulation of advances and retreats. Still in the Jazz Remould bag, but invigorating and loose.

Harrell, Tom

(Born Urbana, Illinois, June 16, 1946)
A considered and deliberate trumpeter, in the Clifford Brown mould, who has been working steadily and unobtrusively as an excellent sideman for two decades, Harrell has, only recently, emerged as a leader in his own right, and his pensive originality of phrasing has marked him out. Harrell first appeared as a member of the late Woody Herman's band, and subsequently worked with Bill Evans, George Russell, Lee Konitz, Gerry Mulligan and, through the Eighties, as a regular member of altoist Phil Woods' group. Diagnosed as a schizophrenic, Harrell's solo career has been hampered by self-doubt, yet his harmonic awareness, poignant sound and original melodic imagination, may yet make him a contemporary trumpeter worthy of more musical accolades than his celebrated peers.

★*Sail Away* (Contemporary C 14054)

Fine Harrell lyricism, and good support from the underrated saxophonist Joe Lovano, a man similarly capable of quiet surprises. But for all the distinctive soloing, the album is let down by its material. Though DAVE LIEBMAN plays some unexpectedly free-sounding saxophone, a blandness creeps in with the ordinariness of the Herbie Hancockish, 'Dream in June', and the elevator-music neutrality of much of the rest.

Harris, Eddie

(Born Chicago, October 20, 1936)
Eddie Harris is one of those musicians who formerly used to spark

off regular debates about whether he was really a jazz player or not – a controversy now gone quiet, since the eclecticism of the new jazz generation has made boundary-jumping commonplace. A keyboard player, reed player, singer and composer. Harris has been a pop-jazz expert for decades – often through adapting material of existing mainstream popularity, like his first hit, the 'Exodus' theme in 1960.

Harris was raised with gospel music and served an apprenticeship in an army band. After the success of 'Exodus' he remained in jazz-flavoured commercial music but, within his limitations, he has been an experimenter – even developing a form of trumpet that used a sax-like reed. He has also creatively used electronics within a pop context, and has at times been a composer of attractive music – notably 'Freedom Jazz Dance', which has been played and recorded by many jazz artists.

★*Swiss Movement* (WEA/Atlantic K781 365–2)

Best-selling collaboration between Harris and pianist-singer Les McCann, at the 1969 Montreux Jazz Festival. Brash, repetitive, funky set which has its moments of compulsive grooving and splashes of colour from Harris – but McCann's performance of his own hit song, 'Compared To What', hasn't been treated kindly by the intervening years.

Hill, Andrew

(Born Port Au Prince, Haiti, June 30, 1937)
Jazz, like all arts, has thrown up its pioneers in each era, and shoals of more or less dutiful disciples. On piano, Bud Powell produced a generation of Powellites in the Fifties. HERBIE HANCOCK and KEITH JARRETT, a similar mixture of clones and independent embroiderers, in the Seventies and Eighties. But, like Thelonious Monk, Andrew Hill has always remained in a school of his own. Like Monk also, Hill has stripped down conventional jazz materials and explored rhythmic dislocations. Unlike Monk, he has not become jazz legend – but personal circumstances hampered his musical life, and if he continues to flourish now, he may yet attain his rightful due.

Hill was born in Haiti, but raised in Chicago. He worked in blues bands, and then with leading Chicago musicians, including Von Freeman and Johnny Griffin. In the Sixties, Hill – because of his obvious hard bop leanings – became a regular figure on the Blue Note roster, extending that label's experimentalism as far as it went toward more unorthodox jazz. Latterly Hill has taught more than he has played in public.

★*Black Fire* (Blue Note CDP 784 151-2)

Powerful 1963 debut for Hill, in a demanding trio format, also featuring Richard Davis, on bass, and Roy Haynes, on drums. *Black Fire* demonstrated the leader's inclination toward a rattling, percussive music full of sudden rhythmic zigzags and odd intervals – and, furthermore, established that his harmonic extension of regular jazz materials, was as audacious and visionary, for his generation, as had been Monk's twenty years before.

★*Point of Departure* (Blue Note CDP 784 167-2)

Hill's early, best album; this time for sextet, including Kenny Dorham, on trumpet, Joe Henderson and Eric Dolphy, on reeds. Though relatively inexperienced in a larger group format, Hill reveals here one of the most valuable qualities in jazz – the ability to combine the unorthodox and the supportive, in sufficient balance, to awaken hidden powers in soloists. Prominent features of the disc are two takes of the haunting and poetic 'Dedication', together demonstrating Hill's handling of his musicians, to achieve maximum colour, and to serve the atmosphere established by the work.

★*Shades* (Soul Note 121113-2)

One of Hill's most impressive later records, a 1986 quartet session, with the magisterial Clifford Jordan, on tenor, Rufus Reid, on bass, and Ben Riley, on drums. 'Monk's Glimpse' is a fascinating insight into the similarities and differences (the latter being principally measured in the contemporary player's greater intensity and volubility) between Hill and his departed mentor.

Holland, David

(Born Wolverhampton, October 1, 1946)
Dave Holland is not only one of the world's leading bassists, but a musician for whom a dream came true. He was still a student at London's Guildhall School of Music, when his clean articulation and unwavering, percussive beat quickly established him on the local jazz circuit, and with the London avant-garde. Holland was noticed, at Ronnie Scott's Club, in 1968, by MILES DAVIS, and invited to the States. He worked on the powerful Davis fusion albums, *In A Silent Way*, *Bitches' Brew* and *Filles De Kilimanjaro*, then left to join CHICK COREA's advanced acoustic trio.

A variety of work with legendary jazz artists (including Thelonious Monk) and with members of the avant-garde followed, including a productive partnership with saxophonist Sam Rivers on *Conference of the Birds*. Holland also recorded some devastating unaccompanied bass and cello improvisations, *Emerald Tears* and *Life Cycle*. Recently he has been leading his own remarkable small groups blending bebop, the innovations of Ornette Coleman and tributes to Charles Mingus, in the company of some of the finest younger New York jazz stars, including STEVE COLEMAN.

★*Jumpin' In* (ECM 817 437-2)

The debut of the excellent free-bop ensembles, that Dave Holland put on the road in the 1980s. This recording dates from 1983, and includes the Canadian trumpeter Ken Wheeler, Julian Priester, on trombone, Steve Coleman, on alto, and Kenny Washington, on drums. Holland left a lot of space to his musicians, but ensured there would be sufficient structure to the interplay of the frontline, to preserve a sensation of life and exuberance, suggestive of earlier and simpler jazz. Holland's devotion to Mingus, both in the jostling bluesiness of his compositions, and his own extraordinarily propulsive bass lines, is immediately apparent.

★*Razor's Edge* (ECM 8330482)

The brilliant Steve Coleman was still present, for this 1987 set, with the group continuing to sound like a smoothed-out Monk or Mingus band. Holland delivers a ringing bass tribute to Mingus, on the intro to 'Blues for CM', which turns into exactly the kind of smoky, bleary-eyed theme Mingus was famous for Robin Eubanks' trombone trails swathes of loose counterpoint beneath it, and Coleman plays an alto solo, on the same track, that manages to be both stately and tantalising. Not such an urgent session as *Jumpin' In*, but very classy.

*Triplicate (ECM 837 113-2)

A trio set for Holland with JACK DEJOHNETTE, on drums, and Steve Coleman, on saxophones, with the latter delivering his best-ever playing with the band. The detail in the music is enthralling, Coleman playing the concluding theme statement of Holland's 'Quiet Fire', as an ascending series of silvery breaths, accompanied by tiny pings from DeJohnette's kit, and a final, gentle shower of cymbal sound. On Ellington's 'Take The Coltrane', DeJohnette's accompaniment is an endless badgering of explosive cymbals, angular crashes on the snare, bumpy, broken, but propulsive ride cymbal patterns, and Holland purrs like a Rolls throughout. Over-perfection is the group's only problem, with Holland's tunes, outwardly purposeful, displaying an occasional touch of cosy folksiness.

Hollyday, Christopher

(Born Boston, 1970)
Christopher Hollyday is one of the most widely-heralded, of the young, tradition-conscious, jazz virtuosi who have arrived on the scene in the late Eighties – and, unlike most of the others, he is self-taught. A technically astonishing altoist, in a style close to those of both Charlie Parker and Jackie McLean (who helped launch his career) Hollyday made his debut in his brother's hard bop band at fourteen, cut his first album, as a leader, a year later, and, four years after that, recorded *Reverence* with Cedar Walton, Billy Higgins and Ron Carter. He has already toured with the Maynard Ferguson band, and is the youngest musician ever to have led a band at New York's Village Vanguard.

Hollyday's elder brother Richard, a trumpeter, introduced him to the music of Charlie Parker, and, even as a ten year old, he was amazed by Parker's tone and strength. Hollyday taught himself to sing Parker solos first, before applying them to the saxophone, learning them off records and, by word of mouth, from other musicians in Boston. He made his first record, with his father's help, on his own label, but currently records with RCA/BMG.

★*Christopher Hollyday* (BMG PD 83055)

On this CD version of Hollyday's 1989 BMG debut, four tracks are uprated bop, from Jackie McLean's pen, two are bop classics ('Ko-Ko' and 'Bloomdido') and one is Dizzy Gillespie's ('Bebop') with Gershwin's, 'Embraceable You', as the additional feature. Hollyday is still happiest at fast tempos and unsteady on ballads, his tone turning sour on, 'Embraceable You'. He negotiates 'Bloomdido' with a husky, tenor-like sound giving way to hurtling double-time, releases turbulent sustained lines, ending in bagpipe-like wails on 'Ko-Ko', revealing himself as a nimble and spontaneous musical thinker; and, overall, varies the semiquavers with a repertoire of smears, cackles and bluesy sounds, that come originally from Jackie McLean's awakening to Ornette Coleman in 1963 (seven years before Hollyday was born). Expert repro-jazz, but repro just the same.

Hussain, Zakir

(Born Bombay, March 9, 1951)
Zakir Hussain is an Indian tabla player, who has effected some of the most creative and genuinely communicative links between Indian music and jazz. Like his fellow countryman, Trilok Gurtu, Hussain has worked with the expatriate British guitar virtuoso JOHN MCLAUGHLIN – and, also like Gurtu, he represents a new generation of Indian musicians who have an enthusiastic awareness of the jazz tradition.

Hussain was the student of the famous tabla player, Alla Rakha, who had himself worked with Buddy Rich, Elvin Jones and Yusef Lateef, and was able to familiarize Hussain with jazz. Hussain first heard Charlie Parker when he was twelve, and found it easy to assimilate jazz into Indian music. He has recorded with pop-jazz saxophone star, John Handy, and with Ali Akbar Khan, and been a member of McLaughlin's Indo-jazz band, Shakti.

★*Making Music* (ECM 831 544-2)

One of the most successful albums of east-west collaboration, featuring Hussain, on tabla, with McLaughlin on acoustic guitar, flautist Hariprasad Chaurasia, and Norwegian saxophonist, JAN GARBAREK. Garbarek's ghostly tone and long, hooting lines blend atmospherically both with the flute and the reserved sway of the rhythm, and McLaughlin cuts down on both his speed and the banter of exchanging phrases that he sometimes goes in for, in favour of substantial support of the ensemble. Thoughtful, softly glowing world-jazz.

Ibrahim, Abdullah (Dollar Brand)

(Born Cape Town, South Africa, October 9, 1934)
With the trumpeter Hugh Masekela, Abdullah Ibrahim has become the most prominent exponent of South Africa's unique version of jazz music in the world. Originally recording as Dollar Brand, Ibrahim gained a devoted following for a music that was moving, dignified and exuberant, and he was equally acclaimed as a pianist (with some clear allegiances to Duke Ellington and Thelonious Monk) and as a composer of themes that frequently combine the edgy immediacy of jazz and the composure and unity of church music.

Ibrahim's grandmother was a church musician, and his exposure to hymns and gospel through the African Methodist Episcopal Church was crucial to his musical development. But indigenous dance-music was also central to Ibrahim's culture as, in the Forties, was American jazz – picked up over the radio, and on expensively imported records. Ibrahim's first professional jobs were in vocal groups performing American pop and spirituals, then in dance bands. But when he and HUGH MASEKELA formed the Jazz Epistles in 1960, which became the first black group to record an album in South Africa, Ibrahim's future was transformed. After the Sharpeville massacre, he left South Africa to work at first in Europe and then in the States. His work so impressed Duke Ellington that Ellington arranged for him to record, and Ibrahim even took the piano chair with the Ellington band on tour. Influenced extensively by the free scene of the Sixties, Ibrahim nevertheless reverted to more song-like, accessible music following his conversion to Islam in 1968. He worked frequently as a hypnotic solo performer, but also formed larger groups, notably a fine seven-piece, Ekaya. Since the recent changes in South Africa, Ibrahim has returned to his home country, organising concerts and jazz education.

★*Blues for A Hip King* (Kaz Records KAZ CD 104)

Kaz Records has been performing an invaluable task in reissuing many of Ibrahim's performances from his South African early days and this disc, from several sessions in the company of the finest South African modernists of the Sixties, links local music, the jazz tradition and the avant-garde with pieces including 'Ornette's Cornet', and Thelonious Monk's 'Blue Monk' and 'Misterioso'.

★*The Mountain* (Kaz Records KAZ CD 7)

Ibrahim with his fine small-band, Ekaya, which was formed in 1983. The individuality of such instrumentalists as Carlos Ward (alto) and Ricky Ford (tenor) isn't cramped by Ibrahim's rich and distinctive settings, and the music (much of which was drawn from an earlier recording, 'Water From An Ancient Well') is powerful, emotional, and among the leader's best group work of recent times.

Irakere

Cuban rhythms have been combined with jazz for decades. Dizzy Gillespie was one of the most enthusiastic supporters of the idiom, using Cuban percussionists in the Forties. But Castro's revolution cut the practical connections between Cuba's vigorous jazz scene and America's – until Irakere appeared.

In 1977, a jazz cruise featuring Gillespie, plus Stan Getz and Earl Hines, among others, docked at Havana, in the first such US-Cuban link. A local group, with an African name, Irakere, performed alongside the Americans and caused a sensation. The result was that CBS signed its first non-expatriate Cuban artists for decades, and the following year this boiling, energetic ensemble toured America and Europe.

Prominent in its ranks was ARTURO SANDOVAL, one of the most

remarkable trumpeters in the world. Sandoval, a classical as well as a jazz trumpeter, astonished listeners with his tireless invention, effortless control of stratospheric high notes and rumbling low-register sounds. With altoist Paquito D'Rivera, as well, Irakere was a world-class band. They could generate immense heat from virtually any materials and their music contained bebop, classical music, salsa, tributes to Ellington, and thematic suites, frequently on African history, that blended jazz improvisation, dance music and theatre.

Irakere's recording career was not as consistently impressive as their live shows; it veered increasingly toward pop-jazz. The departure of Sandoval and D'Rivera was also hard to recover from.

★*Misa Negra* (Messidor 15972)

One of the better, and less pop-inclined, Irakere recordings, with a bracing mixture of jazz, funk and programmatic music. The title track is an extended tone-poem referring to Yoruba music, rather self-consciously portentous and over-long, but the remainder of the disc is a good sample of this animated, ambitious and, at times, moving band at work.

Jarrett, Keith

(Born Allentown, Pennsylvania, May 8, 1945)
Pianist Keith Jarrett prefigured New Age romanticism and Eighties eclecticism, a decade and a half ago, and his European romantic leanings and adaptation of musics other than jazz, have brought him both rapturous audiences and some critical disapproval. At its most apparently self-satisfied, Jarrett's work is a marketing-department model for sale to a white, upwardly-mobile audience, wanting something cleverer than pop and gentler than jazz. At its strongest, it represents genuinely adventurous improvisation, vaulting over bar-lines and chorus patterns, with a spontaneous symmetry, that fitfully puts Jarrett in the league of jazz piano giants.

Jarrett was a child prodigy, taking up piano at three, giving lengthy solo recitals at seven, and touring as a child, with a repertoire of his own pieces and classical standards. Jarrett studied in Paris with Nadia Boulanger, went to Berklee for a year, and left to start his own band. In the late Sixties, Jarrett played with Art Blakey's Jazz Messengers, then with CHARLES LLOYD's early fusion quartet. Lloyd's group was very popular and toured the world (including Russia) and its funky inclinations clearly attracted Jarrett, whose style was already becoming recognisable as a mixture of impressionism, bebop, country music and driving rhythms. When Jarrett left Lloyd, he formed his own trio, operating at times in territory close to one of his principal influences, Bill Evans. But it was the association with MILES DAVIS, in 1970–71, that lifted Jarrett's reputation, and in the Seventies he was mainly associated with the ECM label in Germany, performing massively popular (and usually completely improvised) solo concert tours throughout Europe and virtually securing ECM's financial future with the sales of one live recording in particular, the 1975 *Koln Concert*. Jarrett also success-fully continued with small-group music in America, working in an engaging territory suggestive of both the offbeat jauntiness of Ornette Coleman's faster pieces and the clangy, intricate tuneful-ness of a country-flavoured GARY BURTON session.

In the Eighties he performed more with European musicians, adapting his style to a more introspective, and at times melan-cholic music under the influence of partners including, JAN GARBAREK, Palle Danielsson and Jon Christensen. Jarrett has also participated more in completely composed music, in recent times, both interpreting his own works and giving concerts of the classical repertoire. To more traditional jazz listeners, some of Jarrett's most satisfying music has been delivered by his Standards Trio (with JACK DEJOHNETTE on drums and Gary Peacock on bass), a vehicle for classic materials of an older jazz repertoire, often operating very close to the sound of the Bill Evans trio. The absence, on CD, of Jarrett's lively 1970s American small-group recordings (*Death and the Flower* and *Byablue*) is regrettable.

★*Arbour Zena* (ECM 825 592-2)

One of Keith Jarrett's more successful pursuits of the methods of the romantic classical composers, this early Eighties collaboration, with Jan Garbarek and the Stuttgart Radio Symphony Orchestra, nevertheless retains an atmosphere of pensiveness and melancholy brooding, through most of its length. Oddly, Jan Garbarek's horn manages to lift the proceedings rather than compound the atmosphere of isolation.

★*Belonging* (ECM 829 115-2)

One of Jarrett's finest recordings with his European quartet, of Jan Garbarek (reeds), Palle Danielsson (bass) and Jon Christensen (drums). Of the six Jarrett compositions, two are ravishing ballads, while the remainder display a more abandoned, rhythmically-driving aspect of the leader, that's engagingly reminiscent of his early and less self-preoccupied work. Garbarek, his tone austere and hypnotically tranquil, almost steals the show.

★*Koln Concert* (ECM 810067-2)

A 1975 solo gig, and vintage Jarrett. From the opening dew-drop melody, through the passages of roaring riffs and folksy, country-music jauntiness, Jarrett is one hundred percent on the case, with the brake firmly applied to the sentimentality and archness he can fall into.

★*Nude Ants* (ECM 829 119-2)

A refreshing alternative to Jarrett navel-contemplation, this live set features the Scandinavian band, including Garbarek, at New York's Village Vanguard, in 1979. 'Sunshine Song', not only recalls earlier Jarrett and triggers more purposeful work from a rhythm section, often discreet to the point of evaporation, but also displays an earlier and more animated Garbarek.

★*Standards Live* (ECM 827 827-2)

The Standards Trio of Jarrett, Jack DeJohnette and Gary Peacock, in urgent mood, on a 1985 live performance from Paris. Jarrett recovers his lightness and fluency on the standards material, not least because he's being propelled by two of the best rhythm-section players in jazz, and the band breezes gracefully through material including, 'Stella By Starlight', 'Falling in Love with Love', and 'The Way You Look Tonight'.

★*Paris Concert* (ECM 1401)

Another Paris show and one of Jarrett's most recent releases. This time he's unaccompanied, but the formula reveals more of this controversial musician's faults, than his virtues. In particular, his odd tendency (odd for a musician of such proven improvisational imagination) to so frequently opt for exactly the figure you think he's about to. He opens 'October 17 1988' at his most baroque, with a central, repeated bass-note pattern enveloped in flaring, flamenco-like figures, falling eventually to dewy, pensive ripples of sound. But the favourite Jarrett devices (dogged rhythmic figures against stabbing licks inflected with country and blues voicings, intensity generated by repetition and volume, heart-on-sleeve emotionalism) are eventually irritating, as are his howls of ecstasy whilst pounding one note for that seems like hours.

Jazz Renegades

The Jazz Renegades came up with the British dance-jazz movement of the mid-Eighties, specialising in a mixed repertoire of jazz, blues, latin, soul and punk. Led by a broadminded rock drummer, Steve White, the band was one of the first on the British scene to reawaken the pounding bluesy sound of the Hammond organ.

White took up drumming after listening to jazz, but his most commercially successful work was performed with rock singer Paul Weller's band, Style Council. When he decided to return to jazz, he formed the Jazz Renegades, with Alan Barnes, an excellent hard bop altoist who had learned his craft with Tommy Chase's bands. White added John Dankworth's son, Alec, on bass, and David Newton on keyboards. The result has not been a music that exactly justifies the group's title, in terms of rebellion against the traditions; the effect has been quite the reverse. But the Renegades have been an intimate part of the movement that has kept the new enthusiasm for jazz on the boil. White, moreover, hasn't restricted his fondness for the Hammond organ to his own band; he has also played drums for another British dancefloor favourite, organist James Taylor.

★*Freedom Samba* (Polydor 839 651-2)

With a broader repertoire, than on their first independently-

produced album (*A Summer To Remember*), the Renegades feature
ex-Communards singer, Sarah-Jane Morris, on 'Do It The Hard
Way', several originals by Alan Barnes, and variations on Sonny
Rollins' 'Mambo Bounce', and Freddie Hubbard's 'A pec A sec'. Not
exactly an improvisor's masterpiece, but, as a foot-tapper, it keeps
the pressure up.

Jazz Warriors

From the postwar expansion of Britain's West Indian and Asian
populations, relatively few of the new citizens took to jazz;
though, in the 1960s, reed players Joe Harriott and Harold
McNair, trumpeters HAROLD BECKETT and Shake Keane, and Indian
classical violinist John Mayer, were exceptions. Twenty years
later, when jazz was expanding substantially in popularity, there
still appeared to be no role models for aspiring black jazz artists in
the UK.

But, nevertheless, some things were changing in the 1980s.
Public funding for local jazz education had increased slightly, and
a number of local authorities and arts organisations were
specifically encouraging black participation. Furthermore a
proportion of black youngsters were pursuing a formal musical
education; an option that had seemed economically impractical to
the previous generation. Several of the latter – including the
talented ex-reggae saxophonist, COURTNEY PINE and multi-
instrumentalist Gail Thompson, have gone on to develop a
significant black contingent in British jazz.

Pine and Thompson (the former having developed his jazz skills
in a class run by the adventurous London drummer, John Stevens,
and in Stevens' idiom-hopping big band, Freebop) played together
in the eccentric swing/bop big band led by Rolling Stones
drummer Charlie Watts, in 1985, and began to explore the
possibilities of a young, all-black, big band. They discovered a
powerful, Herbie Hancockish pianist, Julian Joseph, a raw, but
ferociously dedicated drummer, Mark Mondesir, and a rugged
and reliable bassist in Gary Crosby, who together formed the
Warrior's first rhythm section, and also the basis of the Pine's own
band.

The Jazz Warriors opened for business at the Fridge, Brixton, in

January 1986, and the reaction from a packed house was ecstatic. The band proceeded to avoid orthodox jazz venues, in favour of places drawing a non-jazz audience. They also set to writing original work, despite their inexperience, being considerably assisted by two skilled composer-arrangers – trombonist, Fayyez Virji and veteran trumpeter, Harry Beckett. Playing opportunities increased (including an Arts Council Music Network tour) and, though personnel changes accelerated as founder members Pine, Steve Williamson and vibraharpist, Orphy Robinson, left to pursue their own careers, enthusiastic new players were constantly found, and resourceful regulars, like saxophonist Ray Carless and Fayyez Virji, continued to underpin the band's new ventures.

*_Out of Many, One People_ (Antilles ANCD 8712)

An erratically played album, recorded live at the Shaw Theatre, in the spring of 1987, and not all of its material suggested that musical virtues, like contrast, surprise and rhythmic drive, were commandingly in hand. But what did resoundingly echo from it was the independence of the band in its choice of material, and the foregrounding of the African heritage, as the principle message that the Warriors wanted their audience to absorb. Fayyez Virji's compellingly accelerating and choppily-accented 'Minor Groove' was a standout of the record, and remains in the Warriors' repertoire.

Johnson, Marc

(Born Texas, 1953)
A formally-educated bass player who was working with the Fort Worth Symphony Orchestra, when in his teens. At the same time, Johnson discovered jazz, and, thereafter, made rapid headway with a succession of pedigree leaders; first Woody Herman, then Bill Evans, Mel Lewis and eventually Stan Getz.

But by the mid-Eighties, Johnson had musical ideas of his own and they were closer to his own generation's notions of jazz and rock collaborations, than they were to the textural and harmonic preoccupations of his former employers. Johnson thus formed the band, Bass Desires, with two fast, up-and-coming, electric guitarists of completely different types; the abstract, multi-idiomatic BILL FRISELL whose work often resembled studio overdubbing, rather than live guitar playing and the rhythmic, bluesy, ex-Miles Davis accompanist, JOHN SCOFIELD. Pete Erskine joined on drums. The group came together, on and off, for occasional tours and visits to the studio during the Eighties, but its music remained a distinctive blend of contemporary elements; blues, free-playing, stretches of driving jazz, moments of pastiche.

★*Bass Desires* (ECM 827743-2)

Frisell, in demonstrative form, in his sound-effects guise, Scofield in his bluesy-bop persona, in a guitar-band set in which the instruments are frequently used to create slow-motion waves of sound, distant banshee hootings and churchy chimings, against themes, eerily like KEITH JARRETT tunes, which swell and fade.

★*Second Sight* (ECM 833038-2)

Bass Desires, in 1987. This is, altogether, a more contemplative affair and lacking in the melodic variety of the above album. Johnson's own piece, 'Prayer Beads', is an effectively ambiguous use of space, but the tunes don't stick in the mind – apart from amiable surprises, like Scofield's rocker, 'Twister'.

Jordan, Stanley

(Born Chicago, July 31, 1959)
Stanley Jordan appeared as a street-musician, in New York, in 1984, producing an entirely new effect with the electric guitar. It consisted of playing, simultaneously, two independent melody lines on the instrument. Jordan hardly strums or picks, nor does he anchor his non-fretting hand to the bridge end of the instrument. He allows both hands to roam the fretboard freely, 'hammering' the strings against the frets to produce the notes, and thus freeing both hands to develop melodic ideas independently.

Stanley Jordan was taught classical piano, from the age of six, and at eleven – inspired by the sound of Jimi Hendrix – he took up the guitar. Partly because of a Hendrix-inspired disrespect for conventional guitar technique, Jordan began experimenting with tunings, and, from the age of sixteen, the two-handed tapping technique.

In 1981, he made his first album, *Touch Sensitive*, on his own label, and, in spring 1984, he began playing on the streets outside music shops, like Manny's and Sam Asch's on 48th Street. But appearances at the Kool Jazz Festival, and then Montreux, in 1984, were Jordan's break, and the Blue Note label signed him up. Jordan's records have been variable, his technique, so far, more revolutionary than the music he makes with it, but his promise remains considerable.

★*Standards Vol 1* (Blue Note CDP 746 333-2)

Jordan's notion of standards includes recent hit songs, like Bobby Hebb's, 'Sunny', and Simon and Garfunkel's, 'Sound of Silence', as well as more traditional jazz vehicles. Fitfully graceful, rarely moving.

★*Magic Touch* (Blue Note CDP 746 092-2)

A massive hit, in both the jazz and pop charts, in the States. *Magic Touch* takes in a variety of material, from the Thelonious Monk classic, 'Round Midnight', to the Beatles', 'Eleanor Rigby'; but though the breadth of the material makes the album superficially varied, Jordan's packed, technically dazzling, blizzard of notes, leads virtually all of his solos to take on a similar character, without apparent development of either the theme, or distinctively different concepts of his own.

Kennedy, Nigel

(Brighton, England, December 28, 1956)
Nigel Kennedy is a young fiddle virtuoso who is beginning to devote as much of his time and energy to jazz, as he has to classical music. Kennedy is a rare kind of conservatoire rebel, whose involvement with jazz looks like neither a flirtation, an affectation, nor a naive obsession with the vernacular. He plays jazz

material with insight and respect, though he still betrays the runaway classicist's unsteadiness at establishing a truly organic relationship between improvisation and the compositions underpinning it. Despite his enthusiastic and imaginative cracking of the mould which made him, Kennedy is still not always sure of his ground. His variations are frequently dazzling, repeated patterns rather than cumulative melodic developments, and his own, jazz-flavoured, writings can seem conventional and almost coy, in their artlessness. He is often happiest with the most direct versions of jazz swing, for example on a song like, 'Sweet Georgia Brown'.

★Strad Jazz (Chandos Records CHAN 8350)

Typical accumulation of the virtues and faults of the Kennedy method; improvisations, often boldly and dramatically attacked, but without the long-range logic and the accumulating excitement of the best jazz solos. The materials, though, represents Kennedy's favourite kind of jazz repertoire, and includes 'Body and Soul', 'Autumn Leaves' and 'Lover Man', and the influence of Stephane Grappelli has a powerful impact on the entire session.

King, Peter John

(Born Surrey, England, August 11, 1940)
One of the finest of all English saxophone players, Peter King emerged at the end of the 1950s, as a Charlie Parker disciple, and delivered his accolades to Parker with a swing and sureness of phrasing rare for non-American jazz players at the time. Age certainly has not withered King, since in recent times – partly through adding some of Coltrane's innovations to Parker's – he has improved, even on his own impressive record. His phrasing, albeit on the fastest themes, still sounds like the best of a number of competing options, all racing neck-and-neck in his brain.

King's first major appearance was at the opening of Ronnie Scott's Gerrard Street club, in 1959. The assurance of his performance quickly marked him out, and he began to find work with prestigious bands, including JOHN DANKWORTH's, Maynard Ferguson's, and Tubby Hayes'. Through the Sixties and Seventies, Parkerish bebop was his forte, and he appeared in this mode, with innumerable British bands, and in the company of visiting Americans, such as Zoot Sims and Hampton Hawes, as well as joining the Ray Charles orchestra for a European tour. In recent years, King has occasionally softened his playing on record, seeking to broaden his appeal, to include the fusion market, but it is as a heated bop artist, that he continues to be at his most effective.

★*Crusade* (WEA K2461172)

One of Peter King's more influential admirers is Ben Watt, of the pop band Everything But the Girl, who is also the producer of *Crusade*. The album is thus unsurprisingly pop-influenced, with a velvety studio atmosphere, tunes by Smokey Robinson, Donny Hathaway and Joni Mitchell, even a funk version of 'Blue Monk'. King's CD representation should be more of a likeness of him than this, but underneath it all there is the same fluidity, the same lightning double-time runs, the same sense of shape, as of old. The bland materials do, however, inevitably lessen the impact.

Knitting Factory

Despite the recent revival of older jazz forms, particularly the post-bop style of the Fifties and Sixties, some musicians have continued to swim against the tide by developing unusual compositional methods, combining idioms, using unfamiliar instrumentation, and seeking untried settings for improvisation. A highly successful home for such activities has been the Knitting Factory, at 47 East Houston Street, in New York's Greenwich Village. The Knitting Factory has been run by an enterprising promoter, Michael Dorf, and it has played host to a variety of (mostly younger) musicians from avant-garde jazz, experimental rock and pop, and straight music. The succession of musicians who have played there, includes the violent sound-effects guitarist, SONNY SHARROCK, British art-rock improvisor, FRED FRITH, and composer, musical-collagist, thrash-metal and bebop alto improvisor, JOHN ZORN.

★*Live at the Knitting Factory, Vols 1 & 2* (Enemy EMCD 111/112)

An eclectic blend of experimenters and oddballs, among them, a septet, the Jazz Passengers, who mix scrambling violin passages, fitful stretches of breezy jazz time and bricks-through-windows electric guitar eruptions. Also noteworthy are a lyrical, violin-led trio that plays as if it was trying to sell Elgar to East Side street-gangs; a soloist who improvises on Albert Ayler tunes, country-style, on a steel guitar; plus electronics, banshee chanteuses and much more. The second volume, featuring the jagged sound of SONNY SHARROCK and the inventive Fred Frith, is more abstract, yet more dramatic, than the first.

Lacy, Steve (Steven Lackritz)

(Born New York, July 23, 1934)
Like his inspiration, Sidney Bechet, Steve Lacy is a soprano saxophone specialist. Lacy's command of this instrument is immense, but still utterly personal. He doesn't aspire to the kind of technical wizardry exemplified by Charlie Parker, or on trumpet by WYNTON MARSALIS, but to a more oblique, unassuming virtuosity, for which he has been employed by some of the most sophisticated jazz minds, Thelonious Monk, Cecil Taylor and Gil Evans.

Lacy isn't primarily a bebop player, or a performer of fiddly tunes and dazzling runs, but his range (four-octaves) and tonal purity are highly expressive. He is as subtle an architect of delicate, glancing effects, as anyone in jazz. For at least a decade, he has been developing his own music in bands that are both compositionally strong and that leave considerable room for improvisation (his wife, the cellist and singer, Irene Aebi, is regularly featured, as is a long-time alto partner, Steve Potts). He has also been open to free-improvising situations and the European avant-garde, unconcerned by the indifference to Afro-American traditions displayed by many of these partners.

As a student, Lacy had abandoned his music courses, in favour of playing New Orleans-style jazz, emulating, in particular, the swing, intensity and passion of Sidney Bechet. With time, he came to appreciate jazz's more recent guises, but never explored bebop closely, moving straight to a complex, thematic improvising style, influenced by Cecil Taylor. Lacy and Taylor were associates until the late Fifties, when Lacy developed an obsessive interest in Thelonious Monk, learning all his tunes and, eventually, joining his band for a season in 1960. Lacy kept to the Monk repertoire until, in the mid-Sixties, he began playing in Europe, particularly Rome, where for three years he worked with the non-jazz, experimental group, Musica Elettronica Viva.

In the 1980s, Lacy and his quintet played a remarkably integrated synthesis of composed music, wry, slippery improvisation (his own soprano sound is predominantly a high-pitched, inquisitive sound) and collective interplay reminiscent of Cecil Taylor.

★*The Door* (BMG PD 83049)

Steve Lacy's first recording, in 1988, for BMG/Novus; the first major label in years to have shown an interest in him. Excellent introduction to recent Lacy, featuring his restless, needling, endlessly-reconstructing soprano style, in collaboration with various permutations of his regular group, including Steve Potts, on alto, and Kent Carter, on bass.

★*Straight Horn of Steve Lacy* (Candid CCD 9007)

The best CD, so far, of Lacy in his earlier and more orthodox guise, working here, in 1960, with drummer Roy Haynes, and performing three challenging Monk tunes, some Cecil Taylor material and the bebop classic, 'Donna Lee'. His solos are effervescent and artfully constructed, and the contrast between Haynes' unstoppable rhythmic propulsion and Lacy's disruptive instinct for sidestepping the beat, gives the session a unique quality.

★*Anthem* (BMG/Novus PD 83079)

A Lacy exploration of the territory between jazz and contemporary straight music, partly put together, at the request of the French government, for the 200th anniversary of the French Revolution. One of Lacy's favourite subversive ploys is to pitch bebop time against regular, on-the-beat, time; a feature here of

'No 1', with its bleary trombone line thumping downstairs in a conventional march, whilst Steve Potts' alto hovers and whirrs, in the mid-range, and Lacy's bright, keening soprano flutters upwards against it. Other aspects are, an approximation of Greek *bouzouki* music, Irene Aebi's solemnly unjazzy vocals, a recital of a revolutionary text (ending in a boiling collective interplay) and pianist Bobby Few, in Cecil Taylor mode.

Lake, Oliver

(Born Marianna, Arkansas, 1944)
Altoist Oliver Lake is best known for his role in the World Saxophone Quartet, but, the WSQ apart, he leads an independent musical life as well. Raised in St Louis, Lake was originally a percussionist, only starting on alto saxophone at sixteen. In the 1960s, in sympathy with the Civil Rights movement and black liberation politics, Lake joined the Black Artists' Group in St Louis, and for much of that period was associated with the avant-garde, as well as political activity. He moved, as did the ART ENSEMBLE and several other experimental bands, to Paris, in the early Seventies, but by 1977 he was back in the States, as a founder member of the World Saxophone Quartet. As a result of his abrasive high-output playing, in the Sixties, and his later absorption into the WSQ's group sound, Lake's subtleties and individuality have rarely got their due; but in more recent times he has become involved in a variety of bands, apart from WSQ, including the funk outfit, Jump Up, and the free-ensemble, Blue Star.

★*Otherside* (Gramavision 188901-2)
Lake, in a 1988 collaboration, with a highly gifted recent partner, pianist Geri Allen, with tracks featuring both small groups and a big band. *Otherside* features an Eric Dolphy dedication, as do all Lake's own albums, and a challenging collection of his typical, knife-edge balancing acts between waywardness and offbeat lyricism.

Laws, Ronnie

(Born Houston, October 3, 1950)
A bluesy, exciting saxophonist who displays the broad tone and

leisurely gait, so familiar of Texan horn men; but also a player whose undoubted talents have been masked by the formulaic disco styles on many of his records. In the late Seventies, Laws became the highest-selling debut artist ever to have recorded for Blue Note, with *Pressure Sensitive*, astutely produced by the CRUSADERS' trombonist, Wayne Henderson.

Many of the members of Laws' family were musical. His grandfather was a harmonica player, his mother, a gospel pianist, and his brother, Hubert, a successful flute-player. Laws studied music, then moved to Los Angeles at twenty one, joining the rock bands, Von Ryan's Express, and later, Earth Wind and Fire. He has also lent his wide, rolling sound to projects by South African trumpeter, HUGH MASEKELA.

★*Classic Masters* (Capitol/EMI CDP 746 585-2)

The CD of *Pressure Sensitive* has been deleted, but this moderately varied selection of Laws' fusion work at least includes from it, 'Always There', its best track, with the saxophonist mixing a tenor sound, both plaintive and exuberant, over an irresistibly propulsive keyboard figure.

Liebman, David

(Born New York, September 4, 1946)
Even an occasional jazz listener quickly loses count of the number of Coltrane disciples there are among contemporary saxophonists. Dave Liebman is one whose style is founded on Coltrane, but who has added a fragile, tremulous quality to his upper register playing, on soprano sax, that is quite his own.

Liebman learnt to improvise with one of the most eccentric exponents of the practice, Lennie Tristano. His working life took in the rock band, Ten Wheel Drive, and, eventually, the early MILES DAVIS fusion ensembles. It was only in 1980 that he shifted exclusively to the soprano saxophone, and throughout that decade, was principally absorbed in developing, Quest: an adventurous collaboration, including pianist, Richie Beirach, that used a kaleidoscopic collective improvisation as background and catalyst for soloists. Quest, a quartet, worked both original material and startling transformations of standards.

The quartet apart, Liebman appeared in other situations, notably performing highly idiosyncratic tributes to John Coltrane.

★*Quest 2* (Storyville/Moss Music STCD 4132)

Quest, in 1986, with Liebman and Beirach, plus Ron McLure, on bass, and Billy Hart, on drums. This is good, fast-moving, contemporary jazz, the focus of the playing is sharp, the interweaving of the parts deftly economical and the coaxing of spiky themes in unexpected ways, a source of fresh phrasing.

★*Homage To John Coltrane* (Owl/France LC 046)

Liebman on Paddlewheel's *Tribute to John Coltrane*, might have been better for a CD reissue, but this album is almost as strong and wilful, with Liebman showing how resourcefully he can improvise, at length, over repeated figures; a particular skill of Coltrane's, for which most of his disciples, compared to Liebman, lack sufficient harmonic knowledge.

Lloyd, Charles

(Born Memphis, Tennessee, March 15, 1938)
Saxophonist Charles Lloyd has displayed a remarkable talent for both putting promising players on the map (JACK DEJOHNETTE and KEITH JARRETT in earlier times; more recently, French pianist, MICHEL PETRUCCIANI) and for spawning versions of the post-Sixties avant-garde that have popular appeal. But, as an improvisor, Lloyd has rarely seemed more than another good Coltrane disciple, and still seeks the edge of surprise that distinguishes a player such as DAVE LIEBMAN.

Lloyd scored two significant firsts, in the Sixties, with his highly successful quartet (Keith Jarrett was in it); his was the first jazz group to perform at San Francisco's Fillmore stadium and the first American group to play jazz at a Soviet festival. The reasons for Lloyd's success are not hard to discern. His tenor playing is fierce and direct, bursting with gospel and blues (a legacy of early experience with singers, BB King, and, Bobby Bland) and also influenced by the funky jazz performed by his one time partner, Cannonball Adderley. Nor was he, at the time, shy of using Beatles' tunes in his repertoire, and so helped pave the way for the development of the fusion movement.

Lloyd has kept his head down since, becoming both a teacher of music and of transcendental meditation, but makes occasional returns to playing and recording.

★*Fish Out of Water* (ECM 1398)

A spacious and contemplative disc, which presents Lloyd's late-Eighties work. All of the musicians, for the most part, avoid anything more strenuous than a brisk walking pace, preferring a rather drowsy riffle through the pages of the Scandinavian rhythm-section's soft-licks catalogue. Eventually there is some acceleration to an African feel, which does animate Lloyd into some searing Traneish phrases. But it comes too late to prevent this from being a drifting, uncertain session, and unlikely to put Lloyd back in there among the powerbrokers.

Loose Tubes

(Formed 1984, dissolved 1990)

Loose Tubes, only recently defunct, was a London-based big-band that, by blending distinct genres of music, such as African hi-life, bebop, soca, funk, rock 'n' roll, sambas, marches and bursts of extrovert electro-pop, broke the conventions of big-band playing and gained a wide following in Britain. Its records became respectable sellers, in jazz terms, and it attracted the attention of distinguished professionals, such as Teo Macero, the Miles Davis/ Gil Evans studio producer, who mixed the final album, *Open Letter*; Macero insisted that Duke Ellington would have enjoyed the band. The Tubes became headline news, virtually selling out the Albert Hall for a Promenade concert in 1987, touring widely in Europe, even playing live on the BBC's chat flagship, 'Wogan Show'.

It was in early 1984 that Graham Collier, a highly-regarded British composer, experienced bandleader, and teacher at the Guildhall School of Music and Drama, set up a workshop orchestra for adventurous up-and-coming jazz musicians. The project soon gathered such steam that the orchestra ceased to be just a workshop band, acquired the name Loose Tubes, and began to feature original material; mostly by pianist, DJANGO BATES, and bassist, Steve Berry.

In 1985, after a concession by the Musician's Union, the band played for a week at Ronnie Scott's Club, and raised the roof. It then began to appear in concerts and at music festivals all over Britain. Some other venues of the band were determined by its association with the anti-nuclear movement and it frequently lent its services to street-protests. The collective energy generated by the band galvanised the careers of many of its individuals, and it was the competing commitments of sidemen like Bates, IAIN BALLAMY, Mark Lockheart, and others, that brought about its demise.

★*Open Letter* (Editions EGED 55)

Loose Tubes' third, and best album. The full title is *An Open Letter To Dudu Pukwana* in reference to the late Port Elizabeth altoist, who had lived in London – and the South African influence, a particularly strong feature, offsets the Tubes' occasional tendency to musical fidgetiness with its warmth, rhythmic exuberance, and song-like directness. The soloing doesn't always gleam, as much as the ensemble work does, though the mercurial, Eric Dolphy-like, Iain Ballamy and the fierce trumpet of DAVE DEFRIES, make up most of the difference.

McFerrin, Bobby

(Born New York, March 11, 1950)
Whether vocalist, Bobby McFerrin is a circus act or a musician, is a question that puzzles jazz observers. The son of opera singers, McFerrin was taught piano as a child, and developed a jazz style on the instrument, close to KEITH JARRETT's. But at the age of thirty three he turned to singing, encouraged by the successful bop vocalist of the Fifties and Sixties, Jon Hendricks. McFerrin quickly indicated that he was not simply a singer with an attractively light, buoyant tone, but an uncanny mimic too, able to sound like most of the instruments of an entire band.

His early successes were on tours with George Benson, Grover

Washington, HERBIE HANCOCK and WYNTON MARSALIS but it is latterly, as a unaccompanied performer, that McFerrin has made a special mark. He dazzles audiences with a combination of indrawn breaths and chest beating (with the microphone held close) to represent percussion sounds and low, gargling noises to represent funk bass figures and synthesiser effects.

McFerrin has explored the vocal arts, in a variety of directions, in recent years; working with free-improvising singers, making successful, pop-oriented records (*Don't Worry Be Happy*) and, latterly, concentrating more on lyrics than wordless vocals to further improve his commercial prospects.

★*Simple Pleasures* (EMI/Manhattan CDP 748 059-2)

McFerrin's most successful album, from 1988, saw the singer making his most committed moves yet toward the pop market – but though the audacity of some of his live shows, with jazzier partners, is missing, McFerrin's expertise, swing, and choice of songs ('Suzie Q', 'Sunshine of Your Love', and, 'Don't Worry Be Happy') makes much of it a pleasure, and, sometimes, a marvel to listen to.

★*Medicine Music* (EMI/Manhattan CDP 792 048-2)

McFerrin, in 1990, displaying two further developments in his approach: more lyrics, and a kind of hip piety, as befits his religious interests and endorsement of traditional family values. Some of this highly eclectic album is irritatingly devout (the song, 'Discipline', is taken from the Epistle to the Hebrews, and the 23rd Psalm is also there, dedicated to the singer's mother) but the ensemble sound that McFerrin achieves through overdubbing, plus some support from the vocal group, Voicestra, is nevertheless remarkable. Idioms touched on are American Indian, African and gospel music. The more abstract sound-effects pieces, like 'The Train', and 'He Ran All The Way', may appeal more to McFerrin's pre-pop fans.

McLaughlin, John

(Born Yorkshire, England, January 4, 1942)
Nobody can accuse guitarist John McLaughlin of jumping onto

the world-music bandwagon. Following an illustrious stint with MILES DAVIS, at the end of the Sixties, he formed the Mahavishnu Orchestra, inspired by his fascination with the East. His next group, Shakti, featured three Indian musicians, and tried to unite western jazz and pop to traditional Indian forms. McLaughlin has latterly been leading a more jazzy ensemble, often featuring himself on an amplified acoustic guitar (occasionally mildly stretched to resemble the sounds of heavier metal, or even organ) and including, the remarkable Indian percussionist, Trilok Gurtu.

McLaughlin was raised in a musical family, but was mostly self-taught on guitar. He played blues on it at first, and then fell under the spell of the Belgian guitarist, Django Reinhardt. Playing at first in rhythm & blues and bebop groups around Newcastle, he moved to London, in the early Sixties, and took part in the British rhythm & blues boom of that era; but he was also a skilled improvisor and composer, and his brilliant debut album, in 1969, *Extrapolation* (in the company of some of Britain's finest younger jazz soloists) confirmed his class. McLaughlin attracted the attention of the Miles Davis circle, initially worked for Davis' talented drummer, TONY WILLIAMS, then for the trumpeter himself, on the landmark fusion albums, *Bitches' Brew*, and, *In A Silent Way*. McLaughlin, by now a student of Indian philosophy, was ready to launch his own band. He envisaged, for this venture, a marriage between a playing style based on jazz-rock fusion, and a thematic inspiration drawn from his studies of Eastern mysticism.

The result was the Mahavishnu Orchestra, formed in 1970; initially one of the most sophisticated and popular of all fusion bands. After the first version's break-up, McLaughlin experimented with personnel, and, at the same time launched the softer, acoustic band, Shakti, with Indian musicians, including the violinist, L Shankar. From 1975 to the present, McLaughlin has moved back and forth between revamped Mahavishnu bands and acoustic groups. His own playing has moved toward a more seamless, densely packed and technically dazzling phrasing, rather than the more fragmented and surprising shapes his solos took in his Miles Davis period and before. He has also written a guitar concerto for performance with full orchestra. Most of McLaughlin's best records are currently not available on CD; notably *Extrapolation*, *My Goal's Beyond*, and, the Mahavishnu debut album, *Inner Mounting Flame*.

★*Adventures in Radioland* (Polygram SOSCD, 2020)

The albums of the earliest, and best, Mahavishnu Orchestra, have been deleted; this is from a less successful remake of the band, in the mid-Eighties. McLaughlin sounded bemused about electric music after the first two Mahavishnu discs, and he doesn't sound much more convinced here, and though his characteristically dazzling bursts of sound are still much in evidence, their underlying logic is difficult to track. The personnel, in the main, consists of noisy funksters, though, ex-Miles Davis saxophonist Bill Evans, lends the kind of vitality, intelligence and atmosphere that he always seems to be able to concoct, however manic the surroundings.

★*Live at the Royal Festival Hall* (JMT 834 436-2)

McLaughlin in 1989 in London, with his trio featuring bassist Kai Eckhardt and the remarkable drummer Trilok Gurtu, an Indian who has studied both the percussion methods of his own culture and those of Elvin Jones as well. Inevitably it's fast, over-clever music, but Gurtu's presence gives it a gleeful energy that overcomes the glibness of technique.

Mantler, Mike

(Born Vienna, August 10, 1943)
A classically trained trumpeter and composer, Mike Mantler has been involved, both organisationally and compositionally, with some of the most adventurous activities of the New York avant-garde of the Sixties and Seventies. His own music, however, is predominantly slow-moving, and bleakly dissonant to the point of desolation, and his choice of thematic inspiration – the works of Pinter, Beckett and Edward Gorey – have represented an existential angst, which owes more to his mid-European roots than to his American acquisitions. With hindsight, Mantler's greatest claim to fame may have been to write the composition, *Communications*, for the Jazz Composers Orchestra, that helped propel one of Cecil Taylor's finest recorded performances.

Mantler helped found the radical Jazz Composers' Guild, in

New York, in the mid-Sixties, and also played trumpet with Cecil Taylor's group. He married composer CARLA BLEY, playing in her band and in that of the saxophonist, STEVE LACY, and coordinated and promoted Bley's epic jazz opera *Escalator Over the Hill*. Mantler has written semi-classical works for orchestral performance, and continued his involvement in independent production and distribution for uncommercial music.

Hapless Child (ECM 831 828-2)

Mantler's musical adaptation of the whimsically ghoulish child-hood world of illustrator and writer Edward Gorey – remarkable, not especially for compositional ingenuity, but for the utterly appropriate contribution of ex-Soft Machine percussionist and singer, Robert Wyatt, a man with one of the most distinctive voices in new music. Worth it for Wyatt alone.

Something There (ECM 831 829-2)

One of the most successful of Mantler projects, a mix of fusion, serial composition and a rich and thoughtful arrangement (by MICHAEL GIBBS, who has brought colour to the normally pallid Mantler) featuring a spectacular performance by Miles Davis guitarist, Mike Stern, Pink Floyd drummer, Nick Mason, and the London Symphony Orchestra. Unexpectedly accessible and pro-vocative music.

Mann, Herbert Jay Solomon 'Herbie'

(Born New York, April 16, 1930)
A technically adept and commercially opportunistic performer, on a distinctly marginal jazz instrument, the flute, Herbie Mann didn't simply make waves, in the Sixties, as an unusual voice on a little-used instrument, but as one of the closest things to a pop star the jazz world throws up. Before the late-Sixties jazz-rock bandwagon really rolled, Mann – like saxophonist CHARLES LLOYD – put together a band that deployed funk rhythms with the more provocative contributions of jazz-based players, to make a major hit, *Memphis Underground*, one of the seminal fusion albums. For

years afterwards, Mann topped the press polls as everybody's favourite jazz flautist. When that star waned, Mann nevertheless remained a popular festival draw, and he had a Seventies disco hit with his more recent ensemble, Family of Mann.

Mann was originally a clarinettist, and worked for three years with a US Army band, in the early Fifties, following that up with successful studio work on the West Coast. The musics of other cultures interested him, and he later toured both Africa and Brazil, with his own group, adapting his sound to absorb the bossa nova boom. Later in the decade he became more rock oriented, which led to *Memphis Underground*, and, in the following decade, he investigated both reggae and disco music. Largely an uninspiring soloist, Mann has nevertheless shown a remarkable knack for tuning in to dance idioms, though he may stop at the 1990s.

★*At the Village Gate* (Atlantic/WEA 781350-2)

One of the better, early Mann records to have remained available, and his first major hit. As with most of the successful Mann recordings, this one displays a tightly organised, highly percussive band, though without much sense of anything in the music being spontaneously discovered, as they play. But the leader's grasp of the danceable essentials of Latin music is shrewd, and sometimes exuberant.

★*Memphis Underground* (WEA K781 364-2)

A virtual definition of Herbie Mann's particular alchemy – a powerful, headlong blend of two quite dissimilar guitarists (the harmonically subtle LARRY CORYELL, and the bludgeoning, SONNY SHARROCK) plus funky vibraharpist, Roy Ayres, and an inexorably swinging Memphis rhythm section.

Maria, Tania

(Born Sao Luis, Brazil, May 9, 1948)
It is as an artist who comprehends the intricacy and impro-visational demands of bebop, and the rhythmic energy of Latin music, that Tania Maria has made her mark. An inventive

keyboard player and a wild, blazing singer, Tania Maria is also a live performer of an immense vigour and drive which isn't always achieved in her recording sessions.

In the 1970s, when the world already knew of ASTRUD GILBERTO and FLORA PURIM, Tania Maria was still building the foundations of what was to become her mature style. She was invited to work in a Paris nightclub on a three-month contract, and stayed for the next seven years, recording several albums, powerfully highlighting her Brazilian roots, for the Barclay label. During her European stay, she continued to make an occasional impact in the States – performing, on the same bill as Sarah Vaughan, at the 1975 Newport Festival. By 1981, through the encouragement of Charlie Byrd, (a guitarist who had long sought to further the Brazilian connection, and who had played on the Getz/GILBERTO samba classics of the 1960s) Tania Maria had cut an American album, *Piquant*, and moved to New York City to live. She made a number of successful albums for Concord, during the Eighties. More recently her work has lost much of its reckless bravura and is beginning to adopt the kind of showbiz polish that she was once such a refreshing change from.

★*The Real Tania Maria – Wild* (Concord CCD 4264)

One of the few Tania Maria albums to capture her true flavour; this 1984 recording was a live set that included some of her most famous tunes, including the rat-tat-tat uptempo scat classic, 'Sangria', the driving, 'Yatra-Ta', and percussion displays likely to set even the most weary feet on the move.

Mariano, Charlie (Carmine Ugo)

(Born Boston, November 12, 1923)
A creative and original reed player, far more highly regarded by his colleagues and musical partners than by the public, and one who has constantly challenged his own musical assumptions and looked for inspirational new settings to work in. He was originally a bebop altoist, in the Charlie Parker mould, and later affected by Coltrane and by the music of the East, which he has intelligently absorbed and adapted.

Mariano was taught piano as a child, later playing in an army band and then studying saxophone at the Berklee School. He spent part of the Fifties working in the Stan Kenton band, and performing with various of its sidemen around Los Angeles. In 1959 he married the Japanese pianist and composer Toshiko Akiyoshi, and performed with her. Then came work with Charles Mingus' group and as a teacher at Berklee. He also travelled to Malaysia to coach a local orchestra, it was on that trip that he discovered the oboe-like South Indian instrument, the *nadaswaram*, which he has extensively studied and still plays. Mariano has also worked a good deal with European musicians, notably the composer of gentle fusion tone-poems, German bassist, EBERHARD WEBER.

★*Jyothi* (ECM 811 548-2)

Mariano in his Indian incarnation; a 1982 collaboration, in Bangalore, with the Karnataka College of Percussion. The leader reveals the depths of his commitment to Indian music, in his weaving, wraith-like lines on the *nadaswaram*; a richer collaboration between cultures than the recent crop of more celebrated examples.

Marsalis, Branford

(Born New Orleans, August 26, 1960)

The saxophone-playing member of the Marsalis family (a dominant surname in contemporary jazz), Branford is a brilliant reeds-player. He personifies the best of the 'neo-classical' period of jazz, in which a variety of post-bop styles are being re-examined and redeployed. His own recent preferences have been toward the collective agility and rhythmic ambiguity of the pre-electric MILES DAVIS bands of the mid-Sixties. But Marsalis is no copyist. His bands have a characteristic quirkiness, wit and subtlety, and his own playing is frequently Sonny Rollins-like in its mixture of bristling runs and sudden indignant squawks, with at times, echoes of Lester Young, in passages of light, skittering, nearly-evaporating phrases, like someone absently doodling. Marsalis is also a strong-minded defender of young musicians and their new internationalism, and a movie actor of promise as well.

With his brothers, Marsalis insists that their piano-playing father, Ellis, didn't push them toward their jazz careers. Their mother, however, did ensure that their musical interests were backed by the resources of a thorough education and Marsalis attended Southern University, Baton Rouge, studying clarinet with a legendary New Orleans traditionalist, Alvin Batiste. He then went on to Berklee, and from there straight into Art Blakey's Jazz Messengers, eventually playing side-by-side with his younger brother, Wynton, who was on trumpet.

In 1983, Branford Marsalis made his debut album – an inconsistently impressionistic piece of urban-streets programme-jazz based on Charles Mingus', *Scenes in the City*. Later in the decade he worked in pop-singer Sting's backing band. Marsalis' recorded output has been of irregular quality so far, despite his considerable skill as an improvisor.

★*Trio Jeepy* (CBS 465 134-2)

A trio album of Branford Marsalis, plus the remarkable polyrhythmic drummer Jeff 'Tain' Watts, and octogenarian bassist, Milt Hinton. The result is a session of immense vitality and wide-ranging references, with a spaciousness deriving both from the trio format and the generousness of Branford's approach, that enables the improvisatory talents of all three to flower. Marsalis plays a dazzling fast solo on, 'Three Little Words', (an old Rollins favourite) without a repetition or a cliche, and there's hardly a dull moment on the disc.

Marsalis, Wynton

(Born New Orleans, October 18, 1961)
A strikingly gifted young trumpeter, who took the jazz world by storm in 1980, when he was just nineteen years old. Wynton, one of six sons born to pianist Ellis Marsalis, was named in honour of the pianist Wynton Kelly. Almost inevitably in such an environment, he learned music early, quickly mastered the classical trumpet to the extent that he took the solo part in Haydn's Trumpet Concerto, with the New Orleans Symphony Orchestra, at the age of fourteen. Three years later he arrived at the Juilliard

School, New York, supplementing his allowance by playing in the pit band for the Broadway musical *Sweeney Todd*. That indefatigable talent scout, Art Blakey, heard him play and soon Wynton Marsalis had joined that array of trumpet stars who have, over the years, fronted the Jazz Messengers.

From 1983 onward, Wynton Marsalis has worked virtually on his own terms, having won, in that year, two Grammies – one for his second album, *Think of One*, and another for a collection of classical trumpet concertos. He toured with HERBIE HANCOCK's VSOP band, which was devoted to sustaining the style of the classic MILES DAVIS group of the early and middle Sixties, and the Davis sound of that era was clearly a powerful inspiration. With the release of his album, *Standard Time*, Wynton Marsalis firmly demonstrated the mixture of realism, dedication and respect for the past that shapes his music. Convinced that jazz technique suffered during the free-music era, Marsalis argues that if it's accepted that classical performers should interpret and embellish the music of earlier periods, then, by analogy, there's no reason why jazz players should not treat earlier jazz music the same way. This is a view that has led some critics to observe that while Marsalis clearly knows what *has* happened in jazz inside out, he doesn't yet appear to be overly concerned about what should be happening to it in the future.

★*First Recordings with Art Blakey* (Kingdom CDGATE 7013)

Wynton Marsalis in 1980, aged nineteen, demonstrating his flair and confidence in an excellent edition of Art Blakey's Jazz Messengers, including Ellis Marsalis, on piano, and the exciting saxophonist, Billy Pierce. The trumpeter sounds brisk and surefooted, though a little over-inclined to displays of speed. Tracks include 'Angel Eyes' and 'Wheel within A Wheel'.

★*Standard Time* (CBS 451 039-2)

Twelve lyrical, lovingly burnished jazz evergreens performed by the quartet of Marsalis, plus Marcus Roberts (piano) Bob Hurst (on bass) and Jeff 'Tain' Watts (on drums). 'Caravan' is delivered like a long cackle and dipped briefly into salty dissonance. 'Cherokee', appears in two versions, with a stunning muted solo over Watts' scurrying brushwork in the first, the coda taking the form of ever more urgent ascents of the register, finishing abruptly on a ledge as if suspended in space. Marcus Roberts displays both his pearly Herbie Hancock manner and his history-of-jazz-piano expertise. In his phrasing, rhythm and long-range imagination, Marsalis can conceive a seamless solo over far longer distances than most improvisors.

★*Live at Blues Alley* (CBS 461 109-2)

One of the loosest of Wynton Marsalis' records, made in 1986, and featuring the *Standard Time* quartet. Most of the regular criticisms directed towards Marsalis – namely, uptight orderliness, brilliant but disengaged coasting on favourite jazz and classical phrases, solos sounding like exercises, unwillingness to leave spaces – are despatched by this album, in which the quartet demonstrates immense rhythmic flexibility and the leader displays a cliffhanging adventurousness on 'Delfeayo's Dilemma', and rare relaxation and pacing on 'Just Friends'.

★*The Majesty of the Blues* (CBS 465 129-2)

Marsalis with a tribute to his New Orleans roots, full of the growls, wah-wahs, jangling vibrato and chugging rhythms of early jazz; nevertheless, it isn't a straight pastiche. Though Marsalis's own playing is largely devoted to capturing the raunchiness of a pioneer brass player like Bubber Miley, the group continues to flavour its reminiscences with modernisms, particularly from the piano and reeds. If the album is dedicated to any individual, it is to early Ellington, but it lacks the idiosyncrasy of a Twenties-jazz tribute that the ART ENSEMBLE OF CHICAGO, for instance, is capable of. The twenty-minute spoken sermon on the 'noble sound' of jazz has a stirring, Luther King-like delivery, imparted to a ploddingly banal text.

Masekela, Hugh

(Born Witbank, South Africa, April 4, 1939)
Trumpeter Hugh Masekela is nowadays probably the best known

of the black South African jazz musicians to have merged townships dance music together with the Afro-American traditions – and the all-embracing entertainment value of his work makes him attractive way beyond the jazz scene. Masekela's music is jubilant, phlegmatic and defiant, at one moment political satire, at another a celebration of the sunshine, or an impassioned rendition of Bob Marley's 'No Woman No Cry'.

Masekela began firmly in the jazz lineage, an imaginative instrumentalist with the beginnings of the rounded, lustrous sound he has now, and doubly famous for blowing a trumpet given to him (at the behest of the liberal cleric, Father Trevor Huddleston) by Louis Armstrong. Masekela formed the Jazz Epistles, the first black band to make an LP in South Africa, but, in the political circumstances, working opportunities were fraught and few. He left South Africa, in 1960, in the wake of the Sharpeville massacre, coming first to London to take up a Guildhall School of Music place, fixed for him by JOHN DANKWORTH, then going to study in New York. As well as evading apartheid, Masekela was fulfilling a dream he had had since his first exposure to jazz through the records of Ellington, Count Basie, Charlie Parker, that of visiting the source, the United States.

Since the Sixties Masekela has lived variously in America, Britain, Zimbabwe and Botswana. Some of his American albums – in seeking to blend jazz-rock fusion and South African music – have blurred the distinctive identity he originally had. His trumpet solos have also tended to repetition in recent times. But Masekela's live performances are often sophisticated and, sometimes, thrilling world-music shows rather than jazz acts alone, though the impact is hard to duplicate on disc.

★*Uptownship* (BMG/Novus PD 83070)

Good representation of late-Eighties Masekela, performing a mixture of music with a strong African flavour and his later American acquisitions. There isn't a substitute for hearing the trumpeter live, however, and this set does have a lingering formulaic quality.

Metheny, Pat

(Born Kansas City, Missouri, August 12, 1954)
Guitarist Pat Metheny has, since the 1970s, enjoyed a worldwide
reputation as a dealer in some of the most melodic of fusion music,
often sustained over long, suite-like pieces, and highly evocative
of rural landscapes and of country music as well. But there is
another side of Metheny, which is sometimes submerged in his
carefully-wrought programmatic music, that of the spontaneous
improvising guitar player, who assiduously studied Wes Montgomery's guitar bop as a child, but was growing up in an era in which
it had to be accommodated to the new influences of the Beatles
and Jimi Hendrix. The result was that Metheny's own guitar work
became an attractive and highly distinctive blend of bebop,
country music, blues and rock – free-swinging, and full of tonal
colour and atmosphere.

Metheny took up the guitar at thirteen, learning so fast that he
was a skilled guitar teacher and a sophisticated sitter-in, in Kansas
City clubs, before he had even gone to music college himself. He
joined vibist GARY BURTON's group at nineteen and then established
such an instantly recognisable composer's trademark with his
own albums, that his recorded output was divided between the
release of 'blowing' jazz records, with the likes of MIKE BRECKER and
Dewey Redman, and his own, largely composed, works that
almost inevitably led to movie scores. With the scorching and
largely soloistic, 'Song X', session of 1985 (Metheny in partnership
with another idol, saxophonist Ornette Coleman) the young
guitarist proved also that he hadn't deserted his earliest loves.

In recent times he has alternated between his highly textured
fusion projects and small, improvising bands. In 1990, Metheny
helped form two inventive versions of the latter: a quartet, with
HERBIE HANCOCK, on piano, DAVE HOLLAND, on bass, and JACK
DEJOHNETTE, on drums, and a boppish trio, with Holland and
drummer Roy Haynes.

★*80/81* (ECM 815 579-2)

One of Metheny's most productive recording dates, made when
the title suggests, and bringing together the talents of saxophonist Mike Brecker (so inspired by the occasion that he rebuilt
much the same band for his own debut album in 1987) and

drummer, Jack DeJohnette, plus two celebrated alumni of Ornette Coleman in tenorist Dewey Redman, and bassist, CHARLIE HADEN.

Metheny's affection for the skewed lyricism of Coleman is one of his most unexpectedly attractive characteristics, and the Coleman influence is strong on several tracks. Brecker's urbane eloquence and Redman's quirkier style make an effective contrast. Metheny demonstrates his improvisor's, rather than his special effects, talents and the rhythm section is terrific.

★*As Falls Wichita, So Falls Wichita Falls* (ECM 821 416-2)

Made around the same time as *80/81*, *As Falls Wichita* was a total contrast. Spacious, less explicitly jazzy, and full of electronically synthesised evocations of rural landscapes, it is an imaginative, texturally rich collaboration between Metheny and, pianist, Lyle Mays, that took the guitarist's work to the borderline with easy-listening. It nevertheless retained a poignant warmth and a tonal adventurousness that set it apart from the New Age music it was affiliated to.

★*Offramp* (ECM 817 138-2)

One of Metheny's most enduringly popular and attractive records features the leader, on guitar synthesiser (on which he achieves a sound mingling charisma and whimsy, like a violin section crossed with a harmonica choir) proceeding through a repertoire of inventive and laid-back funk, with occasional bursts of near-abstract wildness.

Miller, Mulgrew

(Born Memphis, Tennessee, 1955)
The return of hard bop, in the 1980s, has – paradoxically – not always helped young bop musicians to establish their own sound. The orthodoxies of the idiom, and the formalities of current jazz-school teaching have reproduced some of the featureless expertise that caused a backlash against the first wave of bop in the early Fifties. But pianist Mulgrew Miller by a mixture of restraint,

broadmindedness and an unconventional model, in Herbie Nichols, has stood out from the crowd so convincingly that he has been in demand for innumerable prestigious bands – including those led by BRANFORD MARSALIS, Freddie Hubbard, Frank Morgan and TONY WILLIAMS.

Miller's apprenticeship took in many persuasions of jazz – the Duke Ellington Orchestra, led by Mercer Ellington, in the late Seventies, the singer, BETTY CARTER, the drummer, Art Blakey, and eventually one of the finest and most original bands operating loosely in MILES DAVIS' Sixties territory, that led by Tony Williams. Miller dislikes bravura and technical displays, which makes him both a supportive accompanist and a soloist who tantalises audiences with space, as well as with fusillades of sound.

★*Wingspan* (Landmark LCD 1515-2)

Subtle hard bop, in which Miller demonstrates not simply his own originality of phrasing and avoidance of the obvious, but a creative empathy with the other members of the rhythm section, rare for the neo-bop generation. Miles Davis saxophonist, Kenny Garrett, another bop player with an unconventional touch, is also present.

★*From Day to Day* (Landmark LCD 1525-2)

Miller's fifth and most recent recording for Landmark, with a trio of Kenny Washington, on drums, and WYNTON MARSALIS' bassist, Bob Hurst. Miller reveals his usual sophisticated foresight about the overall construction of a solo, notably on the opening original, 'La Chambre', which begins with choppy time-changes and fragmented figures which gradually coalesce into fluent legato patterns, and on the standard, 'What a Difference A Day Makes', which opens with softly suggestive chords and shifts gear into a lazily driving mid-tempo improvisation. The CD version also has a galloping rendition of the bop standby, 'Four', with Miller gliding and skating over Washington's hustling brushwork. Unpretentious, strongly rooted in bop and pre-bop orthodoxies.

Mitchell, Roscoe

(Born Chicago, August 3, 1940)
A multi-reed player best known for his association with one of the

most communicative of all Sixties avant-garde descendents, the ART ENSEMBLE OF CHICAGO. As well as being a visionary composer, Mitchell is a virtuoso saxophonist, particularly on alto, but he has eschewed most of the styles by which jazz musicians sell records, and his skills have thus been neglected. He has a scalding, urgent tone, and a driving built-in rhythm that maintains its momentum independently of accompanists. When many of the 1960s avant-ists were attempting to outdo each other for sheer firepower and noise, Mitchell remained faithful to the virtues of space and implication and – though some of his records have been contemplative to the point of stasis – he has, over a twenty five-year recording career, produced some of the more enduring works of free jazz.

Though primarily a free player, Mitchell intimately familiarised himself with bop through work in army bands in the Fifties, and early in the following decade he participated in hard bop groups. He then led his own bands, and participated in the Association for the Advancement of Creative Musicians (AACM) which led to the formation of the Art Ensemble. With albums such as *Congliptious* and *Sound* (neither on CD) Mitchell revealed a hushed and dramatic version of the avant-garde, widely-spaced sounds wheeling in dark spaces. Mitchell continued to explore these methods in the Eighties with his own Sound Ensemble as well as touring with the Art Ensemble.

★*LRG/The Maze* (Chief Recs CHIEFCD 4)

LRG is a trio featuring Mitchell, plus trumpeter Leo Smith, and the revolutionary trombonist and computer-music innovator, George Lewis, and these recordings of its intricate and faintly precious work were made in 1978. 'The Maze' is an unhurried and compelling extended piece for eight percussionists, and Mitchell also plays a long solo soprano feature, 'S II Examples', which doesn't display his improvising talents at their best. Not ideal Mitchell, but better than nothing.

Moore, Ralph

(Born Brixton, London, 1956)
A Brixton-born New York resident, Moore is a tenorist with the

dry, grainy tone of John Coltrane, but without the packed arpeggios. He instead displays a blues player's punchy articulation and willingness to let the rhythm section fill space.

Moore is one of the new heroes of the bop revivalist movement, who emigrated from Britain to the States to join his American father when he was fifteen. A star pupil at the famous Berklee Conservatory in Boston, Moore quickly found work with bebop artists of the quality of drummer Roy Haynes, and soul-bop pianist Horace Silver. He has also appeared with Mingus Dynasty, with Dizzy Gillespie, and with the recent ex-Art Blakey sidemen, TERENCE BLANCHARD and Benny Green.

*_Furthermore_ (Landmark LCD 1526-2)

A fast-moving, hard-driving neo-bop disc, mostly devoted to the swaggering Art Blakey manner, though without Blakey's sudden volcanic eruptions at the drums. Roy Hargrove is on trumpet, Benny Green on piano, Peter Washington on bass, and Kenny Washington or Victor Lewis, on drums. Moore's measured pace and sinewy tone are appropriate for the salty Thelonious Monk feature, 'Monk's Dream', and he also crisply and succinctly negotiates the attractive mid-tempo blues, 'Girl Talk', inventively pushed and prodded by the others. Expert and streamlined, if short on originality.

Morrison, James

(Born Sydney, Australia, 1963)

It's increasingly hard to amaze jazz audiences with technical displays, now that instrumental virtuosity among young players is commonplace; but Australian, James Morrison, can still occasion a sharp intake of breath. Morrison is not only capable of making sense at blistering speed on the trumpet, he can do the same on trombone, alto saxophone, euphonium and piano as well. And though much of Morrison's music betrays an as-yet unformed view of what to do with his prodigious skills, he delivers these fusillades of sound with such amiable panache as to sidestep most of the self-aggrandisement these displays usually convey.

Morrison was an early starter, in a Dixieland band at nine, a big band in his early teens, and his own successful ensemble not long after. He was invited to play the Monterey Jazz Festival while still a student in New South Wales, was hired by ex-Charlie Parker trumpeter, Red Rodney, in 1987. He made his debut album the same year and began playing international jazz festivals alongside such celebrities as WYNTON MARSALIS. The following year Morrison took to working with the skilled mainstream pianist, Adam Mackowicz, a partnership that brought the best out of the Polish musician, whose star had been on the wane by the early Eighties. Morrison's speed and accuracy impressed even jazz music's most venerable giants, and he began working occasionally with Dizzy Gillespie.

★*Postcards From Down Under* (WEA K255 697)

Dazzling display of Morrison's technical virtues on many instruments. He begins 'You Are My Sunshine', with a buttonholing high squeal and performs it with many of the old jazz trumpet virtues of brassy tone and bluesy intonation, the music littered with tricks, like throwaway whispered squeals between phrases and furious double time. He also plays some smooth romantic alto saxophone ('Shadow of Your Smile') and a less mellifluous version of 'Autumn Leaves', opened with unexpectedly growling chords. But generally, on all his instruments, Morrison is a light, airy player, full of good humour – though not a particularly idiosyncratic one. The plush big-band sound is, thanks to overdubbing, largely Morrison's own unaided work.

Motian, Stephen Paul

(Born Providence, Rhode Island, March 25, 1931)
Many drummers are spectacular, but truly musical ones are harder to find, and those that do exist are often undervalued. Paul Motian is one such, a highly musical accompanist (who has been such for nearly forty years) who is one of the few drummers in jazz whose solos resemble well-constructed tunes, who is reluctant to play to the gallery, and who, in his work, has demonstrated an original conception of new directions jazz might take. This has not always made Motian's own music the most accessible in the

world, yet he generally emphasises the more conversational and detailed aspects of freer jazz, even when his partners aren't observing orthodox tonality.

Motian's most famous job was accompanying the late Bill Evans, from 1959 to 1964, in which situation – like bassist Scott LaFaro – he helped further emancipate the rhythm section into operating in a contrapuntal partnership with the leader. Motian had been a crisp bop performer whose partners, in the Fifties, included mainstream tenorist, Zoot Sims. Following the stretch with Bill Evans, he spent almost a decade in KEITH JARRETT's band, forming a close association with the innovative bassist, CHARLIE HADEN, in the process, and, through Haden, mingling with the younger radicals of the Sixties New York avant-garde. The extent of Motian's open-mindedness was indicated by his choice of the young sound-effects guitarist, BILL FRISELL, for his own group in 1980 – to play a repertoire which permutated tight structure, loose structure, regular and suspended metres, tonality and atonality.

★*It Should've Happened A Long Time Ago* (ECM 823 641-2)

Compelling and richly ambiguous performance from the early Eighties by a Motian trio featuring Bill Frisell, on guitars, and Joe Lovano, on reeds. Some of Frisell's most effective forays have occurred in Motian's company and Lovano's playing is altogether a more satisfying mixture of patience and impulsiveness, than is usual among most of his saxophone contemporaries.

Murray, David

(Born Berkeley, California, February 19, 1955)
Bridging the period from the Sixties, when the rejection of earlier jazz styles was at its height, to the end of the Seventies (when the re-evaluation of the tradition returned) is the saxophonist David Murray. Murray has packed so much into a relatively short career that his status, in his mid-thirties, as a standard bearer for progress and fertile thinking about jazz, is no more than he deserves. He has been a fierce avant-garde improvisor, an organiser of adventurous big-bands, leader of an enthralling octet that sounded like a free Ellington group, a lyrical soloist in the

tradition of the swing masters of the Thirties, even a recreator of Ellington's famous 1956 Newport performance of 'Diminuendo and Crescendo in Blue'.

Murray's tenor playing went back to childhood, and he learned harmony from his mother, a church pianist. He studied music at college in Los Angeles (having already led his own rhythm & blues groups) and, by the age of twenty, had moved to New York to lead his own bands. Free music interested him, and he performed with both Cecil Taylor and ANTHONY BRAXTON initially, though he quickly moved toward a more balanced position between abstract improvisation and structure. Murray's career has proceeded by systematic development and with idiosyncratic tangents, his music in the Seventies being ethereal, Albert Ayler-like, impassioned reveries, his later work as a leader drawing him closer to Charles Mingus, though with less troublesome undercurrents. Murray has also appeared with JACK DEJOHNETTE's Special Edition, and in the World Saxophone Quartet.

★*Home* (Black Saint BSRCD 055)

A 1981 octet, with some of Murray's best compositions on it, including, 'Last of the Hipmen', and, '3D Family', as well as the title track. 'Home', is a ballad, a mixture of frankness and off-register probings, and Murray's chemistry of vigorous contrapuntal work and rhythmic surprises, in his ensemble writing, gives the entire session an integrated quality that both makes already vivid compositions shine, and makes the band sound bigger than it is.

★*Morning Song* (Black Saint BSRCD 075)

Murray's quartet, in 1983, featuring, John Hicks (piano) Ray Drummond (bass) and ED BLACKWELL (drums) including a brilliant rendition of 'Body and Soul', that shows how realistically Murray can now be bracketed with the best improvising lyricists, like Coleman Hawkins. He proves himself entirely worthy of the responsibility, with his sureness of touch at the extremes of the register, variation of dynamics and melodic adroitness.

Myers, Amina Claudine

(Born Arkansas, March 21, 1943)

An underrated performer, genuinely at home with contemporary music, blues and gospel, Amina Myers was a member of the Association for the Advancement of Creative Musicians in Chicago, in the mid-Sixties. A pianist, organist, composer and vocalist, Myers sang and played piano from the age of four, and was arranging music for church choirs by eleven. Her background was gospel music, which gave a particularly earthy twist to her experiences with the avant-garde jazz musicians of the AACM.

Myers has performed in the most illustrious circumstances through the Seventies and Eighties, which has made her relative obscurity hard to understand. She wrote an ambitious 'Suite for Chorus, Pipe Organ and Percussion', for a nineteen piece band, and took the Ellington piano chair on a Kool Jazz Festival tribute to the Duke. Her keyboard playing is as emphatic and insistent as her voice.

★*Salutes Bessie Smith* (Leo CDLR 103)

The most telling example of Myers' blues and gospel playing on disc. Her versions of Smith's 'Wasted Life Blues', and 'Jailhouse Blues', go way beyond the usual fake-soulful remoulds of vintage blues, revealing her profound grasp both of the idiom and of Bessie Smith's particular grandiose unease.

Newton, James

(Born California, May 1, 1953)

Composition has always been a thorny issue in jazz, though less so for those jazz composers (notably Ellington and Mingus) whose compositions were intimately related to the sounds that jazz soloists already made. But some performers who have shown considerable interest in jazz have been as powerfully drawn by straight music, and sought to unite techniques associated with both. In the past, these meetings have been largely unsuccessful (Paul Whiteman's symphonic jazz, Stravinsky's Woody Herman collaboration, Third Stream chamber-jazz in the Sixties) but

ANTHONY DAVIS and flautist, James Newton, have investigated it with more promise during the 1980s.

Newton is not another saxophonist who also plays flute, but a flute specialist with a delectable tone and such delicate control over his sound that he is able to use unusual intervals, as well as audaciously expanding the vocabulary of simultaneous voice and flute-playing – even to the extent of being able to sing one theme and improvise an instrumental one independently.

Eric Dolphy was his inspiration, though he had formerly been a rock musician in school bands. At college he was comfortable in both classical and jazz groups, and, after graduation, he began working regularly with Anthony Davis. Newton has written a variety of chamber-jazz pieces, some using woodwind groups, including oboes and bassoons, some featuring the cello of Abdul Wadud. His range of interests continues to make him one of the most intriguing of musicians, on the outer limits of contemporary jazz.

★*African Flower* (Blue Note CDP 746 292-2)

One of Newton's finest, a 1985 recording (it made Record of the Year in the 1986 *Downbeat* critics' poll) featuring the impassioned alto of Arthur Blythe with Jay Hoggard on vibes, Anthony Davis, and the excellent violinist, John Blake.The album is devoted to Ellington's music and makes graceful and probing work of, 'Black and Tan Fantasy', 'Cottontail', 'Sophisticated Lady', and others.

★*Romance and Revolution* (Blue Note CDP 746 431-2)

Another dedication, this time to Charles Mingus, with the incisive young pianist, Geri Allen, in a powerful octet that also includes trombonists Steve Turre and Robin Eubanks. Apart from the loping elegance of Ornette Coleman's, 'Peace', there is a dazzling display of Newton's flute virtuosity, on his own theme, 'Forever Charles'.

Oregon

A pioneering and immensely sophisticated band exploring what would, nowadays, travel under the title of 'world music'. Oregon was formed in 1972, to combine the talents of guitarist **Ralph Towner**, reed player **Paul McCandless**, violinist, flautist and pianist **Glen Moore**, and tabla player and percussionist, **Collin Walcott**. Towner had already revolutionised acoustic guitar improvisation, drawing large-scale orchestral effects as well as subtle detail from the 12-string instrument, McCandless and Moore had worked in both conservatoire experimental music and jazz, and Walcott had extensively worked with the best Indian musicians, including Ravi Shankar, as well as recording with MILES DAVIS. Walcott's breadth of view was such that he could not only play classical Indian music on the sitar, but also sound like a jazz bassist or a jazz guitarist on it, and his talents were so sharply missed by Oregon, when he was tragically killed in a road crash in Europe, that the band folded afterwards, and has only recently reformed.

★*Oregon* (ECM 811 711-2)

A graceful 1983 set by the band, made a year before Collin Walcott's death. The music represents a revival of the group's vigour (often inclined to wilt beneath the formidable techniques of the players) after a series of virtuosic, but uninspiring, discs made in the late Seventies.

Osby, Greg

(Dates unknown)

Greg Osby is one of the most striking of the M-base players; that group of young virtuosi (STEVE COLEMAN, Geri Allen, CASSANDRA WILSON are others) whose dominance, absorption of, and then evolution from bebop, has given them the freedom to try those harmonically driven skills against quirkier rhythmic and orchestral ideas drawn from funk, hip-hop, rap, and bits and pieces of contemporary straight music. Osby graduated from Berklee Conservatory, Boston, in 1983, and joined the quintet of trumpeter Jon Faddis, following that with a stint in JACK DEJOHNETTE's Special Edition. In the remainder of the decade Osby's ability to gain vivid effects without hyperbole, and his openness to the ideas of his employers, resulted in appearances with Dizzy Gillespie, McCOY TYNER, PAT METHENY and many others.

But it has been the M-base group, and Steve Coleman in particular, which have involved Osby the most. As with Coleman, it has been other leaders' work that seems to have loosened up Osby the improvisor, and his own sessions – though intriguing – have yet to take wing.

★*Mind Games* (JMT/Germany 834422-2)

An Osby session from 1988, featuring pianist Geri Allen. At its best, it offers a freshness of ensemble sound that is an encouraging change from the retro-jazz work of many of Osby's contemporaries, but some over-deliberation calculated to achieve new jazz structures (a problem with many of the M-base artists) prevents the improvisors from finding their voices.

★*Season of Renewal* (JMT 834 435-2)

More hallmarks of the M-Base style here; shuffling, staccato, rap-derived tracks, like 'For the Cause', a piece that quickly shifts into its solo sax mode (against a tambourine and occasional rimshot clatters) after a spinechilling soprano wail and STEVE LACY-like, high blipping sounds interweaving with the rhythm. The essence, as with so much of the genre, is rhythmic counterpoint. Bursts of funk patterns culminate in cymbal splashes, against repeated scurrying keyboard figures, legato vocals, horns diving between them, boiling down to an ambitious, but only patchily compelling, session.

Papasov, Ivo

(Born Kardjali, Bulgaria, February 16, 1952)
Some are already comparing reed-player Ivo Papasov's impact on jazz with that of Django Reinhardt's, in the Thirties. Both men shared a Romany origin, both have been preoccupied with hybrids

of jazz and the indigenous music of their own communities, and both have delivered music of immense excitement and panache.

Papasov's musical development has been shaped by a combination of the traditional Balkan wedding music of his locality, the influence of Charlie Parker and Benny Goodman on his reed playing, and the international language of funk, which has affected his choice of rhythm section.

★*Orpheus Ascending* (Hannibal HNCD 1346)

Papasov's British record debut, with a feverish, whirling display of jazz-influenced improvising pitched against the complicated dance rhythms of traditional Bulgarian music. It's mostly high-energy collective playing but Papasov's unique bitter-sweet intonation and interspersing of hurricane runs against solemn, declamatory passages compounds the all-round amiable freneticism.

Parker, Evan Shaw

(Born Bristol, England, April 5, 1944)
Of all the saxophonists originally inspired by the example of John Coltrane, Evan Parker is one of the most unusual. Now an internationally respected virtuoso improvisor with explicit jazz inclinations, Parker came to prominence in the Seventies as a purely abstract player. He went much further than his idols, or most other British free players – in recording and performing technically remarkable researches into harmonics, split-note formation, playing of chords on the horn and two or more lines at once, very little of it referring to regular jazz structure or tempo. Over twenty years, he has worked with the most inventive improvisors in the world.

★*Atlanta* (Impetus IMPCD 18617)

A formidable 1986 recording with bassist BARRY GUY and drummer Paul Lytton, vividly representing the collaborative, texturally rich, sometimes austere music of this school.

Pascoal, Hermeto

(Born Lagoa da Canoa, Brazil, June 22, 1936)
Hermeto Pascoal, a man as visually charismatic as he has been musically influential (bearded, and with flowing white hair) has been a model for the careers of many Latin-American musicians, notably percussionist Airto Moreira and singer FLORA PURIM – and he is also sometimes quoted as one of the less obvious influences on MILES DAVIS later exploits.

Pascoal plays a variety of instruments including flutes, keyboards, and a huge, tusk-like, horn, that sounds like an elephant announcing dinner. He and his musicians are also prone to lacing the proceedings with unearthly manic cacklings and gibberings, and sometimes to anchoring the themes on a churning, repeated-pattern, that sounds like a cross between circus music and old Frank Zappa records. But they never become lost, in this maze, because there are always sudden breaks into the sunny clearings of straight-ahead Brazilian swing, often coloured by the dubbed-in chantings of children, sardonic conversational exchanges between the players, or what sounds like radio commentaries on horse races. Pascoal has even been known to enlist the services of a live piglet onstage, inducing the unlikely improvisor to squeal at key moments – an innovation for which he found the RSPCA joining his audiences on his last British tour.

★*Pascoal* (West Wind WWCD 009)

Uneven but engaging mixture of Pascoal's typical rhythmic insistence, unusual textures and strong composition.

Peacock, Annette

(Dates unknown)
Unclaimable by the entertainment corporations, vocalist and synthesiser player Annette Peacock is an artist, who for twenty five years has been consolidating her own definition of style, through variations on jazz origins, that have neither been attempted nor imitated by anyone else. Her compositions are unsentimental, devoid of orthodox lyricism, monochromatic, and

taut as toned muscles. Her voice is clear, but razor-edged rather than rounded, often working over jumps of wide intervals and occasionally, surprisingly slight and withdrawn (rather as Blossom Dearie might sound, if she'd been a lifelong member of the Mothers of Invention). Her keyboard playing is spare but telling, in both its quirky melodic shapes and its tonal variation. On the synthesiser (she was a pioneer of the instrument, having been presented with a 1968 version by its inventor, RA Moog) Peacock gives her short, needling figures the texture of vibes or pianos.

Annette Peacock's association with the jazz community began with her relationship with the brilliant bassist, Gary Peacock, with whom she moved to New York in the 1960s. She became involved with the psychedelic movement of the period, and with one of its gurus, Dr Timothy Leary, and then began to contribute highly personal themes to the piano repertoire of PAUL BLEY, much as CARLA BLEY had done before her. After discovering the synthesiser she made a series of recordings that imaginatively used the new instrument on jazz materials, then turned to an off-the-wall kind of jazz-rock fusion in the late Seventies, and moved to free-improvising jazz, in the next decade. She has performed with many of the most original musicians in Europe and the States.

★*Skyskating* (Ironic IRONIC 2CD)

Annette Peacock's first album for Ironic, her own label; a selection from her own solo live shows, in which she handles all the instrumentation with her usual impassive intensity.

★*I Have No Feelings* (IRONIC 4CD)

Peacock with a frequent partner, the free-improvising percussionist, Roger Turner. The album is notable for one of Peacock's most telling compositions, originally written for Paul Bley, 'Nothing Ever Was, Anyway'.

Petrucciani, Michel

(Born Montpelier, France, December 28, 1962)
An explicit admirer of the work of Bill Evans, KEITH JARRETT and

McCOY TYNER, French pianist Michel Petrucciani, is evolving beyond the legacy of his primary influences well before he reaches thirty. Petrucciani is one of the most striking members of the new generation of non Afro-American jazz-influenced virtuosi, who are of the right age and background, and with sufficient independence and open-mindedness, to bend jazz history their way.

Petrucciani was discovered at the age of eighteen, by the *International Herald Tribune*'s Mike Zwerin (himself a musician) and a French tour, with Lee Konitz, followed. Two years later, he was on a social visit to a California friend when CHARLES LLOYD, the once fashionable saxophonist, who had been in retirement for the previous fifteen years, heard him and was sufficiently inspired to come out of retirement and hire Petrucciani himself. Two years later his career touched an early high when, at impresario George Wein's instigation, Petrucciani played a solo concert at Carnegie Hall, to acclaim in *Time* magazine and the *New York Times*.

The pianist came from a musical family, and was inspired to take up piano, at the age of four, when he saw Duke Ellington on a TV show. He also enjoyed drums, partly as therapy for the wasting disease that has resulted in his miniscule physical stature. His triumphs over the practical obstacles to being a jazz pianist are, however, aspects he prefers to play down. He has worked in recent years with many of the best musicians in jazz, including guitarists Jim Hall and JOHN ABERCROMBIE, and saxophonist WAYNE SHORTER.

★*Power of Three* (Blue Note CDP 746 427-2)

Petrucciani live, from the 1986 Montreux Festival, with an excellent partner, the veteran bop guitarist, Jim Hall; a discreet and oblique contrast for Petrucciani's flooding exuberance. Wayne Shorter joins the band, for a spacious workout, on 'Limbo', Hall's calypso 'SRO', and Petrucciani's rich and evocative, 'Morning Blues'.

★*Music* (Blue Note CDP 792 563-2)

A 1989 album, from the stage in his career when Petrucciani was declaring that he didn't want to be typecast, as a jazz pianist in any specific styles. But rather than abandoning material that might categorise him, the pianist seems simply to have thinned out the density of his improvisational attack and produced a more relaxed and creatively eclectic album with bebop, ballads, and nods to the Latin-dance exuberance of TANIA MARIA.

Pine, Courtney

(Born London, 1964)

Though many other players of distinction have recently emerged from the fervent expansion of jazz enthusiasm among Britain's young black population, Courtney Pine remains the most prominent and a rallying point. Originally a funk and reggae saxophonist, Pine became interested in jazz in the early Eighties, powerfully affected by the influence of Sonny Rollins and John Coltrane. He learned fast, and quickly established himself as a player for whom technical breakthroughs came readily. Never much inclined toward reticence in his early years, Pine brought a heated and energetic approach to most situations in which he found himself, and was not intimidated by the company he was in, however experienced.

Pine's first regular jazz appearances occurred in a workshop led by the London drummer, John Stevens. Not long afterwards Pine's interest in fostering jazz enthusiasm among his contemporaries, extended to the founding of a community group, Abibi Jazz Arts, dedicated to helping teach jazz to keen young black musicians. He also encouraged the formation of an orchestra, the JAZZ WARRIORS. Pine worked with the Warriors and with his own, Coltraneish, small groups, often featuring fast-learning young sidemen, like pianist Julian Joseph, and drummer Mark Mondesir. He has also worked with American musicians, including orchestra leader GEORGE RUSSELL, the late Art Blakey, Elvin Jones, and Ellis Marsalis.

★*Journey to the Urge Within* (Island CID 9846)

Pine's debut album, in 1986, a tour around his musical interests and skills that shifted the astonishing total of 70,000 copies. By the time this disc appeared, Pine was already a popular figure in the jazz press (particularly those ends of it dealing with younger readers) and it would have been difficult for any young artist to justify the musical, spiritual and philosophical insights being attributed to him. Though it touched on many idioms, early-Sixties Coltrane was its principal inspiration, particularly those incantational aspects of Coltrane – and Pine confirmed his preoccupation with this music, and his technical sophistication as well, in the tunes 'I Believe', and 'Peace'.

Destiny's Song and the Image of Pursuance (Antilles ANCD 8725)

More Coltraneish Pine, but less inclined to sound like a sampler than the above. By this stage (1987) both the leader and his partners are more on top of the music and their advances in craftsmanship have enabled the technical challenges to take second place to imagination.

The Vision's Tale (Antilles ANCD 8746)

Pine seemed to have embarked on a Coltranesque spiritual quest, with his first album, but instead of taking a journey further into musical no-man's-land, he retreated to the safer terrain of standards for his third disc. Although the least adventurous of Pine's albums (and despite the leader's slight discomfort with the open spaces of ballads) *The Vision's Tale* was one of the more satisfying, not least because of the confident restraint of a highly original American rhythm section, Ellis Marsalis, on piano, and, Jeff 'Tain' Watts, on drums. The material includes, 'In A Mellow Tone', 'God Bless The Child', and (in a nod to Rollins) 'I'm an Old Cowhand'.

Pinski Zoo

Pinski Zoo was formed, in 1981, by saxophonist, Jan Kopinski. Until 1990 it rarely made jazz headlines in England, though it had done so in Poland, Switzerland and Austria. It can't have helped that the band devoted itself to free-funk, along Ornette Coleman lines, just at the time when the bebop revival was beginning, and that it mostly avoids the idea of promoting a star soloist, and is based in Nottingham.

Pinski Zoo is a quartet, featuring saxophones, keyboards, bass and drums, and it performs at a sustained level of slightly baleful energy, unfashionable sounds gleefully mingled with fashionable ones, and with an immediately apparent four-way empathy. Typically its sounds take in: vibrato-laden horn playing over spacey, Miles Davis-like organ chords, Rollins-like calypso, Prime Time's thrashing pugnacity, Albert Ayler in his rhythm-and-blues phase, and moments when the beat could quite respectably have sustained a guest appearance from Michael Jackson.

Each of the band's members, without mounting any self-conscious displays, contributed imaginatively to these colourful and mobile effects. Karl Wesley Bingham, the electric bassist, is a specialist in playing both catapulting funk riffs and smooth, gliding Weather Report bass lines. Steve Iliffe is a powerful and dramatic keyboard player, sometimes drenching his partners with fountains of organ-like noise, sometimes tantalising with brooding synth riffs. And Jan Kopinski himself, mercifully disinclined to pepper the proceedings with bebop runs and preferring the squalling sound of PHAROAH SANDERS and the quavering swoops and wails of Albert Ayler, is a breath of fresh air.

Rare Breeds (Jazz Cafe JCRCD 903)

Excellent example of the formidable energies that Pinski Zoo unleash; a disc that won *Wire* magazine's Top British Group award, in 1988. Over a full-length session, Jan Kopinski's emotional flailing on tenor does stop being a welcome alternative to bebop, becoming merely repetitive, but the drive of the rhythm section, the audacity of the bass lines, and the sheer bolshie elan of the whole ensemble are a delight. 'Sweet Automatic', the Aylerish funk tune, with one of the most rivetting bass riffs in contemporary music, appears in two versions on the CD.

Ponty, Jean-Luc

(Born Avranches, France, September 29, 1942)
Ex-classical violinist, Jean-Luc Ponty, has spent much of his career attempting to camouflage the effects of his musical upbringing,

yet his breadth of view and lyricism still demonstrate a strong connection with it. He is of the generation of jazz violinists, who grew up with the sound of Coltrane in their ears, and who, therefore, tended to eschew the jaunty swing or kaleidoscopic bop styles of earlier practitioners, in pursuit of a denser and more energetic manner. To that end, and also to further confound his classical origins, Ponty extensively explored electronics.

Ponty's parents were both music teachers and the boy was a star student on classical violin. In the early Sixties, though working with a straight orchestra, he became increasingly involved in jazz, and began to make an impact in the idiom, at festivals in Europe, and eventually at Monterey in the USA. During the Seventies, Ponty took to working in America with his own fusion outfits and with eccentric rock artist Frank Zappa's adventurous band, Mothers of Invention, notably on the great 'Hot Rats' session. In another experiment, Ponty joined forces with the London Symphony Orchestra to record JOHN MCLAUGHLIN's, rather overblown, 'Apocalypse'. In more recent times, the violinist has returned to his gentler earlier incarnations, playing a small group modal music, that is often engagingly tuneful and romantic without undue schmalz. Ponty's live sessions are his most exciting recorded work, but they aren't on CD as yet.

★*Open Mind* (Polydor 823 581-2)

Good studio session by Ponty, revealing how successfully he has kept the electric violin from destroying the tonal virtues of the acoustic instrument. Pianist, CHICK COREA, and guitarist, GEORGE BENSON, neither of them strangers to Ponty's favoured jazz-rock blend, lend some more than usually musical support.

Pukwana, Mututuzel 'Dudu'

(Born Port Elizabeth, South Africa, July 18, 1938; died London, June 29, 1990)
Dudu Pukwana, the South African altoist, who lived in London from 1966 until his death, was one of the most formidable of South Africa's jazz musicians. He admired the work of Ornette

Coleman, but, at the same time, also the luxurious, romantic styles of the early swing players. His playing reflected his twin allegencies: wild swoops of sound ending in cantankerous honks, tender, vibrato-laden rhapsody, raucous guffaws turning into sly, knowing seductiveness, tantalising displays of quivering romanticism.

Pukwana's parents were both musicians, and he originally worked as a piano player. He took up the alto saxophone, in his mid-teens, and won the 'Saxophonist of the Year' prize, at the Johnnesburg Jazz Festival, in his early twenties. It was as an altoist, and composer, that Pukwana helped Chris McGregor, a white pianist, form the Blue Notes, a band that became notorious in South Africa, for its then unique mixed-race lineup.

In exile, in England, Pukwana had successes with various McGregor groups, including the spectacular, Ellington-meets-kwela, big band, Brotherhood of Breath. In the Seventies, he formed his own group, Spear, and toured South Africa, with HUGH MASEKELA, and then the USA. Pukwana's musical interests ranged wide, he liked reggae, and even the distinctly un-songlike sounds of the European free-improvisors, with many of whom he shared some bizarre and often astonishingly fertile evenings. In 1978, he formed, Zila, a sometimes ragged, but unfailingly exhilarating band, with which he worked until his final illness.

★*In the Townships* (Earthworks/Virgin CDEWV 5)

A reissue of a typically headlong and uneven Pukwana session, recorded with his ensemble Spear in the 1970s. There are seven tracks, and the African flavour dominates the set – but the leader's improvisational flair, both in violent abstract playing and in moods of a kind of manic tenderness, display Pukwana's rich jazz awareness.

Pullen, Don Gabriel

(Born Roanoke, Virginia, December 25, 1944)
Don Pullen's dramatic piano style is often compared to Cecil Taylor's, and in its complexity, mercurial variety, bursts of hammering dissonance, and tightly packed phrasing, it does resemble it – but Pullen is less Europeanised, and less unforgiving

than Taylor. His playing can be boppish, rhapsodic, or even resemble the bop-gospel organ style (he frequently plays organ) when he isn't forcing listeners back in their chairs with hurricanes of sound.

Pullen's most valuable apprenticeship was served with the Chicago avantists, in the Sixties, most notably with MUHAL RICHARD ABRAMS. He also established a creative partnership with the drummer Milford Graves; their recordings together being mostly, independently-produced, free music. In the Seventies Pullen began to work with more high-profile artists, including, NINA SIMONE, and Art Blakey, and finally established his reputation as a member of the Charles Mingus band, between 1973 and 1975. His percussive piano style was ideally suited to the forceful Mingus manner. Also in that Mingus band was GEORGE ADAMS, with whom Pullen established as fruitful a partnership as he had done earlier with Milford Graves, and the two have worked together a great deal since. (See page 225).

★*Sixth Sense* (Black Saint BSR 0088)

Powerful lineup for Pullen's mid-Eighties band, with Olu Dara, on trumpet, Donald 'Duck' Harrison on alto, Fred Hopkins on bass, and Bobby Battle, on drums. Powerful, improvisationally resourceful music, with one of the most imposing of all modern bass players, Fred Hopkins.

Purim, Flora

(Born Rio de Janeiro, March 6, 1942)
Flora Purim has achieved a deceptively artless vocal style, in which she makes considerable rhythmic subtlety sound easy. She established herself in New York, in the late 1960s, working with Stan Getz and Gil Evans, then joined CHICK COREA's highly successful, Latin-funk band, Return to Forever. Since then she has mostly worked with her husband, the percussionist Airto Moreira, in a variety of Latin-jazz ensembles, and occasionally with other artists, such as HERMETO PASCOAL.

Purim's musical background was highly varied, both her parents were classical musicians, one Rumanian born, the other

Brazilian. She learnt the piano and guitar as a child, and took to singing when a teenager, most prominently with Quarteto Novo, which featured Moreira and Pascoal. As well as appearing in Moreira's bands, she has also been a featured vocalist with Dizzy Gillespie's multi-national United Nations Band.

★*The Midnight Sun* (Venture/Virgin CDVE 21)

An over elaborate, but fitfully engaging, outing for Purim on a collection of standards, including, 'Angel Eyes', 'Light as A Feather' (from her Chick Corea days), 'Good Morning Heartache', and a selection of the kind of Latin material in which she is much more at home. The funk pianist, GEORGE DUKE, and the English, all-saxophone band, Itchy Fingers, are among an unlikely mix of supporters.

Rava, Enrico

(Born Trieste, Italy, August 20, 1943)
Enrico Rava is the Italian trumpeter who has, for years, been one of the most attractive European defenders of the 1955–65 MILES DAVIS manner. He has added a Mediterranean warmth and light to that poetry of curling long notes, tantalising pauses and unexpected accents, that formed Davis' most expressive and economical style.

Rava was self-taught, though his mother was a pianist. Miles Davis, Chet Baker, Coltrane and Ellington figure among his influences. In the mid Sixties he played with Argentinian saxophonist GATO BARBIERI, then with STEVE LACY, and later with trombonist Roswell Rudd, and, in more recent times, both with prominent European experimentalists (such as drummer Tony Oxley) and the legendary American avantist, Cecil Taylor.

★*Volver* (ECM 831395-2)

A curiosity of a band, featuring Dino Saluzzi on bandoneon (an accordion-like instrument) with guitar, bass and drums. A lot of it is backed by the kind of shimmering cymbal sounds, ethereal tomtom rolls, and flickering hi-hat patterns, now commonly associated with the ECM label, and such frequent suspension of a beat sometimes leaves Rava's fragile sound high and dry. But the leader is an imaginative enough performer to keep his playing simmering most of the time, and the bebop bandoneon playing of Saluzzi – far from being simply a novelty – contains a good deal of fresh phrasing.

Remler, Emily

(Born Englewood Cliffs, New Jersey, September 18, 1957; died May 4, 1990)
Emily Remler was a superb exponent of the guitar style based on the work of Wes Montgomery and which has been modernised by PAT METHENY. Had she not died at the age of thirty two, she might well have refined her own exploits in the genre. A consummately musical performer, whose soloing was smooth and fleet, she was also an excellent accompanist and collaborated with some of the best jazz musicians.

Remler was a student of the Berklee Conservatory, Boston, but she moved to New Orleans, in 1976, and worked there with singers Nancy Wilson and ASTRUD GILBERTO, and later, trumpeter WYNTON MARSALIS and singer BOBBY MCFERRIN. She also met a veteran bop guitarist, Herb Ellis, who got her a record deal. The result was the 1982 session, *Firefly*, for the Concord label. By now living in New York, Remler continued to appear with Astrud Gilberto (with whom she may have acquired a good deal of her accompanist's delicacy) and formed her own trio in the Wes Montgomery, soft-bop, manner. By the mid-Eighties, the music-business pressures, that also led her to alcoholism, began to interrupt her work, but by 1988 she appeared to be back on line. Her death, in 1990, was one of the more acute of several jazz losses in that year.

★*East to Wes* (Concord CCD 4356)

Remler in her Montgomery mode, a little too neat and ordered to drive the temperature right up, but full of original melodic angles on good material, including Clifford Brown's, 'Daahoud', and, 'Softly as in A Morning Sunrise'. A significant reason for the discreet *joie de vivre* of the session is a terrific supporting trio of Hank Jones (piano), Buster Williams (bass) and Marvin 'Smitty' Smith (drums).

Roadside Picnic

London fusion ensemble, Roadside Picnic, was originally set up as a vehicle for the dense, Weather Report-derived, compositions of bassist, Mario Castronari, and its early repertoire was a blend of luxuriously shaded tonality, abrupt dynamic shifts and dramatic, labyrinthine counterpoint. It is an expert, complex, inventively melodic band; its influences coming from both within jazz and outside it, including Indian music, African drum ideas, and King Crimson.

Castronari has been a widely-admired bass player on the London scene for many years, and has worked in avant-garde groups, with adventurous musicians, like pianist Howard Riley. Dave O'Higgins, the saxophonist and other high-profile member of the band, is of the new generation of jazz-playing Britons, a Coltrane-influenced alumnus of the National Youth Jazz Orchestra, who had made a mark for musicianship, if not commercial appeal, through his work with the driving trio, Gang of Three. Though a formidable technician, O'Higgins is still in search of his own muse and, despite the careful complexity of Roadside Picnic, he has not, so far, found it in that band either.

★*Roadside Picnic* (BMG Novus PD 74002)

On the mid-tempo, 'Morning Song', O'Higgins' soprano playing displays a purity of tone and a mixture of lazy composure and impulsiveness, reminiscent of WAYNE SHORTER (though without those phrases that used to levitate the hairs on your neck). While the capacity of the band to sound both glowingly full-bodied and gently ruminative (keyboardist John Smith a constantly attentive injector of atmosphere) emerges in the swirling, ballad-like, 'Cairo', and the programmatic 'New Canterbury Tale'. The latter is constantly tugged and driven by contrapuntal bass lines (from the powerful Castronari), tempo changes and church bell effects, but O'Higgins hits an implacably determined tenor groove, in its climactic conclusion, that blends luxuriant, satiny long notes with elegant eruptions into the upper register. Roadside Picnic wear their elaborate preparations a little too explicitly on their sleeve for improvisation to thrive, but they've got plenty of time to loosen up.

★*For Madmen Only* (BMG PD 74581)

The new album's title track, 'For Madmen Only', was either misnamed, or the group's idea of madness is everyone else's notion of mild eccentricity. It starts with electronic grunts and huffings, which eventually give way to a stretch of open-road funk that could be a vehicle for MIKE BRECKER, with Dave O'Higgins assured, if melodically unchallenging, on tenor. (O'Higgins, a promising saxophonist, may be suffering the same fate, in this kind of tight, synth-dominated band, as befell Wayne Shorter, in Weather Report.)

Another piece inspired by Herman Hesse is, 'The Lonely Wolf', which begins with a slowly whirling bass figure, electronic wolf noises drifting through it, and eventually gives rise to some of the most gripping improvisation on the set, in an attractive journey in and out of structure, from John Smith's keyboards.

Roberts, Marcus

(Born 1963)

For some years pianist, Marcus Roberts, was one of the most interesting elements in the WYNTON MARSALIS band, a young guardian of the traditions, who exhibited both the smooth swing of a Wynton Kelly and the crabbiness of a Thelonious Monk. As his solo career blossomed, this promise wasn't entirely upheld, but Roberts remains a keyboard artist of considerable stature and encyclopaedic knowledge, with a genuine vitality about his work, which is often missing from neo-classical jazz.

Roberts studied at Florida State University and, in the early Eighties, began to win piano competitions with apparently effortless ease. He joined Marsalis, in 1985, and the comprehensive sweep that he demonstrated, across the entire jazz piano repertoire, particularly in his unaccompanied sections, gained him a recording opportunity under his own leadership. If Roberts can bypass the urge to use his remarkable technique as a jazz travelogue, he is likely to become one of the music's most substantial figures in the 1990s.

★*Truth is Spoken Here* (BMG/Novus PD 83051)

Marcus Roberts' debut album of standards, originals that sound like standards, and tributes to Monk, and a session on which his sometime group leader Wynton Marsalis also appears. As with many of the current batch of respectful 'classical jazz' sessions, the blunting of expectations by the lack of anything surprising happening, takes the edge off the fun, and even a supporting cast, including drummer Elvin Jones, and ex-Monk tenorist, Charlie Rouse, can't dispel the sense of inevitability; yet Roberts' easy migrations, between stride piano and the borderline of abstraction, are undeniably impressive.

Roney, Wallace

(Born 1960)

As if to prove that younger trumpet players, in thrall to earlier MILES DAVIS, shouldn't be dismissed out of hand, Wallace Roney has been consistently demonstrating, through the 1980s, that he has grasped the elusive essence of Davis, as well as the oblique, muted, tightly-edited sound. As with Davis, Roney's use of space and delay not only creates more dramatic and involving music, but it also makes rhythm sections more creative – and interestingly, Roney has lately worked with two of the finest drummers in jazz, Elvin Jones, and TONY WILLIAMS.

Roney recorded with CHICO FREEMAN first, in 1982, and four years later made a distinctive contribution to Art Blakey's Jazz Messengers, as one of the few trumpeters in that band not to have attempted to swarm all over the music. Roney's sound was ideal for Tony Williams' return to a measured, reserved acoustic ensemble sound, in the manner of the mid-Sixties Miles Davis band, and since 1986 Roney has appeared regularly with Williams.

★*Intuition* (Vogue VG 651 600607)

A modal session that recalls the Miles Davis band of 1966. The quality of the playing is high, and saxophonist Gary Thomas' dry, unsentimental sound is strongly reminiscent of WAYNE SHORTER. The graceful, labyrinthine, 'For Duke', is outstanding, as is Ron Carter's buoyant bass and the work of an excellent, vigorous drummer, Cindy Blackman. Roney, on trumpet, is Miles-like in his shapes and cadences, Clifford Brown-like in his eruptions of poised speed. Saxophonist Kenny Garrett enhances the proceedings with a nice sour tone and skidding edge to his phrasing.

Russell, George

(Born Cincinnati, June 23, 1923)

Composer and arranger George Russell's music bursts with life, and a colliding, ricocheting life at that, informed by the leader's intellectual and emotional grip on bebop, African rhythmic ideas, Western modern classical devices, and orthodox big-band swing. He may slowly fan a 15th century madrigal into a rhythmic inferno, or enhance free-sounding slitherings and wrigglings, between the ensemble sections, into sustained blasts of uptempo rock time and blazing trumpet riffs, abandoning melody in favour of sheer energy and driving tempo.

As a child, Russell heard jazz on the riverboats, and, by his early twenties, was a drummer good enough to be invited to join Charlie Parker in New York. But though the tuberculosis, that plagued him in the 1940s, prevented him from accepting, he had got the encouragement that he needed to begin writing. He started with pieces for Gillespie's big band ('Cubana Be/Cubana Bop', was his most celebrated contribution to it) and was not much more than twenty five, when he wrote, 'A Bird In Igor's Yard', a marriage of bebop phraseology and rhythmic textures closely related to, 'The Rite of Spring'.

Russell's investigations into compositional methods became profound and extensive, over the next years, and in 1953 he published a complex theoretical work on the subject, *The Lydian Chromatic Concept of Tonal Organisation*, which singlehandedly influenced the shift from chordal to modal (scale-based) playing, during the Fifties, and which underpinned the most independent work by MILES DAVIS and John Coltrane. The scales Russell drew on were adaptations of the Greek Lydian modes. His writings indicated the ways in which these scales could be used to reconcile soloists, at various points, with the given key or the harmonic activity of the rhythm section, but not continuously, as was the case with bop. The essence of Russell's life's work, in the border territories between improvisation and composition, is the exploration of how far from tonal centres improvisation can stretch, while still illuminating the perceptions of both improvisor and composer.

During the Sixties, as well as teaching, Russell regularly led sextets (at times featuring the great reed player, Eric Dolphy) that audaciously blended free and structured materials, and the success of these groups in Europe in particular, led him to live in Sweden for five years. He returned to the States, at the end of the Sixties, to teach at the New England Conservatory, and from that time on has continued to perform regularly, on occasion with substantial orchestras.

Russell's ideas have strongly influenced contemporary musicians on both sides of the Atlantic, notably CARLA BLEY and Miles Davis, in the USA, and JAN GARBAREK, Palle Mikkelborg and ANDY SHEPPARD, in Europe. In recent tours of Britain, with a mixture of American and local players, Russell, in his late sixties, has shown no signs of losing that remarkable rhythmic impact nor the ability to enthuse musicians into accepting methods, which are often unfamiliar to them. In 1989, he won the MacArthur prize, one of the most prestigious American tributes for services to intellectual and cultural life. Though his work is reasonably well-served by CD, his recent Blue Note recordings (*African Game* and *So What*) are currently deleted.

★*Jazz Workshop* (Bluebird/BMG ND 86467)

One of the best of all Russell discs, *Jazz Workshop*, is the most consistent example of his early efforts to splice improvisation and complex organisation. It was recorded in 1956, and features pianist Bill Evans and trumpeter Art Farmer, among others, in bands perfectly attuned to the complex demands of the composer. Russell's Lydian Concept not only offered fascinating alternatives to improvisors, but also reshaped the nature of jazz melody, and, 'Jack's Blues', and, 'Night Sound', both exhibit a needling unorthodoxy and subtle transformation of blues materials, that came as a breath of fresh air in an era dominated by bop. 'Round Johnny Rondo', is one of Russell's most original themes and, 'Witch Hunt', is a classic instance of the teeming energy, and variation of texture and tone colour, that the composer is capable of at his best.

★*New York Big Band* (Soul Note SNCD 1039)

A 1978 outing for Russell's powerful New York orchestra. The lineup is excellent, the soloing vigorous, and the material is more varied than in many of the leader's sessions of the past fifteen years.

Sanborn, David William

(Born Tampa, Florida, July 30, 1945)
Dave Sanborn has helped shaped the techniques of a generation of saxophone players, as well as lending his talents to innumerable recording sessions. But though he's fleet, inventive and, in most respects, the complete virtuoso, Sanborn remains the most direct of players.

When still a boy, Sanborn took up the saxophone as respiration therapy, during his recovery from polio and as an escape from dependence on an iron lung. A school-band alto saxophonist of promise and a prodigious teenage saxophone accompanist to Albert King and Little Walter, Sanborn went on to study music at Northwestern University and then at the University of Iowa. He received his professional musical baptism with the Paul Butterfield Band, from 1967. In which outfit, he learnt to handle the timbres of soul and rhythm-and-blues, that have dominated his playing since.

Everything Sanborn does is inflected with the blues, which gives him both his instant communicating power and his popularity. He listened closely to the most blues-derived of musicians, like Ray Charles and, saxophonist Hank Crawford, as well as to the most subtle yet forthright blues saxophonist of all, Charlie Parker. Sanborn's wailing eloquence made him a regular partner of the composer and arranger of genius, Gil Evans, but the same penetrating voice has also appeared on the work of many soul and pop artists, like James Taylor ('How Sweet It is') David Bowie ('Young Americans') and Stevie Wonder.

★*Voyeur* (WEA 256 900)

Typical setting for Sanborn's searing tone and dancing momentum, *Voyeur* is a 1981 collection of funk and bluesy music that won a Grammy for the saxophonist. Exuberant, direct and earthy music.

Sandoval, Arturo

(Born Cuba, 1949)
A showman to the tips of his toes, and about as nonchalantly in command of the resources of the trumpet as anyone in jazz, Arturo Sandoval is nothing short of a phenomenon. His whistling, accurately pitched, high notes, bull-charging runs, tiptoeing muted figures, machine-gun bebop and tongue-in-cheek showband finales, shower over his listeners, and if the effect is sometimes dazzling to the point of saturation, Sandoval nevertheless delivers it all with an exuberance that is highly communicative in itself.

Sandoval originally came to the attention of Americans and Europeans through his work with the exotic Cuban ensemble IRAKERE. He was already, at the time, a music teacher at the Havana Conservatory, adept on piano, as well as on trumpet, and fluent in the classical repertoire too. As Irakere moved increasingly toward dance music, Sandoval quit, and found that his reputation had expanded so fast that he was in demand everywhere. He played with Dizzy Gillespie – his original primary influence in jazz – from the beginning of the Eighties onward, and became a prominent feature of Gillespie's United Nations big band. Sandoval also performs, around the world, with his own groups and local musicians, in a mixture of bursts of oblique Miles Davis-like electric music, breakneck bebop and feverish Latin-American outings. He has recently begun recording for the funk-oriented, GRP label, a fact that is unlikely to restrain the increasing superficiality and technical bravura of his work on disc.

★*Tumbaito* (Messidor 15974)

Fast, furious, high octane music from Sandoval and supporting small group, that comes close to the atmosphere he generates in live performance; but little of it sticks in the mind, after the dust settles.

Sanders, Pharoah

(Born Little Rock, Arkansas, October 13, 1940)
When Pharoah Sanders joined the John Coltrane group, in the mid-Sixties, it was taken by some as marking the point at which Coltrane's music sped even faster into outer space and left conventionally comprehending mortals behind. Whereas Coltrane was striving for a trance-like music, derived from an ever-more-dense compacting of jazz's harmonic complexity, Sanders took a more direct route to the same end, with a sound that was, predominantly, an abrasive, blues-drenched wail, with little use of orthodox melody. His playing was influenced by Albert Ayler, and he had been closely connected with the New York avant-garde, before he worked with Coltrane. Now that jazz listeners have grown acclimatised to the innovations of that period, Sanders has latterly come to sound attractively salty and direct, particularly since he now applies his distinctive tonal palette to regular tunes.

Like so many of the Sixties avantists, Sanders began in blues bands. He later worked, in California, with such artists as Dewey Redman, and Philly Joe Jones, and then came to New York to join SUN RA. Ayler's influence affected Sanders strongly from the mid-Sixties, and he worked with Coltrane from 1966 until the great saxophonist's death, the following year. This event caused a long period of disorientation for Sanders; though he continued to work with Coltrane's piano-playing widow Alice, he barely recorded in the Seventies. Latterly he has discovered the textural appeal of inserting a refined version of his flamethrowing sound into conventional settings, as well as turning in some of the most affecting ballad performances of recent times.

★*Journey to the One* (Theresa TRCD 108)

A 1980 Sanders set, marking his return to the studio, after years of indecision which were partly the result of his efforts to make a, Coltrane-derived, search for inner tranquillity, whilst possessing a saxophone sound fit to wake the dead. *Journey to the One*, seemed to represent arrival at a balancing point for Sanders; and his ravishing, slow tenor exploration of the ballad, 'Kazuko', is a genuinely moving performance.

Scofield, John

(Born Ohio, December 26, 1951)

The electric guitar emerged from jazz, but it has largely sounded tame and tonally limited in jazz musicians' hands. Blues and rock guitarists made more exciting use of it, from the Fifties onwards, and in the Sixties, the jazz and the blues tributaries were effectively fused together by a group of artists, including PAT METHENY, JOHN MCLAUGHLIN and John Scofield. Scofield, a gifted Berklee student, who worked with Chet Baker, funk drummer BILLY COBHAM, Charles Mingus, vibist GARY BURTON, and the imaginative saxophonist DAVID LIEBMAN, came to big-time fame with MILES DAVIS's comeback to playing, in the early 1980s. Scofield and fellow guitarist, Mike Stern, collaborated in helping the long laid-up Davis, back to form.

Scofield is a fascinating instance of what happens to a musician, whose first love is jazz, but who happened to fall in love with it in the middle of a rock and roll boom, in which guitar virtuosity and a blues revival took first place. The result is that much of Scofield's work, both in composition and improvising, constantly suggests bebop. The finish he applies to it, however, takes into account BB King as well as Jim Hall, Muddy Waters as well as Pat Martino.

Scofield's distinctive tone is moody, glowering; his vocabulary full of reverberating, fiercely struck low notes and arching treble sounds. He even does this on old pop tunes like 'Secret Love', imparting to them an ironic, cantankerous quality straight from the sassiest of blues. It was this combination of jazz literacy and earthiness, that endeared him to Miles Davis. In recent times, Scofield has returned to jazz, but his directness and musicality avoid any suggestion of a superficial adherence to the bop revival.

★*Flat Out* (Gramavision 188903-2)

A 1988 session, with Scofield in his jazz-funk incarnation. Almost everything he plays turns into something like blues; though with tunes like 'All The Things You Are', he is beginning to demonstrate a revised interest in older jazz forms, away from thunderous funk. Dated, but exhilaratingly unpretentious at times, with a useful contribution from drummer Terri Lyne Carrington, on three tracks, who should have been made more use of.

★*Time on My Hands* (Blue Note CDP 792 894-2)

Probably Scofield's best ever album. The blues intonation is still strong, and there are insinuating hints of rock 'n' roll hovering around it, but, as a blend of his influences, it's a delightful record with barely a slack moment. The presence of JACK DEJOHNETTE, on drums, and the excellent Joe Lovano, on saxophones, helps a lot. Scofield's writing is consistently good, and the Mingus influence, that informs some of the ballad playing (distinct echoes of 'Goodbye Pork Pie Hat') imparts a new poignancy to the work of a musician sometimes thought of as a high-class macho artist.

Sharrock, Sonny

(Born New York, August 27, 1940)
Sharrock is not the kind of guitarist who devotes himself to tripping arpeggios and rippling chords. His style is a cross between punk, free-jazz and Seventies' 'jazz-rock', but he was playing like this before punk was invented and his sound, though it has a kind of ghetto-rhetoric, is primarily an attempt to sidestep all the generations of bop-dominated pluckers in jazz, who have made guitar solos sound like fingering exercises. Skyrockets bursting, brakes squealing, an arcade of video games, are some of the bracing noises that Sharrock's playing brings to mind.

He was a Berklee student for a time, but – unsurprisingly – he dropped out, and began working with the New York free players of the Sixties, until he was, unexpectedly, hired by the fusion flautist, HERBIE MANN, for the commercially successful, *Memphis Underground*. MILES DAVIS used him, as a sound effects player, on, *Jack Johnson*, and, in the Seventies, Sharrock toured with a band, which featured his wife, the singer Linda Sharrock. In the Eighties, he was involved in the formation of the ferocious, free-electric, ensemble, Last Exit, with drummer Ronald Shannon Jackson, saxophonist Peter Brotzmann, and bassist Bill Laswell. Sharrock prides himself on knowing virtually no standard jazz phrases, as is evident from the briefest exposure to his disconcertingly distinctive work.

★*Live In New York* (Enemy EMY 108 CD)

Mostly Sharrock's regular application of violent, splintering guitar music, recorded in 1988, but also exhibiting a curious kind of gruff tenderness, on the swaying, 'My Song'. As he has grown older Sharrock has definitely become more mellow (though Sharrock's mellowness is most people's dementia) and this raucous confection of abstract sounds and fragmented blues is an oddly satisfactory antidote to all the prim and studiedly dramatic conventional jazz-guitar performances, that regularly do the rounds.

Sheppard, Andy

(Born Bristol, England, January 18, 1957)
Andy Sheppard is one of Britain's foremost new saxophone stars. Whilst, almost inevitably, indebted to both John Coltrane and Sonny Rollins, Sheppard's combination of whimsy, abrasiveness and danceable swing has a distinctive flavour of its own. Apart from the Americans, Coltrane, Rollins, and STEVE LACY, Sheppard counts British players, like Don Weller, Art Themen, and the avantist, Evan Parker, among his saxophone influences. Other British influences includes pianist, Geoff Williams, a player of self-possessed eccentricity, who worked with him in the early fusion band, Sphere, and KEITH TIPPETT, a fellow West Countryman, and unquestionably one of the finest homegrown improvising pianists of the past twenty years.

Unusually, Sheppard, a former choirboy, didn't discover jazz until he was nineteen, but quickly absorbed the idiom and was soon playing with Sphere, and then with the French performance-art group, Urban Sax. He came a highly-rated second in the Shlitz Young Jazz Musicians' contest in London, in

1986, after which his career blossomed. Having landed a record-ing contract with the Island/Antilles label (who were also producing COURTNEY PINE) he made two good small group albums (see below) and has latterly cut an orchestral record, *Soft on the Inside*, with a multinational big band, that raised the roof on its one London performance last year. He has also been a regular member of groups led by two very distinguished American composer/arrangers, CARLA BLEY and GEORGE RUSSELL, for their European tours.

★*Andy Sheppard* (Antilles ANCD 8720)

Sheppard's first album, a 'blowing' session, with a strong boppish feel, and equally strong shades of John Coltrane. 'Coming Second', is a breezy exploration of driving bop, and the American trumpeter, Randy Brecker, makes some deft and glossy interventions.

★*Introductions in the Dark* (Antilles ANCD 8742)

Sheppard's second disc, stretching his writing more, and ranging beyond the jazz tradition. Much of it is devoted to a suite, 'Romantic Conversations', which includes the ensemble's inge-nious African percussionist, a frequently-returning, mid-tempo, Latin-flavoured saxophone theme (graceful but a bit obvious) and some impressively funky contributions from Sheppard's vibra-harp player, the effortlessly swinging Orphy Robinson. The later stages are less integrated, but more representative of the sound of new band in live performance, and they include: the high-speed, free wail, 'Rebecca's Glass Slippers', a slow ballad that explores the deft and fertile intricacies of Sheppard's phrasing, and some springy dance music that suggests an African hi-life band.

★*Soft on the Inside* (Antilles ANCD 8751)

Sheppard's ambitious, multi-national big band, operating on the principle, drawn from his work with George Russell, that the whole orchestra should be played as a single instrument, rather than simply used for shading and emphasis behind soloists.

Though it begins innocently, with some disarming, West Coast-studio style low trombone licks and wide-grin trumpet figures, it quickly turns into a much more distinctive confection. 'Rebecca's Silk Stockings', opens grippingly with baleful, sonar-like, one-note blipping from the brass, turning into a multi-voiced clamour. The dedication to Carla Bley is appropriately sardonic, with reverberating low trombone sounds against paint-blistering trumpets, which give way to a James Bond riff, and while the first part of 'Rave Trade' is pure Gil Evans, the second part is a gospelly nod to Mingus, ending in a wild drum thrash.

★66 Shades of Lipstick (Editions EG EEGCD 64)

Sheppard and Tippett West Country musicians a generation apart, but united by the love of improvisation, here offer no grooves, dance invitations or set repertoire, but are nonetheless more conventionally tuneful, than the more abstract, free-improvising bands. Tippett sometimes sounds harpsichord-like, as he plucks inside the piano lid, then unleashes thundering bass-register patterns, over which Sheppard mingles keening, Coltrane-like ballad sounds and minimalist repetitive cycles assisted by circular breathing.

Shorter, Wayne

(Born Newark, New Jersey, August 25, 1933)
When he arrived on the jazz scene more than twenty five years ago, saxophonist Wayne Shorter's doings quickly became the subject of intense and enthusiastic scrutiny. He was a Coltraneish performer who, nevertheless, didn't sound like a copy; with a clipped, gritty Humphrey Bogart-like tone, and a fast, staccato manner of phrasing. He was also shaping into a peerless composer for small jazz groups, which he demonstrated with Art Blakey's Jazz Messengers and then with MILES DAVIS. But as a soloist, Shorter has rarely been audible in his old imperious form at any time, in the past dozen years. Jazz-rock, or fusion music, which claimed him during a long tenure with Weather Report, mostly reduced his work to blurted accents and unresolved lines, as if he were taking the line of least resistance in someone else's music.

Shorter learned his craft as a university student, and then in the army, joining Blakey in 1959, and Miles Davis five years later. With Davis, Shorter blossomed as a soloist, since all the melodic originality he had been refining, in the previous years, was shaken into new shapes by the rhythmic openness of that remarkable band that also included Ron Carter, HERBIE HANCOCK and TONY WILLIAMS. Several of Shorter's compositions (notably, 'ESP', and, 'Nefertiti') became regular features of the Davis repertoire, and the saxophonist extended his imaginative contributions into Davis' electro-funk era, adopting the soprano horn for *In A Silent Way*, and delivering haunting, beautifully structured solos on it.

Shorter collaborated in the formation of Weather Report, in 1970, an inventive fusion group that used electronics orchestrally, but his own playing receded within such an integrated group sound. He has continued to lead small groups since (with the distinctiveness of his compositions still apparent) and has recently taken an impressive new quartet on the road, including, drummer, Terri-Lyne Carrington, and the young English pianist, Jason Rebello. For the most part, the wrong Shorter records have been released on CD, while the earlier sessions, like *Etcetera*, *All Seeing Eye*, and *Schizophrenia*, all worthy contenders, have been passed over.

★*Super Nova* (Blue Note CDP 784 332-2)

This album represents Wayne Shorter as he was moving closer to Miles Davis' fusion position, with the release of *In A Silent Way*, and *Bitches' Brew*. It features the obligatory guitars (but an interestingly abrasive blend in JOHN MCLAUGHLIN, and SONNY SHARROCK) and multiple percussion, and Shorter himself plays soprano throughout, on which his curling lines are intermittently delicious. The generally drifting, meditative atmosphere, however, isn't sufficiently illuminated by these flares.

★*Speak No Evil* (Blue Note CDP 746 509-2)

Shorter with Freddie Hubbard, too brash and direct a trumpeter to really mesh with the saxophonist's ambiguities and ambivalencies. There are, however, two sublime ballad performances, 'Dance Cadaverous', and, 'Infant Eyes', the latter a tightly edited and faintly unnerving set of melodic variations, well supported by Herbie Hancock's piano.

Simone, Nina (Eunice Waymon)

(Born Tryon, N Carolina, February 21, 1933)
Brittle, unpredictable, yet a great entertainer and, at times, appropriately bracketed under 'jazz', for her reworking of familiar materials and the gospelly drive of her piano playing, Nina Simone came back to popularity with British audiences in the 1980s. To some extent this might have resulted from a cultural tourism engendered by the prosperous Eighties, but the fierce and idiosyncratic directness of her shows was also an antidote to corporate-planned entertainment, and a big part of her appeal.

Simone's background was in both gospel and classical music. She sang in the local choir as a child, and went on to study music at the Juilliard School, in New York, and then in Philadelphia, and became a piano teacher. Her voice, however, with its incisive, unforgiving bite, became her true calling card. In 1959, she had a hit with her version of, 'I Loves You Porgy', and, through the Sixties, she was successful both in the USA and in Europe, with a strong of gospel-tinged songs, some strongly influenced by her involvement in the civil rights movement. Simone celebrated the work of poets Paul Dunbar and Langston Hughes, in her work, and songs of civil rights' politics, 'Mississippi Goddam', 'Backlash Blues' and 'To Be Young, Gifted and Black', became staples of her repertoire.

Simone continues to be an idiosyncratic performer, sometimes hard on audiences, and always making her listeners aware of the political slant in being an Afro-American performer in a business dominated by whites. But she hasn't wavered from being the woman she is, onstage and off, and that bruised integrity has served her for thirty years in the forefront of music.

★*My Baby Just Cares for Me* (Charly CDCHARLY 6)

Nina Simone's first album, from 1959; the session that brought her to fame. It includes her hit song of the period, 'I Loves You Porgy', a great deal of exploration of the possibilities of, 'My Baby

Just Cares For Me', 'Mood Indigo', and a mixture of standards and blues. More defiant and spring-heeled, not fractured and doubtful like later Simone, but with the same imperious dignity then as now.

★*Live at Ronnie Scott's* (Hendring HEN 6017Y)

Nina Simone's performances, in the mid-Eighties, were theatrical and spinechilling affairs, and though her British drummer, Paul Robinson, is a little inclined to hot, Cobham-like, tom-tom licks, this album brings the sessions instantly back to life. 'See Line Woman', and, 'God God God', locate Simone at her baleful best, and 'My Baby Just Cares For Me', imparts a characteristic suspicion to a usually jaunty vehicle.

Smith, Thomas 'Tommy'

(Born Luton, England, April 27, 1967)
A consummate technician, Scots-raised saxophonist Tommy Smith mastered the fundamentals of bebop saxophone by the age of fifteen, and his precocity has enabled him to move away from that garrulous style toward the haunting, understated manner of the Norwegian, JAN GARBAREK, The only risk Smith faces is that, without really startling compositional insight, the Garbarek style can treacherously turn from the reflective to the diffident. Smith's pieces are often reminiscent of Garbarek, at slow tempos, and CHICK COREA, at fast ones.

Smith took up the saxophone at twelve, and made national TV in a trio, with pianist, Gordon Beck, and bassist, Neils-Henning Oersted Pedersen, at fifteen, recording two albums for Scottish labels shortly afterwards. Smith studied at Berklee Conservatory, Boston, and formed a band, Forward Motion, then joined GARY BURTON, in 1986. The following year Smith's fame spread, through a BBC documentary devoted to him, and he made his debut recording for the Blue Note label, in 1988. Smith has also appeared in a variety of pop contexts, notably with the Scottish band, Hue and Cry.

★*Step By Step* (Blue Note CDP 791 930-2)

Smith's debut for Blue Note, accompanied by the kind of

illustrious partners increasingly becoming obligatory for the first recordings of newcomers. Drummer JACK DEJOHNETTE, bassist Eddie Gomez, and guitarist JOHN SCOFIELD, all took part, but though Smith's playing successfully demonstrated his growing tonal sophistication, the disc didn't altogether avoid the trap of sounding like a high-class demo.

Sun Ra (Herman Sonny Blount)

(Born Birmingham, Alabama, May 22, 1914)

Though the theatricality of his stage act (space-suits, elaborate make-up, illuminated hats, exotic dancers) has diverted attention from the substance of his work, and though his own insistence, that he is an astral traveller with a spiritual calling, hasn't increased the sum of factual information about him, Sun Ra is one of the most adventurous and genuinely progressive of big-band leaders. From the 1950s, his orchestral work anticipated many of the advances of the free-jazz of the next decade, and one of his regular saxophonists, John Gilmore, is commonly credited as being a direct influence on John Coltrane. The sound of his band mingles swing-era bravura (he arranged for Fletcher Henderson, in the 1940s), electronic-synthesiser fury, stormy percussion and abstract horn flights, and Sun Ra himself, remains one of the most imaginative exponents of the frequently treacherous synthesizer.

His early records, in the Fifties, mainly displayed swing and hard bop allegiances (there is a strong flavour of Monk and Ellington) though he soon began to explore the potential of the organ and extended percussion. Based in Chicago, he collected a group of loyal musicians around him, who became the nucleus of his, 'Arkestra', for years, and he also became an early pioneer of independent record production, making a succession of challenging discs for his own, Saturn, label, when no regular record company, and only a few faithful fans, showed any interest. In the period of consolidation of the past decade, when the structural changes of Sixties free-jazz have percolated down into the mainstream of jazz, Sun Ra's vision of the music has seemed increasingly logical and farsighted and he continues to tour, as well as finding his music belatedly of interest to the record business. The early discs, now collectors' items on ·vinyl, aren't available on CD.

★*Solar Myth Approach* (Affinity/Charly CDAFF 760)

Good, mid-period, Sun Ra session, from the point at which the leader had begun to incorporate electronics into an already seething soundscape. Far from overburdening the Arkestra's music, it extended an already startling stock of voicings and texture even further, and the disc (originally issued as two vinyl albums) includes Sun Ra perennials such as, 'Outer Spaceways'.

★*Love in Outer Space* (Leo CDLR 154)

Uneven, but fitfully interesting and more conventional live recording made in Utrecht, in 1983. The only-approximate accuracy of the band's ensemble sound generally doesn't matter in the heady atmosphere of its live shows, but it's more intrusive on disc. John Gilmore, however, delivers some rugged, restless solos, the percussion effects (Sun Ra often gets virtually all his musicians to hit things in unison) are dramatic and the leader's keyboards exhibit their customary elaborate melodrama.

★*Purple Night* (A & M 75021 5324)

The Arkestra recorded in late 1989, featuring DON CHERRY, on trumpet, and Julian Priester, on trombone, in addition to the usual galaxy of talent. It's a typically lurching, witty, occasionally petrifying display, with Sun Ra's keyboards passing from urbane whimsicality to wild, swirling abstractions, notably on, 'Neverness', in which John Gilmore also plays a throaty, barrelling solo. Don Cherry bubbles engagingly.

Surman, John Douglas

(Born Tavistock, England, August 30, 1944)
Like ANDY SHEPPARD in the Eighties, John Surman was the West Countryman who arrived like a whirlwind on the British jazz scene of the mid-Sixties. He was, like most of his contemporaries

all over the world, devoted to the saxophone technique of John Coltrane, characterised by an intense, seamless tumult of variations on arpeggios and modes, but Surman's version was performed on the baritone saxophone, a cumbersome instrument usually used in a more sedate manner. Even if he had not later developed his musical personality in many other ways, this extension of the resources of the instrument, so that it was capable of operating within the range of the tenor saxophone as well, would have guaranteed the young virtuoso a place in the jazz history books.

Surman's involvement with jazz had begun at school in Plymouth, when he attended local workshops run by a local jazz talent, MIKE WESTBROOK. In the early 1960s, Surman and Westbrook went to London, where the saxophonist's fire and energy, and his mentor's blend of Ellingtonian sophistication and art-school subversiveness, marked them out as the coming jazz generation in Britain. Surman then developed his skills both with his own immediate contemporaries and with older musicians, like Ronnie Scott – beginning to select intelligently from the more orthodox jazz tradition and from the possibilities offered by 'free-form'. The Westbrook band went from strength to strength, and Surman was its most inventive soloist through the 1960s.

At the end of that decade, the saxophonist joined forces with two Americans, the drummer and bassist, Stu Martin and Barre Phillips to form The Trio, a band in which the spontaneity and empathy between the performers transcended both the written material and the limitations imposed by such a line-up. In 1970, Surman took the World Expo, Osaka, by storm, in a firebreathing performance with the European Francy Boland Band, and throughout the following decade he experimented endlessly: with electric guitars (Morning Glory), with all-saxophone ensembles (SOS), with brass (John Surman Brass Project), and briefly with the German trombone genius, Albert Mangelsdorff (MUMPS). In more recent times he has increasingly devoted his energies to unaccompanied playing, using electronics and multi-tracking, and investigating a pastoral musical territory somewhere between the existential chilliness of JAN GARBAREK and the jaunty warmth of English folk music. Surman has also enjoyed a fruitful, free-improvising partnership, with American drummer and pianist, JACK DEJOHNETTE.

★*Amazing Adventures of Simon Simon* (ECM 829 160-2)

Duet performance by Surman and Jack DeJohnette, which won plaudits in America and Europe. Though it's informed by Surman's long-term interest in English folk music, the interplay between the two musicians is strongly motivated by the jazz tradition, and its melodic variety is dependent on the creative tension between two dissimilar sources.

★*Private City* (ECM 835 780-2)

About half of the music here was written for a ballet, of the same name, which premiered at Sadler's Wells, London. The title is faithful to the music, which is, at times, a faintly navel-gazing exploration of multi-tracking and computer-generated rhythms, full of Surman's affection for song-like melody, avoidance of transatlantic jazz cliches and rather preoccupied romanticism. Without prodding from partners, the solos do take on a rather static, inexorable air occasionally, but Surman is as affecting and inventive at this kind of music as anyone currently at work.

Thompson, Danny

(Born London, February 4, 1939)
The credentials of British bass player, Danny Thompson, extend from employment by the late, Tubby Hayes, and the young, JOHN MCLAUGHLIN, via Pentangle (the successful folk-pop ensemble, of the late 1960s) Ralph McTell, and Kate Bush. Currently he has achieved a lyrical and resonant blend of Swedish and English folk music, Charles Mingus' magisterial bass sound, and the one-touch receptivity of the best small-group jazz. Thompson, taking his lead from the majestic Mingus and the rich, poetic methods of Ornette Coleman's bassist, CHARLIE HADEN, dislikes the speediness of bop-influenced bass, advising superfast practitioners to play guitar instead. Thompson's bass notes roll like breakers, over-tones humming like wires, the deeper sounds closer to a roar than a boom, the lighter ones bouncing and springy. Like an earlier generation of bassists, he favours the middle and lower register, a gravitas that is a perfect foil for his partners.

From the late Sixties to the mid Eighties, Thompson was all but invisible on the British jazz scene, despite continuing to appear sporadically with excellent musicians, including drummer John Stevens, and pianist STAN TRACEY. But Thompson's pop assignments kept him busy until his decision to form Whatever, in 1987. The name came from Thompson's impatience with pigeonholing, and the group played tunes by composers, as far apart as Sonny Rollins and the anonymous English folk traditionalists. Thompson augmented Whatever with an extra reed and guitar, for his second album, but the first version was the strongest.

★*Whatever* (Hannibal HNCD 1326)

An immensely classy debut for Whatever, the melodic strength of the band being utterly accessible, amenable to jazz improvisation, and yet for the most part utterly different from the jazz tradition. Saxophonist Tony Roberts is wistful and romantic, or Coltraneish and reflective, on the ballads, and guitarist, Bernie Holland, fast and clangy, like early JOHN McLAUGHLIN. The repertoire includes the folk-jazz hybrids of the Swedish musician, Jan Johannsen, English traditionals like, 'Lovely Joan', and dedications to Scottish folk singer, Alex Campbell, and a strong underpinning of swing.

Threadgill, Henry Luther

(Born Chicago, February 15, 1944)

Hindsight indicated that the expressionist improvisational explosion of the 1960s achieved less than it might have because of its uncompromising rejections of structure. In the period since, some of the musicians associated with it have gone on developing forms appropriate to the solo styles. One such is the Chicago saxophonist and composer Henry Threadgill, a powerful improvisor whose style drew on Sonny Rollins, Ornette Coleman and the blues tradition. Threadgill was a prominent member of Chicago's Association for the Advancement of Creative Musicians (AACM, see page 224) in the Sixties, who produced some of the most original improvising to have emerged from the movement, as well as attractive syntheses of free playing with the music of Scott Joplin and Jelly Roll Morton in the trio, Air.

Threadgill had been formally trained, but worked with gospel groups and blues bands in the early Sixties, before becoming involved with AACM and also working as a music teacher. Air, which also included the great bassist Fred Hopkins and drummer Steve McCall was one of the most prestigious offshoots of the Chicago school of contemporary jazz players. In recent times, Threadgill's work as a composer has become a more prominent feature of his career, and he has deployed audacious configurations – including all-bass and saxophone bands – and consistently celebrated the early jazz past. Threadgill's work since his 1986 signing to BMG Novus is on CD, but little of his earlier work is.

★*Air Lore* (Bluebird/BMG ND 86578)

Air's sixth album, made in 1979, representing Threadgill, Hopkins and McCall at their most sweepingly mature, spinning rich variations on material by Scott Joplin and Jelly Roll Morton. Unlike many of the retreats into the archives by contemporary jazz musicians, this set both illuminates the originals and emphasises the remarkable empathy that the trio had established by this time and Hopkins' bass is in full imperious flow.

★*Rag Bush and All* (BMG PD 83052)

Threadgill's augmented group, a sextet recorded in 1988 – retaining both the group interplay of Air and the balancing of expressionism and classicism that the leader had been refining through the decade. In the later stages of Air's work, Threadgill's writing had grown increasingly dolorous, and the sextet session was a welcome lightening of the atmosphere, as well as enhancing his reputation for independence from jazz fashions.

Tippett, Keith

(Born Bristol, England, August 25, 1947)
In an era of highly technical jazz keyboardists specialising in linear improvisation, West Country pianist Keith Tippett is a rare exception – a consummate textural pianist, whose hailstorms of bright, spangly sound or the dark, pounding rhythms of his low

register playing, mark him out, and since he is able to maintain rhythmic drive for long periods by the sheer density of fast arpeggio playing (rather like Cecil Taylor), he is often his own percussionist.

Tippett began his career as a wide-ranging performer who became something of a cult. He formed one of the first British jazz-rock bands with Long John Baldry and sidemen Elton Dean and Marc Charig, was briefly embraced by the record business and thus enabled to move on to wide-screen projects like the 50 piece orchestra Centipede, which included musicians from the classical, rock and jazz spheres. He also married a talented and offbeat rock star of the era, Julie Driscoll, whose hit record with the Bob Dylan song 'Wheels on Fire' had been a classic of the era. But for much of the 1980s, Tippett's career was quiet, especially in Britain, though he went on developing out of all proportion to his reputation, recording extensively for the German label FMP. In recent times, Tippett has performed regularly with a sensational improvising quartet (Mujician) and with his young West Country playing partner, saxophonist ANDY SHEPPARD, with whom he recorded the duo album *66 Shades of Lipstick* in 1990.

★*Couple in Spirit* (EG EEGCD 52)

Almost a pastoral record by Tippett's sometimes fierce standards, gentle, feathery (and fitfully bluesy) multi-tracked singing over chiming, swaying keyboard sounds, all of it improvised from scratch. Though Tippett is a brilliant jazz-based improvisor, very little of the music on this session is directly derived from jazz but frequently displays a soulful, unadorned, pentatonic quality obliquely suggestive of both gospel music and English folk songs. The rich, chanting vocals of Julie Tippett bring a solemnity and calm to the proceedings, and though there is a fey and sometimes faintly unconvincing children-of-nature guilelessness about *Couple In Spirit*, its musicality and originality are indisputable.

Tracey, Stanley William 'Stan'

(Born London, December 30, 1926)
After working with the British pianist Stan Tracey in the 1960s, Sonny Rollins asked in the music press, 'does anybody here know

just how good he really is?'. Until the later Eighties, by which time he was an elder statesman of British jazz, Tracey received a good deal less than his due from the record business and the public in his homeland.

Tracey was a forces entertainer during the latter years of World War II, became a full-time professional in the 1950s and worked both in the insular and dedicated world of British modern jazz and in the commercial sphere during that decade – most notably as the pianist in Ted Heath's famous dance orchestra. Unfashionably for a British pianist in the Fifties, Tracey's inclinations lay with the ornery, elbowing piano style of Thelonious Monk, and though Tracey is recognisable within the first few bars, his percussive, rumbling piano style always suggests links with Monk and with Duke Ellington. It is a method of working that has endeared him to several generations of musicians and listeners – he has worked with this country's most resourceful avantists, as well as those of more orthodox persuasion – and even led to a successful recording (*Playing In the Yard*) with the American saxophonist Charlie Rouse, a partner of Thelonious Monk's for nearly a decade. Tracey has a different kind of clout as a composer, and one that is closely related to the methods of the late Duke Ellington – but with an infectious rhythmic impact also reminiscent of Count Basie.

★*Genesis, and More* (Steam Records – catalogue number on proof)

A 1986 Tracey composition, 'Genesis' is a seven-part work musically depicting The Creation. It has warmth, wit, intimacy and bravura, and finds Tracey the composer at the height of his powers. The CD adds two of the composer's big band classics ('Afro-Charlie' and 'Murdering the Time'). Genesis is exhilarating and exuberant orthodox big-band music of a kind rarely played with such punch anymore and the sharpness of the CD enhances the brash, headlong momentum of the music.

★*We Still Love You Madly* (MOLECD 13)

A big band set of Tracey's tributes to Duke Ellington, his compositional hero. Though Tracey deals with Ellington almost entirely in one or other of two moods (rhapsodic and slow, or bullish and fast) the writing here has a humorous and jubilant panache which is pure Tracey, and some of the soloing is excellent. Peter King's alto coda to 'In A Sentimental Mood' is sensational, as is the work of the eager queue of four trumpet soloists on the fast blues 'Festival Junction', and Art Themen's Rollins-like mixture of sensuality and splutter on 'Lay By'.

Tyner, McCoy Alfred

(Born Philadelphia, December 11, 1938)

McCoy Tyner is one of the most widely imitated pianists in modern jazz. His membership of the John Coltrane quartet in the 1960s, a band of phenomenal group interplay that also sustained an exhausting level of dynamic pressure extensively approximated but almost never equalled, paved the way for his present eminence. Tyner appeared to have taken the piano – an instrument usually used in bebop-derived music for either harmonic support in a group or melodically complex soloing over a minimal chord framework – and turned it into something closer to the drums.

Tyner came up in the Jazztet, an excellent, tightly-knit outfit led by trumpeter Art Farmer and saxophonist Benny Golson. He moved straight from there to the Coltrane group in 1960. Coltrane had reached a stage in his musical life at which he no longer wanted to play on chords but on rocking, hypnotically repeated vamps over which he could spread the dense and throbbing tapestry of notes that came to be known as 'sheets of sound'. It required stamina as well as inventiveness from accompanists, and Tyner, a muscular player with an immense finger-span, could hammer out the same trancelike pattern under sustained improvisations that could run for an hour or more, still able to erupt into fresh solos when his turn finally came.

Tyner left Coltrane in 1965, as the saxophonist moved further out into the territory of free and atonal music. The first years of this independence were taxing to the point where the pianist pondered giving up, but in a series of recordings for Blue Note and then Milestone, Tyner discovered an independent appeal to the public again. With the Milestone records that included *Enlightenment*, *Atlantis*, and *Sama Layuca*, he reforged the furious and unrelenting Coltrane style with a lyricism that still recalled his old allegiances to Bill Evans and an interest in the ethnic musics outside of the immediate orbit of jazz. The excellent earlier Milestone albums aren't available on CD.

★*Live at the Musicians' Exchange* (Kingdom CDGATE 7021)

Tyner's trio in 1988, at its feverish best (Avery Sharpe is on bass and Louis Hayes on drums) in a pyrotechnic display of tidal arpeggios and avalanche chords which nonetheless strives for the spiritual content of the material, rather than simply bouncing technicalities off it. The material includes an attractive, 'Lover Man', and, 'You Taught My Heart to Sing'.

★*Uptown/Downtown* (Milestone M-9167)

A big plush, highly varied big band recording, cut over two nights at the Blue Note, in New York, in 1988. The thumping chordal pivot of 'Love Surrounds Us' firmly establishes that this is a Tyner set, soon engagingly shot through with spears of trumpet sounds. On the fast, high-stepping 'Uptown', the horns are constantly rubbing against each other, brass flares dying away, wild riffing ending in explosive crescendos, then sudden silences into which stalks Tyner's piano, over the soft, springy beat of Louis Hayes cymbals. The highlight is a Tyner classic – 'Genesis' from the old *Enlightenment* session – given a mysterious, diffuse quality by Robin Eubanks' arrangement.

Vasconcelos, Nana

(Born Recife, Brazil, August 2, 1944)
The reputation of that graceful coiled-spring of a Brazilian percussionist, Nana Vasconcelos, has been built over twenty years on collaborations with other employers – and the Brazilian's breadth of view is embodied in the diversity of his partners, who have included Milton Nascimento, BB King, Talking Heads, PAT METHENY and DON CHERRY. His records are showcases for his remarkable repertoire of sound effects, for which he combines vocals, percussion and musical exotica.

Vasconcelos came into the music business as a bongo player during the samba boom, and was brought to New York by the Argentinian tenorist GATO BARBIERI. He toured Europe with Barbieri, remaining in Paris afterwards to play and to work with handicapped children, and also occasionally performing with trumpeter Don Cherry – a liaison that has continued into the Nineties. He has also specialised in the *berimbau* – an African-derived instrument used to accompany martial arts in Brazil, and which looks like an enormous bow and arrow with a gourd on one end. Whether evoking the sound of a jew's harp, mice on a wheel, clattering drumbeats or ghostly voices, there is always a driving rhythm behind all Vasconcelos' work.

★*Bush Dance* (Antilles ANCD 8701)

Vasconcelos' typical sound-forest forays of the mid-Eighties, but of a highly communicative kind – rhythmic, highly textured, supported by an empathetic quartet, and blending north-western and Latin-American influences in the creative manner that the percussionist's name has come to be a byword for.

Watson, Robert Michael 'Bobby'

(Born Lawrence, Kansas, August 23, 1953)
Saxophonist Bobby Watson is one of the few recently emerged performers (a young veteran of bands led by Art Blakey, George Coleman, even Panama Francis) who can, in Rollins fashion, silence a room with unaccompanied alto expeditions uncannily reminiscent of the fluid eloquence of the late Cannonball Adderley, but with jolting contrasts of spinning, repeated motifs against yawing flights across the register, modulations of key and interweaving of glossy semiquavers against offpitch sounds and bluesy smears that avoids Adderley's glibness. He is a complete musician whose fluency and range is also informed by emotional strength and the capacity to move an audience.

The son of a saxophonist, Watson studied music at the University of Miami, having already organised and orchestrated for his high-school band. Watson's skills as an arranger as well as a soloist won him the musical director's position in Art Blakey's

Messengers between 1977 and 1981, and he worked with a variety of groups afterwards, including those led by saxophonist George Coleman and drummer Charlie Persip. In 1983 Watson co-formed the 29th Street Saxophone Quartet, with Rich Rothenberg (tenor), Jim Hartog (baritone) and Ed Jackson (alto) and it quickly developed into one of the most exciting of the all-sax bands.

The Inventor (Blue Note CDP 791 915-2)

Watson's second record for Blue Note (June 1989) and an excellent collaboration between the saxophonist and the young pianist Benny Green, plus Melton Mustafa, on trumpet. Watson's soaring alto takes off with an assurance he has more usually displayed in his work with the 29th Street Saxophone Quartet.

Weber, Eberhard

(Born Stuttgart, Germany, January 22, 1940)
Eberhard Weber is remarkable for his development of a completely unique composing and improvising territory for the bass. Originally a virtuoso bop bassist, occasionally involved in free-music too, Weber moved toward a kind of pastoral, electronically-symphonic music heavily dependent on synthesisers and multi-tracking. In solo recital, his preferred performance vehicle, Weber will develop contrapuntal structures by electronically delaying an earlier phrase and threading it in a few seconds later, after which he will then improvise against it, often with slurred sitar effects in the upper register. There is no other bassist in jazz who sounds like him, though his recorded projects sometimes take on a drifting, somnambulent air. Like several other ECM recording artists, his work anticipated New Age music nearly two decades ago.

In the Sixties, Weber played in a Bill Evans-like trio with pianist Wolfgang Dauner, and continued to work in Dauner's jazz-rock band Etcetera, in the next decade, and in Volker Kriegel's Spectrum. But Weber moved into his more impressionistic territory with his own invention of the 'electrobass', a skinny upright instrument electronically designed to sustain notes as if they were bowed and to produce exotic textures. Weber recorded with GARY BURTON, after this breakthrough, then formed his own imaginative ensemble Colours, with saxophonist CHARLIE MARI- ANO. He has also regularly appeared with Norwegian saxophonist JAN GARBAREK, for whom his slightly dolorous romanticism is entirely appropriate.

★*Colours of Chloe* (ECM 833 331-2)

Weber in 1973, in partnership with keyboardist Rainer Bruningh- aus and a classical cello section, achieving the beginnings of effects that Weber would eventually find ways to concoct on his own. Very spacious, graceful music, and entirely accessible (it won prizes and much critical acclaim on its appearance), though the improvisational content is strictly subservient to the material, a consistent feature of Weber's outlook.

★*Orchestra Solo Bass* (ECM 837 343-2)

An impression of Weber's unaccompanied performances, though a brass section collaborates here and there. Sonorous, liquid melody lines, arching sustained sounds and reverberating chords confirm Weber's status as one of the great contributors to the bass vocabulary, even if the overall atmosphere is a little too tranquil in the end.

Westbrook, Michael John David 'Mike' and Katherine Jane 'Kate'

(Mike Westbrook, born Buckinghamshire, England, March 21, 1936; Kate Westbrook, born Surrey)
Mike Westbrook's band dominated the British jazz scene of the late Sixties and early Seventies, an unruly and imaginative collection of the best of the younger local players of the period having much the same impact as LOOSE TUBES was to do in the Eighties. Westbrook was an art student who loved jazz and was mainly self taught on piano and trumpet. In Plymouth, in 1960, he ran a jazz workshop and formed a six-piece that included a precocious young saxophone talent in JOHN SURMAN. The band came to London, created a considerable stir and built a big local

audience through regular Saturday-night appearances at Ronnie Scott's Gerrard Street, 'Old Place'. It then played at European festivals, began to record, and expanded to as many as 26 pieces on occasion, as Westbrook explored larger-scale writing – influenced primarily by Ellington, but also by the free scene. He was also intrigued by theatre, joining forces with the group Welfare State for mixed-media shows, and by the notion of street-performances using a completely mobile brass band instrumentation. An ambitious and flexible artist, Westbrook has designed jazz contexts for the poems of William Blake, Rimbaud and Lorca, the songs of the Beatles, and the works of Rossini.

Kate Westbrook was a painter originally, and worked as a performance artist in the States in the Sixties. She joined Mike Westbrook's Brass Band in 1974, and devoted herself entirely to music – performing as a jazz-cabaret vocalist and English horn player with Westbrook, and as a solo artist with radio orchestras in Europe and in partnership with the oboist and composer Lindsay Cooper. Separately and together, the Westbrooks represent some of the most independent musical thought and unique transformations of jazz to have been achieved in Britain. One of the Westbrooks' most substantial and successful works, _The Cortege_, deserves CD release.

★*On Duke's Birthday* (Hat Hut ARTCD 6021)

One of Westbrook's most triumphant recordings, a project commissioned in France, in 1984, to feature the leader's 11-piece band. Dedicated to Duke Ellington, Westbrook's compositional inspiration, it intelligently seeks Ellington's essence in textural richness, subtle settings for the soloists' particular qualities and ensemble unity, rather than replicating 'classic works'.

Wheeler, Kenneth 'Kenny'

(Born Toronto, Canada, January 14, 1930)
A brass virtuoso, Canadian-born Kenny Wheeler has appeared in virtually every kind of jazz band in Britain since his arrival in the country in 1952 – performing with dance bands, then the JOHN

DANKWORTH Orchestra, the free-playing Spontaneous Music Ensemble, the Gil Evans-influenced MIKE GIBBS band and the American avantist ANTHONY BRAXTON's group. Wheeler has a cool, sparse sound, but he displays a controlled athleticism in careering runs and wide leaps of intervals that makes his work a blend of rigorous control and tantalising hints at abandon – MILES DAVIES, Booker Little and Art Farmer are among his trumpet heroes.

A diffident and modest man, Wheeler has rarely believed in his own talents and therefore did not lead his own bands until comparatively late in his career. When he did, he revealed that his embrace of all music, regardless of degrees of abstraction from regular rules, produced an orchestral sound close to that of Gil Evans, but which combined mainstream and free-playing soloists in intriguing juxtaposition. Wheeler's talents are now widely recognised in America and elsewhere in Europe and he has regularly performed in bassist DAVE HOLLAND's groups alongside New York star saxophonist, STEVE COLEMAN.

★*Gnu High* (ECM 825 591-2)

Wheeler's debut as a group leader for ECM, an event that helped bring him to the notice of American musicians subsequently. It's a typically oblique, rather reserved session, and thus synonymous with exactly those qualities in the trumpeter's own playing. But Wheeler's clear, soaring sound and unusual phrasing is well supported by a fine American band that includes KEITH JARRETT (piano) and JACK DEJOHNETTE (drums).

Williams, Anthony 'Tony'

(Born Chicago, December 12, 1945)
Along with Elvin Jones, Tony Williams was *the* colossus of jazz drumming from the 1960s onward, and he has retained much of his impact today. Like Max Roach, who was an early influence, Williams' style is constantly active, even hyperactive – his four limbs display astonishing independence even in the most complex figures, his constant eruptions and clatters of sound link spaces in the music or emphasise soloists' phrasing, his accompaniment is an orchestration rather than a timekeeping exercise, and his sense

of where the beat is, is so acute that he can accelerate or delay it with unerring accuracy. Williams has been a model for jazz drummers for nearly three decades, and he lends vitality and aplomb to almost every situation he plays in.

Tony Williams' impact on the jazz scene came very young. His father was a saxophonist, and the boy began on drums at the age of ten, studying with Dave Brubeck's drummer Alan Dawson. By his teens, Williams was playing with the avant-garde saxophonist Sam Rivers, and in 1962 he was working with altoist Jackie McLean. At age seventeen, Williams was with MILES DAVIS, and the combination of the young drummer, pianist HERBIE HANCOCK and bassist Ron Carter, made the rhythm section of that band the envy and wonder of the jazz world. No other Davis band displayed such flexibility and reflexiveness. After he left Davis, in 1969, Williams formed a raucous and experimental fusion band (Lifetime, with JOHN McLAUGHLIN, on guitar, and Larry Young, on organ) which broke up too early, and by the late Seventies he had reverted to celebrating the Sixties Miles band, without Miles, in the popular VSOP ensemble. He has also recorded with rock musicians, including Johnny Rotten and Santana.

★*Angel Street* (Blue Note CDP 748 494-2)

A delightful 1988 blend of the intense, brooding, edge-of-darkness sound of the pre-electric Miles band and an irresistible rhythmic bounce. 'Dreamland', with its chiming funky piano and driving horn lead could have figured on a 1960s Herbie Hancock disc, and is worth the album on its own. Williams' compositional strengths are considerable by this point in his career, and the solo and collective contributions of saxophonist Billy Pierce, trumpeter WALLACE RONEY and pianist MULGREW MILLER, illuminate and amplify them.

Williamson, Steve

(Born London, 1956)
Like COURTNEY PINE, his more celebrated contemporary, Steve Williamson's lineage is Britain's West Indian community. He emerged as part of the wave of young black music that reinvigo-

rated the British jazz scene in the 1980s – initially as a clarinet player and an enthusiast of the soul sound of Al Green, Marvin Gaye and James Brown. When he turned to saxophone, Williamson was initially inspired by funk horn players like Grover Washington and Wilton Felder – until he heard Charlie Parker.

As the profile of jazz music rose in Britain toward the end of the 1980s, Williamson assembled his own band and began to build an enthusiastic following for a style that was hard to categorise. On tenor, his sound has always crackled with a fierceness and urgency that suggests John Coltrane and WAYNE SHORTER, but his affection for the rhythmic grooves of dance patterns gives him an enthusiasm for the more direct and convivial style of an artist like Sonny Rollins, with elements of the reverberating funk of Ornette Coleman's Prime Time, also apparent in earlier periods of his work. Playing alto rather than tenor, he also recalled the memory of a long-departed saxophone hero from the West Indian community, Joe Harriott. He performed in the alto chair on a JAZZ WARRIORS big-band project devoted to the altoist's memory, and in the reformed Indo-Jazz Fusions band, a vehicle for Harriott in the 1960s.

*A Waltz For Grace (Polydor Verve 843 088)

Debut album of immense alertness and sophistication and rhythmic variety. It was recorded in both Britain and America – the leader being determined to involve the brilliant New York saxophonist STEVE COLEMAN as producer – and the session thus included key figures from the British scene like the brilliant young drummer Mark Mondesir, and powerful New York sidemen like Art Blakey's bassist Lonnie Plaxico. Funk, African, jazz and blues, with fine contributions from M-base guitarist, Dave Gilmore.

Wilson, Cassandra

(Born Mississippi, 1963)

That group of radical young black New Yorkers going under the collective name of M-Base (currently producing some of the most unexpected departures from the long traditions of jazz and the shorter ones of hip hop and rap) includes in its ranks one of the most powerful emerging talents in the world of jazz singing in Cassandra Wilson. A forthright campaigner for the continuing cause of black nationalism in America, and an attentive listener to the barrage of sound from the street that assails her apartment in Brooklyn, she has absorbed the kind of influences that produce independence, depth, flexibility and technical assurance – and the abundance with which she possesses all these, rather undercuts the manner in which she's now being touted in hip circles as a jazz artist for the Nineties.

Cassandra Wilson debuted in New York, in 1982, quickly revealing allegiances to BETTY CARTER and Abbey Lincoln, but also a flexibility that enabled her to work successfully in adventurous contexts, such as saxophonist/composer HENRY THREADGILL's band in 1983. She resembles at times a less fanciful and more muscular Betty Carter, mingled with an abrupt and spinechilling mid-register fierceness that even suggests NINA SIMONE, and these qualities have been easier to detect in more conventional contexts than in the collectivised sound of the STEVE COLEMAN Five Elements group.

★*Blue Skies* (JMT 834419-2)

A 1988 Wilson recording of jazz standards, delivered in her intriguingly displaced, reflective style, with bursts of emphatic, exclamatory scatting and sudden four-wheel skids on the accents. She's accompanied by an excellent trio of MULGREW MILLER (piano), Lonnie Plaxico (bass) and Terri-Lyne Carrington (drums).

Zorn, John

(Born New York, 1954)

Zorn is the New York composer and improvisor who erupted to public notice (after nearly fifteen years underground with the avantists and performance artists of the Lower East Side) with a captivatingly personal interpretation of the movie music of Ennio Morricone in 1987. Morricone, who not only penned all those baleful spaghetti western themes for the Sergio Leone/Clint Eastwood partnerships but also scored *Battle of Algiers*, *Once Upon A Time In America* and a raft of others, said admiringly of Zorn

'My ideas have been realised not in a passive manner, but in an active manner which has recreated and re-invented what I have done'.

Zorn is a tireless beachcomber of contemporary culture and his reference points are movies, the line of jazz and blues that runs into pop, and urban soundscapes. He is devoted to Japan because he admires that culture's openness about borrowing and remixing ingredients from elsewhere. Though Zorn's written works appear superficially to function on lines of Cage-like randomness, it is quickly clear that they are sharply honed and orchestrated. But, like a jazz composer (though he restricts himself to no single school of composition) Zorn now constructs works that are both hooked to an overall theme and open to the eccentricities of spontaneous players. His own playing (he is an excellent saxophonist, but perversely camouflages it) mixes bop alto, duck calls, heavy metal music and pounding, horror-movie cliches. His first musical interests were in Cage and Ives, but a period of his life spent in St Louis attracted him to jazz – particularly bebop and the post-bop avant-garde. He has described the music for kids' cartoons as being a significant influence with him (Bugs Bunny melodist Carl Stalling is a hero) and his work is often a restless confection of jump-cuts, like an insomniac endlessly switching TV channels. It is packed with nervous energy it is also packed with explosive humour and a sly wisdom about the fast, coded, disposable media culture it feeds off.

★*Big Gundown* (Nonesuch 979 139-2)

Zorn's extraordinary Morricone tribute, a display of bebop, funk, blues, free music and musical collagism, that not only calls on the leader's regular repertory company of off-the-wall players but also blues guitarists and even the legendary harmonica-playing composer Toots Thielemanns.

★*Spy Vs Spy* (Nonesuch K960 844-2)

Ornette Coleman's early themes (some of the most beautiful jazz tunes since the bebop era) merged bop lines, free improvisation and a rough-hewn early-New Orleans intonation, but often delivered in a superfast, blurted, jerky fashion quite different to the lava flow of bop. Zorn here plays seventeen tracks spanning much of Coleman's extensive composing career. The first half of this album is performed as frantic thrash-jazz, the horn sounds writhing and squealing over unbroken barrages of percussion, seven of the tunes lasting not much more than a minute. The remainder is more open, bluesy and yearning, closer to Coleman's original conception. Crazed, affectionate, headbanging elegance.

INDEX OF BIOGRAPHICAL ENTRIES